Praise for *The Pulitzer Prizes*

"The articles, photographs, and cartoons that have put their creators into what Wills rightly dubs 'journalism's most exclusive, yet unofficial club.' "

—Alida Becker,
The Philadelphia Inquirer

"It is a pleasure to report that in the case of this volume best really is best . . . an inspiring blend of literary technique and old-fashioned conscience. . . . I can easily envision an entire course around the invaluable lessons provided by this book."

—Madeleine Blais,
Associate Professor,
Journalism Department,
University of Massachusetts at Amherst

"For scholars and students of journalism as well as practitioners and citizens, this compilation is a valuable addition to the growing body of work that illuminates the very best craft skills of a dedicated group of professionals."

—Edward P. Bassett,
Dean, The Medill School of Journalism,
Northwestern University

A TOUCHSTONE BOOK
PUBLISHED BY SIMON & SCHUSTER INC.
NEW YORK LONDON TORONTO SYDNEY TOKYO

THE PULITZER PRIZES

1989

EDITED BY

KENDALL J. WILLS

TOUCHSTONE
Simon & Schuster Building
Rockefeller Center
1230 Avenue of the Americas
New York, New York 10020

Designed by Bonni Leon
Manufactured in the United States of America

10 9 8 7 6 5 4 3 2 1
10 9 8 7 6 5 4 3 2 1 (Pbk.)

Library of Congress Cataloging in Publication Data
The Pulitzer prizes 1989.

"A touchstone book."
1. Journalism—United States. 2. Pulitzer prizes.
I. Wills, Kendall J.
PN4726.P82 1989 071'.3 89-21780
ISBN 0-671-68748-4
ISBN 0-671-68749-2 (pbk.)

Pulitzer Prize nominating letter by Howard C. Weaver, Managing Editor of the *Anchorage Daily News.* Reprinted with permission of the *Anchorage Daily News.*
"Alakanuk's Suicide Epidemic," by Sheila Toomey, January 10, 1988. Reprinted with permission of the *Anchorage Daily News.*
"A Culture in Crisis, A People in Peril," editorial, January 10, 1988. Reprinted with permission of the *Anchorage Daily News.*
"Youth's Despair Erupts," by Debbie McKinney, January 12, 1988. Reprinted with permission of the *Anchorage Daily News.*
"A River of Booze," by Richard Mauer and Hal Bernton, January 14, 1988. Reprinted with permission of the *Anchorage Daily News.*
"Haven for Bootleggers," by Hal Bernton, January 15, 1988. Reprinted with permission of the *Anchorage Daily News.*
"A Revolution of Hope," by David Hullen, January 19, 1988. Reprinted with permission of the *Anchorage Daily News.*

Pulitzer Prize nominating letter by David V. Hawpe, Editor of the *Louisville Courier-Journal.* Reprinted with permission of the *Louisville Courier-Journal.*
"Many Feared Dead, Dozens Hurt in Fiery I-71 Bus Crash," by *Louisville Courier-Journal* staff, May 15, 1988. Reprinted with permission of the *Louisville Courier-Journal.*
"Fiery Deaths of 27 Leave Questions, Anguish," by Tom Loftus, Al Cross, and Judy Bryant, May 16, 1988. Reprinted with permission of the *Louisville Courier-Journal.*

(continued on page 529)

ACKNOWLEDGMENTS

I am most grateful to the Gannett Foundation for granting me a fellowship to study Asian Affairs at the University of Hawaii, followed by research in Asia. Professor Daniel W. Y. Kwok, as a founder of the fellowship program, has done much to foster understanding between East and West and has been a great inspiration to me. I would also like to pay tribute to the other Gannett Foundation fellows this year with whom I have shared many Chinese meals and enjoyed many hours of lively discussion: Laura King, Nie Lisheng, Ann LoLordo, Sylvia Nogaki, Bill Raftery, and Greg Victor.

I must thank my parents, Robert H. Wills and Sherilyn L. Wills, who have given me far more than I can ever repay.

Finally, I would like to thank my editors at Simon & Schuster, Carole Hall and James Nichols, for their continued backing of this project.

To my wife, Margaret Piaskoski-Wills

CONTENTS

SEVEN "Rescue Attempt" 313
1989 Winner in the Spot News Photography Category
St. Louis Post-Dispatch
Ron Olshwanger

EIGHT "A Class Act" 317
1989 Winner in the Feature Photography Category
Detroit Free Press
Manny Crisostomo

NINE "City Government's Folly and Fraud" 321
1989 Winner in the Editorial Writing Category
Chicago Tribune
Lois Wille

TEN "Literary Heroes and 'Creative Writing' " 343
1989 Winner in the Criticism Category
The Raleigh News and Observer
Michael Skube

ELEVEN "The People's Republic of Chicago" 371
1989 Winner in the Commentary Category
Chicago Tribune
Clarence Page

TWELVE "Being Black in South Africa" 397
1989 Winner in the Feature Writing Category
The Philadelphia Inquirer
David Zucchino

THIRTEEN "Anatomy of an Air Crash" 433
1989 Winner in the Explanatory Journalism Category
The Dallas Morning News
David Hanners, William Snyder, Karen Blessen

FOURTEEN "Death in the Dark" 493
1989 Winner in the Specialized Reporting Category
The Orange County Register
Edward Humes

ABOUT THE WINNERS 519
ABOUT THE EDITOR 527

INTRODUCTION

As you begin reading each chapter in this book, pause a moment and briefly imagine the "thud" of a newspaper landing at your doorstep, bearing the latest news from around the world or from across town. The freshness of those daily reports is preserved here in the latest annual volume of *The Pulitzer Prizes.* This year's collection of prize-winning news stories, photographs and editorial cartoons presents some of the most important news of the day, covered by some of the country's best journalists.

These are the articles, photographs and cartoons that were selected as the best of the year by the winners' peers—juries of fellow journalists, some of whom are themselves former Pulitzer Prize winners. The final selections were made in March by 18 members of the Pulitzer Prize Board, composed of journalists and academicians. (A list of the board members is on page xvii.)

The winning entries this year in the 14 Pulitzer Prize categories cover a broad range of writing styles and emotions.

There is drama—the compelling photograph taken by Ron Olshwanger, for instance, showing a St. Louis firefighter in a desperate attempt to revive a young girl pulled from a burning building. Or the coverage by the staff of *The Louisville Courier-Journal* of the design and regulatory lapses that contributed to the deaths of 27 people in a tragic church bus accident on a Kentucky highway.

There is humor—*Chicago Sun-Times* editorial cartoonist Jack Higgins lampoons some of your favorite politicians and spills some India ink on other public figures as well.

There is "watch dog" journalism at its best. Donald L. Barlett and James P. Steele of *The Philadelphia Inquirer* sink their teeth into the quiet deals that keep your taxes high while friends and business supporters of politicians grab millions in the biggest tax giveaway ever. These two reporters name names.

There is great writing. David Zucchino, also of *The Philadelphia Inquirer,* masterfully presents a series of articles that vividly portray the often unexpected struggles of daily life as a black in South Africa.

There is thoughtful analysis. Clarence Page, columnist, and Lois Wille, editorial writer, both at the *Chicago Tribune,* strike at injustice and abuses of the public trust. They also offer refreshing new thinking on old issues, such as racism and the elusiveness of affordable housing. Michael Skube holds many of the nation's top scholars and authors to a tough standard in his book columns for *The News and Observer* of Raleigh, North Carolina.

There is investigation. Bill Dedman, in his series of articles for *The Atlanta Journal-Constitution,* sniffs out widespread discrimination practiced by Atlanta's lending institutions as they decide who will and who will not receive housing loans.

There is discovery coupled with a warning. Manny Crisostomo, after spending a year in a Detroit public high school, offers a photographic essay in the *Detroit Free Press* that helps us comprehend the often mystifying behavior of our teen-aged youth. Don't just look at these photographs; listen to the story they tell.

There is writing that will educate. Edward Humes of *The Orange County Register* saw a pattern in the deaths of military pilots who wore night-vision goggles and asks why no one in official positions had ordered an end to their use. David Hanners, a reporter at *The Dallas Morning News,* teams up with photographer William Snyder and graphic artist Karen Blessen to give an insider's view to an air crash investigation by the National Transportation Safety Board.

There are historic developments. Glenn Frankel of *The Washington Post* reports from the Middle East on the persistence of the *intifada,* the uprising by Palestinians in the West Bank and the Gaza Strip. Bill Keller, reporting for *The New York Times* about the dramatic changes that are transforming the Soviet Union under the guidance of Mikhail Gorbachev, spotlights the social upheaval and some unintended consequences.

Howard C. Weaver, managing editor of the *Anchorage Daily News,* which won the Gold Medal for Public Service, perhaps speaks for many of these winners. In describing his paper's coverage of the social ills that cause Alaskan Natives to commit suicide and engage in other self-destructive practices, he says: "The story continues."

Indeed, most of the stories in this book are ongoing. These articles are not destined to obscurity in the newspapers' "morgues," where old clips are filed. They form the basis of related stories that fill today's newspapers and that will shape the news of tomorrow.

Finally, there is the story behind the story. As in past volumes, the winners here introduce their work by explaining how they go about their craft. In the winners' own words, these essays offer the behind-the-scenes descriptions of the efforts that went into the works before they could appear in the newspapers. They describe false starts, setbacks at the hands of those who did not want the articles to be published and, finally, triumphs.

These letters from the winners are as engaging as the winning works. Glenn Frankel, for instance, describes the difficulty of reporting as a neutral observer from the tension-filled Middle East. "Perhaps it was inevitable," he writes, "that in a conflict in which both sides routinely invoke history, morality and religion for their cause, no one would be allowed to remain neutral for very long and that the press itself would be quickly perceived as a combatant."

On the local front, Manny Crisostomo, a photographer at the *Detroit Free Press,* gained a new perspective on the state of this country's public high schools. He writes: "If it is said that our schools mirror our society, then these images and words should be of concern."

Clarence Page explains how his columns reflect an outlook shaped by an early encounter with racism. "I would be lying," he admits, "if I said that I was not profoundly influenced to this day by the bitter experience of being told at the age of six that I could not go to a nearby amusement park because 'little colored children ain't allowed in that park.' "

David Hanners relates how he and *The Dallas Morning News* photographer William Snyder tried to fade into the background as they shadowed federal air crash investigators. "We quickly learned it was a small, closed community that was suspicious of outsiders, particularly reporters and photographers," Hanners says. "Looking back," he adds, "getting the aviation community to trust us was perhaps our biggest hurdle. . . ."

There's more. These Pulitzer Prize–winning articles, photographs and editorial cartoons, plus the reflections of the winners, provide a storehouse of stimulating reading about the issues at the top of this nation's agenda and on the front pages of American newspapers. It's worth saying again: The stories continue.

Kendall J. Wills
Beijing, China
1989

THE PULITZER PRIZES

PULITZER PRIZE BOARD

MICHAEL I. SOVERN, president, Columbia University

ROGER W. WILKINS, senior fellow, The Institute for Policy Studies, and Robinson Professor of History, George Mason University

JOAN KONNER, dean, Graduate School of Journalism, Columbia University

RUSSELL BAKER, columnist, *The New York Times*

SISSELA BOK, associate professor, Brandeis University

MICHAEL G. GARTNER, president, NBC News, and editor, *The Daily Tribune,* Ames, Iowa

MEG GREENFIELD, editorial page editor, *The Washington Post*

JAMES F. HOGE JR., publisher, *The Daily News,* New York

PETER R. KANN, publisher, *The Wall Street Journal*

DAVID A. LAVENTHOL, president and chairman, The Times Mirror Company

ROBERT C. MAYNARD, editor and publisher, *The Tribune,* Oakland, California

C. K. MCCLATCHY, editor and chairman, McClatchy Newspapers, Sacramento, California*

BURL OSBORNE, president and editor, *The Dallas Morning News*

EUGENE L. ROBERTS JR., executive editor and president, *The Philadelphia Inquirer*

CHARLOTTE SAIKOWSKI, chief of the Washington bureau, *The Christian Science Monitor*

HOWARD SIMONS, curator, The Nieman Foundation, Harvard University*

CLAUDE F. SITTON, editorial director and vice president, *The News and Observer* and *The Raleigh* (North Carolina) *Times*

ROBERT C. CHRISTOPHER, secretary of the board

*C. K. McClatchy and Howard Simons both died shortly after the 1989 Pulitzer Prizes were announced.

ONE

A PEOPLE IN PERIL

1989 WINNER IN THE PUBLIC SERVICE CATEGORY

"For a distinguished example of meritorious public service by a newspaper through the use of its journalistic resources . . . a gold medal."

Anchorage Daily News
Staff

"In rural Alaska," the *Anchorage Daily News* states in an editorial, "alcohol is misery's mask. One hundred economic and social problems may lie behind it, but until the mask is laid aside no one can see them clearly." With this series, the mask starts to come off.

We knew before we published it that our series on suicide and self-destruction among Alaska Natives would have dramatic impact. The facts are too horrible and the desperation too great to be otherwise.

But we were unsure about two other critical questions: How would the rural Eskimos, Indians and Aleuts receive the report from our urban, mostly white newspaper? And would anything really change?

Although the issues illuminated in the series are of course far from resolved, both those questions have been answered conclusively. We learned how Alaska Natives felt about the series when our reprinted version sold 30,000 copies—more than half of them in rural areas where our paper does not regularly reach. (That amounts to about one copy for every nine people outside our regular circulation area in Anchorage.) They were purchased by individuals, health cooperatives, school districts and Native regional corporations and were used in school curriculums and community awareness programs.

Since the publication of the series, I have been asked many times to speak about our findings. To challenge listeners to take some action and not leave responsibility entirely on "those people in the villages," I included a long list of things our investigation suggested needed changing.

I am greatly encouraged to report that my speech was quickly out of date. The changes came so fast that I had to keep updating my remarks to incorporate them.

• Under the law as it existed when our series appeared, it was a felony to guide a moose hunt in Alaska without a license, but only a misdemeanor to bootleg whiskey in the villages. The legislature quickly changed that. In addition, the legislature promptly adopted new laws to strengthen villages' authority to regulate or ban alcohol, and require packaging intended to make it easier for authorities to discover and reject shipments of booze.

• A special grant program was instituted to encourage development of suicide prevention programs in rural Alaska. Significantly, the program specifically requires local autonomy and control of the plans, recognizing that detachment and powerlessness at the local level have contributed greatly to the problems.

• The state Alcohol Beverage Control Board has reversed two controversial decisions illuminated by our series, denying renewal of the Nulato liquor store license and foreclosing a new liquor store in Kasilof. Two new members have been appointed to the board—both men identified in our series as critics of the board's current practice.

• And the money order telegraph office in Bethel, the last of its kind in Alaska and operated purely as a convenience to air freight booze orders into the dry town, has been closed. The parent company, Alascom, shut it down.

Only a few things can now be said with certainty. The first, and most important, is this: Our series, whatever else its accomplishments, legitimized discussion of the formerly taboo topics of alcoholism—abuse and self-destruction. It galvanized responses in towns, villages and community halls across Alaska. It amplified lonely voices as they cried for help. It brought Alaskans' focus on the future of the Native people into sharp relief.

The story continues. We have assigned a staffer full-time to the exploration of rural affairs, and we increased attention throughout the newspaper on the issues raised in this series. Like Alaskans throughout the state, we have rededicated our efforts to search for solutions.

—Howard C. Weaver, managing editor
Anchorage Daily News

Addendum: *C.K. McClatchy, a member of the Pulitzer Prize Board and the editor and chairman of McClatchy Newspapers, died unexpectedly just 17 days after learning that the Public Service prize had been awarded to the* Anchorage Daily News, *one of the McClatchy newspapers. His passing diminished all of us who knew him. The* Anchorage Daily News *was near folding when he bought it 10 years ago. With his steadfast support and steady direction, it became Alaska's largest newspaper, a flourishing competitive success and a Pulitzer Prize winner. This prize is dedicated to him, with affectionate memory and the determination to further his ideals and meet his standards.*

Howard C. Weaver

ALAKANUK'S SUICIDE EPIDEMIC

SUNDAY, JANUARY 10, 1988

BY SHEILA TOOMEY

ALAKANUK—In March 1985, a young man walked out onto the tundra behind this Yukon River village and carefully, neatly shot himself in the heart.

"I guess I've always looked for a reason to do it," said the note near Louie Edmund's body. "And I found it."

The sound of the shot rolled across the flat delta land, through the supper time darkness of a cold spring day. It breached the walls and windows of the wooden houses, marking the moment as a beginning, for Louie Edmund had begun a 16-month suicide epidemic that ended the lives of eight young villagers.

In a community of 550 people, eight suicides is the equivalent of more than 3,000 in Anchorage. It is an unimaginable tragedy.

In a community of 550, every name on the roll of the dead is someone you know: Louie Edmund, 22; Melvin Tony, 23; Steven Kameroff, 19; Jerry Augline, 21; Karen George, 17; Benjamin Edmund, 21; Timothy Stanislaus, 25; Albert Harry, 29.

"I never went through this before," said Louie's mother, Adeline Edmund, who lost two sons before it was over. "My whole body hurt. . . . I never did get mad at God (before) but I find myself getting mad at Him."

Alakanuk had known many unnatural deaths, yes. Too many. From violence and recklessness, on land and on the river. Most of the victims were drunk when they died. But none officially labeled suicide. Other villages had suicides but not traditional, Roman Catholic Alakanuk.

The village looked for a reason for Louie's death. He was exceptionally bright, an honor student when he graduated from high school in 1982. He had gone to college in Fairbanks and planned to go back. But there was another side to Louie, one shaped by a childhood of alcohol and violence.

"We were a team of abused children," he wrote in his suicide note.

He was suspected of stealing. "I left a wave of uncaught crime in my past," the note said. "The future is shit. I've been clashed into a rapidly changing culture. Tried my best to keep up, but we're losing and the past histories of Americans (is that) Natives have lost all. And it's happening again and I don't want to see it when them land claims (illegible) breaks us apart."

Was Louie involved in a store burglary the night before he died, as suspected? Was he afraid of arrest or jail? Or just depressed by the suspicion? There seemed to be "reasons" for Louie's suicide and people were prepared to accept it.

"Being the first one, it was an oddity," said Sister Ann Brantmeier, a Catholic nun who has lived in the village for five years. "It was like, 'I can't believe he died and I don't know why he did it, but that was Louie and it just happened.' "

Nothing happened for seven months. But a new idea had been born, a new door opened. On Oct. 2, Melvin Tony shoved the muzzle of a shotgun under his chin and pulled the trigger. Melvin was a quiet, pleasant man who rarely drank, but he was black-out drunk when he died. His blood alcohol was .35, three-and-a-half times the legal limit for driving. He had spent the day drinking himself into a despondent stupor over a broken love affair and a baby lost to abortion.

Suddenly the village that never had a suicide had two.

After Melvin, the deaths came fast. At one point, five in 14 weeks, and as many as 40 attempts, ranging from gestures that were clearly imitative cries for help, to one where a father found his son hanging but was able to cut him down in time.

Grief flooded the village. And fear. Alakanuk families are all related, by blood or marriage. Few were left unscarred. Three of the victims were first cousins.

"I never heard of anybody killing themselves before, except for those big movie stars like Marilyn Monroe," said Valentina Black, a high school senior who lost two cousins and a close friend. "After Melvin killed himself, I thought maybe they were copying. . . . It sounded and looked so crazy, all those people killing themselves, sometimes for no reason at all."

"It had a life of its own, it seemed," said Ralph Baldwin, a high school teacher.

Each death stretched out for weeks as the bodies were taken from the village to Anchorage for autopsies. Before the mourning for one was over, someone else was dead.

"Some parents were openly asking their children to stop this, right on (CB) channel 11," said former Mayor Elizabeth Chikigak. "Like a plea."

Routine death, or what passes for routine death in rural Alaska, didn't stop during this time. Four people drowned, a young woman was raped and beaten to death, one died of illness, an unarmed 20-year-old village police officer was murdered.

"We hated to hear the CB," said Kitty Curren, who has taught in Alakanuk for 12 years with her husband, George. "We hated to hear a late plane. It meant an emergency. It meant death."

Then, in the summer of 1986, the suicides stopped. The epidemic was over and Alakanuk began to heal, slowly. But it was not the same village it had been. The people had learned things about themselves and their children, things they hadn't known before. This fall some villagers agreed to talk about their experiences.

"We have to try to help other villages," said Mary Black, Valentina's mother.

PEOPLE KNOW THE ENEMY

Alakanuk is 15 miles from the Bering Sea, strung out for four miles along the banks of a Yukon River slough. People get from one end of town to the other by three-wheeler, by boat or by walking along one of two rutted dirt roads. The villagers live mostly in the standard wooden Monopoly houses that dot the Bush, up on stilts here to protect them from flooding.

Twentieth-century technology is the norm—chain saws and outboard motors, stoves and freezers, CB, cable TV and a Laundromat. In addition to more than 50 paying jobs, many families fish commercially. But the men still hunt seal, standing in flat-bottomed boats to hurl their spears. They hunt to put food on the table and to feel right—subsistence is both a responsibility and a religion.

Because of its location so far down the Yukon, problems caused by the intrusion of Western culture came late to Alakanuk. But they did come. Ask the villagers to name the worst problem and they'll tell you:

Alcohol.

Not just in Alakanuk, in many villages.

Ask why husbands beat their wives, why men are shot. Ask why women are raped and children hate their lives. Ask why love drowns in anger and guilt. The answer is always alcohol.

Alakanuk is officially dry—no importation or sale of liquor is allowed. But the law has little relevance where the drink of choice is brewed from sugar and yeast in five-gallon plastic pails.

Alcohol shapes most of the death and all of the violence in Alakanuk. Sister Ann estimates that about 85 percent of the adults abuse alcohol or marijuana or both. Many individuals are sober, alcohol counselor Arthur Chikigak said, but he couldn't think of a single family where everyone is sober.

Johnson Katchakoar, 81, remembers that alcohol first came to Alakanuk in the 1950s, brought downriver by cannery workers and soldiers, a "traditional" feature at Fourth of July picnics.

"Remember how them Indians were in early-time history," said Mary Ayunerak, translating for Katchakoar, her father. "They take the whiskey, drink it like it was juice. That's how (the Yupiks) were. . . . They drink it foolishly."

In the 30 years since, alcohol has laid waste to many villages. Elizabeth Chikigak, the former mayor, can list 38 alcohol-fueled deaths in Alakanuk since the late 1970s. But the effect of alcohol is much more complicated than people getting drunk and falling in the slough. Or beating up their parents. Or killing their neighbors. It is destroying the family, once the strength of the Yupik people.

Alcohol loaded the gun or knotted the rope in only four of the Alakanuk suicides, but nearly all those who died came from drinking families.

'I REALLY HATE MYSELF'

Steven Kameroff, 19, was the third to die. He hanged himself in an empty dormitory at the boarding school in St. Mary's. It happened Jan. 22, 1986, shortly after Steven returned from a Christmas visit home. At his inquest, a witness said he was upset by his family's drinking during the visit, although he had gotten drunk with them almost every night. He had been expelled for a while from school for using marijuana but had asked to be let back in. He had no drugs or alcohol in his system when he died.

While he was home, Steven said he was going to kill himself when he got back to school. But he was drunk when he said it, so the threat wasn't taken seriously.

Most people saw in Steven the nice boy he was, shy and self-conscious. His friends at Alakanuk High School dedicated their 1986 yearbook to him. "A fun loving, joyful person," the dedication says.

Here, from the last entry in his private journal, written a week before he died, is how Steven saw himself:

"I really hate myself. I really wish I had a pistol right now so when I feel that feeling again, that funny feeling, that way I act and the way I am. I hate it. I wish I was a bird in the air and get eaten by my parents. The way I feel right now, I'm going to commit suicide for sure. I took one full bottle of aspirin. Then I took it again. Didn't succeed. Try again asshole. You're too chicken, Kameroff. Eat your heart out or take two boxes of pills this time, you scar face. . . . The way your life is going, you need help badly and quickly, before it's too late."

FROM FATHER TO SON

"Nobody suddenly commits suicide," said Tim Sergie, once a drinker and village drug dealer, now a city council member and minister of the Assembly of God Church in Alakanuk.

"It is not spontaneous. No one gets to hate their life instantly. No one loves instantly. It's a growing process that we walk through day by day."

Sergie had just finished Sunday church services. Outside, low gray clouds dropped early snowflakes into the thickening river. Inside, he remembered his past.

"My mother and father used to drink a lot," he said, "and I started drinking at a very young age too.

"The most awful experiences for me . . . would be my father beating on my mother. . . . I used to say to myself, 'I'll never be like my family, I'll never be like them.' And I became like them."

His parents eventually stopped drinking, but too late to save Sergie, now 34. He believes God is the only reason he survived his youth.

"It got to that point where I started hating my life. I wanted to quit (drinking) but I was incapable of quitting. . . . I became like my father. . . . I got to where I didn't love anymore. I hated everybody. I hated what I stood for. I hated my life. I hated what alcohol was doing to me. I hated living. . . . And after one especially hard night, I almost committed suicide.

"I remember. I wasn't drunk to the point where I didn't know what I was doing."

"That particular night, when I was really high, we ran out of dope. We ran out of booze. I was dry and I wanted some more. And I was angry, and the first person who happened by was my wife. . . . I hit her and I beat her and I threatened to kill her.

"And she said, 'It's OK. Go ahead and kill me.' So I took a shotgun. I loaded the shotgun and I pointed it right on her head. . . . And I said, 'I'm going to kill her. And then I'm going to kill myself.'

"And what she said—'Go ahead. We don't have any life.' And I realized . . . there was no meaning to what we were doing. . . . There was no happiness, no love for each other, no caring. It was just existing. . . . I took the gun off from her head and pointed it at my head and I was going to . . . push the trigger.

"It's easy. It's easy. I've tried many times . . . after the incident, while I'm out hunting, just to see how stupid I was. I'd go like that, and the trigger's right there. I could see it. I could push it.

"And I said, 'How did I *not* kill myself that night?' "

CRIES IN THE NIGHT

The fourth young man to die was Jerry Augline, two months after Steve Kameroff. Jerry was 21. He was big and would fight if he thought he had to, but he was also very shy. He made the cross for Louie Edmund's grave.

Jerry had lived for a while with Paula Ayunerak, then the village health aide, now regional health supervisor. "I practically raised him when his mom and dad used to be drinking," she said. "Pretty soon, Jerry never went home anymore." In high school he lived for a while with the Currens.

Some people said they had heard Jerry sobbing that night, inside a dumpster. They found him the next day, by a pond out on the tundra, still alive. He died minutes later. He had shot himself in the heart.

Jerry's blood alcohol was .08, not legally drunk, most likely left over from heavy drinking the night before. A friend told police Jerry had been drinking a lot lately and talking about killing himself because he thought his parents didn't want him around.

OUT OF CONTROL

"Sometimes I used to be scared, when I was young, 12 years old or 11," said James Tony, brother of Melvin Tony, the second suicide victim. James' and Melvin's parents don't drink anymore, but they used to. James is 21 now, but he remembers.

"I didn't like those years, on weekends, 'cause everything used to go out of control. If I have kids, I don't ever want them to see me high, not ever, not once in my life."

Scared. Out of control. He left out angry. And ashamed.

"Young people bottle up their pain," said Arthur Chikigak, 30, the alcohol and drug counselor. They drink, like their parents, "to kill the pain that's inside. . . . probably from their past, the abuse they had from their parents.

"A lot of the hurt they're going through, I feel it because I felt it too. . . . I grew up in an alcoholic environment. My parents drank a lot by the time I was in elementary. . . . When they were high and talking bad about me, I'd leave and walk in the trees. . . . The hurt would still be there, but it would make me feel a little better, just walking."

Once Chikigak drank and used drugs himself. Once he took his boat out on the river and tried to flip it, a suicide attempt that probably would have been called an accident if it had succeeded.

"I had been hollered and screamed at 'til I felt really small.

"I didn't go around telling people how I felt inside," he said. "I'd put up an act, like there's nothing wrong. I think a lot of the students are like that today. We're trying to reach them now. There's a lot of people who are willing to devote their time to help."

THE BEST AND BRIGHTEST

"Hey! Happy 1986," Karen George wrote to a friend on New Year's Day. "My year has finally come."

Queen of the prom, president of the student body, valedictorian of the class of '86. Pretty, self-confident and popular. Karen at 17 was Alakanuk's brightest star.

By May 1986, seven months after Melvin Tony's death, some people in the village understood they had a suicide epidemic on their hands. Sisters Susan Dubec and Ann Brantmeier; Paula Ayunerak; public safety officer Willie Smalley; some school staff and parents were watching for danger signs. But Karen George wasn't on anyone's endangered list. Drugs and alcohol were used in her home and she had what one teacher called "a small alcohol problem," but she was successful, a leader.

Karen's father had drowned several years earlier, another drinking death. In her valedictory address, she choked up when she spoke of him, telling the audience how proud her dad would be if only he could see her now.

Two days later, shortly after midnight, Karen walked out on the tundra behind her house and shot herself. Twice. She used a stick to push down the trigger of a shotgun. She shot herself in the shoulder first, then tried again and shattered her heart.

Because of the two wounds, police initially wondered if it might have been murder, but Karen's mother was able to settle the question. She heard the first shot, she said, and looked out a window in time to see her daughter fire the second.

Karen killed herself over boyfriend trouble. She acted impulsively and with little understanding of the finality of her act. The notes she left behind make that clear. Romantic, silly notes. Teen-age dramatics. "Bye everyone. . . . I miss you a whole lot. . . . But I've got to go."

Unfortunately every suicide leaves blame and shame in its wake. Karen's boyfriend was Benjamin Edmund, 21, brother of Louie Edmund, the first suicide.

Everyone knew Benji was going to kill himself. Some people tried to get him shipped out to a hospital in Bethel or Anchorage, but somehow they couldn't arrange it in time. His family and friends posted a 24-hour watch on him, but he told them, "If I want to kill myself, no one can stop me."

He was right. Five days after Karen died, he slipped away and shot himself.

Now every parent was frightened. If kids like Karen and Benji could act so crazy, whose children were safe?

"It was scary," recalled Chikigak, the alcohol counselor. "You never knew who was going to be next. It was frightening, a feeling of not being able to do anything about what was going on in the village."

After Karen's death, one of her teachers said she had made no real plans for her life after school. Maybe she would go to a training program, she had said, maybe not. Maybe she would get married and have a baby, a friend said.

But maybe she would become just another bored and aimless village youth.

In a 1964 article, anthropologist Seymour Parker described an Alakanuk in the first stage of acculturation. Villagers were borrowing Western technology but adapting it to Eskimo needs. Children wanted to become hunters or housewives. They could be what they wanted to be and were respected for doing so. They were successful in the eyes of the community and in their own eyes. They had self-esteem.

But unless something was done to avoid it, Parker warned, Alakanuk would soon find itself in the second stage of acculturation. The youth would begin to adopt Western values. They would look at themselves, at their parents and their lives through Western eyes and find it all of little value. They would aspire to professions Westerners valued, but wouldn't be able to compete successfully for them. They would come to despise themselves and their world. They would have no self-esteem.

Village kids love their parents, said Kitty and George Curren, the teachers. "But they don't admire them."

FEW JOBS, LITTLE TO DO

"There's nothing to do but only drinking," said James Tony, brother of the second victim. "They think drinking will make them have fun." James used to drink and smoke marijuana, but says he doesn't do it anymore. "Everybody's emotional feelings would pour out," he said. "Some people would get into fights."

After kids graduate from high school, there's not much for them to do in the village. James is luckier than most. He has a part-time job giving fluoride treatments to Head Start children. But in general, few local jobs are available to people his age. He helps cut wood for his father's sauna and is trying to organize a youth club, but in his eyes, that's not a life.

There are also few ways for kids to have fun in Alakanuk—no community center, no place for dances or concerts, no bowling alley, movie theater, hamburger hangout, no library. But there's always a bucket of home-brew around, to dip a cup or two or six from.

James has plans for his life, but to have plans, he must leave Alakanuk. In preparation, he has been to Mountain Village four times for computer courses, to Anchorage for a vocational program called RSVP, working for two weeks as a clerk at the state human rights commission. A bright, ambitious young man, he feels he has learned a lot that will serve him in the future.

"I learned how to use the streets, how to use the bus—to get on and off, how to ask for help. I learned how to use a postage meter."

Like many others his age, James wants a future more like the life he sees on television. He wants to move to Anchorage and get a job.

"I would do anything to live there," he said.

NEW SURVIVAL SKILLS

Alakanuk High School sits above the beach, around a curve in the shoreline—a big, yellow Pandora's Box. Yupik children go there to learn things their parents don't know in a language their grandparents don't speak.

"We're the major change element here," said Principal Mike Hull, a 10-year veteran of Bush education. From 8:30 to 3:30, we are the value system. We set the standards for whether they succeed or fail, which may be different and not always in harmony with what's going on in the village."

The school raises expectations, then sets the children back down in an environment where their hopes cannot be fulfilled. "We're part of the problem," Hull said.

Even so, he believes school is the Eskimos' best hope for survival. Yupiks must master the skills of the invading culture, he said, then turn around and use those skills to fight the invaders, to keep from being destroyed.

"For the Yupik nation to survive, it has to become Anglo so it can defend itself . . . defend its right to live the way it wants. . . . They have to take our culture and come back."

In the process, "some people are going to be lost."

Longtime teachers George and Kitty Curren agree with Hull. Two of the suicide victims sought refuge in their home, lived with them for long periods. Four of their five children married Eskimos.

Nothing angers George faster than a suggestion that Eskimo villages are economic dinosaurs, doomed to extinction. A town of 550 people can support any number of small businesses, he said. A barber, a bakery, an optometrist. A family can combine a small business with subsistence hunting and fishing and make a good life.

The school prepares kids for more education. Never mind that few actually go to college and fewer graduate. The school does no vocational training or counseling, nothing to help kids make successful lives in the world right outside the door.

"You tell kids to graduate from high school. Then they graduate and so what? I think the poor kids are batting their heads against the wall. Is that the only choice? To sit in your house and drink and watch TV?"

The Currens teach a business course in which high school students run a snack store every day after school. They learn to order stock, keep books, make change. George hopes one day to help graduates set up successful village businesses.

SOBER AND LONELY

On June 25, 1986, the night he hanged himself, Tim Stanislaus wore a T-shirt that said, "I got drunk and lost in Alakanuk, Alaska." Which was just about right. His blood alcohol was .23.

Tim's death puzzled people even more than Karen George's. He was so very bright, a success, the Yupik teacher at the high school. But those who knew him well say he was two people: During the week, an impressive achiever, but on weekends and during the summer, a staggering drunk and drug user. He wanted to be a leader and sober, but he needed his friends, and they drank.

"He couldn't walk that line," George Curren said.

Walking the line means staying sober and off drugs when your friends are drinking and smoking. Fredrick Joseph walks that line every day. He is part of a budding sobriety movement, encouraged by the Catholic sisters, by Paula Ayunerak, by Chikigak, the alcohol counselor, and others.

Joseph was a heavy drinker by the sixth grade. By ninth grade he was also smoking marijuana. Once he stayed sober for more than a year, then fell off the wagon, hard. "I guess I got crazy. I started not caring about anything. . . . My girl couldn't talk to me anymore, couldn't communicate with me anymore and I couldn't understand why. And it led to hitting her, slapping her. And . . . I broke her arm by kicking her. And then I tried suicide."

Joseph ended up at the Alaska Psychiatric Institute in Anchorage for a month. "I was too depressed, lonely, unwanted, not cared for. . . . I went through emotional stages, regretting everything I did." He returned to Alakanuk sober and determined to remain so.

The hardest thing about sobriety, Joseph said, is the aloneness of it. His old friends still drink. His girlfriend won't come back to the village with their two daughters until she's sure he is serious about staying sober, so he is alone. Each night he walks the village, counting the hours and killing them, visiting safe places—the priest, the alcohol counselor, the police station, the Sisters.

"I try to find a job. I read the 24-hour book (from Alcoholics Anonymous). I read some chapters of the Bible. . . . I feel a lot better than I used to feel. I think a lot more than I used to think."

Across the river, Sally and James Leopold have been sober for a year. It's a little easier for them because they walk the line together with the help of their children. Their home is clean and tidy, the atmosphere relaxed. Outside, a cold sleet blows in the wind. Inside, Sally washes dishes. On the radio, Willie Nelson sings, "San Antonio Rose."

Even in a story about eight suicides, Sally Leopold's family history is horrifying. One of her brothers beat up their father, who died. The brother went to jail. Another brother killed a village police officer. Her sister and mother drowned in separate incidents while drunk. Another sister was killed in one of the bloodiest murders in lower Yukon history. One of Sally's babies accidentally suffocated during a family drinking session.

Still, Sally and James didn't stop drinking until she almost died from an ulcer.

The Leopolds have eight children, from a baby to a 19-year-old boy. The older ones have vivid memories of their parents' drinking. Cecelia Leopold, 13, said she used to get scared when Sally and James would "fight, argue with each other. Loud. We used to go to our auntie's house. Sometimes we used to stay out until they sleep, then come."

"I hardly used to cook for them," said Sally. "I never used to think of their stomach or clothes. . . . When we used to drink, they hardly used to come home from the school. Now that we quit, they listen to us more than they used to.

"Sometimes I think of the past, you know. It was living in the darkness. Now everything is so bright, it seems."

But not all is bright. In November, one of Sally's sons was charged with raping an old woman—his aunt. For a few days after that, alcohol beckoned the Leopolds back to oblivion, but they clung to the light.

BREAKING THE PATTERN

"It's one thing to stop drinking," said Sister Susan. "You stop drinking, the problems are still there. The parenting skills are gone, children still have a poor self-concept. . . . Just like it took one or two or three generations to get to suicide and the problems we have now, it's going to take one or two or three generations to get out of the problem again." Fifty years, she estimated.

Maybe it doesn't have to take that long for everyone. Tina Black, 17, is one generation away from an alcoholic grandfather. "He got drowned, maybe by drinking, when he was in his camp," said Tina's grandmother, Agnes Shelton. "One of my boys was drowned with him. It was very hard for me."

Shelton was a non-drinker who preached abstinence to her children and chose a non-drinker for her second husband. But for a while it looked like the familiar pattern would assert itself anyhow. Her daughter and son-in-law, Tina's parents, drank. Twelve years ago, Tina's mother, Mary Black, stopped drinking and Tina's father eventually stopped drinking in the village. In this family, the destructive cycle seems to have been broken.

Tina is a top student at the high school and president of the student body. She seems a sensible girl, having the usual teen-age rough spots with her mother but close to her father. She drinks occasionally at parties, she said, but never in kill-the-bottle bouts. She seems undaunted by the high school stars of yesteryear who are in the village, doing nothing much.

"Sometimes I think it's stupid," she said. "They're just hanging in town. They can be anything they want. . . . I don't want to hang in the village, doing the things they do, partying."

THE END AT LAST

While Tim Stanislaus was hanging himself in Alakanuk, Albert Harry, an Alakanuk fisherman who spent his winters in Anchorage, was dying in a bed at the Alaska Native Medical Center.

About 2:45 a.m. on June 24, Albert went into the bathroom of his Anchorage apartment, sat down on the floor with his back against the closed bathroom door, and fired a revolver into his right temple. Three people, including his brother, were in the next room. He lingered for a day before he died.

A few weeks earlier, Albert had called his brother back in the village and said he was going to kill himself. Through the phone, his brother heard the mechanism of a gun. The night he died, Albert had been drinking heavily, vodka and beer. He left no note. One of the men in the next room was so drunk he slept through the suicide.

With Albert's death, the epidemic ended.

SILENT HURT

In the early morning the village is silent except for the crunch of feet now and then along the frosted paths. The air feels good—cold and wet against the skin. More snow has fallen, but the river is still liquid, not yet an ice highway. Early risers smile, say hello. If something bad happened last night, it remains behind closed doors. If people are troubled, the trouble is hidden away. The village is silent.

But silence is an enemy. People don't talk to each other about their feelings and have little understanding that they can reach out and shape the future.

"They never talk to us, those young people, when they have problems," said Agnes Shelton, the grandmother who has never been a drinker. "It's too bad. I just don't know how come they do that. . . . Their minds get them scared to be alive sometimes after they do something wrong. . . . Some always never have a good home. . . . Some always getting tired of moving around when the parents drink too much."

When people get drunk, "a lot of words pour out," James Tony said, hurtful words. Guilt and shame are part of every hangover. Silent hurt radiates from those who have been abused.

Even healthy teen-agers in healthy families have trouble talking. "It's hard to tell your parents that you love them," Tina Black said, "to tell your grandparents that you love them. I don't know why."

Chikigak, the alcohol counselor, Sisters Susan and Ann, John Thomas, who runs the Alcoholics Anonymous meetings, and others are trying to get people to talk. Progress is slow, but it's there. Two years after Louie Edmund's death, members of the Edmund family have begun talking to each other about it. Last month, 15 young people showed up for an overnight retreat.

Adults in the village did not immediately rally around suicide prevention efforts. Few appeared at a suicide prevention workshop last year. Many people in Alakanuk seem to view violence and early death the way they view bad weather and poor fishing—as natural disasters. As for shaping the future, how can you stop a snowstorm? "We'll just have to wait and see what happens, won't we?" one woman said.

'I QUESTION WHY'

It's late, nearly midnight. Adeline Edmund has stopped at the Sisters' house on her way home from work at the village sauna. She is a small middle-aged woman with short black hair laced with silver. Sorrow animates her face. Her silence is intense. She has heard that a newspaper story will be written about the suicides. She lost two sons and has some things she wants to share.

"Some days . . . I question why, why could they, after they care so much for us. . . . There's some days it's really hard. You can't take it anymore. . . . Some days it's really strong that I don't want to live no more. Then God comes.

"Write it down," she says, for other villages to read and learn from.

Stop all the hurting in the home, she says. "Stop all the blaming. Try not to get mad even when they get mad at you. . . . Love is the most important. If you're not loved . . ."

'THEY WANT TO BE LOVED'

Will there be more suicides in Alakanuk? Probably, say the people most likely to know. But not another epidemic. "I don't think our village is at a trigger point anymore, that if one happens, there's going to be five. I think we're past that," said Sister Ann.

"I think (the young people) see that the suicides didn't accomplish what they thought they would. Yeah, there was that glory of everybody over the bodies, but I think that's not there anymore."

Still, an empty space remains in the hearts of the young, said Sergie, the Assembly of God pastor. "They want to be loved. They want to be shared with. They want caring. . . . And if they can't find pleasure, love and caring in any direction, well, what's the use of living?"

"When I stayed with one who was going to commit suicide," said James Tony, "I had to keep saying, 'Come on, everybody loves you. They don't act like it, but in their hearts they love you.'

"They say, 'Aaaagh, who loves me? Nobody loves me.'

"I say, 'Well, I do.' "

Editorial A CULTURE IN CRISIS, A PEOPLE IN PERIL

SUNDAY, JANUARY 10, 1988

If it happened in any city in the country, it would make headlines nationwide: a rash of suicides and violent deaths punctuated by rapes, beatings and child abuse.

But the crisis in Alaska's villages is a quiet crisis. When hope dies, it dies silently. And the epidemic of despair that is robbing an entire generation of its birthright happens far from city lights.

Today, the Daily News begins a series that will detail that crisis. These stories run not as a criticism but as a warning to us all. The Native culture that is the heritage of all Alaskans is endangered, threatened by alcoholism, helplessness and despair. From Fort Yukon to Kake, Alaska Natives are dying in vastly disproportionate numbers.

The causes are complicated and varied, but one constant appears over and over again—booze.

In rural Alaska, alcohol is misery's mask. One hundred economic and social problems may lie behind it, but until the mask is laid aside no one can see them clearly.

Make no mistake, Alaska's predominantly white cities offer their own share of grief. Violence born of liquor is no stranger here. But the statistics gradually emerging from the Bush point inexorably to an entire culture in peril.

- Alaska Natives are four times as likely to commit suicide as other Alaskans.
- Alaska Native men between the ages of 20 and 24 are 10 times more likely to kill themselves than non-Natives nationwide.
- Fetal Alcohol Syndrome, where a pregnant woman's drinking damages her unborn child, is 2½ more times more common among Native women than non-Natives.
- Natives comprise only 16 percent of Alaska's population, but make up 34 percent of its prison inmates.

- While the official U.S. Department of Labor unemployment figure for the Yukon-Koyukuk region is 15.5 percent, experts say that if "discouraged workers"—those who have given up—were included, that figure would be two or three times higher.
- And even when they come to the cities in search of jobs or a new life, Natives in Anchorage are three times more likely to be raped, four times more likely to die violent deaths than non-Natives.

Yet the numbers remain cold and impersonal. One cannot remain impersonal in the Bush. There are no statistics in the villages, there are husbands and wives, cousins and neighbors—entire families whose potential is lost, and whose despair passes from one generation to the next.

Gradually, though, the code of silence is being broken and the people themselves are talking, exploring ways to break the cycle. By confronting the hegemony of the white culture, they hope to retain their own. It is a sobriety movement born of pain, and it is the best hope for village Alaska.

We talked to many villagers in preparing these articles, including a woman who has lost two sons to suicide. Adeline Edmund's son, Louis, was 22 and a former Alakanuk honor student when he shot himself in the heart on the tundra behind his village. Louis' brother, Benji, was 21 when he killed himself 14 months later.

"Write it down," Adeline Edmund said, so others can learn. In that spirit, we have.

YOUTH'S DESPAIR ERUPTS

TUESDAY, JANUARY 12, 1988

BY DEBBIE MCKINNEY

Sophie Larson was the first to be shot. A bullet slammed into her hand, knocking her off the three-wheeler as she and Loren Abyo tried to escape. As she fell, the machine's engine sputtered and died.

Loren ran, but Sophie panicked. She crawled behind the three-wheeler in an attempt to hide. But the gunman kept coming.

It was Sunday, July 31, 1983, in Pilot Point, a fishing village of about 70, surrounded by cold, gray ocean and roads to nowhere on the northern coast of the Alaska Peninsula. The day had begun with a bottle of vodka.

That afternoon, some friends from a neighboring village flew into town with a case of whiskey and six cases of beer, as good a reason as any to party. Someone kicked in marijuana, and a couple of guys shared a gram of cocaine. The group of 10 devoured the drugs and drained the last drop of whiskey at the village airstrip, then topped off the party with a bottle of blackberry brandy.

It was a good time. Then suddenly it wasn't. A fight broke out over one of the women. The blows triggered an explosion deep within the darkest abyss of Chris Conners' mind. The 15-year-old boy, blinded by cocaine, whiskey and a lifetime of hurt that could never be spoken, stormed off and returned with a gun.

In Pilot Point, it's not unusual for children to grow up knowing how to drink. Loren Abyo, 17, and Chris Conners had been drinking together since Chris was in the fifth grade. Now Loren was running for his life and shouting for Sophie to run, too. He sprinted across the tundra and dove over an embankment just as a bullet grazed his back.

Chris Conners then walked up to 19-year-old Sophie, who was crouched behind the three-wheeler. He raised a .357-caliber revolver, aimed and fired. Later she would remember that the bullet burned as it ripped through her neck.

By the time the last shot was fired hours later, three people were dead, four were wounded and the residents of Pilot Point, who had watched Chris Conners grow up cornered by rampant family alcoholism and severe neglect, were left terrified and perplexed at his sudden surge of madness.

His mother, investigators believe, was the last to die. Evelyn Conners was sleeping off a head full of booze when her son walked into her room. Chris was Evelyn's middle son, the son she never could bring herself to love. He pointed a 10-gauge shotgun at her head and squeezed the trigger.

Whatever flipped the switch that day was trivial. The best anyone recalls, Chris tried to kiss Sophie. He thought she wanted him to, but she pushed him away. This was the last rejection he could bear.

Chris was never one to talk about feelings. He never talked about the father who abandoned him. Or the man who killed himself with a bullet through the brain inside his mother's house. Or the way his mother ruined his only hope for a future in the village. After years of burying his emotions, the boy finally broke.

Chris remembers only bits and pieces of what happened that day. Two psychiatrists who examined him believe he was in an alcoholic blackout at the time of the murders. Chris recalls a fight at the airstrip and standing over someone, he doesn't know who, with a gun. He remembers firing a shot at a passing three-wheeler. And he remembers one of the men he wounded saying: "Chris, what are you going to shoot me for? I never did nothing to you." But he doesn't remember shooting the man. He remembers nothing about killing his mother.

His recollection begins on the plane ride to jail, when he looked down at his hands and saw them cuffed and stained with blood.

It wasn't until months later, when Chris saw photographs of his victims, that he fully understood and believed what he had done. As the tears streamed down his face, his emotional suit of armor began to corrode.

For the first time in his life, Chris wanted to talk. The following story is the result of three days of prison interviews with Chris Conners in St. Cloud, Minn., investigators' transcripts, court documents, witnesses' testimony, psychiatrists' reports and telephone interviews with village residents and officials involved in the case.

AN EARLY OUTCAST

Christopher Conners is the product of a summer fling between his mother and a man from a neighboring village. Chris, a mixture of Aleut, Eskimo and Caucasian blood, was born in a cabin in Pilot Point on Feb. 27, 1968. He was the second of three sons born to Evelyn Conners, all of whom had different fathers.

Chris was 10 when he saw his father for the first time. His father had been in the village and was waiting for a plane out when he and Evelyn ran into each other.

Back home, Evelyn told Chris he could go down to the airstrip and take a look at his father. The boy jumped on his three-wheeler and raced off.

The man he saw standing there behind dark, mirrored glasses was tall, broad-shouldered and expressionless. He looked at Chris and Chris looked at him. The boy just kept on riding.

Unlike his two brothers, Chris was extremely overweight as a child, which led to teasing by other children.

Janice Ball, president of the Pilot Point Village Council, said Chris seemed like an outcast for as long as she could recall, particularly with respect to his mother. "Evelyn would call Chris all kinds of names—not even really treat him as a son," she said.

"Christopher could never do anything right, and his mother was always picking on him," is the way another villager put it. "It was just like she treated him like a dog."

No one can say for sure why Evelyn banished Chris from her heart. Some people say they believe she was so hurt by the father she couldn't bring herself to love the son.

Evelyn Conners was a good woman and a hard worker, village people say. She wouldn't intentionally hurt anyone.

But she was a drunk. Chris remembers hiding bottles from her as a child. When she would drink herself sick, he would throw rags over her vomit.

The alcohol seemed to unleash Evelyn's own anger and frustration at a life that hadn't worked out the way she wanted. Chris remembers times when his mother and grandmother were drinking, and hearing his mother sob: "Why would you throw me out when it was 20 below zero?" His grandmother, her head hung, would just say, "I know, I know."

Chris and his mother made life hell for each other. That was no secret in the village. Some people talk about the day they saw Chris shouting at his mother, telling her how much he hated her. Others talk about the time Evelyn chewed him out over the CB radio for everyone to hear.

All the drinking, yelling, cursing and slapping became too much. By the time he was 6 years old, Chris refused to live with his mother.

Instead, he lived down the road with his grandparents, Nick and Titianna Meticgoruk. They drank, too, but not nearly as much as his mother. From Chris' perspective, the booze didn't make them mean the way it seemed to with her.

Chris said he didn't mind taking care of them during their occasional binges. He would lend them a steady shoulder as they staggered off to bed and fix hot soup for their hangovers.

Sometimes the binges would last a week or more. During these times, Chris' grandparents would shout at each other. Chris learned that if he just waited it out, eventually peace would return to the house. Then he could look forward to a month or two of them staying sober.

These were Chris' happiest years. His grandparents would hug him when he got home from school, and ask whether any of the kids had been picking on him. He was his grandfather's favorite.

The old man taught Chris to hunt game and smoke fish, and to tell the difference between husky and wolf tracks in the snow. He took Chris out on his trap line and told the boy stories about his days as a reindeer herder up north. At home at night, Chris would climb into his grandfather's lap with a cup of hot chocolate, and together they would indulge in the adventure of Br'er Rabbit on the Uncle Ben Radio Show.

Early on, Chris decided that when he grew up he would become a commercial fisherman like his grandfather had been. Chris' brother, Alan, would inherit his grandfather's fishing permit because he was the oldest. But grandmother's permit would go to him.

THE GOOD TIMES END

The good times in Chris' life ended abruptly when he was 9, at the tail end of one of his grandfather's binges. Chris was about to fix soup for his grandfather's hangover when he walked into the bedroom and found the old man sitting on the floor clinching his teeth and holding his left side. He tried to hide his pain. He slowly stood up, took a few steps into the hallway, stumbled and fell to the floor.

When the village health aides arrived, they suspected a heart attack or stroke, and loaded him into a plane to Dillingham. Chris and his grandmother flew out later. They arrived at the hospital five minutes after he died.

Inside a brightly lit room of stainless steel and sterilized linens, the old man lay still, tubes still poking from his nose and arms. The boy went numb.

That night, a family friend spent half an hour trying to convince Chris it was OK to cry. But Chris couldn't. He had never seen his grandfather cry.

The drinking began early the day of the funeral. Chris' mother, grandmother and other family and friends were at it by 9 or 10 in the morning, mixing alcohol with tears.

At the funeral, Chris' grandmother sat between the boy and his mother. A priest sang and waved a pot of incense, filling the church with a sweet smoke that made Chris queasy. But it wasn't until later, as men lowered the coffin into its grave, that emotion finally punched through. Chris burst into tears, turned and ran.

Back at home, still dressed in a stiff new suit, he lay on his bed and stared at the ceiling. Grieving family and friends returned to the house, and the drinking resumed in the front room. On the other side of a blanket that served as a door, Chris waited for someone to come in to his room, hug him and ask him how he was doing. But nobody came.

Soon after the funeral, Evelyn moved in to help take care of her ailing mother. Chris didn't want to be home much after that. People in the village gave him a place to sleep when he needed one. If they questioned why a 9-year-old child couldn't bear to be home, they kept it to themselves.

DRUGS AND DRINKING

Six months after his grandfather's death, Chris started smoking marijuana. It made him laugh. Although Chris had been sneaking sips here and there for as long as he could remember, he became a drinker soon thereafter.

The first time Chris drank enough to pass out he was in the fourth grade. He and one of his aunts were in a Ford Capri. Chris helped himself to the large plastic cup of whiskey she placed on the dash, and she was too drunk to notice.

Chris woke up the next morning at a friend's house with a pounding head, unable to remember how the evening had ended. It didn't bother him much; he had learned long ago that hangovers and blackouts were normal.

One night at a friend's house, he wanted to impress a woman who had been flirting with him. She was 26; he was barely 13. He grabbed a bottle of whiskey and chugged it. Ten minutes later he stumbled outside, tripped and passed out with his face in a puddle.

Chris woke up the next morning upstairs, with his clothes gone. Whoever had taken care of him that night had pulled him out of the puddle and tossed his muddy clothes in a heap outside the door. Chris walked home wrapped in a sheet.

As much as Chris was humiliated by his mother's drinking, he was starting to become just like her. She begged him not to. Yet Chris says he occasionally drank with her, beginning at age 13. He says they smoked pot a couple times together, too.

"You know, I think that's what really made her angry at me," said Chris. "I wouldn't listen to her. She would tell me not to drink, and I'd drink anyway. And I believe I drank just to get back at her. That's the way I could get under her skin the most.

"And there was nothing else to do."

'DAD KILLED HIMSELF'

Although Chris said he cared about his mother, he hated the way she was. His resentment carried over to her boyfriends.

Evelyn was with Paul Matsuno back then. Matsuno was an OK guy by Chris' standards, but they still didn't get along. He was a commercial fisherman, part-Aleut, part-Japanese. When he drank, he drank hard, but never raised a hand against the kids.

Chris' 6-year-old brother, Guy, was particularly fond of Matsuno. Guy called him "Dad." Chris tried to, but it didn't feel right.

One winter day in 1980, Chris forgot to stop for the mail on his way home from school. Matsuno was angry; he told Chris to go back and get it. Chris refused. An argument ensued in which Chris said words he would later regret. He called Matsuno something like "a dirty Jap," then stormed out of the house. On his way out, he passed his mother. She was slumped in the seat of a snowmachine, woozy from too much booze. He was so furious, he said he could kill Matsuno.

Later that night, after a drunken argument with Evelyn over a snowmachine, Matsuno picked up a hunting rifle and blew his head all over her living room. Chris' brother Guy was there when he did it; he ran from the house in horror. "Dad killed himself in the face," the boy screamed.

Evelyn silently blamed Chris for Matsuno's suicide, although she said nothing. Chris said nothing. Guy said nothing.

Relatives say Evelyn drank harder than ever after that. Chris did, too. Weekend parties were pretty much the same—drink, pass out, get up, do it again.

The year after Matsuno's death, Evelyn sold her mother's fishing permit—the one that was to have been Chris' inheritance—to her new boyfriend, a white man named Bud Reina. She needed the money. Chris saw the permit as his only chance to make something of himself, to follow in his grandfather's footsteps.

He never talked about it.

ANOTHER NEW HOME

The more Evelyn and Chris drank, the less they could stand each other. Sometimes Evelyn would call Chris' aunt and uncle in Port Heiden, John and Annie Christensen, and ask them to take Chris. They were always willing. Invariably, Evelyn was drunk when she made the calls.

The Christensens got along with Chris. Their home was the epitome of family life, with a constant stream of neighbors, children and dogs through the house. The couple was well respected in the community. John rarely drank, and Annie, like her parents, didn't drink at all. She didn't even allow alcohol in her house.

Chris continued to sneak out and drink once in a while, and a couple of times he got caught. Annie would let him know how much she disapproved and explain why she felt the way she did.

Chris spent two years with John and Annie. In many ways, the

Chris Conners who lived in Port Heiden was a different kid from the one his mother knew. In a stable home, he was polite and helpful around the house, Annie says, chopping wood and helping with chores without having to be asked. Back home, his mother couldn't get him to lift a finger.

"He was just like one of my kids, you know," Annie told investigators after the shootings. "He really behaved well here. . . . He didn't ever show any anger when he was talking to me.

"He always seemed concerned and worried about his mom and her drinking. He'd always call and, you know, check on (the family)."

One time, Annie remembers, Chris wanted to go home for his birthday. When he called the village phone, the person who answered told him his family had moved to Anchorage.

"He even started crying, he was so upset over it," Annie recalled. "It was just like he wasn't important. He didn't know (why) they didn't bother to call him and say they were moving."

Chris spent the last couple of years between Pilot Point, Port Heiden and Anchorage. The winter before the murders, while staying with John and Annie, Chris again wanted to be with his family, this time for Christmas. He called his mother; she said she would pay for his brother Alan's plane ticket, but not his.

Chris took the news hard. Although there were presents for him under the tree and Annie had fixed a big turkey dinner, Chris spent all of Christmas Day in bed. He finally got up to pick at some leftovers that evening.

RETURN TO PILOT POINT

Chris quit school that spring and returned to Pilot Point to strike out on his own. He landed a job as a deckhand on a fishing boat, and slept wherever he happened to be—on the boat, at friends' houses, at his mother's place.

One day Chris got drunk and asked to borrow his mother's pickup truck. Although he was told he couldn't, he took it anyway, and blew the engine driving 40 miles an hour in low gear down the beach. It wasn't much of a truck, but Evelyn depended on it to work her setnet site. The two of them screamed it out in front of several villagers.

About a month before the murders, Chris and Evelyn, drinking as usual, started arguing as usual. Out of nowhere, she said what she had been thinking for three years. "*You* killed Paul!" she screamed.

"She was crying," Chris says. "I believe that she really believed I killed him. Maybe what I said did have an effect. I'll never know."

Chris became increasingly agitated as the summer progressed, and people in the village started to notice. Janice Ball said Chris seemed restless. Others said Chris was becoming more and more hot tempered.

Chris earned $5,000 fishing that summer. He bought a couple of three-wheelers—one as a gift for his little brother, Guy—and blew the rest on cocaine, marijuana and booze. He stayed constantly stoned, and on several occasions drank until he blacked out.

Finally, Evelyn had had it. She kept telling people that her son was out of control. The night before the murders, she told Chris she was thinking of putting him in a reform school.

"At that point," Chris said. "I didn't really care what happened to me. I kept telling myself nobody cares about me. I was mad at everyone. I hated everyone."

THE FINAL REJECTION

When Sophie Larson spurned him the next afternoon, the rejection overwhelmed him. When the years of accumulated anger finally burst through, Chris lashed out at everyone—people he cared for, people he hated, people he hardly knew.

According to authorities, the shootings went something like this: After seriously wounding Sophie at the airstrip, Chris took off on his three-wheeler and fired a shot at Sonny Greichen, the man who had hired him to work on his boat. At first, Sonny thought it was a prank, that the gun was loaded with blanks, until a bullet came close enough to his head to make his ears ring.

Chris traded the .357 for a 10-gauge shotgun, then walked into the bedroom of Bud Reina, the man he believed had swindled his mother out of his fishing permit. He blasted Bud in the neck, but he didn't kill him.

By now, word was getting around on the CB that Chris had gone berserk. James Achayok couldn't have known because he had been out riding his three-wheeler. As James' machine rounded the top of a hill, Chris raised the shotgun and fired.

Achayok, age 22, died instantly.

Three pellets from the blast struck the 9-year-old boy who sat hidden behind him. It was Chris' little brother, Guy.

Guy jumped from the three-wheeler, ran a few yards, crumpled to the ground and died.

A schoolteacher was next. Lance Blackwood was home watching "Falcon Crest" when he heard Bud Reina on the CB calling for help. Blackwood grabbed his .44-caliber Magnum, put a handful of bullets in his pocket and headed out the door. As he approached the hill above Evelyn Conners' house, he found James and Guy lying on the ground. He called to them, shook them and tried to get a pulse. Nothing.

He stood over the bodies a long time, not knowing what to do. He finally loaded them into his pickup. As he closed the tailgate, a shotgun pellet struck him in the buttocks, wounding him.

Finally, it was Evelyn's turn.

From a half-mile away, Sonny Greichen watched through binoculars as Chris struggled to load a heavy yellow bundle onto the back of his three-wheeler. The bundle kept sliding off. Sonny saw Chris tie it behind his three-wheeler and drag it across the tundra out of town.

The troopers found Evelyn's body late that night, about a mile from the village. She had been shot in the head, a yellow sheet tied around her neck and bite marks on her face, neck and chest.

Prosecutor Charles Merriner called the murders among the most brutal and senseless he could imagine.

'A SCARED LITTLE BOY'

Chris was like a cornered animal when first brought to McLaughlin Youth Center to await trial for murder, attempted murder and assault. He was described at the time as unemotional, self-centered and volatile.

The murders would be easier to understand if he were psychotic. But psychiatrists who examined him found that wasn't the case.

"When I first heard about this murder, I thought, 'Oh God, I hope I don't get this case because it was so gruesome,' " said Polly Morrow, who did get the case as an investigator for the public defender agency. "When I went to meet him for the first time I expected someone who was sinister, and he was a scared little boy. I think with so many public defender clients, there's no remorse, no sadness about their crimes. This kid was grief-stricken.

"You know the most profound interview I had was with Chris' grandmother, who is now dead. She said to me, 'I don't blame Chris for this. I blame Evelyn.' And this is Evelyn's mother who said this."

Morrow said she believes if someone had intervened earlier, Chris never would have done what he did. She was so moved by her work with him, she left the agency to pursue a master's degree in social work.

The turning point in Chris' attitude came after he was shown photographs of his victims. "I didn't want to accept the fact that I did it," he said. "I knew they were dead, but I didn't want to believe it. After (I saw) those pictures of what I did, I knew I needed somebody to talk to."

After that, psychiatrists and counselors started seeing drastic changes. Later evaluations described him as bright, articulate, sensitive and extremely distraught over what he had done.

Psychologist Jon Burke told the court Chris had lived most of his life overwhelmed. In jail, he was finally safe, safe because he didn't have to worry about people being abusive. Only now could he let down his defenses.

Psychiatrist Irvin Rothrock, who originally examined Chris on behalf of the prosecution and found him "cold," was later called to testify for the defense. "I would say he's one of the more favorable people I've seen," he told the court, "more favorable in terms of potential rehabilitation."

Along with these changes came nightmares. Chris would see himself flipping through those pictures, the bodies of his mother, little brother and James. He would wake up in a cold sweat, and be afraid to go back to sleep for fear the images would return.

At one point, he broke the plastic off the light fixture in his cell and slashed a wrist and forearm deep enough to require stitches and leave a trail of scars. During court hearings, Chris threw up as a pathologist summarized autopsy reports.

Before Chris' case could go to trial, the court had to decide whether to try him as a juvenile or an adult. Chris was 15 at the time of the shootings. If he were to remain in the juvenile system, he would be free by his 20th birthday.

Chris' public defenders fought hard to keep the case in juvenile court. They were convinced that he was a "salvageable" human being. Just removing him from his home environment had produced remarkable changes; with extensive counseling, they argued, Chris could turn his life around and pose no threat to society.

Because of the seriousness of the charges, Superior Court Judge Seaborn Buckalew decided Chris should be tried as an adult. That meant he could spend the rest of his life in prison.

The case never went to trial. Instead, Chris pleaded no contest to the charges against him. At his sentencing, Judge Buckalew considered Chris' relationship with his mother and the role of alcohol and neglect. The judge considered the theory that Chris was so drugged he didn't know what he was doing. Buckalew thought, too, about Sophie Larson, hospitalized with bouts of paralysis for months after the shootings. And he thought about those who died.

Despite prosecution pleas that Chris remain behind bars for the rest of his life, Buckalew was persuaded that Chris could be rehabilitated. He gave the boy 55 years to serve.

PAROLE IN 2001?

It has been more than four years since the shootings. Chris is imprisoned in St. Cloud, Minn., but may be returned to Alaska when the new prison in Seward opens. He will be eligible for parole in 2001. Chris said he hopes to get a college education while he is locked up so he can make something of himself once he is free.

Until then, home is a 6-by-9-foot cell with a bed, television, nightstand, fan, toilet and sink. Chris starts each day with a cigarette and a cold shower. He shuffles through his daily routine trying not to think too much. When he does think about what has happened, he becomes intense.

Chris has written to his victims' survivors and those he wounded to say how sorry he is. He doesn't expect them to accept his apology. His older brother, Alan, lost his entire family that night. Chris doesn't expect to ever hear from him again.

"They say time heals all wounds. But I don't think time will heal theirs," Chris said.

He said he plans to sell the shares he holds in his Native corporation, put the money in a savings account to accumulate interest, then give money to those he hurt to help pay medical bills. It's something he said he needs to do to be right with himself.

"To tell you the truth, I will never know why I did what I did. I still have a hard time dealing with it. It's going to be with me all my life. There's no escape from it. Ever."

CIRCLE NEVER ENDS

Back in Pilot Point, the tragedies continue.

Three years after the Conners murders, a volley of shotgun blasts left a 6-year-old boy dead and his stepmother shot in the face. There had been drinking and an argument. The dead boy's 16-year-old brother was charged with the crime.

Loren Abyo, the boy who ran from Chris' bullets at the airstrip four years ago, is dead. He drowned three days after his 21st birthday. He and some friends were drinking on a boat. Loren got tossed off the boat. Nobody on board could swim. His friends just watched him wash out to sea. The man who threw him overboard was convicted of negligent homicide.

"It's just like you're at a dead end or a circle that you never reach the end of," says Janice Ball, one of several people in Pilot Point who don't drink at all. "You just see it happening over and over.

"After all we've been through. . . . You know, you would think they would learn or something. But the drinking just goes on."

A RIVER OF BOOZE

THURSDAY, JANUARY 14, 1988

BY RICHARD MAUER AND HAL BERNTON

BETHEL—A sole Alascom telegram office has survived the communications revolution that brought telephones to nearly every village in the Bush.

The office is in Bethel, and it owes its staying power to a steady accumulation of crumpled currency shoved through a slot beneath tinted, bullet-proof glass.

The cash, $100 and $200 at a time, comes from bootleggers and whiskey drinkers wiring money orders to Anchorage liquor stores.

The office is a humming pump, nourishing the headwaters of Alaska's fearsome river of booze.

Though Alascom shut its other Bush telegram counters over the past decade, the Bethel office is different. The continuous flow of alcohol business rings up $800,000 a year in money orders and represents 95 percent of the money wires out of Bethel. Though the liquor stores are 225 miles away, the network linking them with Alascom and the airlines guarantees same-day delivery and mocks Bethel's voter-approved ban on in-town liquor sales.

Alascom is one of dozens of legitimate enterprises whose decisions and policies, sometimes passively, sometimes not, have kept the floodgates wide open for bootleggers and consumers of low-grade whiskey in villages, both wet and dry.

Alascom, like most of the others, says it shouldn't be asked to play policeman and go beyond the restrictions imposed by society itself. "It's a judgment call we can't make," said spokesman Tom Jensen.

Yet the aftermath of those business choices is widespread death, violence, abuse and neglect—for adults whose choice it is to binge, and for children and other victims who find themselves trapped inside another's nightmare.

A passive state liquor agency with a history of toothless regulations, an ineffective local option law, flagrant bootlegging and ambiguous community standards have kept the flood of liquor unchecked. Because liquor starts out as a legal commodity, unlike marijuana or cocaine, gray- and black-marketeers openly take advantage of the network that ties together even the remotest parts of Alaska for legal commerce.

In recognition of the role of alcohol in human misery, the legislature has offered communities a menu of options for its control, ranging from community-owned liquor stores to a complete ban on possession. Some 82 places, from the Kuskokwim Delta center of Bethel, population 4,462, to the Athabascan hamlet of Birch Creek, population 40, have chosen to restrict the sale or possession of booze.

But residents of those places and the authorities who enforce the laws readily admit that even in the most restrictive villages, where arriving travelers are frisked for flasks, there are still ways for the booze to get in.

Some of it is due to the ingenuity of bootleggers. By uncorking a jug and filling it to the brim before hiding it in a suitcase, they can avoid the telltale gurgle a conscientious baggage handler might detect. Plastic bottles have eliminated the risk of breakage—and the giveaway odor.

It is 1:15 p.m. on a Friday afternoon in October. A steady flow of customers has journeyed to the silver-sided building, beside the huge satellite dish, where Alascom conducts its telegram business. It is just up a dirt street from the Kuskokwim River and the office of Bush Air Service, whose owner was recently charged with transporting liquor to a dry village.

In walks a man with bushy-blond hair. "You must be glad it's Friday," says the Alascom agent, making small talk. "What difference does it make to me?" replies the customer. "One day of the week is the same as the next." He wires $172 to Party Time Liquor in Anchorage.

The next customer, a Native man with the smell of liquor on his breath, sends $219.74 to International Liquor, also in Anchorage.

"Hello, Al," a clerk says to another man. "$189.50, Party Time," he replies. He pushes a wad of bills through the window, she gives him back some change. Then she walks to the teletype machine. In seconds, the message beams from the dish outside to the satellite Aurora, and back down to the Alascom office in Anchorage. In minutes, a check is ready for Party Time.

ORDERS FROM ANIAK

Like Bethel and a half-dozen other communities in Alaska, the Kuskokwim River village of Aniak has banned the sale of booze, but not its possession or importation.

On a Friday afternoon last October, Postmaster Leonard Morgan was on the phone to a customer. The weather outside was rotten—snow, wind and low clouds—and Morgan told his customer that the Northern Air Cargo plane would be late, so there was still time to get a postal money order shipped by Express Mail to a liquor store in Anchorage.

The one-day Express Mail service provided by the Aniak post office attracts booze customers from as far away as Kalskag, 25 miles down-river. In the summer, they make the two-hour journey by boat, and in winter, in a quarter of the time, by snowmachine or truck on the frozen river. If they make the mail deadline, they'll be back the next day to pick up their shipments at 1:30 p.m. when the Northern Air Cargo DC-6 roars into town.

Where do those orders go?

Primarily to a half-dozen liquor stores in Anchorage and Fairbanks that specialize in the Bush trade, some of which have teamed up with airlines to offer drinkers a package deal.

20-GALLON LIMIT

Since territorial days, Alaska has allowed people to place orders for alcoholic beverages through the mail for shipment by common carrier. In 1980, the legislature revamped the liquor code and eliminated restrictions on the amount that can be shipped.

Alcoholic Beverage Control Board regulations that went into effect in November require the liquor store to notify the board when an order is 20 gallons or more—the equivalent of about 8½ cases of Windsor Canadian in plastic bottles. Though the rule was supposed to detect bootleggers, loopholes remain, conceded Bill Roche, the commission's chief investigator. Bootleggers selling a case or two a week don't need to place single orders in such a large quantity, he said, and even if they did, they could avoid detection by splitting their orders among several stores, or having confederates place orders.

If 20 gallons proves too loose a restriction, Roche said, the board may change it.

The new rules will mainly affect the few stores that specialize in mail-order sales. In Anchorage, according to ABC board staff, they are Party Time Liquors, Value Liquor, International Liquor, Our Liquor and Brown Jug Warehouse.

According to records filed with the Alaska Department of Revenue, Party Time No. 2, on Spenard Road, where the Bush sales are made, sold an average of 1,400 gallons of hard liquor a month over the past year, the equivalent of 5,000 "jugs." That's more than twice its nearest mail-order competitor, Value Liquor No. 3 on Jewel Lake Road.

The records don't show the proportion of liquor sold over the counter as opposed to mail order, and Party Time owners Michael and Paula Gallagher won't discuss their business. But their competitors estimate that as much as 75 to 80 percent of their sales from the Spenard store goes to the Bush.

In an interview in Bethel, a self-described bootlegger said he prefers Party Time because it understands his needs. Clerks ship the bottles in innocuous cartons, like those for potato chips, he said, so "no one can see what you are getting in the box."

And evidence now in court indicates that Party Time may have been increasing its sales by actively courting the bootleg trade. In addition to opening the operations of Party Time to public view, the unusual lawsuit, brought in Superior Court in Bethel, has shown the state liquor board to be ineffective in policing mail-order sales.

The suit, filed in 1986 and not yet tried, was brought by the parents of Moses Strauss Jr., a 20-year-old minor when he was struck by a Bethel city bus on Jan. 14, 1986, and suffered severe head injuries. The suit charges that Strauss was drunk at the time and that he bought his liquor from Malachy Polty, a customer of Party Time.

The Gallaghers declined to be interviewed. Through their attorney, they denied the Strausses' allegations. "We are confident we will be found blameless when all of the facts are presented to a judge and jury. However, we and our attorneys believe it is highly inappropriate to try cases in the press," they said in a prepared statement.

Depositions and documents obtained by the Strausses' attorney, Kneeland Taylor, include the record of a previously undisclosed 1985 investigation by the beverage commission into allegations that Party

Time flouted mail-order rules, shipped to customers from dry villages, and was likely dealing with bootleggers.

In visits to Party Time's store at 4006 Spenard Road over a six-month period, agency investigator Virginia Holland found that the store was helping its large-order customers over regulatory hurdles designed to slow the flow of booze to the Bush, keep liquor from the hands of minors and discourage impulse consumption and binge drinking.

Among the requirements of the law then and now, according to Roche, the beverage board's enforcement officer, was that mail-order customers send the liquor store a signed, written request for each purchase.

Party Time took a creative approach to the rule. According to the depositions, it told customers to mail a batch of signed order forms filled in with huge quantities of anything they could possibly want. Then, when they decided to actually make a purchase, they called Party Time, directed which part of the order to fill, and wired the cash by Alascom. The Party Time clerk scratched off the portion of the order that was filled, leaving the remainder for the next call.

About 2:30 each afternoon, the Party Time truck would leave the liquor store for the MarkAir SpeedMark package express window at the airport for same-day delivery to Bethel.

On a single day, April 12, 1985, most of the orders that left Party Time for the Bush came from forms with matching handwriting but different names, according to the investigation report. In a later visit to the store, Holland uncovered orders from residents of Napakiak and Nunapitchuk, two dry villages in the Yukon-Kuskokwim Delta.

On Jan. 6, 1986, ABC board Executive Director Patrick Sharrock signed the report of his investigators recommending suspension or revocation of Party Time's license for a pattern of on-going violations: accepting telephone orders, shipping liquor to customers in dry villages and failing to correct deficiencies pointed out during the course of the investigation.

Three days later, Party Time attorney Dan Coffey responded that the fault was not with the store, but with vague regulations. He accused investigator Holland of writing "rules and regulations herself."

In a letter to the beverage board on March 10, 1986, Assistant Attorney General Kay Gouwens recommended against prosecution.

"I understand and sympathize with your concerns about package stores such as this that have a large volume of Bush sales and seem undaunted by the fact that some of what they sell almost certainly finds its way to villages that have banned importation, to bootleggers, and to individuals with drinking problems," she wrote. "However, our existing statutes and regulations are poorly equipped to deal with the problem."

The ABC case was shelved. It took a year and a half to implement new regulations that clarify the absolute ban on telephone orders.

PLENTY OF 'LOOPHOLES'

Holland quit her job in March 1986 and moved to Seattle. In a recent interview, she said her tenure at the liquor board was an exercise in futility. The kinds of violations she observed at Party Time could be found in other liquor stores that ship to the Bush, she said.

"My foremost frustration was the way the regulations were written. They were very vague and nebulous and although anyone can read them and know the intent of the law, they leave all sorts of loopholes for someone who doesn't have a conscience to violate them," she said.

She said she didn't find much official support from either the attorney general's office or the ABC board. The people in positions of authority didn't seem to want to make the effort to fight bootlegging by controlling sales.

"If there is a general consensus, it is that (bootlegging) is one of those victimless crimes. People up there want liquor. People in Anchorage are willing to send it. And nobody gets hurt."

Roche and Sharrock said they sympathized with Holland's frustrations, but they said she quit before the last chapter of her investigation was written. Roche said the liquor board saw the need for tighter rules, and responded with the new regulations.

AMAZING NUMBERS

In their suit against Party Time, the Strausses built their case upon the ABC investigation. By using a computer to examine subpoenaed records, they've taken it much further.

During 1986, the Strausses reported, Party Time shipped $475,445.19 in booze to Bethel.

They also documented that the 11 biggest Party Time customers bought 12,175 bottles of whiskey and 2,430 cases of beer during the year, for a total of $125,775.89.

That averages out to three bottles of whiskey and 72 cans of beer a day for each buyer.

Assuming the proportions of beer to whiskey are roughly comparable among all buyers as they are with the top 11, Party Time's sales to Bethel would translate to a hard liquor per capita adult consumption rate of 3.6 gallons—more than one and a half times the national rate.

And Party Time is only one of five Anchorage liquor stores selling directly to Bethel. Adding to the consumption would be whiskey carried in luggage or booze purchased over the counter and shipped by individuals themselves.

It all goes to a town where the sale of liquor is officially outlawed.

Between Jan. 6 and June 18, 1986, defendant Polty spent $6,471.46 at Party Time, and among his purchases were 480 bottles of whiskey, according to the court record.

To preserve the privacy of the other Party Time patrons, their names were not disclosed in the court filings. But a computer printout showed that one of them, identified as "Customer 1," bought 283 bottles of whiskey between June 2 and July 12, 1986, a period that includes the busy Fourth of July holiday. The most orders went to "Customer 11," who spent $23,239.47 during the calendar year on 2,423 bottles of whiskey, six bottles of other hard liquor and 21 cases of beer.

The July 14, 1987, affidavit of a former employee, Edith Turkington, accused the Gallaghers' son-in-law, Richard Marietta, of forging signatures on Bush order forms.

From a back-room office crammed to the ceiling with booze, she and Marietta would take orders over the telephone or by mail. "Each day we would call Alascom and see who had sent money in," she testified.

When a phone order arrived from a regular customer, she or Marietta searched the customer's file for an order form. The forms were often blank, with only the signature of the customer at the bottom, she said.

"On many occasions, we would not have a signed blank order form and Richard just forged the signature," she said.

The Gallaghers kept a ledger for each customer, Turkington testified. "On some of the pages in the book, the word 'bootlegger' was written. I asked Richard Marietta what that meant, and he just said it was a person who sold booze out in the Bush.

"We shipped large liquor orders to persons who were marked as 'bootleggers' in the book. As far as I know, we treated bootleggers just the same as anyone else, although Mike Gallagher often would give discounts and free booze to persons ordering large amounts of liquor."

Attempts to locate Marietta were unsuccessful. An employee of Party Time said Marietta was in California, but didn't know where. Paula Gallagher said she couldn't provide his location or a way to reach him.

AIRLINES' ROLE

In Aniak one Friday afternoon in October, a Northern Air Cargo DC-6 touches down on the runway in the center of town, a few minutes behind a MarkAir jet. It taxis to the terminal area. A forklift goes to work on the freight pallets. Within an hour, both planes are back in the sky.

The Northern Air Freight plane leaves four shipments of booze, three of them—cases of whiskey and beer—for men suspected of bootlegging by the local police. Shipping records show that one of the men has received three cases of whiskey over the past six days.

Outside, two men, each with a case of beer tucked under an arm, tread from the MarkAir terminal toward a river slough. They are met by a woman who helps them load the beer into a pair of boats. After pausing for a drink, they take off up the slough and disappear around the bend, a tiny current in the big river of booze.

Half an hour later, Tommy Toms of Aniak is perched on a bluff above the same slough. He and a friend are holding the cases of beer and whiskey that arrived under his name at Northern Air, and they have cracked the beer case and are drinking.

He's no bootlegger, Toms says, but he also doesn't believe it is wrong for anyone to buy or sell liquor. "It's their money, they could do what they want. There should be no law in spending money the way you want."

A third friend emerges from the thicket below. He ambles up the hill, chats for a few minutes, then hoists the two cases to his shoulders and turns back the way he came.

The next day, Aniak police report a complaint from Kalskag that Toms was bootlegging there.

FLIGHTS FOR BOOZE

Airlines large and small are huge channels for Alaska's river of booze. Their role was recognized last year by an elders council of the Seward Peninsula and the northern Bering Sea islands. In a formal resolution, they asked air carriers to refuse liquor shipments to the Bering Straits villages.

A more discreet role is played by private planes.

James Michelangelo, chief of the National Transportation Safety Board's office in Anchorage, said he believes that booze is the cargo aboard some of the hundreds of planes that take off each day from Merrill Field, one of the nation's busiest airports. The only time anyone knows for sure, though, is when something goes wrong.

That happened Jan. 24, 1987, when a single-engine plane crashed on takeoff at Merrill. The pilot survived, but was uncooperative with authorities, Michelangelo said. He gave his address as General Delivery, Bethel.

When authorities went through the plane, they found it loaded with liquor.

"They had booze up the kazoo," Michelangelo said.

Michelangelo said alcohol, in small amounts, is suspected as a hidden cargo on a Yute Air mail plane that crashed and exploded May 7, 1987, on a hillside near Chefornak, killing the pilot. The flight manifest listed no volatile liquids, yet the plane burned with a ferocity that could only have been fueled by an extremely flammable cargo, he said.

Most booze, at least to Bethel and the surrounding wet villages, moves on scheduled airlines and air taxis. For some, the business can be an important part of the profit picture.

Phil Hoversten, once an official for now-defunct Wien Air Alaska, said the expedited booze packages that arrived on Fridays brought in enough money to cover the entire weekly payroll of the Bethel staff. "We'd get 100 to 150 packages at 50 bucks a crack," he said.

Audi Air, a commuter airline based in Fairbanks that serves the Inupiat and Athabascan communities of the North Slope and Interior, has a pad of order forms from International Liquor of Fairbanks stuck on the wall of its Fort Yukon terminal.

MarkAir has had promotions with liquor stores. Brown Jug has distributed flyers saying it has teamed up with MarkAir to bring speedy and convenient service to Bethel. MarkAir will pick up checks and money orders at its counter in Bethel, whiz them to Anchorage for delivery to Brown Jug, and have the booze waiting for the customer by the next day—with no Alascom charges.

MarkAir's express package rates are the best to Bethel. Clerks at Party Time and Our Liquor in Anchorage recommend the price and convenience of the daily 3:45 p.m. MarkAir flight to Bethel. The cost for up to 70 pounds is $36.75 for a SpeedMark versus $47 for an Alaska Airlines Goldstreak, they said.

MarkAir's former Bethel station manager, Kent Harding, says the airlines should shoulder more responsibility for controlling booze.

"Anyone that lives in a community—management or employees—should like to see bootlegging controlled," said Harding, now a sergeant with the Bethel police department.

But that attitude got him in trouble when he worked for MarkAir, he said.

"When a box (not marked as liquor), came in and would go slosh, that had obvious signs of liquor, we would bring it to the attention of police. They would get a search warrant. And it would be safe to say that what was reported turned out 100 percent of the time to be alcohol."

Harding said the concealment of the liquor indicated that it was bound for the bootleg market and justified a search warrant.

But his attitude made his bosses unhappy, he said. "You can either be an employee of MarkAir and keep the revenue, or go back to being a cop," he quoted them as saying. So he quit.

MarkAir President Ralph Brumbaugh declined to respond to Harding's comments.

Officials of airlines in Alaska say they refuse to ship liquor to dry villages. But most say they are duty-bound to carry all legal cargo—and booze to Bethel and most western Alaska villages is legal.

MAKING A STAND

One airline is different. Bering Air decided to just say no.

The airline offers commuter service to 17 northwest villages out of Nome and serves as a contract carrier for continuing Alaska Airlines passengers and cargo.

Bering Air President Jim Rowe said the airline will carry no booze to any village, wet or dry.

"It was my choice," said Rowe, who has flown in the area for 14 years.

"I'm responsible for the impact of this company on the people it serves. The fact is that we do provide a lot of services for the troopers, and we're on medevac duty. When there's an emergency call to go out to a village, if you're the pilot and it's 2 o'clock in the morning, and you're looking at somebody about to go into a body bag, and the troopers ask where they got the booze, I don't want them pointing their fingers at me.

"Anytime I get a call that someone's hurt in a village, it's somebody I know. There are villages where there are 13-, 14-year-old kids having alcohol problems, and I may have flown the mother to the hospital to have those kids. So it's personal."

Rowe said he has no delusion that his action is diminishing the flow of booze into the villages. With the exception of Little Diomede, at least one other carrier serves each of his destinations, and none flies by his rules.

Alaska Airlines was not happy with his decision because of concerns that it would run afoul of common carrier regulations. Rowe said he sympathizes with their concerns.

"Even though we're certified the same as MarkAir or Alaska, it's harder politically (for them) to make the stand we have. Alaska Airlines doesn't support our stand. They're a publicly held company. If they make a stand such as we have, it goes all the way back to Washington, D.C. When Bering Air does it, there's only one person it comes back to, Jim Rowe.

"One hundred percent of all the mail we had was positive," he said, including letters from local councils and elders. "No one has even suggested we were out of line. Having alcohol in the villages is not a position that's easily defended. There are not many good points for alcohol abuse."

While other airline companies have not followed Rowe's example, some individual pilots have.

'NO MORE BOOZE FLIGHTS'

It is a cool, windy morning in October, 8 a.m., and there is no hint yet of dawn. Pilot Jim Twedo walks into the Ryan Air Service terminal at Unalakleet.

"No more booze flights," he tells the ticket counter clerk, with a note of disgust in his voice. "I'm not doing any more."

Later, during the flight to Nome, he talks about the last straw: a flight chartered the previous day by two women to the nearest liquor store. It was in Galena, 130 miles away.

"People's permanent fund checks have just come in, and they're taking charters to get booze," he says. "They don't have food for their kids at home. Their kids don't have good shoes and jackets for the winter. I don't want to be a part of it anymore. It makes me feel guilty.

"You just got to draw the line," he says. "I'm just tired of seeing the kids of parents I've taken sitting outside crying because their parents are home drunk."

If recent history is any example, Twedo's action would only divert the business somewhere else, like a small weir in the river of booze.

HAVEN FOR BOOTLEGGERS

FRIDAY, JANUARY 15, 1988

BY HAL BERNTON

BETHEL—On a damp Sunday in October, two youthful brothers from a village along the Kuskokwim River motored up to Bethel for whiskey to drink with the second game of the World Series. To make the bootleg buy, they didn't have far to go.

They pulled up their boat on a beach littered with empty plastic bottles of Windsor Canadian and walked across a sandy boardwalk to a collection of plywood shacks and A-frame huts.

One of the two disappeared into a hut, then reappeared a few minutes later. He had a bottle hidden under his clothes, his brother said. They hopped back into the boat and turned downriver for the half-hour trip home.

Such sales are the mainstay of Alaska's bootleg liquor industry, and Bethel is its capital. Bootleggers find the city's tentative approach to prohibition—allowing the importation of alcohol, but not its sale—and its role as an air and river crossroads, an ideal climate.

The cases of liquor that arrive each day from Anchorage are sold, bottle by bottle, from riverfront shacks, the trunks of taxi cabs, abandoned freezer vans or the backpacks of teen-agers. Law enforcement officials estimate the illegal trade at $2 million to $5 million a year.

"Right now we see pallets, literally pallets of alcohol arrive at the airport," said Bethel Police Chief Kevin Clayton. "We know where it's going. We know what's going to happen with it, but we're powerless to stop it."

Much of the liquor is sold to local residents or the people who visit Bethel from the villages that dot the broad delta of the Yukon and Kuskokwim rivers. Some are social drinkers, but many are binge alcoholics unwilling to wait for liquor to arrive by air freight from Anchorage. They want their whiskey immediately, and will pay up to $40 for a $7 bottle of it.

Other bootleggers use Bethel as a base from which to smuggle booze into villages where both importation and sale are banned. In the "dry" villages, that same $7 bottle can sell for $120.

Aniak, a village along the middle Kuskokwim River that also allows unlimited importation of liquor, is another distribution hub for bootleggers. Cargo and passenger planes bring in daily shipments of booze, which a half-dozen bootleggers sell to local clients or send up and down the river.

In both towns, the bootleggers operate just out of sight, often using "runners," some as young as 12 years old, to make the actual sales. The runners dispense bottles from small packs, then turn over the cash, minus a $5- to $10-a-bottle commission, to the bootleggers.

Bootleggers who sell directly to customers protect themselves by refusing to deal with strangers.

In the early '80s, some of the biggest bootleggers were ethnic Albanians from Yugoslavia.

"I remember when Albanians from Bethel came in they would buy about 10 cases of Windsor whiskey in plastic bottles," recalls Edith Turkington, a former employee of Party Time Liquor in Anchorage. "That is 10 cases for each person."

A BIG MARKET

"There's plenty of business for all," said one bootlegger in his early 20s who agreed to be interviewed only if his name were withheld. He is a handsome man who would look more at home on a California surfing beach than the soggy tundra of the delta. He tried a 9-to-5 job, he said, but bootlegging proved more alluring, first as a way to earn quick cash, and then as a full-time occupation. Today he peddles whiskey from a small freezer van in the seedy section of town known as Bootlegger's Alley.

"I just kind of got into this and things started working out real good," he said.

He spoke on a Friday evening while at the Bethel airport awaiting a shipment of beer. The order was for another bootlegger, who planned to smuggle it into a dry village.

The young man said he launched his bootlegging operation two years ago with a special introductory offer: $25-a-bottle whiskey, which he hoped would quickly attract a core of customers. The price created "quite a bit of conflict" with other bootleggers, he said, so he raised it to $30.

Now, in a good day, he may sell two 12-bottle cases of whiskey at a profit of more than $500. Less enterprising bootleggers, the ones he calls "subsistence bootleggers," order only a half-dozen bottles at a time, earning just enough to support their own alcohol habits.

At first, he said, he used his van as both an illicit liquor store and a tiny, one-room apartment. But last fall he finally tired of drunken clients pestering him through the night—even after the booze was all gone—and moved out. Now he operates only part of the day from a different van. But that approach has caused him other hassles: "I've had problems with break-ins three or four times. And my windows have been shot up."

He also had trouble with alcoholic runners who drank his booze instead of selling it. Now he uses only sober ones. In early October, his three runners were aged 16, 17, and 25.

Despite the problems, he estimates he earned more than $20,000 last year. "When I didn't drink," he said, "it was really quite profitable."

Sales of bootleg booze peak in July as hundreds of fishermen converge on Bethel to sell their catches. On the Fourth of July alone, he said, he earned more than $2,000. Demand stays strong through the summer, then drops off sharply as villagers stalk moose in September. As permanent fund dividends begin to arrive in October, business picks up again and remains brisk through New Year's.

On a typical weekend, he gathers with other bootleggers in the parking lot of the town shopping mall. They smoke, drink, talk and watch for potential clients across the street at the Brass Buckle, a low, ranch-style building that serves as the delta's only nightclub. By midnight, the Brass Buckle is jammed with Eskimo, Indian and white rock 'n' rollers.

The bar can't sell alcohol, just soft drinks, but that isn't obvious from the customers. Many are staggeringly drunk. On the crowded dance floor, two women argue over a man; across the room, two men fight over a woman, or would, if they were sober enough to manage a serious scuffle.

"It's a hot spot," the bootlegger said. "People don't go there unless they're really f——d up."

At 1:30 a.m., as closing time approaches, the action shifts outside.

Around the back of the building, amid a clutter of 55-gallon drums and fuel tanks, a young Eskimo woman sips from a cup. "I'm getting drunk and looking for a good piece of a——," she says with a laugh.

Out front, the parking lot of the Brass Buckle looks like a giant block party. "I'm on shruuums," says one woman who apparently has been eating psilocybin mushrooms. A young man standing nearby pulls out a plastic bottle of Windsor Canadian from his blue-jean jacket. When he draws a few stares, the bottle quickly disappears behind his back.

A half-dozen cabs ring the parking lot, the drivers ready to make quick runs for booze, and the ever-present, backpack-clad runners wander through the crowd.

The bootleggers stay as long as there is money to be made.

'THERE'S NO FUTURE'

"People will beg you and beg you," the bootlegger said. "They pay in food stamps . . . everything they got. One guy gave $65 in food stamps for one bottle." Sometimes they trade ivory.

Asked whether he worries about the ravages of alcohol on his customers and their community, he replied: "When it gets to the younger neighborhood kids, that makes you feel kind of bad. Knowing you are f——ing these kids' lives up."

Briefly last summer, he said, he feared a police bust. Then the heat slacked off. "Bootleggers are winning the war now. . . . It seems like nobody cares," he said.

Does he ever think about quitting? "I just got into this and things started working out real good." He thought about it some more. "This is so easy. . . . But there's no future."

THE 'BUSH AIR COMPLEX'

Carl Berger spends much of his time trying to heal the wounds caused by alcohol. The Yukon-Kuskokwim Health Corp., which he directs, provides suicide prevention and rape counseling, and helps villages cope with accidental death and acts of violence.

From the second-story window of his riverfront office, Berger can look down at the beachfront conglomeration of A-frames and shacks with a reputation as one of the town's most notorious bootlegging sites.

Locals call it "the Bush Air complex" because of the air taxi headquartered there.

During the fishing season, Berger recalled, he watched in frustration as village seiners, their pockets stuffed with cash from salmon sales, lined up to buy bootleg whiskey and then scattered up and down the river to drink.

Some headed down the beach toward the neighborhood of state Sen. Johne Binkley, a forceful spokesman for local option laws that allow voters to ban alcohol. Others milled around the health corporation building. "It got to the point where we had to hire security so that people could get in and out of the building without getting harassed," Berger recalled.

The complex sits on a half-acre of land owned by the Moravian Church. The Moravians came to Western Alaska in the 1880s and helped found Bethel. The federal government deeded 129 acres of land to them in 1911. A church was built on one part, a school on another. Some of the land has been washed away by the river; much of what remains is being "held in trust for the Native people," according to Kurt H. Vitt, director of theological education for the church.

For the last 13 years, a portion of the "trust" land has been leased to Ron Peltola, the 44-year-old proprietor of Bush Air. Peltola has been charged with flying booze into a dry village and is awaiting trial. He has a history of problems with authorities.

In 1974, he pleaded guilty to a misdemeanor charge of selling wild game illegally and was fined $2,400. The state temporarily shut down his charter operation in 1985 because he lacked the required insurance.

Last year, his pilot's license was permanently revoked for doctoring his medical records, according to the Federal Aviation Administration. On June 22, he pleaded no contest to a misdemeanor charge of harassment for repeatedly threatening to kill a police officer.

The Moravians first gave Peltola a 10-year lease in 1974, according to court records. He built a plywood shack to serve as an air taxi office, and a collection of other shacks and A-frames, some of which he later sold.

When the lease expired in 1984, the Moravians sued to evict Peltola for non-payment of rent. So far they have been unsuccessful.

'ONE-STOP SHOPPING'

In the meantime, the complex has developed into a base for bootlegging, according to Berger and Bethel Police Chief Clayton. It is the base for one of a half-dozen major bootlegging operations in Bethel, Clayton said, with revenue estimated at more than $100,000 a year.

Because the beach at Bush Air is one of the few breaks in a riverfront largely walled off by old cars and metal pilings, it is a favorite pull-in spot for villagers arriving by boat. The beach also serves as a waiting area for charter passengers traveling to or from nearby villages.

"It was easy to get customers, when you knew (Bush Air) could give you a bottle and fly you," said Simon Brown, a state trooper who investigated Bush Air. "This was one-stop shopping."

On Aug. 2, troopers, with the aid of an undercover agent, busted Bush Air. They seized Peltola's floatplane and arrested him on misdemeanor charges of importing alcohol into the dry village of Tuntutuliak and enlisting a minor to aid in the crime.

The minor was a young female employee of the air service. She told Trooper Brown she went to the Bethel airport to pick up liquor and delivered it to Peltola, who handed it over to Joe Newman, an occupant of an A-frame next to the Bush Air office, according to an affidavit by Brown.

Peltola instructed the employee to send any liquor customers to the A-frame, Brown said she told him. After the booze was sold, Newman brought the money to her, and she put it in a Bush Air money bag.

Bush Air still has a floatplane, and the charter service is open for business. Peltola spoke indignantly of his arrest, and flatly denied the employee's statements to police. He said passengers may have carried liquor on his planes, but he didn't know about it.

Peltola sold two of the three A-frames in May 1982, according to Peltola and his attorney. Some huts may be used for bootlegging, Peltola said, but they have no connection to Bush Air.

$120 A BOTTLE

Hooper Bay, a community of 776 people spread along the Bering Seacoast, is one of more than 30 villages along the Kuskokwim River that prohibits the importation and sale of alcohol.

But the prohibition, rather than stemming the flow of liquor, has merely altered its course by creating a powerful economic incentive for bootlegging. A bottle of whiskey that sells for $7 in Anchorage or $40 in Bethel can sell for $120 in a village like Hooper Bay.

As a result, subsistence or professional bootleggers bring booze into virtually every village—by snowmobile or skiff, in the baggage of air charter passengers, or in a concealed package through the U.S. mail.

In Holy Cross, a village on the lower Yukon River, bootleggers use private planes to fly in liquor shipments from the nearby wet village of Anvik, or smuggle it in on cargo flights delivering groceries and other essentials.

"We get it every Friday. . . . There'd be a lot of repacked boxes for people," said Bill Turner, a convicted Holy Cross bootlegger who recently went through an Anchorage alcohol rehabilitation program. "Like, it might be a milk box or an egg box. And it'll be all taped up so you can't get in it real easy. And inside the egg box would be booze."

Where cash is scarce, drinkers often turn to sour-tasting batches of home-brew made from crackers, yeast, sugar and fruit cocktail.

Last summer in Hooper Bay, a teen-age boy killed himself during a game of Russian roulette, and four other youths attempted suicide, according to Ed Graham, the principal of Hooper Bay High School. Only one of the attempted suicides was directly linked to drinking, Graham said, but "without any question, the real problem is alcohol."

"Everybody in the village is affected by even one single drunk," he said. "The village is so small and so close that every little incident has an effect on everybody."

Much of the hard liquor sold in Hooper Bay is imported by home-grown entrepreneurs lured by the easy money. While fishing, fire-fighting and basket weaving all provide some income, much of life is still subsistence hunting and fishing. So when someone needs a new snowmachine, bootlegging is a quick way to raise the cash. A bootlegger can buy a round-trip ticket to Anchorage, party in the city for a few days and still turn a profit on the trip by bringing home a single, 12-bottle case of whiskey purchased for $86.

Other village bootleggers go only as far as Bethel, where an established bootlegger will, for a fee, order booze from Anchorage and have it delivered to the airport. From there, it can be concealed in luggage and flown into a dry village.

Once in a dry village, bootleggers offer liquor to a select group of customers, or use runners to peddle it. A case of whiskey can be sold in a half-hour or less, according to one part-time bootlegger. Sometimes, the last bottle in a shipment is auctioned off to the highest bidder.

The bootleggers "know the people who like to drink," said one 30-year-old resident of Hooper Bay, "and they know the power of the craving. They know people need it."

A REVOLUTION OF HOPE

TUESDAY, JANUARY 19, 1988

BY DAVID HULEN

GLENNALLEN—Almost everyone had a horrible story to tell, stories of suicides and despair and deaths that shouldn't have been. These were the kinds of things people talked about openly. More discreetly, they whispered of sexually abused children and women beaten by husbands and boyfriends in bursts of drunken rage.

People in the villages of Alaska are like a man being pulled under by the currents of a river, said Walter Charley, a 79-year-old Athabascan from Copper Center. The people sitting around him—Indians, Aleuts and Eskimos from all over Alaska—knew exactly what he meant. Some nodded as he spoke.

"We're struggling for our lives," Walter Charley said.

Here, on a dusty baseball diamond beneath the Wrangell Mountains, the roots of a revolution were quietly taking grip.

For five days last August, a couple hundred Alaska Natives gathered to discuss the problems facing people in the villages. A few were counselors, social workers or political leaders, but most were just regular people—many of them former alcoholics or drug abusers—trying to live a decent life, worried about the future and eager to visit with people from other places struggling with the same issues.

They shared their experiences and talked about solutions. They danced to traditional music, and boogied to a Native rock band. In a ceremony at the end of the retreat, they vowed to stay sober, respect the people they live around and work toward improving life back home.

The gathering was one of the most visible signs of a movement percolating in dozens of villages over the past two years. Known as the "sobriety movement," its goal is a Native world unimpaired by alcohol or drugs, one in which widespread alcoholism is no longer considered normal.

The aim of the movement goes well beyond that, though, and includes reshaping Native communities and culture all over Alaska, places where people are being destroyed by changes and forces they don't understand and haven't been able to control.

GLIMMERS OF LIGHT

It is a long, slow, extreme uphill struggle. The movement is so new it's difficult to tell how much of an effect, if any, it is having.

The problems are so complex that there's no single, proven way to solve them. Villages are trying dozens of approaches, from Alcoholics Anonymous to traditional Native spirituality and ritual, from legal sovereignty to est-like "personal growth" seminars.

"It's not the kind of thing you can look at and see big dynamic successes," said Mary O'Connor, health educator for the North Slope Borough in Barrow. "You can't say, 'Yep, it's working. We're real successful.' You're dealing in people's lives. It's an over-time kind of thing."

What the sobriety movement has stressed above all else is a philosophy that it must be the people of the villages—not health agencies, not the government, not the regional corporations—who take responsibility for their own well-being. With that comes pride, unity with others doing the same thing, and increased control over their lives.

"You've got to start someplace," said Doug Modig, director of the alcohol program for the Rural Alaska Community Action Program, a state- and federally-funded social service agency.

"We started with the idea that people are impaired by alcohol and that has to stop if you're going to deal with these other problems. . . . As long as people are drinking, they don't have a choice. When they stop, they do.

"We're not just talking about alcohol. It's a real broad thing. We're talking about suicides, and sexual abuse, and domestic violence. We're talking about economics and ineffective local government.

"We're talking about personal responsibility that results in self-determination. . . . It suggests a unity, that people aren't doing it alone."

Modig, a Tsimshian Indian from Ketchikan, runs the only statewide alcohol program in Alaska, and has been at the center of the sobriety movement from its beginnings. Two years ago, RuralCap banned alcohol from its functions, a move since followed by several regional Native corporations.

Since then, Modig and his associate, Amy Lohr, have traveled to more than 20 villages, been invited to 25 others and worked with more than 90. They say they listen to what communities want, then help establish appropriate alcoholism and development programs.

"The approach from the agencies in the past has always been, 'We'll come help you.' What we're saying is, 'You got to help yourself. We can maybe help you do that, but you've got to be the one to do it,' " Modig said.

Some regional health corporations and government health agencies have begun to tailor programs to the needs and wishes of specific communities rather than use a single model for all. For example, rather than rely on a single psychologist to make infrequent visits to a village, there have been efforts to train residents to counsel one another.

"Nobody can come in from outside and solve the problems," said Carla Bonney, director of the tribal-run health department in the village of Tanana, in the Interior. "But for so many years, people, Native people, have been told they're not capable of solving their own problems. There's been an erosion of self-esteem that goes back to the missionaries.

"It's not a big flow, something huge that's happening everywhere. It's little glimmers here and there. We'll hear that somebody somewhere else has similar ideas and it's a very positive thing."

Some people in some villages have stopped drinking. Others have voted to ban alcohol and set communitywide goals for living without booze. Progress is slow, but there are small signs of it.

In Alakanuk, a Yupik village in which eight young adults killed themselves in 16 months, an Alcoholics Anonymous meeting was held for the first time last fall. With eight people attending, it was believed to be the largest AA meeting ever on the Yukon River. Regular meetings have been held since.

On the North Slope, perhaps the most affluent local government in Alaska, young adults who have given up booze have gone on borough-owned television to talk about it.

Attendance at statewide gatherings like the one in Glennallen has increased steadily.

While some communities have tried banning booze—with varying degrees of success—there are no examples of Alaska villages that have successfully gone from rampant alcoholism to widespread sobriety. Sobriety advocates hope that, over time, some communities will emerge as examples of what is possible. That will take years, they admit.

TO SHOW THE WAY

More than anything else, Alaska's sobriety movement has been influenced by Alkali Lake, an Indian village in British Columbia that —through the will of its people—went from 100 percent alcoholism to almost complete sobriety. It took 15 years.

Alkali Lake's struggle was depicted in the film "The Honour of All," with residents of the town portraying themselves as the drunks they once were. Cassettes of the movie have circulated extensively throughout rural Alaska for the past year, with demand increasing as more people learn what happened there.

"It's been real influential," said Modig. Dozens of villages in Alaska have problems as bad or worse than the old Alkali Lake, he said. "It's a vision of hope. People see it and say, 'If they can do it, maybe we can do it.' People look at that and they see real live Native people. It's not a Hollywood thing."

Over the past couple of years, people from Alkali Lake have made several trips to Alaska to talk about what happened there, as have people from Four Worlds Development Council, an Alberta-based Native organization that has worked extensively on Native alcoholism in Canada and the Lower 48.

"When things get really desperate, when a whole community is ready to go down, when things get really bad, it's time to do something," Lloyd Dick, a 23-year-old from Alkali Lake, told participants at Glennallen. He told of losing family members and friends, and struggling with alcohol and drugs himself.

"I used to do about five hits of acid in one night," he said. "Really get stoned. I'm really grateful for being alive. I travel maybe thousands of miles, and talk a little bit, maybe one or two, it would be really nice if you'd listen and recognize what's happening with this alcohol. . . . You can't hide a lot of stuff that happened, can't keep it inside. You stand up and share."

Later, David West, a huge man with long, dark braids who leads the Fairbanks-based Crossing Paths drummers, sat in a circle of singers around a big drum in right field. He slowly pounded a beat and, in a high, strong, ghostly wail, sang a traditional Sioux chant. Others also beat the drum and answered his chants, or danced slowly around it.

Between songs, West spoke:

"We share the dream of the people of Alkali Lake, that we can kill this enemy. It's been a prayer of ours for a long time, that it would be the Native people that would show the way out from under the disease of alcoholism, for this is our country. We were put here, we're from here.

"It should be us that has the strength to show the way."

TWO

CAMPAIGN FOR BUS SAFETY

1989 WINNER IN THE GENERAL NEWS REPORTING CATEGORY

"For a distinguished example of reporting within a newspaper's area of circulation that meets the daily challenges of journalism such as spot news reporting or consistent beat coverage . . ."

The Louisville Courier-Journal
Staff

We've all seen them on the highways—secondhand school buses loaded full of youngsters or the church faithful on an outing. A fatal collision involving one such bus in Kentucky triggered investigations into bus safety and drunken driving.

This series of articles begins with the story of a church excursion that ended in grotesque tragedy on an interstate highway in rural northern Kentucky. Patched together from the memories of survivors, it reveals the trauma and confusion through which our staff had to dig.

On the night of the crash, one of our reporters was among the first on the scene. We had an exclusive, full first-day story. Being first gave us an advantage, helping us dominate the news coverage. It also meant we could be first to develop the public policy questions raised by the tragedy, with not one but two series: the first on bus safety, the second on drunk driving.

Why bus safety? Because, as bizarre as the accident was, none of the victims was killed, or even seriously injured, by the impact of the drunk driver's pickup truck slamming into the side of the bus. They died because they could not escape the inferno that followed.

Throughout the coverage, we never lost the respect and cooperation of the victims and their families. That's how we were able to convince 19 youngsters to describe the moments in which they escaped or were saved, while 27 of their friends, classmates and fellow church members suffocated and burned. We had to convince their parents, too.

We argued that it was worth sharing these horrors, in order to make the case for reforms, some of which already have been accomplished and some of which are in the works.

That first night, our copy desk rose to the challenge.

A clerk making routine hospital checks learned about 12:15 a.m. —five minutes prior to the last edition's Page One copy deadline— that some victims of a bus crash were on their way to the emergency room of a Louisville hospital.

A local reporter, a state capitol reporter and a staff photographer were rousted from bed and dispatched to the scene, 50 miles away and about equidistant from Louisville, Cincinnati and Lexington. Copy editors became reporters, phoning funeral homes, hospitals, churches and law enforcement agencies to pin down the details.

Out of that night's chaos, the copy desk built a story that held up in the cold light of day.

On the second day, and throughout the first week of coverage, we pounded away at the issues, while not forgetting the human drama.

In ensuing weeks we fully developed these issues:

• We looked at bus safety from a national and state perspective in our series, "The Search for Safety." We discovered that researchers had been warning of these dangers for two decades.

• We looked at the drunk driving problem in early September, in a series called "Bending the Law on DUI." Kentucky had stiffened its penalties several years before, and Traffic Alcohol Patrol programs had attacked the problem in urban areas such as Louisville and Lexington, but our series showed that enforcement was uneven around the state and that major loopholes existed.

Reaction by Kentucky officials was swift, setting an example for federal officials.

Here's a summary of bus-design and safety changes since the Carrollton crash, all of which responded to issues raised in our reporting.

• Kentucky is requiring two "push-out" windows as emergency exits on standard-sized buses and four on larger buses. The state Board of Education recommended that push-out windows be installed on existing buses that are driven across county lines on field trips and to athletic events. Many districts went beyond the recommendation by installing the push-out windows on many existing buses. The state also is requiring all new buses to be powered by diesel fuel, which is much less flammable than gasoline.

• A task force assembled by Gov. Wallace Wilkinson recommended that buses purchased after November 1990 be equipped with a left-side emergency door. It also said all existing buses—including the aged relics used by churches and youth groups—should be retrofitted with four push-out windows by November 1990, despite complaints from ministers who don't want to spend the money. The task force urged that younger drivers receive additional training and that school districts certify the safety of any buses they put up for sale.

• Kentucky began requiring safety inspections of all privately owned buses. In the first round, more than 700 buses—about one-fifth of those inspected—failed, and more than 160 were in such bad shape that they had to be taken off the road immediately.

The changes have made Kentucky a leader in bus safety.

• The federal government has said it is studying its regulations on emergency exits and flammability of seating materials. Federal officials have said they expect new regulations in both of these areas. The federal government also reissued a manual of school-bus safety operating guidelines, which was last issued in 1973.

• Many bus manufacturers decided to step up research on less-flammable seating materials. And, school transportation directors plan to at least look at the issue of fuel-tank placement at their 1990 conference.

We believe our quick response met the test of daily journalism. We think our follow-through helped to set an agenda for reform that will save lives. Victims of great tragedy always want their loss to have meaning. We hope our work helped that happen in this instance.

—David V. Hawpe, Editor
The Louisville Courier-Journal

MANY FEARED DEAD, DOZENS HURT IN FIERY I-71 BUS CRASH

SUNDAY, MAY 15, 1988

Several people were feared dead and at least two dozen were seriously injured in a fiery bus crash on Interstate 71 near Carrollton last night.

"I've been on the state police for 24 years, and this is the worst so far as the number of people killed, so far as the seriousness of it," Trooper Jim Mudd said this morning.

Mudd said the bus, carrying mostly teen-agers from the First Assembly of God Church in Radcliff, was hit head-on by a pickup going the wrong way and the bus burst into flames. He said 18 people were thought to be dead.

The truck driver was taken to a hospital. No charges had been filed.

Mudd said officials planned to use a crane to lift the bus wreckage onto a flatbed truck with the bodies on it. It would be taken to the National Guard armory in Carrollton, which will be used as a temporary morgue.

No names of victims were released.

The bus, returning from a trip to Kings Island, was carrying 67 people, Mudd said.

The victims were taken to several area hospitals by helicopter and ambulance.

Fifteen—at least six of them critically burned—had arrived at Humana Hospital-University of Louisville by 2 a.m., said Dr. Don Thomas, head of the emergency room. Six were transferred to Kosair Children's Hospital.

Two others had been taken to Humana Hospital-Suburban, but the hospital would not release any information about them.

Dr. Jeffrey Alan Campbell, the emergency-room physician at Carroll County Hospital in Carrollton, said his hospital treated about 20 patients suffering from burns and respiratory injuries.

"Some were seriously injured, but we only got the second wave. The most seriously injured were taken to Humana Hospital-University or Norton's in Louisville."

Campbell said there were no fatalities at Carroll County Hospital.

"There was lots of fire. I don't know if a fire broke out and caused the accident or if some sort of accident caused a fire. But there was fire —a lot of it," Campbell said.

Mary Darling, assistant director at Tri-County Community Hospital in La Grange, said that about eight people were treated there.

She said only one of those victims was seriously injured, and that person was sent to University.

Meade County School Superintendent Stuart Pepper said he received a telephone call after midnight from the Carroll County school superintendent, who thought a Meade County school bus might be involved in the accident.

Pepper said he went to the Meade County police dispatch office and confirmed from state police in La Grange that no Meade County bus was involved. Pepper said the confusion apparently resulted from a Meade County bus that had been sold to a church group two or three years ago. Although the Meade County lettering is always painted out before buses are sold, Pepper said, the bus involved in the accident apparently had burned, revealing the old Meade County lettering.

FIERY DEATHS OF 27 LEAVE QUESTIONS, ANGUISH

TRUCK TRAVELING WRONG WAY BRINGS HORROR TO RADCLIFF TEENS ON OUTING

MONDAY, MAY 16, 1988

BY TOM LOFTUS, AL CROSS AND JUDY BRYANT

CARROLLTON, KY.—The collision that turned a church bus into a hellish fireball and killed at least 27 people—most of them teen-agers—left officials groping for answers yesterday as families of the victims tried to cope with their unspeakable grief.

The tragedy, one of the worst bus accidents in U.S. history, happened about 10:55 Saturday night when the bus collided head-on with a Toyota pickup truck that was traveling the wrong way on Interstate 71 near Carrollton.

The bus, which was engulfed by flames shortly after the collision, was returning its 67 occupants to the First Assembly of God Church in Radcliff after a daylong outing at Kings Island amusement park north of Cincinnati. Many of those on the bus were not members of the church but were guests.

The names of the dead were not released, although the state's chief medical examiner, Dr. George Nichols, said there were 19 females and eight males. Forty-two people were hurt, and 17 remained hospitalized yesterday evening, including nine in critical condition.

Police said the truck, which was traveling north in the southbound lanes, was driven by Larry W. Mahoney, 34, a chemical worker from Moxley in rural Owen County, who was hurt seriously. No charges had been filed last night.

The main questions that investigators said they could not answer yesterday were:

Why was Mahoney's truck on the wrong side of the divided interstate? And why did the bus become engulfed in flames so quickly?

All 27 victims were burned beyond recognition. Authorities said they would identify them all positively, then notify their families.

However, the pastor of the church said the driver, John Pearman, and the church's youth director, Chuck Kytta, were killed. Pearman was an associate pastor of the church and the circuit clerk of Hardin County.

Families and friends of those unaccounted for have been informed and counseled about the likelihood that they have lost loved ones. Many relied on their religious faith to get them through the ordeal.

Debra Dame of Radcliff said that since 5:30 a.m. yesterday, when she could not locate her 11-year-old daughter, Lori, at any hospital, "I've had good feelings she's with peace now."

A group of about 60 relatives and friends of those not yet found and likely to be among the victims drove in vans to Carroll County yesterday morning to see whether they could see their loved ones and to learn more about the disaster.

The vans were provided by Fort Knox, where 65 percent of the church members work, according to pastor W. Don Tennison.

The group went to a meeting room at the Holiday Inn just off I-71 at the Carrollton exit where they conferred with Nichols.

Nichols told reporters before he met the group that he was going to advise them that they not see the bodies.

"Visual identification is impossible," Nichols said, his voice breaking. "I'm going to try to explain to them that the picture of how they want to remember their children is not in that room. It's what's in their wallets and in their minds."

The members of the group took Nichols' advice. Most returned to Radcliff yesterday afternoon.

THE COLLISION

State police troopers Jim Mudd and Glenn Walton, who made periodic reports to reporters all day yesterday, said they are not sure how Mahoney came to be driving the wrong way on I-71.

"There are places he could have crossed over. He could have come on an exit ramp," Walton said. "We are not sure . . . how long he had been there at the time of the collision."

Two students on the bus said last night that they saw a motorcycle racing with the truck. Walton and Mudd said they had no information to substantiate reports of a motorcycle.

They said the truck hit the right side of the front of the 1977 Ford bus.

The bus then veered into a 1977 Cadillac driven by a man from Akron, Ohio, Walton said. Walton said neither that driver nor his passenger was hurt.

Mahoney is an employee of M & T Chemicals in Carrollton. In 1984, he paid a fine after being charged with driving while intoxicated, said Carroll Circuit Clerk William Wheeler.

Mudd said blood was taken from both drivers for testing, as is the usual practice in such cases, but the results probably will not be released until the case is submitted to a grand jury.

Walton said police were "not ruling out anything 100 percent." He said yesterday's investigation focused only on "life-threatening developments" such as monitoring the progress of hospitalized victims and identifying the dead.

Darrell Breeden, who lives about a quarter-mile from the scene, said he heard an explosion, but Walton said investigators have not confirmed that there was an explosion.

Walton said investigators have not been able to determine why the fire erupted so quickly. He did say the truck hit near the bus's gas tank, which he said is beneath the floor just behind the main door.

Tennison and Wayne Spradlin of Elizabethtown, a church board member and mechanic who had prime responsibility for maintenance of the bus, said they believed the collision caused the fuel tank to rupture and explode. Carroll County Coroner Jim Dunn told The Associated Press that the bus had just been refueled.

Nichols said the bus has 11 rows of seats, with an aisle down the middle. Those seats normally are designed to accommodate three passengers, Walton said. If that is true, and if the bus was full, there were 66 passengers aboard, plus Pearman, the driver, Walton said.

However, a list of the injured compiled from area hospitals last night included the names of 42 people—including Mahoney. But it was not clear whether the other 41 were all passengers on the bus.

Walton and Nichols said most of the passengers who escaped did so out of the back emergency exit.

Nichols said late yesterday that there were two groups of victims in the aisle—one between the seventh and ninth rows, and another at the fifth and sixth rows.

He said examinations of the victims at the temporary morgue set up in the National Guard armory show that all 27 died from smoke inhalation, not from burns or the impact of the collision.

He said smoke inhalation can cause death that quickly, depending on the composition of the smoke.

AFTERMATH

The southbound lanes of I-71 were closed by state police, and traffic in the northbound lanes was limited as ambulances rushed the injured to Carroll County Memorial Hospital and Tri-County Community Hospital in La Grange. Many of the more seriously injured victims were flown by helicopter to Humana Hospital-University of Louisville, and some of the injured were taken to three other Louisville hospitals.

Dunn said he thought dental records would be required for positive identification of every victim.

Many family members who came to Carrollton yesterday brought medical and dental records with them. The records of military families stationed at Fort Knox were flown to Carroll County by army helicopter.

Early yesterday morning, hours after the accident, the bus was a gutted hulk, charred gray, its windows and doors gone, the lettering on the side almost completely burned away.

The front end and cab of the pickup, a black, four-wheel-drive Toyota, appeared as crumpled as a discarded piece of aluminum foil.

Police cordoned a long stretch of the southbound lanes and median for several hours while they measured the accident scene and prepared to hoist the bus onto a flatbed truck. Scores of police cars, fire engines and ambulances lined both sides of the road.

Southbound traffic backed up almost five miles. Hundreds of people trapped in the jam—including many youngsters also returning on school buses from a day at Kings Island—walked forward until they pressed against the yellow plastic ribbons outlining the accident scene.

About 7:30 a.m. yesterday, the bus—with victims still aboard—

was carefully put aboard a flatbed truck and driven to the armory in Carrollton, where it was unloaded and put into the large, open motor-pool area.

Walton said the bus will remain on the truck inside the armory until a full investigation is complete. Representatives of the National Transportation Safety Board arrived in Carrollton yesterday. They said they were involved in the investigation because of the number of fatalities and the fact that a school bus was involved.

Late in the morning, Nichols and the chief investigating officer for the case, Trooper Henry "Sonny" Cease, went into the bus and estimated the number of victims at 26. Later, when the bodies were removed one by one, Nichols confirmed the number was 27.

Nichols said the identifications of the victims will be released today "if we're extraordinarily lucky."

About noon, the caravan of vans carrying the loved ones of those missing arrived at the Holiday Inn about a mile from the armory. After being advised by Nichols not to go to the armory, the group remained for a while in a meeting room at the hotel.

Red Cross workers gave the families sheets to fill out, listing identifying marks and other information about their missing loved ones.

Most of the group returned in the vans to Radcliff about two hours after arriving, but some stayed through the evening at the hotel.

Glenn Grubbs, 40, a friend of many of the victims who rode up from Radcliff in one of the vans, said: "They're shocked, but their faith is not shaken. We're a close-knit church although we have almost 600 members."

He said one man lost his wife and his two children.

State police troopers who were at the accident scene were at a loss to try and describe it to reporters.

"It was a very saddened, gut-wrenching experience," Mudd said.

The Carroll County community also was touched by the tragedy. By mid-morning yesterday, the Druthers restaurant across from the armory had changed the message on its highway sign to read, "Our prayers are with you."

THE INVESTIGATION

Mudd said Cease's preliminary report on the crash would not be ready for a few days.

Nichols said the position of the bodies inside the bus indicated passengers made "considerable effort" to flee by exiting through the rear door. Nichols said many of the children may have been asleep when the collision occurred.

Nichols was being helped at the armory by five staff members from his state medical examiner's office, two professors from the University of Louisville Dental School, a colonel from the Army Medical Corps, and Hardin County Coroner Louis B. Lawson, a dentist.

Walton said Nichols and his crew would continue the identification process until about 9 p.m. last night and begin again this morning about 7.

Information for this story was also gathered by staff writer Robin Garr.

SURVIVORS RECOUNT TERROR-FILLED MOMENTS AS BUS BECAME A FIREBALL

MONDAY, MAY 16, 1988

BY ROBIN GARR

The black Toyota pickup hurtled through the night on its oversize tires. It whispered along the fast lane on the wrong side of Interstate 71, sloping down the long grade toward Carrollton from the south.

The long, yellow church bus rumbled southward, pulling the grade, carrying 67 youngsters and church leaders of the First Assembly of God toward their homes in Radcliff.

Most were sleeping, tired after the church's annual outing to Kings Island amusement park near Cincinnati, said Allen Tennison, 15, son of the pastor.

Riding in a car a few hundred yards in front of the church bus, Lisa Sturgeon of Turners Station, Ky., yelped as the Toyota's headlights loomed in the windshield.

"We pulled over real quick into the slow lane," she said.

Behind them, the pickup crashed head-on into the bus.

"We didn't see his brake lights go on at all—and the next thing we knew, we saw the flames go up," Sturgeon said.

On the bus, the crash came with little warning.

"I looked up and I saw a truck and a motorcycle coming at us," said Thomas Hertz, 15, who was sitting in about the third row from the front. "Our bus driver tried to get out of the way but couldn't."

"They were coming at us," he said. "They were drag racing."

Hertz and 13-year-old Jason Booher said the motorcycle's headlight wasn't on.

Then came the crash, and smoke and flames and screams in the night.

It threw 16-year-old Larry Flowers out of his seat near the back of the bus.

"What I mainly remember is hitting the seat in front of me." Flowers said. "And then the front end caught fire and they were yelling for everybody to get off."

Wayne Cox, 14, said the impact jarred him.

Then he saw the flames.

"They spread pretty fast," said the eighth-grader at Radcliff Middle School, whose blond hair was singed by the fire.

"They just sweeped down the middle of the bus real quick," Cox said.

Tennison, who had been sleeping, said he awakened to a nightmarish scene of "bodies on top of bodies and orange everywhere."

On the bus and in trucks around it, several people were about to become heroes.

Trucker Patrick Presley of Dallas, Texas, and another trucker who didn't stay to leave his name leaped from their cabs and ran to the flaming bus.

Suddenly a gas tank exploded, filling the bus with flames and smoke. Intense fire and smoke crept toward the back of the bus, driving screaming passengers ahead of it, and Presley emptied his fire extinguisher with no apparent effect.

Then he and the other trucker opened the rear emergency door, and passengers started jumping out.

Youngsters in the front and middle of the bus crammed to the back to escape the flames. Some remained quietly in their seats; others clambered over seat tops, tried to crawl through windows and, worse, fell, piled in the aisles and jammed the rear doorway.

"I was pinned," said Cox. "I was under a lot of people. That's probably what saved me from getting burned."

Hertz, who had been holding hands with a new-found girlfriend, grabbed her and struggled to get out.

"It was so crowded. I kicked the windows and they would not break through like they're supposed to."

He managed to leap through the jammed exit and ran. "Within 45 seconds it blew," he said.

"Once I got outside I panicked. I didn't know what to do. Some truck driver handed me an extinguisher, but I didn't know how to use it so I handed it to someone else."

John Pearman, the associate pastor and bus driver who did not survive, shouted for everyone to get out of the bus before the gasoline exploded.

"Everyone started screaming and hollering," said 16-year-old Jamie Hardesty. "Everyone was trying to get off as fast as they could."

Hardesty, who had been sitting four seats from the back, was one of the first passengers to escape through the rear exit after the truckers got it open. He suffered burns on the nose and wrist.

"It wasn't the fire that burned us, it was the heat," he said.

He found a lead pipe on the ground near the bus and started smashing windows.

"I thought maybe if I broke out the windows I could help some of them get out or at least let some of the smoke out. I busted windows hoping they could get out, but I don't guess they could. Then the bus exploded two times."

Flowers ran to the back and helped the truckers pull people out the emergency door.

"I helped a few girls get out and this one girl had a burned foot and I was getting her over to the side of the road, and then behind me the bus just burst into flames, and the girls had cans of hair spray and they just started exploding," he said.

Helium-filled balloons bought at the amusement park exploded too.

Hardesty described the hellish scene at the rear door.

"They were just laying down in the back door, stacked up on top of each other, and no one could get out 'cause they all fell down on top of each other. I grabbed their arms and pulled," he said.

"There were 67 of us on the bus, and not very many of us got off."

There was no shortage of heroes.

"There's one thing I'm proud of. Everyone was helping someone else," Tennison said. "Everyone was a hero in their own way."

Juan Holt, 17, places Hardesty high on the list of heroes.

"When I jumped off the bus, I saw him carrying somebody and laid them down, and ran back up and was trying to get some more people," Holt said of Hardesty.

"He ripped off my shirt, and he used it for bandages. . . . He put ice on people. He was like a doctor."

Other students agreed. Tennison said Hardesty directed paramedics to the more seriously wounded survivors, and Booher, an eighth-grader at Radcliff Middle School, said Hardesty "played a big part. He saved a lot."

Hardesty "was pulling everyone out," said Booher, "and the people who were burning, I carried over into the median where it was grass, and rolled them over."

His friends call Hardesty "kind of quiet" and "real nice."

His father, Jerry Hardesty, who farms about 1,000 acres in Meade County, calls his son "my right-hand man."

Hard work on the farm may have given him the strength to rescue his friends. But, he said, "I'd say God helped me."

Information for this story was also gathered by staff writers Tim Roberts, Hunt Helm, and David Cazares and The Associated Press.

KENTUCKY'S BUS TRAGEDY—THE SEARCH FOR SAFETY

CRASH FINALLY MAY PROMPT CHANGES URGED FOR DECADES

SUNDAY, JULY 10, 1988

BY SCOTT THURM AND HUNT HELM

For two decades, scientists, university researchers and some government agencies have warned of the dangers that took 27 lives on a dark section of interstate near Carrollton, when a church bus became a fiery trap.

The unprotected gas tank that ruptured near the front door. The highly flammable seats that fueled the fire. The inadequacy of the lone emergency exit for 67 frightened, desperate people.

Numerous experts have called for improvements, and in a handful of places, dangers have been confronted: safer seats installed, emergency exits added. In newer buses everywhere, the gas tanks are protected by steel cages.

But, for the most part, the dangers remain.

The safety record has been so good for so long that the federal officials who regulate school-bus design haven't thought it necessary to act. Most local school officials—caught between tight budgets and that record of few major accidents—have chosen not to install additional safety features.

As a result, the great majority of school buses being manufactured today have only one emergency exit, have their fuel tanks right behind the front door and have seat cushions made of highly flammable polyurethane.

In addition, thousands of older, more dangerous buses are in the hands of churches and other private groups—their operation unregulated, their maintenance unmonitored and their hazards unknown to their passengers.

Of course, the Carrollton accident, on May 14, never would have happened if a pickup truck had not been going the wrong way on Interstate 71—driven by a man police say was drunk.

But it was fire, not the impact of the crash, that killed.

Now, there are signs the Carrollton accident could forever change government's judgments on these safety issues, and it could change the way school buses are designed and built. In Washington, in Frankfort and across the country, officials are predicting reform:

- The National Highway Traffic Safety Administration, which sets safety standards for new vehicles, is reviewing all of its regulations for school buses.

Three of them—fuel-tank protection, flammability of interior materials and the number of emergency exits—are receiving "a lot of emphasis," said Barry Felrice, the agency's associate administrator for rule-making. Interior materials and exits likely will get "the closest scrutiny," he said.

"The agency has tended not to do much on school buses because it was felt they were so safe to begin with," Felrice said. He expects it to recommend stronger school-bus standards by the end of the year.

In addition, the National Transportation Safety Board, which investigates major accidents, may hold a hearing in Kentucky next month. The board is considering additional safety recommendations for school buses in a report that will be completed next year.

- The Kentucky Board of Education will consider a proposal this week to equip new school buses with two push-out windows that can be used as emergency exits. Only six other states now exceed federal requirements for emergency exits.

Also, Gov. Wallace Wilkinson has ordered mandatory safety inspections of privately owned buses. And this fall, state and local school officials will test a fire-retardant seat cover that may be required on future Kentucky school buses.

The Carrollton bus, built in early 1977, conformed to state and federal design requirements then in effect.

- Outside Kentucky, school officials also are considering additional safety features. A bus manufacturer that offers a fire-retardant seat cover said interest has surged since the accident.

As far away as California, Dan Stephens, director of transportation for San Diego schools, said the Carrollton crash "raised eyebrows all across our state for sure."

HOW SAFE IS SAFE?

At the same time, the accident has rekindled a national debate over the safety of school buses. The debate revolves around two inseparable questions: How safe is safe? And how effective are government safety regulations?

On one side are government and industry officials and safety experts who consider the Kentucky crash a fluke, the unlikely combination of highly unusual events. They point to reassuring statistics showing that only 15 to 20 school-bus passengers are killed every year.

"Do you put a plastic bubble around it (the bus) that no one can ever enter?" asked Ed Donn, transportation director for the Washington County, Md., schools and president of the National Association for Pupil Transportation. "I'm not really convinced we have a bad piece of equipment out there."

In the extreme, Don Ivey, associate director of the Texas Transportation Institute at Texas A & M University, argued that the low death toll on school buses—compared to thousands who die in truck accidents or because of drunken driving—means that "spending safety dollars in this area is like throwing them away. It's like stuffing them down a sewer.

"There probably are safer ways to build school buses," Ivey said. "But I can't argue that it ought to be done."

ROOM FOR IMPROVEMENT

Others contend there is room for improvement in school-bus design.

They point out that each feature of the bus that may have contributed to the loss of life in the Carrollton fire had been identified as a problem in government reports and private studies. And improvements were available.

Replacements for the polyurethane foam used in seat cushions have been available since the 1960s, the federal government has outlawed polyurethane on most city buses since 1977, and top scientists recommended in 1979 that it be taken off school buses. But it cushions the ride of virtually every American schoolchild today.

Additional emergency exits—such as push-out windows and roof hatches—also have been available for decades. But in requiring only a single rear door, federal regulators ignored advice from the NTSB and from bus manufacturers themselves.

And, while the federal government required greater crash protection for fuel tanks in 1977, buses built before that standard took effect are still in wide use—including about 800 in Kentucky.

The 1977 Superior bus involved in the Carrollton crash was such a bus—one of the last built without a metal cage shielding its gas tank.

In addition, the accident history of those old buses is largely unknown. School-bus-accident statistics—the basis for so many of the government's conclusions about bus safety—exclude mishaps involving former school buses in private hands.

"I don't want to hear their statistics about how safe the buses are," said William Bainbridge, a former school superintendent who now runs a public-policy research firm in Columbus, Ohio. "They're not doing everything they can to improve those buses."

Added R. Brady Williamson, a professor of engineering science at the University of California at Berkeley and an expert on fires: "If anybody had put some common sense to it, you could have averted" the deaths with a better-designed fuel system and less flammable seats.

James King, a former member of the NTSB, said government regulators have "done everything on school buses to avoid changing the basic design. It's crazy. The things we're talking about are peanuts. They don't cost all that much."

In some states and local school districts, officials routinely request more safety features than the federal government requires—and bus manufacturers usually comply. But the number of such districts is small.

In part, this reflects local officials' limited knowledge. Carroll Pitts, transportation director for the Cobb County, Ga., schools, recalled watching a school bus burn during a test in 1985, a full decade after scientists had demonstrated the flammability of polyurethane.

"I stood there in amazement," he said. "I never thought a bus could burn" throughout as the result of a fire started with newspaper.

MONEY IS A FACTOR

But Pitts and others said the primary reason safety features aren't more widely adopted is financial.

"All the incentives are to go cheap," said Stephens of San Diego, who heads an association of big-city school-transportation officials. "It takes parent pressure to overcome the controllers, the fiscal people, who say we can't afford" additional costs on buses.

The NTSB offered one answer to that argument nearly 20 years ago. In its report on a 1970 accident in Alabama, the board found a "unique need for protection of innocent children who ride school buses, and who are almost totally unable to assure their safety by their own actions.

"This consideration of justice," the board concluded, "should override the question of whether the cost of (safety improvements) could be demonstrated to be less than the dollar value of the lives saved."

BENDING THE LAW ON DUI

'SLAMMER' LAW FAILS TO SHUT DOWN PROBLEM

SUNDAY, SEPTEMBER 4, 1988

BY GIL LAWSON AND TIM ROBERTS

FRANKFORT, KY.—Despite years of heightened awareness and the passage of a get-tough law aimed at stopping the slaughter on the highways, Kentucky seems to be losing ground in the battle against drunken driving.

The number of alcohol- and other drug-related traffic fatalities is again on the rise, while the number of drunken-driving convictions dropped last year.

Key provisions of the "slammer bill"—passed four years ago amid great fanfare and emotional debate—are being ignored by the very officials responsible for enforcing them.

"The problem is a lot more stubborn than we all imagined," Attorney General Fred Cowan said in an interview last week. ". . . I think there's still a lot of resistance in certain quarters to really crack down on drunk driving. There's still a significant number of people who are saying, 'Heck, I've done that, and let's continue to live with it.' "

But the issue seems to have regained a sense of urgency since May 14, the date of the worst drunken-driving accident in the nation's history.

Late that night in Carroll County, a church bus returning from a daylong outing at an Ohio amusement park was hit by a pickup truck traveling the wrong way on Interstate 71 and driven by a man police say was drunk. Twenty-seven occupants of the bus, 24 of them young people, were killed.

After the accident, The Courier-Journal interviewed dozens of officials and reviewed court records to see how the fight against drunken driving is being waged in Kentucky.

Among the newspaper's findings:

• Charges of driving under the influence are often reduced or dismissed, even when the defendant's blood-alcohol content is well above the 0.10 percent level at which a person is presumed under the law to be intoxicated.

Except in unusual situations, the law prohibits judges and prosecutors from reducing DUI charges when a defendant has a blood-alcohol content of 0.15 percent or more. But it still happens.

State police are investigating a now-defunct program in Breathitt County that permitted DUI charges to be dismissed if defendants attended an alcohol-treatment program. Cowan has advised county officials that the program was illegal.

The 1984 law also required prosecutors to give reasons for reducing charges against defendants with blood-alcohol levels of 0.10 percent or more. Court records checked by the newspaper rarely listed any reasons, although some prosecutors said they explained their decisions in court.

When DUI charges are amended, usually to offenses such as reckless driving or alcohol intoxication, there is nothing in the defendants' driving record to show the original charge.

• Although the new law required courts to sentence repeat DUI offenders to treatment programs for up to a year, some judges aren't complying. Experts say these offenders—they number more than 17,000 since the law took effect—are likely to have serious drinking problems that require treatment.

"I read that (part of the law) as an option," said District Judge Everett Currier, who presides in Estill, Owsley and Lee counties. "It's hard for me to police it."

Even when treatment is ordered, there is apparently little follow-through by the courts, and no state agency is responsible for seeing that it's carried out. Some offenders simply don't attend the programs.

"The client is left to go and get treatment on his own," said Richard Miller, who works in the substance-abuse division of the Cabinet for Human Resources. "Who's going to know?"

• Alcohol-education classes for first-time offenders are criticized as ineffective. Two state agencies—the Transportation Cabinet and the Cabinet for Human Resources—oversee a welter of 28 programs offered by private companies, the state and regional mental health agencies, all of which compete for customers. Their philosophies and practices vary widely.

By completing these classes, first offenders have their licenses suspended for only 30 days, instead of six months. The nine-hour classes once had to be spread out over three days, but the 1986 General Assembly allowed them to be taken in one day. Many experts question the effectiveness of one-day classes, especially for people with drinking problems.

"People aren't looking for quality. It's expediency," said Ray Ochs, an Eastern Kentucky University professor who heads the state Alcohol Driver Education program, which offers first-offender classes throughout Kentucky.

The 1984 law also required all first offenders to have their drinking problems assessed. But interviews with treatment experts and others showed that little, if anything, is done with these assessments.

"We have no tracking system," said Gary Martin, assistant director of the state Division of Driver Licensing. "When they walk out of the classroom, we've lost them."

• In an effort to encourage stronger penalties in serious cases, the 1984 law specified that drunken drivers who kill someone can be charged with murder. (Only a few such cases had been brought in the past.) But, in part because of the many variables involved, there is a great disparity in the way fatal DUI cases are handled.

Some defendants are sent to prison, while others get off without a day in jail.

For example, in 1984 a Todd County man pleaded guilty to one count of manslaughter in a drunken-driving accident in which four members of his family died. He received a suspended 10-year sentence and didn't spend a day in prison.

Earlier this year the same judge sentenced another Todd County man to eight years in prison after he pleaded guilty to the same charge —one count of manslaughter—in an accident in which one person was killed.

Despite the varying outcomes, prosecutors seem to be reaching for the murder charge more often in drunken-driving cases, Cowan said.

"Prosecutors are more willing to seek it, grand juries are more willing to indict with it and juries are more willing to convict," he said.

• Kentucky appears to be lagging behind other states in enacting enforcement tools to fight drunken driving.

In a report last year from the National Commission Against Drunk Driving, Kentucky had in place just five of the 19 countermeasures the commission had recommended; Indiana had 10.

The Insurance Institute for Highway Safety studied three types of laws commonly used to fight drunken driving and found they had reduced the number of fatal accidents. But Kentucky was one of three states that had not enacted any of the three measures.

Mothers Against Drunk Driving has launched a national campaign for seven measures that it believes are effective, including proposals to allow licenses to be confiscated when a DUI arrest is made and to give Breathalyzer results more weight in court. Four of the proposals are not on the books in Kentucky.

Kentucky's law has resulted in repeat offenders serving jail time, paying fines and losing their licenses. But some authorities have called for even stiffer penalties and longer license suspensions. Cowan said that such steps, while important, don't get to the heart of the problem.

"It seems to me the most logical place we're going to have any impact is through effective treatment programs," he said.

After the "slammer bill" took effect in July 1984, it had an immediate impact.

DUI arrests soared from 43,000 in 1983 to almost 48,800 in 1984; convictions increased from 20,978 to 31,426; and alcohol-related deaths dropped from 365 to 315.

But more recently, the numbers have been telling a different story.

Complete arrest figures for 1987 are not yet available, but state police expect them to show a decline from 1986. Convictions dropped from 32,643 in 1986 to 29,903 in 1987. The number of alcohol-related fatalities increased for the second straight year—from 289 in 1985, to 343 in 1986, and to 359 last year.

The conviction rate for DUI cases handled by the state police—overall statewide figures are not available—has risen slightly, from 66 percent in 1983 to 68 percent in 1986, the last year for which numbers are available. By contrast, the conviction rate for all DUI cases in Indiana rose from 72 percent before a new law took effect in 1983 to 91 percent in 1987.

"I don't think the law's living up to its expectations," Cowan said. "I don't think we've seen the kind of dramatic impact on drunk driving that we had all anticipated and hoped."

Capt. John Lile, a spokesman for the state police, said the public's attention can be held for only a few years.

"Maybe they aren't heeding the message; maybe they aren't taking the 'slammer bill' as seriously as they should," he said.

Members of MADD worried that the same thing was true of the 1988 Kentucky General Assembly in light of efforts, ultimately unsuccessful, that they say would have weakened the law. One would have authorized an occupational driver's license to allow some people convicted of DUI to drive to work.

"In the 1988 General Assembly the mood had changed," said Mildred Hilton, president of the Louisville chapter of MADD. "Drunk driving was no longer an important issue. The attitude we saw reflected a change in attitude in general."

But the issue is important because the consequences can be so tragic. Consider the case of 20-year-old Ronald B. Garner of Wayne County:

In 1985 a Monticello police officer arrested Garner on a DUI charge after finding him in the driver's seat of a car stopped with its lights on. The policeman said Garner appeared to be intoxicated. He was unsteady on his feet and had slurred speech, and a bottle of vodka was in the car, according to the arrest slip. Garner refused a blood-alcohol test.

The charge was reduced on Feb. 6, 1986, to reckless driving, and Garner was fined $200, plus $57.50 in court costs. Wayne County Attorney Van Phillips said the charge was amended because officers didn't see Garner driving.

Less than a year later Garner was arrested on a DUI charge in Cumberland County. Again he refused a blood-alcohol test, according to the citation. He pleaded guilty, was fined $407 and lost his license for 30 days. He completed an alcohol driver-education course for first offenders.

On April 9, police say Garner was driving on KY 90 in Wayne County when his car crossed the center line and hit another car head-on. Authorities said Garner, who was hospitalized with injuries, had a blood-alcohol content of 0.22 percent—more than twice the legal limit.

Garner is now facing murder charges because three people in the other car and a passenger in his car died.

BENDING THE LAW ON DUI

COURTS USE 'DISCRETION' TO EASE DUI CHARGES

SUNDAY, SEPTEMBER 4, 1988

BY TIM ROBERTS AND GIL LAWSON

FRANKFORT, KY.—Some courts in Kentucky are reducing drunken-driving charges without following the law, hampering efforts to get habitual offenders off the road.

The 1984 revision of the state's drunken-driving law was designed to reduce the courts' discretion in dealing with such cases. But prosecutors and judges still retain wide latitude, and there is little uniformity in the handling of drunken-driving cases.

As a result, many drivers who should have been jailed or stripped of their licenses for a second offense are still behind the wheel because their first offense has been, in effect, forgiven.

"All prosecutors want their discretion," Assistant Attorney General Andrew T. Coiner said. "But clearly the intent of the law is to keep discretion out of this."

Judges, too, bear some of the blame, he said. "It's the judge's duty to run the court and make sure the law is correctly applied."

The Courier-Journal found two important areas in which the law is not being followed:

- Charges of driving under the influence are being reduced improperly.

Except in rare cases, the 1984 law prohibits a DUI charge from being reduced or dismissed if a defendant's blood-alcohol level is at or above 0.15 percent. (A driver is presumed to be drunk at a level of 0.10 percent.)

The law says that "no prosecuting attorney shall agree to the amendment of the charge to a lesser offense and shall oppose the amendment of such charge at trial, unless all prosecution witnesses are, and it is expected they will continue to be, unavailable for trial."

Violating this provision is what Coiner calls "the big taboo." But it happens nonetheless.

In checking DUI charges in seven counties, The Courier-Journal found 109 cases in which the charges were reduced or dismissed even though the defendant's blood-alcohol content was 0.15 percent or above.

In some of those cases, the one legitimate reason—a lack of evidence or witnesses—may have led to the decision to amend the charge. But in others there appeared to be no authorized reason.

For example, last year in Spencer County a DUI charge against Geraldine Peacock, 41, of Mount Washington, whose blood-alcohol level was 0.19 percent—nearly twice the legal limit—was reduced to public intoxication.

Court records show that the arresting officer did not appear at an April 17 hearing. A note in the case file says the officer "has a new baby and has been at the hospital all week."

The charge was amended that day, although there was no indication in the record that a trial had even been scheduled at that point. Spencer County Attorney E. Lorraine Russell said there was nothing else she could do "if the officer did not show up" at the hearing.

Peacock was fined $100 plus court costs.

In a Boone County case, Paula Kay Alexander, 28, of Walton, was charged with DUI in May 1987 after a police officer saw her car weaving on U.S. 25. Her blood-alcohol level was measured at 0.16 percent.

In November the charge was amended to reckless driving, and Alexander was ordered to pay $47.50 in court costs and attend state traffic school.

Boone County Attorney Larry Crigler said the charge was reduced because reckless driving "appeared to be the better charge." But he couldn't explain further.

"We try to be careful about it (amending charges)," he said. In this case, he said, neither the court nor the prosecutor noticed that the blood-alcohol reading should have prevented an amended charge.

Crigler said he tries to follow the DUI law, even though he believes it unconstitutionally hampers prosecutors' efforts to see that justice is done.

Policies on amending charges vary widely from county to county. Prosecutors in Jefferson County, for example, will not amend when the blood-alcohol level is 0.12 percent or more. But a prosecutor in Carroll County amended a case with a 0.14 percent blood-alcohol level because he considered it low.

A 1983 task force on drunken driving cited the amending of charges as a major problem. Its chairman, former Adjutant General and Justice Secretary Billy Wellman, said recently that it's still a problem—"something that needs to be looked at."

• Prosecutors often fail to give a reason when charges are otherwise properly reduced. The law allows amended charges if a defendant's blood-alcohol level is below 0.15 percent, but it requires prosecutors to explain their decision to do so if the reading is 0.10 percent or higher.

Moreover, the reasons are supposed to be forwarded to the Justice Cabinet. But Gary Bush, head of the state police records section, said that is virtually never done, and the cabinet still has no method for even collecting such data.

"The intent was to keep records, to keep track of what was happening, and why cases were being amended," said Lois Windhorst, founder of the Louisville chapter of Mothers Against Drunk Drivers, whose efforts helped pass the 1984 law. ". . . This is not working like it had been planned."

In Breathitt County, two DUI charges involving Eddie Spencer, the brother of Sheriff Dean Spencer, were either dismissed or reduced without a reason being given.

In May 1986 Eddie Spencer was arrested after being chased by police, and his blood-alcohol level was measured at 0.14 percent.

In February 1987 he was arrested again on a DUI charge. The arrest slip gave no details, but his blood-alcohol level was measured at 0.15 percent.

On June 29, 1987, both cases were disposed of. In the first, Spencer was allowed to plead guilty to a charge of "driving contrary to law" and fined $100. The second case was dismissed because he had attended an alcohol-treatment program.

Neither DUI charge is reflected on his driving record.

County Attorney Mike Stidham and assistant Dawn Watts, who prosecutes DUI cases, said they could not recall either case.

Sheriff Spencer said he had nothing to do with the way the cases were handled. He said his brother got no special treatment.

The change in the law making it more difficult to amend DUI charges was aimed at ensuring that repeat offenders were punished more effectively—and gotten off the road.

But when a driver escapes a first DUI charge, he also escapes one of the law's tougher provisions if he gets caught a second time—automatic license suspension for a year.

Coiner, the assistant attorney general, said that in most cases in which a DUI charge is reduced it "has no impact on their driver's license. The statute is designed to keep drunk drivers off the road."

Some county attorneys, he said, just aren't willing to change "every time the legislature springs something new on them. Some of them just don't change."

Although the law says that a driver is presumed drunk when his blood-alcohol level reaches 0.10 percent, in many counties charges are routinely reduced around that level.

For example, charges against a Warren County man cited for a second DUI offense in February 1987 were reduced to reckless driving. County Attorney Michael Caudill said the man's blood-alcohol level of 0.11 percent was "extremely low."

Caudill calls the range from 0.10 to 0.15 percent "a gray area."

"It's hard to get a conviction on a 0.10 unless there are aggravating circumstances," he said. "Juries are very sympathetic."

Caudill said defense attorneys will tell a jury that a client in that range is only a little over the limit and say, "It's not like he blew a 0.27."

Coiner disagrees.

"The presumption (level) has an impact on juries," he said, "and prosecuting attorneys who amend in that 'gray area' are underestimating themselves and juries."

In Spencer County, where more than half of the 77 DUI charges were reduced in 1987, County Attorney Russell said she seeks the "best end result" in prosecuting DUI cases, even if that means amending a charge.

If a defendant really needs counseling, Russell said, she may seek a longer sentence by amending a first-offense DUI charge to alcohol intoxication and then asking the judge to probate most of the sentence but reimpose it if the defendant doesn't get counseling.

The maximum jail sentence for a first DUI conviction is 30 days; the maximum sentence for alcohol intoxication—a charge that isn't reflected on a driving record—is 90 days.

One problem with that approach, Coiner said, is that there is no first DUI conviction on the driver's record, meaning a lighter sentence if there is a subsequent DUI conviction. Avoiding the DUI prosecution, he said, "would defeat the law's purpose."

In Breathitt County, only 20 percent of the 366 DUI cases in 1987 resulted in convictions.

The low percentage stems partly from the practice of dropping charges against some first-time offenders—including Eddie Spencer—after they received alcohol-education treatment.

At least 15 people who benefited from the program in 1987 had blood-alcohol levels of 0.20 percent or more—twice the legal limit—when arrested. A state police investigation, which is still under way, brought the practice to an end in June.

County Attorney Stidham said he believed the practice, which he called "pre-trial diversion," was allowed as long as the court permitted it. District Judge William Bach has declined to comment on the matter.

In several other Breathitt County dismissals, there was no official explanation.

For example, a DUI charge against Charles L. Noble of Clayhole was dismissed on May 7, 1987. He was arrested by Jackson police on Feb. 2 with a blood-alcohol reading of 0.22 percent.

A notation on the court record reads, "Dismissed on rec. of arresting officer—has declined to prosecute pursuant to superior's orders."

Another note says "move to dismiss by arresting officer Sgt. Ricky Jones." But Jones, who no longer works for the Jackson police department, is not listed as an arresting officer on the citation. Efforts to contact Jones were unsuccessful.

Neither the two arresting officers nor police chief Frank Noble (who is not related to the defendant) could explain the dismissal or the notation.

What discretion the law allows is intended to let prosecutors deal with unusual circumstances in individual cases, Cowan said. But it may be, he said, that each county is treating the law differently.

"To the extent it's being dealt with on a county-by-county basis, that's not fair," he said. "That's not right. There should not be that kind of treatment."

He added: "I think we would probably be better off if we just said, 'No amendments.'"

Information for this story also was gathered by staff writer Judy Bryant.

THREE

THE COLOR OF MONEY

1989 WINNER IN THE INVESTIGATIVE REPORTING CATEGORY

"For a distinguished example of investigative reporting within a newspaper's area of circulation by an individual or team, presented as a single article or series . . ."

The Atlanta Journal-Constitution
Bill Dedman

Home ownership has been the traditional keystone of the American Dream. But despite federal laws prohibiting the practice of redlining, Bill Dedman points out that a disproportionately high number of blacks in America and elsewhere are still denied home loans.

The yellow school bus full of white bankers rolled through the black side of town: a racial re-education school on wheels.

The bus tour of Atlanta's Southside was directed by a black executive of the Chamber of Commerce, who hoped to challenge the perception—the stereotype—that black equals poor. The 30 bank executives from Atlanta's Bank South were skeptical.

For the first mile or so, the bankers saw just what they expected—liquor stores, untidy lawns, vacant storefronts. Some bankers nudged each other, grinned and winked.

But as the bus rolled on, still on the predominantly black Southside, the scenery changed. The bankers began to see big houses, $300,000 houses with tennis courts—built by black developers, bought by black homeowners, financed by black lenders.

"This is an eye-opener for me," one banker said as he tramped across the fresh sod. "I didn't know there were houses down here that big."

Atlanta's bankers covered a lot of unfamiliar turf in 1988, after *The Atlanta Journal-Constitution* published "The Color of Money," a series of articles documenting that banks and savings and loan associations shunned black neighborhoods.

In Atlanta in 1988, separate lunch counters were gone, but not separate loan offices. Banks and savings and loan associations made many home loans in white neighborhoods, even in poor white neighborhoods. But they made few home loans in black neighborhoods, even in Mayor Andrew Young's neighborhood, leaving the market to unregulated mortgage companies.

That segregated system may have been unintended, but it was well known to bankers and real estate agents and black homebuyers. We merely pointed out the obvious, documenting racial segregation with a computer study of lenders' reports to the federal government on $6.2 billion in home loans.

We were stunned by the power of documenting the obvious.

Nine days after the series ended its run, Atlanta's nine largest banks and savings institutions began pouring $77 million in low-interest loans into black neighborhoods.

The largest institutions went further: calling on black real estate agents, increasing the hours of branches and accepting loan applications in black areas; hiring black real estate appraisers; advertising in black media; renovating offices; and even taking their executives on a bus tour.

The heat is on for more change. In April 1989 the U.S. Justice Department began investigating 64 banks, thrifts and mortgage companies in metro Atlanta for possible racial discrimination in mortgage lending. Federal bank regulators, so often the protectors of financial institutions, have taken a few steps toward vigorous enforcement of fair-lending laws. Congressional efforts to strengthen those laws have gained steam.

As a black real estate broker in Atlanta told me later, "It's a good thing the white newspaper told white folks what black folks already knew."

All that reaction was a surprise to me. "The Color of Money" started with an off-hand remark by a white housing developer: He said he was having trouble developing houses in black South Atlanta because banks wouldn't lend money there. He said he'd heard the banks wouldn't lend even in affluent black areas.

That's a hard charge to prove. It's impossible to demonstrate for sure that someone who didn't get a loan should have gotten one. It's even more speculative to translate a few cases into a widespread pattern. I hoped there was a way to take a more systematic look at the system.

From talking to the few academics who work in this field, I learned that banks and savings and loans are required to report to the federal government the location of every home loan, by amount and census tract.

All we at the paper did, to put it simply, was to cross-index the federal computer tapes with a federal census tape, looking especially at comparable black and white neighborhoods. (Of course, it wasn't simple at all: The fruit of our first three days of computer work was to put spaces in the numbers; unfortunately, the tapes from the Federal Reserve Board come with no spaces between columns.)

The results were worth the trouble: Concentrating on stable, middle-income neighborhoods of similar housing age, we found that banks and thrifts were making five times as many loans in white areas as in black areas.

Next we looked at bank policies and practices that might have caused the lending patterns. We found that lenders were not looking for business in black areas, and in some cases their policies discouraged black borrowers.

Only then did I turn to anecdote. From the chairman of the county commission to a retired railroad laborer, I found black residents who had been turned down or discouraged from applying for home loans. And in a sidebar I focused on two neighborhoods: one black, one white.

Finally, in follow-up articles, the paper turned its sights nationwide, examining federal records of $1 trillion in home-loan applications: America's savings and loans were rejecting black applicants more than twice as often as whites.

Beyond the numbers, I think I know the key to the effectiveness of "The Color of Money." The editors took out what I thought were the good parts.

When I wrote that Atlanta's banks were redlining, editor Bill Kovach marked through it. "Just use the numbers," he said. "Let the facts speak for themselves." We left it to others to use the "R" word: redlining.

And just when I thought we had bent over so far backwards that we were looking behind us, Kovach decided we really shouldn't call them bankers after all. "Call them banking officials,"he said. "Bankers might be considered a pejorative term."

That flatness of tone must have infuriated the banking officials. They couldn't argue with the numbers and they couldn't argue with the presentation. All they could do was make some loans to black people.

A final word about editing: Without Kovach's guidance and the persistence of editors Wendell Rawls, Hyde Post and Dwight Morris, these articles would not have been published.

The pressure from Atlanta's banking establishment started out as the normal stonewalling.

The shortest reply to my request for information came from a banker who wrote: "Under no circumstances do we provide this information to anybody. Sincerely . . ."

And the cleverest came from a thrift executive: "Some of the material you have asked for does not exist. Other parts of the material exist but are confidential. The rest of the material exists and is not confidential but is irrelevant to your subject matter."

Others invoked my boss's name. One banking official mentioned in a letter that my publisher was serving on a Chamber of Commerce committee hoping to spruce up Atlanta's image before the Democratic National Convention. "I'm sure that Jay Smith would recognize any article alleging racial discrimination by Atlanta financial institutions as another unmerited potshot at our great city. . . . cc: Jay Smith."

Stronger letters came later to Bill Kovach's desk, but he never mentioned them to me. It seems that's the way it ought to work.

—Bill Dedman
The Atlanta Journal-Constitution

ATLANTA BLACKS LOSING IN HOME LOANS SCRAMBLE

BANKS FAVOR WHITE AREAS BY 5-1 MARGIN

SUNDAY, MAY 1, 1988

BY BILL DEDMAN

Whites receive five times as many home loans from Atlanta's banks and savings and loans as blacks of the same income—and that gap has been widening each year, an Atlanta Journal-Constitution study of $6.2 billion in lending shows.

Race—not home value or household income—consistently determines the lending patterns of metro Atlanta's largest financial institutions, according to the study, which examined six years of lender reports to the federal government.

Among stable neighborhoods of the same income, white neighborhoods always received the most bank loans per 1,000 single-family homes. Integrated neighborhoods always received fewer. Black neighborhoods—including the mayor's neighborhood—always received the fewest. The study was controlled so any statistical bias would underestimate the differences between lending in black and white areas.

"The numbers you have are damning. Those numbers are mindboggling," said Frank Burke, chairman and chief executive officer of Bank South. "You can prove by the numbers that the Atlanta bankers are discriminating against the central city. It's not a willful thing. The banks really are considered the pillars of the community. If somebody walks in and applies, they'll get fair treatment."

Senior banking executives noted that home mortgage lending is not their primary business. Lenders also said any disparities most likely are caused by factors beyond their control, including poor quality housing and lack of home sales in black neighborhoods, fewer applications from blacks, and limitations in the federal lending data. They pointed out that lending patterns are influenced by real estate agents, appraisers and federal loan programs.

For example, banking officials said they would make more loans to blacks if real estate agents sent them more black applicants. Real estate brokers who work in black neighborhoods confirmed that they often don't send black homebuyers to banks or savings and loans, but said that is because those institutions have not been responsive and do not solicit their business.

A federal law, the Community Reinvestment Act (CRA) of 1977, says deposit-gathering institutions have an "affirmative obligation" to solicit borrowers and depositors in all segments of their communities.

Federal bank regulators give passing grades to 98 percent of the nation's financial institutions on compliance with the act. But in recent testimony before Congress, heads of the regulatory agencies conceded that they have not enforced the law as well as they should.

As part of a five-month examination of compliance with the CRA, the Journal-Constitution used lenders' reports to track home-purchase and home-improvement loans made by every bank and savings and loan association in metro Atlanta from 1981 through 1986—a total of 109,000 loans. The study focused on 64 middle-income neighborhoods: In the white areas lenders made five times as many loans per 1,000 households as in black areas.

A companion study of 1986 real estate records for 16 of the neighborhoods yielded similar results: Banks and savings and loans financed four times as many of the home purchases in middle-income white neighborhoods as in middle-income black neighborhoods.

With the banks and savings and loans largely absent, home finance in metro Atlanta's black areas has become the province of unregulated mortgage companies and finance companies, which lenders say commonly charge higher interest rates than banks and savings and loans.

The two lending studies form the foundation of the Journal-Constitution's examination of home finance in metro Atlanta. Among the other findings, which will be discussed here and in subsequent articles in this series:

• Banks and savings and loans return an estimated 9 cents of each dollar deposited by blacks in home loans to black neighborhoods. They return 15 cents of each dollar deposited by whites in home loans to white neighborhoods.

- The offices where Atlanta's largest banking institutions take home loan applications are almost all located in predominantly white areas. Most savings and loans have no offices in black areas.
- Several banks have closed branches in areas that shifted from white to black. Some banks are open fewer hours in black areas than in white areas.
- Lenders are not required to disclose information on loan applications by race. However, two of the largest lenders volunteered that information, which showed they rejected black applicants about four times as often as whites.
- Meanwhile, a black-owned bank in Atlanta, which makes home loans almost exclusively in black neighborhoods, has had the lowest default rate on real estate loans of any bank its size in the country.

'IT'S INSTITUTIONAL RACISM'

The differences in bank lending to whites and blacks in metro Atlanta did not surprise some government observers.

"I think it's obvious that some areas of Atlanta have more trouble than others getting credit," said Robert Warwick, vice president of the Federal Home Loan Bank of Atlanta, which regulates savings institutions. "It's perfectly obvious."

"It's institutional racism," said Marvin Arrington, president of the Atlanta City Council. "While we are patting each other on the back about being a great city and a city too busy to hate, they're still redlining."

Redlining is an illegal practice of refusing to lend in certain neighborhoods on the basis of race, ethnic composition or any standards other than creditworthiness. The definition comes from the alleged practice of drawing a red line on a map around certain neighborhoods to designate them as off-limits.

Senior bank executives said they welcome black borrowers. They also point out they have contributed to many efforts to improve housing in Atlanta, from giving money to build Southside houses for blacks in the 1960s, to forming a mortgage loan pool for lower-income homebuyers in the 1970s, to supporting the Atlanta Neighborhood Housing Service effort to revive Grant Park in the 1980s.

"It's a myth that banks have a map with a red line on it," said Jim Graham, vice president of SunTrust Banks, the parent of Trust Company Bank. "We don't avoid any area."

"I've never known of anybody redlining areas," said W. D. Hosford Sr., president of DeKalb Federal Savings and Loan. "I believe that any qualified borrower can get a loan today."

"Since the 1950s forward, we've had no prohibition, no implied rules. We didn't pay any attention to black or white," said Thomas Boland, vice chairman of First Atlanta. "We advertise, 'Please borrow money from us.' We send our mobile information center to the black side of town and on and on and on. If I spent the time and money on the Northside that I've spent on the Southside . . . If you could locate these people . . . It's an imponderable. Somebody's making the loans. It's just not the banks."

MEASURING IMPACT OF RACE

The impact of race on lending patterns was easier to measure in metro Atlanta than in some other cities, since housing patterns almost always follow racial lines here and since Atlanta has a substantial and identifiable black middle class.

The study focused mainly on 64 middle-income neighborhoods: 39 white, 14 black and 11 integrated. Middle income was defined as between $12,849 and $22,393 in 1979, the base year for the 1980 census.

The study was controlled to ensure that neighborhoods were comparable in income and housing growth. All judgments about which data to include were made conservatively.

For example, to account for Atlanta's rapid suburban growth, the study excluded any neighborhood that grew by more than 10 percent in the number of single-family houses from 1980 to 1987.

Even with these controls, distinct and growing differences appeared. Banks and savings and loans made 4.0 times as many loans per 1,000 single-family structures in white areas as in comparable black areas in 1984, 4.7 times as many in 1985, and 5.4 times in 1986.

Banking officials, while not questioning the accuracy of the lending figures, offered a variety of explanations for the differences.

Some bankers cited the aging of structures in the city.

"Much of the housing in predominantly black areas is substandard, requiring rehabilitation to qualify for mortgage lending," said Willis Johnson, spokesman for Trust Company Bank. "As a result, this cannot be handled through conventional mortgage lending channels."

Officials at Atlanta's black-owned bank disagreed.

"I have difficulty believing that most of the housing in black neighborhoods is substandard," said Ed Wood, executive vice president of Citizens Trust Bank. "That is where the black community of Atlanta really got its name nationally. People who come from outside are amazed: 'Black folks got these kinds of houses here?' "

Several banking officials also said the difference might be caused by more home sales in white areas.

The bankers were partly right. To check the demand, the newspaper analyzed real estate records of all home sales in 1986 in 16 of the 64 middle-income neighborhoods. Homes did sell twice as often in white areas as in black areas.

Of the homes that were sold, banks and savings and loans financed four times as many in the white areas as in the black areas. In middle-income white areas, banks and savings and loans made 35 percent of the home loans. In middle-income black areas, banks and savings and loans made 9 percent.

Even lower-income white neighborhoods received more of their loans from banks and savings and loans than upper-middle-income black neighborhoods. Lower-income white neighborhoods (those with a median income below the $12,849 household income in 1979) received 31 percent of their loans from banks and savings and loans. Upper-middle-income black neighborhoods (those above the metro area's median of $18,355 in 1979) received 17 percent.

In Cascade Heights, where Mayor Andrew Young and other prominent blacks live, 20 home-purchase loans were made in 1986. Of those, two were made by banks and savings and loans, and two by mortgage companies owned by banks. The rest were made by unaffiliated mortgage companies.

BLACKS REJECTED MORE OFTEN

If sales differences do not account for most of the lending pattern, banking officials said, then the number of applications probably would. However, federal law does not require financial institutions to make public information about applications by race or area.

Only two of the 88 institutions in the study divulged application figures by race. These figures, from the two largest savings institutions in Georgia, suggest blacks make proportionately fewer loan applications than whites. But they also show that black applicants for home-purchase loans are rejected four times as often as whites.

Georgia Federal Bank in 1987 rejected 241 of 4,990 white applicants, or 5 percent, but 51 of 238 black applicants, or 21 percent. Fulton Federal Savings and Loan, from 1985 through 1987, rejected 1,301 of 12,543 white applicants, or 10 percent, but 363 of 1,022 black applicants, or 36 percent.

Banking officials also said the racial disparities in the study might be caused by limitations in the lending data. The federal records include only loans made directly through the banks and savings and loans, not through mortgage companies owned by the large banks. All but one bank declined to provide information on loans by their mortgage companies.

However, real estate records show that mortgage companies owned by banks rarely made loans in black areas of any income. In white middle-income areas, 20 percent of loans from mortgage companies were made by those owned by banks. In black areas of the same income, the figure was 3 percent.

Finally, banking officials said home lending is not their primary business. Traditionally, banks made most of their loans to businesses, and still often call themselves "commercial banks." A home loan was a favor for a commercial customer.

In recent years, however, changes in federal and state laws have blurred the lines between banks and savings and loans. Banks across the country are doing more home lending. Metro Atlanta's banks now make more than $1.5 billion annually in home loans, according to 1986 annual reports compiled in an industry directory, Sheshunoff's Banks of Georgia.

LAW REQUIRES FAIR LENDING

Equitable lending practices are required under the Community Reinvestment Act, which says banks and savings and loans have "continuing and affirmative obligations to help meet the credit needs of their local communities, including low- and moderate-income neighborhoods, consistent with safe and sound operation."

The law strives for a balance: Banks and savings and loans should protect the money of depositors and make a profit for shareholders. But the law also says they should seek that profit in every neighborhood.

Banks and savings and loans face this obligation because they receive privileges, particularly government permission to operate and federal insurance of their deposits.

Federal appeals courts have said banking is so "intimately connected with the public interest that the Congress may prohibit it altogether or prescribe conditions under which it may be carried on."

Bankers said they bend over backward to obey the laws, and some said they are eager to make more money in black areas.

"If I could make $10 million or $20 million in these loans, I'd make them," said First Atlanta's Boland. "I don't think a black borrower brings me any more risk per se."

First Atlanta placed last in the Journal-Constitution's ranking of 17 banks and savings and loans based on the percentage of home loans made to minority and lower-income neighborhoods. And it placed 12th of 14 institutions in a ranking based on lending to comparable middle-income black and white areas.

Only the city's two black-owned financial institutions, Citizens Trust Bank and Mutual Federal Savings and Loan, made more home loans in black areas than white.

These institutions, although small, appeared not to be suffering for lending mostly to blacks. Citizens Trust had a lower default rate on real estate loans than the six largest banks in the city and the lowest of any bank its size in the country in 1986, according to the Federal Financial Institutions Examination Council, a government agency that produces reports for bank examiners.

"I don't see our default ratio being any higher because we're working in the black community," said Wood of Citizens Trust. "I wouldn't be in banking if I gave money away."

Several of the institutions that ranked low in the Journal-Constitution lending study capture the largest share of black customers, according to a 1986 market study for the Journal-Constitution. First Atlanta, Trust Company, Citizens and Southern (C&S) and First American, in that order, had more than half the black customers.

In all, metro Atlanta's blacks have an estimated $765 million deposited in financial institutions. That estimate is made by multiplying the number of non-white households in a 15-county metro area (204,802, according to the U.S. Census Bureau) by national black households' average balance of accounts at financial institutions ($3,734, according to a 1984 Census Bureau survey).

The banks and savings and loans appear to invest little of black deposits in black neighborhoods, at least in home loans.

In middle-income black neighborhoods, each single-family home received an average of $339.27 in home-purchase loans from banks and savings and loans in 1986. Using the census estimate of $3,734 in deposits per black household, that's an estimated 9.1 cents on the dollar in lending.

In middle-income white neighborhoods surveyed, each single-family structure received an average of $2,432.82 in home-purchase loans from banks and savings and loans in 1986. Using the census estimate of $17,812 in deposits per white household, that's an estimated 13.7 cents on the dollar in lending—a rate of return 50 percent higher than in the black neighborhoods.

"We're talking about disinvestment, capital flight from the Southside," said Sherman Golden, assistant director of the Fulton County Department of Planning and Economic Development. "When the banks disinvest, the governments also find themselves disinvesting. To accommodate the growth on the Northside, all the public funds flow north. Southside residents put money in the bank and pay taxes, but their money is spent on the Northside."

LOWER-INCOME ALSO AFFECTED

Although the Journal-Constitution study focused on middle-income neighborhoods, the results concern groups working to solve Atlanta's shortage of decent housing for the working class and the poor, regardless of race.

"As long as they won't lend in Cascade Heights, I don't know how we'll get them to lend in Cabbagetown or Ormewood Park or Pittsburgh or South Atlanta," said Lynn Brazen, a director of the Georgia Housing Coalition, a group that encourages housing efforts.

Neighborhoods say they need investment by financial institutions now more than ever because federal housing aid is rapidly dwindling—from $33 billion in 1980 to less than $8 billion in 1987, according to a study by the National Association of Realtors. Atlanta's share of federal housing and community development money dropped from $8 million in 1983 to $4 million last year. The city also earmarked half of that money for its tourist-entertainment complex, Underground Atlanta.

With less federal money, neighborhoods searching for other deep pockets have turned to the banks. And Atlanta has some of the most profitable banks in the country.

Last year First Union Corp. of North Carolina and SunTrust Banks of Atlanta, parents of First Union and Trust Company respectively, led all U.S. banks in net income. First Atlanta, C&S and Bank South have consistently been in the top half of their peer groups nationally in profits, according to the federal examination council.

Neighborhood leaders say they don't want to cut those profits.

"We're not asking the banks to do anything that's not banking. We just want them to make money on the Southside too," Mrs. Brazen said.

Without equal access to credit, community leaders say they watch their neighborhoods slide. When people cannot borrow money to buy or fix up houses, property values decline. Real estate agents direct their best prospects elsewhere. Appraisers hedge their bets by undervaluing property. Businesses close. Homeowners sell to speculators.

Homeownership is the linchpin in the American Dream, the main way that families accumulate and hold wealth. Americans borrow against their homes for education, for vacations, for emergencies, for retirement. The family home often forms the bulk of parents' bequest to their children.

White families are more likely than blacks to build that wealth. They own homes more often, and their homes grow in value faster.

The Census Bureau said in 1984 the income of a typical white family in America was twice the median income of a black family, but the median household net worth of whites was nearly 12 times that of blacks. That's $39,135 versus $3,397.

"It takes money to make money. The problem we have in the black community is there is no base with which to make money," said the Rev. Craig Taylor, a white Methodist minister and Southside housing developer.

Redlining and disinvestment were hot issues in the nation's cities in the mid-1970s, when Congress approved disclosure laws and the Community Reinvestment Act.

A decade later, activists claim red lines are being redrawn, and Congress is considering legislation to enhance enforcement of the law.

"Let's face it: Redlining hasn't disappeared," said Sen. William Proxmire (D-Wis.), chairman of the Senate Banking, Housing and Urban Affairs Committee. "Neighborhoods are still starving for credit."

FULTON'S MICHAEL LOMAX: 'IF I CAN'T GET A LOAN, WHAT BLACK PERSON CAN?'

SUNDAY, MAY 1, 1988

BY BILL DEDMAN

When he went to the banks last year looking for campaign contributions for his 1989 race for mayor, Michael Lomax picked up a donation from every one. He wishes he'd done as well when he wanted a loan.

The Fulton County Commission chairman says he had to go to three banks last year to get a loan to add a guesthouse in Adams Park, an upper-middle-class black neighborhood in southwest Atlanta.

"The first reaction from the bank was, 'Why do you want to invest that much money in that neighborhood?' But that's the neighborhood my house is in.

"If I, a powerful black elected official, can't get a loan, what black person can?"

James Fletcher said he couldn't—at least not from a bank. The 56-year-old retired Southern Railway laborer needed a $5,000 loan to fix his roof. He owned the house in Mechanicsville, a lower-income black neighborhood in southwest Atlanta.

Fletcher went in 1984 to Citizens and Southern Bank (C&S), his bank for 10 years.

"They said they didn't make no house loans. They didn't let us fill out the papers."

So he and his wife, Lizzie Mae, went to Atlantic Mortgage Co., which loaned them $5,773.69 at 18 percent interest—plus $3,180 in "discount points" and other add-ons, raising the effective interest rate to 27.1 percent, according to the loan papers.

Total payback: $30,722.30.

If C&S had made the loan, at its usual terms of 15 percent interest with five points over 10 years, the Fletchers would have paid back $11,764.82.

Fletcher discovered the size of his debt two years after getting the loan. He had paid about $4,000 and took another couple of thousand in to pay off the rest.

"I don't know exactly how the thing went, but when they got through with it, it was $30,000," he said. "I guess they can get by with it."

A spokesman for C&S, Dallas Lee, confirmed that Fletcher had been a depositor, but said he could find no record that Fletcher had ever applied for a loan. "It seems highly unlikely [that he would be discouraged from applying]. We make a lot of home-improvement loans," Lee said.

In Fletcher's Mechanicsville neighborhood, C&S made no home-improvement loans and no home-purchase loans from 1984 to 1986, according to federal records. The bank declined to release any information about the number of its loan applicants.

Michael Lomax and James Fletcher are at opposite ends of the same boat. The Atlanta Journal-Constitution's study of lending in metro Atlanta found that banks and savings and loan associations rarely lend to black neighborhoods, from the lowest-income to the highest, from Mechanicsville to Adams Park.

Lomax said he hadn't thought he'd have any trouble finding a lender when he started planning a renovation.

"I had remarried, and we decided we wanted to stay in the house. I wanted to add 1,400 square feet in a free-standing building—a guesthouse where we can put people up and I can go hide and where we can entertain. We also were adding air conditioning in the house, a new septic tank field and some landscaping."

An associate professor of literature at Spelman College and one of two leading candidates for mayor of Atlanta, Lomax has a family income "between $50,000 and $100,000 a year . . . and I pay my bills." He also has money in the bank but declined to provide specifics.

Lomax wouldn't name the banks that turned him down, but he did say one of them was where he had banked for 25 years.

County deed records show he received the loan from First Union Bank for $115,200. Lomax said he has the ability to pay the money back, although he may never recoup his investment.

"My home to date does not appraise for the amount I've invested in it. With a new guesthouse my appraisal went up only $8,000. I find that extremely frustrating and somehow just plain wrong. I'm not doing anything different from what people do in Morningside or Peachtree Park. You drive through Peachtree Hills and you'll see the exact same houses as in Adams Park, but they're appraised at a third more because white people live in them. Perhaps I'm wrong, but I think I've done the right thing. Since I made my investment, three other homes on my block are being added to."

Banks and savings and loans lend less often in Adams Park than in white neighborhoods of similar household and housing growth, according to real estate records studied by the Journal-Constitution.

In 1986, banks and savings and loan associations financed 17 percent of the home purchases in the census tract that roughly corresponds to Adams Park. They financed 37 percent of the home sales in comparable white neighborhoods.

Banks sometimes make home-improvement loans for more than $120,000 in southwest Atlanta's highest-income black neighborhoods —at least, the black-owned banks do.

According to federal lending records for 1986, the black-owned Citizens Trust Bank made a home-improvement loan for $156,000 off Cascade Road near Lomax's neighborhood. Black-owned Mutual Federal Savings and Loan made one in the same neighborhood for $144,000, in integrated East Point for $134,000, and in integrated southwest Fulton County for $175,000.

No white-owned institution reported a home-improvement loan of more than $120,000 in a predominantly black neighborhood in 1986. They did make larger home-improvement loans in more affluent white neighborhoods. For example, in 1986 Citizens and Southern made home-improvement loans in Druid Hills for $128,000 and in north DeKalb for $133,000.

"If my house were lifted up and put into any neighborhood in northeast Atlanta, with my family income I would have absolutely no difficulty getting a loan to rehab my house," Lomax said. "But I don't want to move. I like my acre of land and my little bungalow. I can look out my window on a park and a golf course behind it.

"What I tried to explain to the lenders was, I'm pioneering. It's an economically mixed neighborhood, but our income levels in Adams Park are higher than some of the intown neighborhoods where they make loans. On my street are the senior black executive at Coca-Cola, myself, two architects and at least one lawyer. We are restrained by the financial institutions from improving our neighborhood."

Lomax attributed his rejections to lack of understanding by bankers.

"I think that, for most Atlanta banks, black continues to equal high risk in their perceptions. It's an educational issue that we need to work on. In the 1970s they didn't want to lend in Virginia-Highland and Morningside, either. They learned they can make money there.

"If we want to see balanced residential development on the Southside, the banks are going to have to evolve aggressive programs to assist black families in acquiring property. Central Atlanta Progress encouraged such a program for Inman Park and Virginia-Highland. Where is the comparable program on the Southside? I think it's in the best interest of the banks to support that. We want a city of strong neighborhoods where home values increase and not decrease."

Lomax says he isn't mad at bankers and doesn't want to increase regulation of them. He even invited several senior bank executives to his Christmas party, the one he threw in his new guesthouse.

"The ones who came to the party weren't loan officers."

SOUTHSIDE TREATED LIKE BANKS' STEPCHILD?

BLACKS MAY SHUN SOME HOME-LOAN LENDERS BECAUSE THEY'RE SHUNNED FIRST, CRITICS SAY

MONDAY, MAY 2, 1988

BY BILL DEDMAN

James Gray is black and he sells real estate for Century 21 on Cascade Road in southwest Atlanta, an area that includes some of the richest black neighborhoods in Atlanta, including the mayor's.

"Banks and savings and loans: We don't use them," Gray said. "First of all, they don't solicit us. Banks and savings and loans do not have loan officers out looking for business. They don't solicit in white areas, either."

But they do. Loan originators from banks and savings and loans "come by every day" at the Century 21 office in Alpharetta, said broker Richard Blalock. He is white, and Alpharetta is almost entirely white.

Where the banks look for business is one of many factors that help explain the results of an Atlanta Journal-Constitution study of lending. The study found that Atlanta's banks and savings and loan associations rarely make home loans in black and integrated areas, even the highest-income black areas.

Some other possible explanations of the study results:

- Most black Atlantans live on the Southside. The Southside mortgage office for Citizens and Southern Bank (C&S) is in Fayetteville—20 miles south of Atlanta. The Southside mortgage offices for Trust Company Bank and First Atlanta are also south of the Perimeter. These three banks, the largest in Georgia, take applications and close loans only at the mortgage offices, not at branch banks.
- Several banks have closed branches in black and integrated areas.

In 1986, Trust Company closed its branch on Wesley Chapel Road after the area shifted from white to black; in Belvedere, which was becoming blacker; and in black East Atlanta, although it kept open 23 branches in white areas with less in deposits. Bank South replaced its South DeKalb branch with an automatic teller machine.

- Many banks keep their branches in black and integrated areas open less often than in white areas. Bank South, for example, advertises that it is open on Saturday to give "the personal attention you deserve." Bank South is open on Saturday in Alpharetta and Snellville, but not in East Atlanta or the West End.
- Some Atlanta banks won't consider home-loan applications for loans of less than $40,000. A lot of homes on the Southside sell for less.

Courts have found similar practices in other cities to be violations of the federal Fair Housing Act and the Equal Credit Opportunity Act, which forbid discrimination in lending based on race or color. Courts have said discriminatory effect, not just discriminatory intent, is enough to prove a violation.

'NOT A CHARITABLE INSTITUTION'

Atlanta bank officials say their lending practices are not discriminatory. They say something else, too.

"We are not a charitable institution," said Willis Johnson, spokesman for Trust Company. "We are not the United Way."

Federal law encourages banks to seek a profit. It also says they have a "continuing and affirmative obligation to help meet the credit needs of their local communities, including low- and moderate-income neighborhoods, consistent with safe and sound operation."

That last phrase, "consistent with safe and sound operation," brings into play one of banking's principles.

"It's called the First Rule of Banking," said James Wallace, vice president of Fulton Federal Savings and Loan. "Don't lend money if you won't get it back."

It has a corollary, the Second Rule of Banking: "When in doubt, don't."

Don't lend more than borrowers are able to pay. In case they don't pay it back, don't lend more than can be recovered by foreclosing and selling the property. Don't lend $100,000 on a $60,000 house. And don't lend $40,000 on a $50,000 house in a neighborhood so bad that the house may someday be worth only $38,000.

In effect, lending money to homebuyers is an expression of faith—faith in the borrower, faith in the property, faith in the neighborhood.

In the United States, such questions of lending faith historically have been influenced by race. That influence used to be easily defined—with a list.

In 1933, a respected economist at the University of Chicago, Homer Hoyt, published a list of racial groups, ranking them from positive to negative influence on property values:

1. English, Scotch, Irish, Scandinavians.
2. North Italians.
3. Bohemians or Czechs.
4. Poles.
5. Lithuanians.
6. Greeks.
7. Russians, Jews (lower class).
8. South Italians.
9. Negroes.
10. Mexicans.

The next year, Hoyt was hired by the federal government to develop the first underwriting criteria—who is a good credit risk and who is not—for the new Federal Housing Administration (FHA). His list wasn't included, but warnings on racial influence were.

The same views were included in the first text of the American Institute of Real Estate Appraisers in 1933, which warned appraisers of the harm to property values caused by the "infiltration of inharmonious racial groups." The list appeared in the bible of appraising, McMichael's Appraising Manual, as late as 1975.

Appraisers were not alone. The prevailing racism in society was institutionalized in the rules of bankers and real estate agents as well. The National Association of Realtors developed a code of behavior forbidding members from selling homes in white areas to minority buyers.

These racial views persisted through the civil rights era. Publications from the U.S. Department of Housing and Urban Development

(HUD), the parent of the FHA, reflected Hoyt's views as late as 1975. In that year, "The Dynamics of Change," a HUD publication, defined racial change, or the fear of racial change in nearby neighborhoods, as the most significant predictor of "incipient decline."

As late as 1977, it took a lawsuit from the U.S. Justice Department before such racial standards were purged from guidelines of the Society of Real Estate Appraisers, the Mortgage Bankers Association of America, the American Institute of Real Estate Appraisers and the United States League of Savings Associations. Appraisers opposed the settlement, contending their right to free speech was abridged if they could not consider the effect of race in their appraisals.

Real estate is still essentially a white person's business—selling it, appraising it, insuring it, financing it. Ninety-five percent of the officials, managers and professionals at real estate companies in metro Atlanta are white. At savings and loans 90 percent are white. At banks and insurance companies, 87 percent, according to the latest figures (1985) from the federal Equal Employment Opportunity Commission. Most appraisers in Atlanta, at least 80 percent, are white too, appraisers say.

Bankers say they have tried to hire more minority employees.

"We make a steady effort to make sure we're hiring officers in sufficient supply to make sure the numbers come out good," said Thomas Boland, vice chairman of First Atlanta.

Most senior bank executives interviewed for this article said differences in lending to black and white neighborhoods in the Journal-Constitution study can be explained by factors beyond their control—such as a lack of applications.

"The realtor usually guides them," said Bill VanLandingham, president of C&S. "If they don't refer the homebuyer, we can't make the loans."

Real estate agents in black neighborhoods, however, said they usually don't refer homebuyers to banks and savings and loans. One reason is that the banks don't come around looking for business.

Ruben James is black and he works in predominantly black south DeKalb County for Precision Realty. "I haven't seen anybody from a bank in a couple of years. There used to be a woman from C&S who came by this office, but I haven't seen her in a long time."

Teresa Jones said bankers don't figure much in her business, either. She is black and she sells houses in predominantly black areas of south DeKalb for Century 21. "Bankers—those are types who just sit at a desk and wait for somebody to come in. They're not really in the mortgage business, are they?"

Bank officers said that almost all of their loan originators—the salespeople who drum up loans—are paid on commission. A good originator will notice two things: First, more homes are sold in the mostly white areas than in black areas. Second, homes in white areas usually cost more.

Two $50,000 houses mean $100,000 in sales. One $100,000 house means the same profit—and half the work.

"A loan originator is going to go where he can make the most money for the least work," said Wilbur Kurtz III, senior executive vice president of Decatur Federal.

Most big banks don't make smaller loans at all. Several make no loans below $40,000, and others charge additional fees below that amount.

Donald Cullins, 34, a black disabled Vietnam veteran, pays rent on a fixed income in the Pittsburgh neighborhood on the Southside. The home next-door was offered for sale at $25,000. Just before Christmas he received a certificate of eligibility from the Veterans Administration and went to C&S for a VA loan. He said he was told C&S has a minimum loan amount of $30,000.

"The funny thing is, I'm paying $380 in rent right now. The man said, if he could have made me the loan, my payments would have been $280 a month," Cullins said.

C&S officials say they have no stated minimum loan amount, "but the reality of the situation does in fact define a minimum," said a C&S spokesman, Dallas Lee. Below about $30,000, because of fixed costs, "it can become not an economically sound situation."

FEWER BANK BRANCHES

Real estate agents also say their black customers have a preference for a bank or savings and loan less often than whites. Community groups say that's because banks avoid black and integrated neighborhoods.

Fifty-two percent of Fulton County residents are black, but 82 percent of the 208,089 residents who live in census tracts without a bank branch are black.

Trust Company, which closed its East Atlanta branch, maintained in a letter to the Federal Reserve Bank of Atlanta that it was "a sound business decision" because the community had failed to "pull itself together and improve."

The East Atlanta branch was located in census tract 209, which was 88 percent black in 1987. In 1985 and 1986 combined, Trust Company made no home-purchase loans and eight home-improvement loans totaling $35,000 in the census tract, which has 2,215 single-family households, according to the bank's reports to the federal government.

"The East Atlanta branch had been unprofitable for eight years and was located in a neighborhood which continues to experience decline," Trust Company told the Federal Reserve Bank last year. "Most of the local merchants and many of the branch's customers have moved out of this area. The area has experienced such an alarming increase in crime that the branch hired off-duty Atlanta SWAT policemen to replace the usual bank guards."

As for branch hours, the chairman of Bank South, Frank Burke, said he was not aware that his branches in black areas were closed on Saturday. He said he is mindful of the Community Reinvestment Act.

"The CRA doesn't say you have to lend to black folks. It says low- and moderate-income. We have tried very diligently to listen to community groups, even though we don't have the branches in the neighborhoods that the other banks do."

Even if a borrower prefers a bank, real estate agents see a difference of convenience.

"The mortgage company man, he'll come see you at the office or at the home after 6 p.m. The bank, a working man's got to take a half-day off to go see the bank," said agent James.

Beth Williams, the receptionist in the Southside office of C&S Mortgage in Fayetteville, said, "If our mortgage officer were to leave, he'd have to travel an hour for an appointment and travel an hour back. If he stays here he can do three appointments in that time."

The Georgia production manager for C&S Mortgage, Jack Johnson, said its mortgage offices are outside the city of Atlanta "because there's just not enough volume there to justify putting in an office."

Some bankers acknowledged that location could be a problem.

"If you're on Campbellton Road and you call and they say, 'Go on up to Galleria,'' that could have some effect," said First Atlanta's Boland. "It may be as simple as that. Maybe we haven't realized that."

Bank officers said it would not be feasible to accept mortgage applications at all banks, since the applications are so complicated.

When black applicants do get to a bank or savings and loan, they're more likely to be turned down, several real estate agents who work with black clients contended.

Banks and savings and loans are required to report their rejection rates for blacks and whites to the federal government; they are not required to disclose the information to the public. But two of the largest savings institutions in Georgia did volunteer that information to the Journal-Constitution for all their offices statewide. Georgia Federal Bank rejected black applicants 4.2 times as often as whites in 1987. Fulton Federal Savings and Loan rejected black applicants 3.6 times as often as whites in 1985–87.

"That could only be explained by a lack of ability to qualify for the loan," said Don Stout, senior executive vice president at Georgia Federal.

"Those are statewide figures. It may be that older properties in some of these rural neighborhoods are not able to qualify for a loan," said Shepherd Marsh, executive vice president of Fulton Federal. "Our underwriters don't look at the color of the applicants."

The rejection rates tell nothing about the creditworthiness of those who applied. However, many real estate agents said they don't refer homebuyers to lenders unless they can qualify at least on the two most important lending criteria: income and debt. Some agents also have lenders check a homebuyer's credit history before an application is made.

"The first thing we do is prequalify them," said Precision Realty's James. "Otherwise we're wasting our time, everybody's time."

APPRAISALS MAY BE SAND TRAP

If black applicants succeed in getting themselves approved for a home loan, they still have to get the property approved. That brings in the appraiser, who is hired by the lender to make sure the property is worth enough to cover the loan. Appraisers also said they don't look at race anymore.

Willie Clyde isn't so sure. He's a real estate agent on the Southside, he's black, and he had a house to sell. He almost sold it last summer—he had a buyer and a signed contract. Then the buyer went to a bank, whose appraiser came down from the Northside.

"He called me and asked for directions. He said he didn't work down here that often," Clyde said. "I knew that was trouble."

Clyde bought and remodeled the house, at 53 Bisbee Avenue off Jonesboro Road in South Atlanta. It's an older neighborhood, mostly black, with a lot of vacant houses and a lot of houses being renovated.

"I showed him that we had put on a new roof, that we had redone the interior walls, sanded and varnished the floors, added a sunroom, new plumbing, cabinets, rehabbed the bathroom, rescreened the front porch, new paint. He didn't say anything negative when he came out."

The appraisal came back at $28,000, about 25 percent less than the contract price of $38,000. Clyde lost the deal.

"They just don't trust the neighborhood," Clyde said.

He later found another buyer, who chose a mortgage company not affiliated with a bank or savings and loan. Its appraiser said the property was worth $38,000.

Willie Clyde's first appraiser wrote nothing on his appraisal report about race.

"A conscientious appraiser will forecast property values as best he can, but to avoid liability he might not attribute it to race," said Jim Verner, who teaches appraising at Georgia State University and serves on the curriculum committee of the American Institute of Real Estate Appraisers. "He might attribute it to something more bland—'wearing out of the public infrastructure'—something that isn't such a dangerous area."

Underappraisals—called lowballs—do more than discourage sales. By definition, they lower property values. Appraisals not only judge the market, they help set it.

The effects can show up in how fast homes appreciate in value.

The median sale prices of homes in Atlanta increased by 58 percent from 1975 to 1984, according to the city Bureau of Planning. Prices increased by 68 percent in white Garden Hills, but by 20 percent in black Cascade Heights; 84 percent in white Sherwood Forest, but 26 percent in black Adams Park; 71 percent in white Peachtree Hills, 6 percent in black Collier Heights.

Low appraisals also deter further investment in a neighborhood by current owners. The amount of a home-improvement loan is usually limited by the owner's equity—property value in excess of debt. If the value of a home drops, there may be no equity left for a home-improvement loan.

LEANING ON FHA, VA LOANS

If a black homebuyer gets the appraiser's stamp of approval, there's still the issue of what kind of loan to get. In a black neighborhood, it's rarely what is called a "conventional" loan. Instead, it's likely to be one guaranteed by the federal government through the FHA or Veterans Administration (VA).

In middle-income black neighborhoods of metro Atlanta, 52 percent of home loans were insured by FHA or VA, according to 1986 real estate records sampled by the Journal-Constitution. In white areas of comparable income, only 13 percent of loans were government-backed. Even in upper-income black areas, 31 percent were FHA or VA.

Few of those FHA or VA loans come from banks and savings and loans. Twelve of 17 banks and savings and loans in the newspaper's survey made no FHA or VA loans in 1986. Bank officials said that was usually because those loans carry lower interest rates and more paperwork.

For many buyers, FHA and VA loans are the best way to buy, because of the lower down payment (or none at all) and low interest rate.

However, FHA and VA loans can have disadvantages for the neighborhood. If an area has many FHA and VA loans, banks and savings and loans may not make conventional loans there.

That may be the case in metro Atlanta. Banks and savings and loans made 50 percent of the conventional loans in white middle-class areas, but only 22 percent of the conventional loans in comparable black areas where FHA and VA loans predominate, according to the real estate records.

Conventional lenders said they believe FHA and VA neighborhoods have higher foreclosure rates, since lenders whose losses are covered by the government may be less likely to choose borrowers carefully.

As far back as 1974, Savings and Loan News, the industry newsletter, issued this warning:

"Since the entry of FHA into the inner-city finance business, these areas have taken on new appearances—mostly depressing. The chronology looks something like this (1) abandonment; (2) board-up and padlock time; (3) the vandalize and burn period; (4) wait-to-wreck interval (playtime in the Rockies); and (5) demolition."

The author, appraisal expert Gregory Opelka, began his article with what he called the "chicken or the egg caveat":

Are these neighborhoods deteriorating because lenders that make FHA and VA loans are there, or because the banks and savings and loans are not?

Opelka said it didn't matter.

"It is not my intention—nor should it be the appraiser's job function—to debate the morality of 'causes' and 'effects.' "

Whatever the cause and effect, homebuyers and homeowners in black neighborhoods can be trapped in an endless catch-22:

- Bank loan officers have become conditioned to steer clear of neighborhoods with a preponderance of FHA and VA loans.
- Without a good mix of credit to fuel it, including conventional lenders, the housing market in the neighborhood sputters and property values stall.
- Stagnant property values discourage investment and reinforce bank skepticism about the neighborhood, and the cycle begins again.

The catch-22 has a second part:

Even if black borrowers can prove they deserve conventional financing, lenders will prefer to work in white neighborhoods, where higher sale prices and more sales mean higher commissions.

That's why Congress created the Community Reinvestment Act—to encourage banks and savings and loans to lend in all neighborhoods. The law has been on the books for 10 years.

A TEST THAT FEW BANKS FAIL—IN FEDERAL EYES

TUESDAY, MAY 3, 1988

BY BILL DEDMAN

Each year the U.S. government grades America's 17,000 banks and savings and loans on how fairly they serve their communities, including working-class and minority neighborhoods.

Across the country last year, 98 percent of the lenders passed. In the South, 99 percent passed, according to federal agencies.

Supporters of working-class and minority neighborhoods suspect grade inflation.

"Regulators seem to think we all live in Lake Wobegon. Like the children of that fictional village, U.S. lenders are all above average," said Sen. William Proxmire (D-Wis.), chairman of the Senate Banking, Housing and Urban Affairs Committee.

Besides the annual exams, regulators are required by law to consider lending patterns when a bank applies for approval of a special action, such as opening a branch or buying another bank.

In the past 10 years, regulators have denied eight of 50,000 special applications because of unfair lending, according to federal agencies.

"I wish I had graders like that when I was in school," Proxmire said. "And I ask myself, how is it that so many neighborhoods are continuing to fail, while so many lending institutions are continuing to pass?"

Although applications are rarely denied, the law does allow for delays while regulators consider citizen challenges of a bank's record. A delayed merger can cost a bank a bundle in lost profits. Increasingly, community groups are filing such challenges.

Banks resent the pressure.

"They're a pain in the neck, and as far as we're concerned it's pure ol' blackmail, and I think we are going to see a lot more of it," Edward Crutchfield, chief executive officer of First Union Corp., said in a speech to a bank marketing convention shortly before First Union moved to Atlanta in 1986.

"They said we did not have some specific things and they wanted $50 million—boom. Well, we would have stayed awake until hell freezes over with that and we wouldn't have done it, and we didn't do it."

Other banks have done it. Banks have agreed to a variety of community demands:

- Specific goals for residential and home-improvement loans: $150 million in Chicago, $50 million in St. Louis, more than $5 billion in all since 1977, according to researchers at the University of Minnesota.
- In Iowa, a promise that a family with a broken furnace could get a $2,000 loan approved in 24 hours.
- In St. Louis, low-cost checking accounts and cashing of government checks for non-depositors.
- In Philadelphia, loans to multifamily buildings.

And in many cities and states:

- Deposits of bank funds in community credit unions.
- Credit counseling services.
- Flexible underwriting criteria for loans to the poor.
- Loans with lower interest rates or lower closing costs or lower down payments.
- Charitable contributions to groups working in working-class and minority neighborhoods.
- Automatic second appraisals if appraisals are disputed.

Community groups say these results have not come from blackmail, just good ol' American pressure. They do, however, use the phrase "pull off" for a successful bank challenge, the same phrase historically applied to a heist.

Instead of a gun they use the Community Reinvestment Act (CRA). Approved by Congress and signed by President Carter in 1977, the law doesn't require a bank to take any specific action or lend to anybody in particular. It creates no pool of money. It vaguely says banks have "an affirmative obligation" to serve all of their communities, including lower-income neighborhoods.

The law was intended to stop redlining, the illegal practice of avoiding areas in making loans because of race or other characteristics.

Ten years later, community groups around the country say redlining persists. Academic studies in Baltimore, Chicago, Denver and Washington, D.C., have found that banks rarely lend in working-class and minority neighborhoods. In Atlanta, even more than in these other cities, lending patterns follow racial lines, according to a study by The Atlanta Journal-Constitution.

The law has had beneficial effects, community groups say. But they say their victories came despite federal enforcement, not because of it.

"The regulators have been haphazard," said Allen Fishbein, general counsel for the Center for Community Change, a neighborhood advocacy group in Washington, D.C. "There's a pattern of the regulators' being very close to the industry they regulate, being very reluctant to vigorously slap the wrist of people who violate the law. In many instances the regulators are defending the institutions more adequately than the lenders are defending themselves."

SAFETY OF DEPOSITS COMES FIRST

"We're not consumer activists—we're regulators," said Ronald Zimmerman, vice president of the Federal Reserve Bank of Atlanta. "It's a terribly subjective law to enforce."

Still, leaders of the national regulatory agencies agree they could do better. They say they have had their hands full with their primary duty, ensuring the safety of deposits in banks and savings and loans. The increasing number of bank failures in this decade has stretched their resources.

According to BankWatch, the Ralph Nader gadfly of the nation's banks, the number of examiner hours per year expended to check banks on compliance with consumer regulations fell by 74 percent from 1981 to 1984 at the Office of the Comptroller of the Currency, the Federal Deposit Insurance Corp., and the Federal Home Loan Bank Board, which regulate most of the banks and savings and loans. The Federal Reserve Board regulates only about 1,000 institutions.

"Our bank consumer compliance effort has not been as comprehensive as it should be," said William Seidman, chairman of the Federal Deposit Insurance Corp.

"As you are aware, in the early 1980s the thrift industry suffered a crisis," said Danny Wall, chairman of the Federal Home Loan Bank

Board, which regulates savings and loans. "I regret to report that, as a result of this situation, we did not allocate sufficient resources to the enforcement of the CRA, or, for that matter, other consumer-related issues. The bank board has recently *increased* its activity in the area of CRA after a long lull. There is still much work to be done."

While the annual examinations have decreased, challenges from *community* groups have increased. For example, the Federal Reserve received three protests in 1984, 19 in 1985, 20 in 1986 and 35 last year. One reason is that more banks are merging or expanding into other states, creating more legal opportunities for challenges. Another reason is that federal housing aid has declined, causing community groups to seek more investment by banks in their neighborhoods.

Bankers who haven't been challenged should get their records in order before community groups start a protest, Glenn Loney, assistant director and community affairs officer of the Federal Reserve, told bankers in Philadelphia last year, according to American Banker, the industry newspaper.

"By the time they get to you in three years, they are really going to be good."

'PROCESS SOMEWHAT ABUSED'

In Atlanta last year, a new community coalition challenged SunTrust Banks, the parent of Trust Company Bank. Trust Company was able to complete the merger without making any specific financial concessions, but it left the yearlong negotiations bitter.

"The process has been somewhat abused," said Jim Graham, a SunTrust vice president in charge of compliance with the CRA. "The law is probably a good law but unnecessary. The banks have been meeting their community needs for some years."

That may be true of many banks, activists agree, but they say the law doesn't allow them to know which less-responsible institutions to challenge. The government keeps the grade for each bank a secret; not even the bank is supposed to know. Only regional and national totals are made public. The only information the public has is the federal reports of home loans, the same information that formed the basis for the Journal-Constitution study of lending patterns.

"It's the traditional style of the regulators to be low-key and behind the scenes, but that stuff should be public," Fishbein said. "It's not going to damage a bank. The public should know that, so they know where they put their money. It might even gain the good lenders some business. If it's secret, a lender can claim to have a good record when it doesn't."

Regulators say releasing the grades would set a precedent for disclosure of more sensitive examination information. They say the grades would be misinterpreted: Banks shouldn't be compared with each other, but with their legal responsibilities. And when a bank does poorly, regulators say, they don't have to give bad grades or turn down applications to enforce the law.

"Denials are a last resort," said Comptroller Robert Clarke, whose federal agency regulates more banks than any other.

"Instead of kicking you out of school because you flunked the course, we give you tutorials so you can stay in school," Martha Seger, a governor of the Federal Reserve, told the Senate Banking Committee last month.

The regional grades show that nine banks out of 792 in 10 Southern states received grades of "less than satisfactory" in 1986, the most recent data available. None was judged to be "unsatisfactory" or "substantially inadequate." Out of 318 savings and loans, four were graded as "needs improvement" and none was "unsatisfactory."

Activists scoff at the higher grades for Southern lenders.

"In the South and Southwest, particularly, you've had banks getting away with murder for years—racial discrimination, redlining and dealing almost exclusively in commercial loans," said New Orleans neighborhood activist Michael Shea, national director of housing and banking campaigns for ACORN, the Association of Communities Organized for Reform Now. "I think the Atlanta Fed [Federal Reserve Bank] is shielding the banks from the public."

Regulators say evidence of disproportionate lending patterns is not enough to cause a bank to be penalized.

"It's not our job to allocate the credit geographically. We don't have hard and fast lines on that," Governor Seger of the Federal Reserve testified.

PROPOSED CHANGES IN THE LAW

This contentious triumvirate of bankers, community groups and regulators is lobbying now as Congress considers several proposals to improve enforcement of the CRA.

The lobbying battle is tied to expectations that Congress this session will probably change the rules on what business a bank can do. A bill approved by the Senate would permit bank holding companies to underwrite and sell mortgage-backed securities, commercial paper, municipal revenue bonds, corporate bonds, mutual funds, and perhaps eventually corporate stock, the most lucrative securities activity. A similar bill is pending in the House.

Viewing some form of expanded bank powers as apparently inevitable, community groups hope to slip in increased regulation through expansion of the CRA at the same time. Several bills to expand the law have been introduced in the House. Their provisions include these:

- Change the grading system so only exemplary banks receive a top grade.
- Disclose each bank's grade, as well as its CRA examination report.
- Allow banks with a top grade to expand their powers or expand into other states. Banks with average grades could expand only if they made specific commitments to improve community reinvestment.
- Create separate community affairs divisions in the four regulatory agencies to conduct the examinations separately from examinations for safety and soundness of banks.
- Require banks to disclose their commercial loans by census tract, as they now must disclose home-purchase and home-improvement loans.
- Require banks to provide low-cost "lifeline" checking accounts and to cash government checks for non-depositors with proper identification.
- Establish a procedure for banks to notify the community and hear comments before they close bank branches.

Bank lobbyists have conceded that some of these changes are acceptable. The most disputed are the lifeline and check-cashing provisions, and some oppose the commercial loan disclosure.

BLACK APPRAISERS SHUT OUT BY HIRING RULE OF MAJOR LENDERS

SUNDAY MAY 29, 1988

BY BILL DEDMAN

Several of the largest mortgage lenders in Atlanta hire real estate appraisers only if they are members of one of two national appraisal societies.

In Atlanta, those societies have no black members.

Lenders who said they have the hiring rule include the largest mortgage lender in America, the largest bank-owned mortgage company in Georgia, and the most active savings and loan in metro Atlanta, according to a sample by The Atlanta Journal-Constitution.

The lenders said they do not intend to exclude black appraisers, but require the memberships only to ensure that appraisals are done professionally. The two societies are the country's oldest and largest, with more than 12,000 members nationally.

But membership in the two societies is no guarantee of professionalism, leaders of the two groups and industry experts agree. Most of the country's appraisers belong to other societies. And they say a 600-member national black society with many Atlanta members has comparable standards.

Leaders of the two large societies say they also do not intend to exclude blacks, but none has joined in Atlanta. Black appraisers say they don't necessarily want to join the other groups; they just want to be eligible for jobs.

Requiring membership in the two societies not only bars black Atlanta appraisers from profitable business but also ensures that much of the appraising in black neighborhoods is done by whites.

Use of white appraisers who are unfamiliar with black areas has been cited by lenders and real estate agents alike as a reason that banks and savings and loans make few home loans in metro Atlanta's middle-income black areas, as detailed in recent articles in the Journal-Constitution.

Real estate agents in black areas say they have trouble closing sales with banks and savings and loans because appraisals by white appraisers often come in below the contract price for a home. A low appraisal can kill a sale; a pattern of low appraisals can depress property values.

A lender who requires membership in one of these societies as a condition of employment may be breaking federal antitrust laws, according to legal experts and U.S. Rep. Doug Barnard of Augusta, who has asked federal agencies that insure or regulate lenders to forbid discrimination.

"Obviously, the federal government should not be supporting or condoning such discrimination, by inaction or otherwise," Barnard, a high-ranking member of the House Banking Committee, wrote in March 28 letters to several federal agencies.

"This, to me, is a classic boycott," said James Ponsoldt, professor of law at the University of Georgia. "If members of a trade organization like an appraisal organization establish exclusionary guidelines or informal exclusionary practices, and membership is economically significant, that could be considered a concerted refusal to deal under the antitrust statutes."

SOCIETY DESIGNATION PREFERRED

In a Journal-Constitution telephone survey of banks, savings and loans and mortgage companies, six of nine that would identify their job requirements prefer or require membership in the Society of Real Estate Appraisers or the American Institute of Real Estate Appraisers.

"They would have to be an SRA or an RM [the membership designations of the Society and the Institute] or we wouldn't approve them," said Rita Azif, metro Atlanta appraisal manager for Citicorp Mortgage, the largest mortgage lender in America.

"We do prefer either the Institute or the Society," said Mary McKinney, a supervisor in the appraisal department of Decatur Federal Savings and Loan, the most active mortgage lender in metro Atlanta.

"We would prefer that you have a designation from the Institute or the Society, or you could get a review appraiser with a designation," said Cammie McCarvey of C&S Commercial Corp., the most active bank-owned mortgage lender in the state.

Black appraisers say some lenders require them to hire a "review appraiser," who is a member of one of the two societies, to check their work. That usually means at least $100 of the standard $250 fee goes to the other appraiser.

The newspaper conducted its sampling by having Pamela Smith, local president of the black society, call lenders and ask what qualifications were necessary to be added to the list of fee appraisers. A reporter monitored her calls, then called back later and interviewed officials of the financial institutions.

Sometimes officials gave Ms. Smith and the reporter different answers. Several of the appraisal managers who told Ms. Smith they require memberships in the two large societies were later contradicted by higher-ranking officials or spokesmen for the financial institutions, who told the reporter the first officers were mistaken.

"Our policy was not clearly communicated to you. That was an error," said Betsy Martin, public relations manager for Citicorp in St. Louis. "[The company policy] is not designed to exclude someone."

Lenders who told Ms. Smith that they require or prefer membership in the two large societies were Citicorp, C&S, Anchor Savings Bank, Bank South Mortgage, Decatur Federal and Trust Company Mortgage.

Lenders who later amended their response were Citicorp, C&S, Bank South Mortgage and Trust Company Mortgage. Senior officials at some other lenders did not return telephone calls. Many lenders would not say what criteria they required for appraisers, telling Ms. Smith to send in a resume.

Ms. Smith and the reporter inquired only about jobs as fee appraisers or staff appraisers of residential property. Black appraisers charged that membership in the two large societies is required more often for commercial appraising.

Officers of the Society and the Institute confirm that they have no blacks among the 250 designated members of their Atlanta chapters, but they said they have no rules barring blacks from joining.

"There never has been any question of, 'Why don't you have any black people?' We just didn't," said Richard L. Razel, immediate past president of Atlanta Chapter 8 of the Society of Real Estate Appraisers. "Why didn't we have any Oriental people? You can put this in the record: I have lots of black friends, and I happen to be a Christian, and I don't ever turn anyone away because of the color of their skin. Jesus never did that."

Both organizations said they have black candidate members, who may attend meetings and take courses. But candidate members do not receive the designations, or initials after their names, that open the door to work at many lenders.

Leaders of the two larger societies admit their membership is no certain sign of good work.

"I know some Society appraisers that I wouldn't recommend to my own worst enemies," said Razel.

"All the banks and financial institutions recognize these two groups, but it shouldn't be a requirement," said Joseph Ferry, president of Georgia Chapter 21 of the American Institute of Real Estate Appraisers. "First of all, it would be wrong. Second, it's impractical. There are not enough designated appraisers out there to do all the work. If I was a good appraiser and I couldn't get work because I didn't have a designation, I would be mad."

The two societies and industry leaders also agree that a black appraisal society, the National Society of Real Estate Appraisers, has high standards.

"To my knowledge, their standards are completely adequate," said Bob Morin, chief legislative counsel for the Society of Real Estate Appraisers.

A 1986 study by the Mortgage Bankers Association of America found that the black society has some standards that are higher than the two larger societies.

Yet membership in the two larger groups is required by many lenders across the country, industry leaders say.

"It's definitely a significant portion of the lenders, particularly the banks and savings and loans that do conventional lending," said Brian Chappelle of Washington, senior director of the Mortgage Bankers Association of America, which represents 2,500 lenders. "But it wouldn't be a racial problem in most places, because the Institute and the Society have black members in most cities."

RULE 'A FREQUENT PRACTICE'

In Atlanta, requiring membership in one of the two large societies "is a frequent practice," said David Brantley, executive vice president of Bank South Mortgage. "Having a designation is not absolute [at Bank South], but it's a good indication [of ability]. We don't do as much investigating with somebody who's designated as somebody who's not."

Black appraisers say they have no quarrel with the large societies, but would like to be eligible for more work.

They point out that they are allowed to work for any bank, savings and loan and mortgage company when the loan is government-backed, such as by the Federal Housing Administration (FHA) or the Veterans Administration (VA)—because the government picks the appraisers.

But when the lender is putting its own money at risk, the blacks say they have trouble getting the work.

Some lenders recognize a third large society, the National Association of Independent Fee Appraisers, which has only one black member in the Southeast, according to that member, Elbert Jenkins of DeKalb County.

"You should not have to join an organization to get a job. That is not the American way," said Otis Thorpe, the Atlanta-Fulton County tax assessor and national president of the black appraisal society. "That's like telling me I can't get a job without going to the University of Georgia or Emory, when I want to go to Morehouse."

The quality of appraisals in black areas was an issue in a recent series of articles in the Journal-Constitution. The articles disclosed that banks and savings and loans make five times as many home loans in white areas as in black areas of similar income.

Nationally, qualifications of appraisers have been hotly debated in recent years because of the failure of many banks and savings and loans. Many of the failures were blamed on bad real estate loans made with faulty or fraudulent appraisals.

Barnard has submitted legislation that would establish national standards for appraisers, who are essentially unregulated. The two large societies, the black society and five others joined in helping write those standards, although appraisers differ on the need for federal regulation.

Some lenders said Barnard's bill increases the pressure to hire appraisers from recognized societies. Barnard agrees that lenders should be wary of "diploma mill" societies that grant membership for nothing more than a fee, but he says more than two societies are qualified.

"None of these organizations can fairly claim to impose uniformly higher standards than the others," he wrote to federal agencies.

"Indeed, subcommittee investigations have disclosed that many of the most egregious abuses in real estate appraisals have involved appraisers with the most 'prestigious' designations."

CITICORP SKIPS OVER REAL ESTATE AGENTS IN BLACK AREAS

MONDAY, DECEMBER 4, 1988

BY BILL DEDMAN

Only real estate agents located in predominantly white Atlanta neighborhoods have been invited to join the referral network of Citicorp Mortgage Inc., America's largest lender to homebuyers.

Citicorp's "targeted source list," obtained by The Atlanta Journal-Constitution, shows that all of the 298 real estate agencies solicited for the company's MortgagePower program in metro Atlanta have their offices in neighborhoods that are more than 75 percent white. MortgagePower accounts for 90 percent of Citicorp's business in Georgia.

Homebuyers who apply to Citicorp without going through an agent or broker in the referral network must pay higher fees, fill out more paperwork and wait an extra 30 days to find out if they get the loan.

Citicorp denies that it discriminates, intentionally or unintentionally.

Len Druger, national director of sales for Citicorp, said the internal documents are "clearly not a current list of what's being done. We cover the extreme Northside to the extreme Southside. If we're excluding any areas, it's not how we're doing business. The information you have is either outdated or inaccurate."

He would not provide a more current list, saying it was irrelevant because the company had not been successful at signing up many agents in any area.

Citicorp points instead to its success in signing mortgage brokers, including several who receive referrals from real estate agents in black neighborhoods. Mr. Druger named six minority-owned companies and three more that he said work in minority areas, accounting for 17 percent of the MortgagePower members.

"We're kind of proud of that record," Mr. Druger said. "We think that's a respectable showing. It's self-evident that we are not discriminating."

One of the firms that Citicorp cited as active in minority communities was Standard Home Equities, a white-owned firm in Conyers.

"You're not going to find any discriminatory actions on the part of Citicorp," said Jim Strickland, the company president. "I've sent about six applications, three of them black, and the only one I've gotten approved was one of the blacks."

Yet many of the most successful black real estate agents in metro Atlanta said they have not been invited to participate in MortgagePower. That includes officers of the Empire Real Estate Board, the black real estate society.

"I have never heard of this program or been solicited for it," said Barbara Clay, Empire's real estate agent of 1988, who has sold more than $1 million in real estate 12 years in a row.

Mr. Druger responded: "It beats me, frankly. I can't believe she never heard about it or never received any marketing material. We have been aggressively sourcing members in that market [Atlanta] for the last year and a half."

REVOLUTIONARY LOAN PROGRAM

Eight years ago, Citicorp Mortgage was not among the top 100 mortgage lenders in America.

Last year it was No. 1.

Its rocket to the top is called MortgagePower.

Citicorp calls the program revolutionary, innovative, the no-hassle loan of the future.

To apply for a MortgagePower loan, a homebuyer must go through one of the nearly 4,000 real estate agents, mortgage brokers and financial counselors in 37 states who have signed agreements to refer clients to Citicorp Mortgage, a subsidiary of Citicorp, the largest banking company in America.

The homebuyer usually pays a fee of one-half percent of the loan amount to the agent or mortgage broker for the referral but receives a break of 1½ percent of the loan amount off the normal Citicorp loan origination fee.

The homebuyer also fills out a shorter application, and the company promises a quick response, usually within 15 business days.

The program has been criticized by competitors, who claim it violates the 1974 Real Estate Practices Act, which prohibits kickbacks, or payments from lenders to brokers for referrals. But in 1986 Citicorp secured from the U.S. Department of Housing and Urban Development a legal opinion saying the program was not prohibited because the fee is paid by homebuyers, not the lender.

A second criticism is that real estate agents, who work for the seller of the home, not the buyer, might steer buyers to Citicorp because of the signed agreements, although Citicorp may not have the lowest interest rates in the market. In Atlanta, Citicorp is consistently above the market rate.

Nevertheless, MortgagePower works. It accounts for 90 percent of Citicorp Morgage's $160 million business in Georgia, and 75 percent of the company's $13 billion business last year across the nation, company officials said.

RUN BY WHITE STAFF

Citicorp runs its MortgagePower program for Georgia from a Northside Atlanta office at Perimeter Center with an entirely white sales force, an entirely white corps of real estate attorneys and an entirely white group of real estate appraisers, according to Citicorp documents and employees.

It apparently has also called almost exclusively on white agencies in Atlanta's highly segregated real estate market.

Citicorp's list of targeted real estate agencies was given to the Journal-Constitution by a current Citicorp sales account executive and was verified last week by two former account executives. The current employee said the list, dated April 27, was the most current list.

Citicorp officials said they could not explain why agencies in black areas are not on the list. They said sales agents choose which real estate agents and mortgage brokers to solicit based on sales volume, not location or race.

"We just look for the largest volume potential. It's not hard to see who the biggest firms are," Mr. Druger said.

A former Citicorp marketing planner in the St. Louis office, who spoke on the condition that he would not be named, said MortgagePower was indeed targeted at high-volume agencies—but only in certain upper-income postal ZIP code areas around the country.

"They called it targeted marketing. 'Attractive areas' had a high 'ZIP quality' based on occupational type, educational level, household income and home value" the planner said. "They would come up with a map, then find out what real estate firms had what market share, then go after the big ones.

"They knew that they were leaving out probably every minority ZIP in the country, but their view is that this is perfectly legal," the planner said. "It's cookie-cutter time. They have streamlined making money to an extreme."

Citicorp officials deny that any ZIP code maps have ever been used in MortgagePower.

COVERED BY FAIR HOUSING ACT

Citicorp is not covered by the federal Community Reinvestment Act, which requires banks, but not mortgage companies owned by banks, to meet credit needs throughout their communities. However, Citicorp is covered by the Fair Housing Act and the Equal Credit Opportunity Act, which prohibit discrimination in marketing and credit decisions on home loans.

Legal experts said that marketing to a target audience by ZIP code or other geographic pattern, while a common practice of department stores and political fund-raisers, is dangerous ground for lenders.

"A McDonald's can do that. A dry cleaner's can do that. A mortgage company cannot do that," said Stephen M. Dane of Toledo, Ohio, a leading attorney who has represented plantiffs in fair housing cases. "You can still be the market leader, still make a lot of money, still do a lot of business, but your marketing must include minority areas.

"If they are using ZIP codes, can you think of a better way to screen out minority neighborhoods than to use income or housing value?" Mr. Dane asked.

FOUR

A CARTOONIST'S TICKLE AND JAB

1989 WINNER IN THE EDITORIAL CARTOONING CATEGORY

"For a distinguished example of a cartoonist's work, the determining qualities being that a cartoon shall embody an idea made clearly apparent, shall show good drawing and striking pictorial effect, and shall be intended to be helpful to some commendable cause of public importance . . ."

Chicago Sun-Times
Jack Higgins

Jack Higgins has been around politics long enough to know that mischief often lurks just behind the smiling faces. His political cartoons start with the accepted version of things, and then he sketches in a twist.

I was born and raised on Chicago's South Side. There you cannot escape being involved in politics, from cradle to grave and beyond.

An election always seemed to be in the offing. I was only 10 years old when I got my first job. My assignment was to put on a White Sox cap, sit near the entrance of the polling place and slip palm cards to people as they passed by on their way to vote. I thought it was exciting. I didn't question the legality of my actions. At the end of the day the precinct captain would buy us ice cream and pop. It was like a game. Did we win? Of course! The Democrats always won! Eventually I moved into the world of journalism—when I was 11, I got a paper route.

A passion for local politics and art placed me in political cartooning. It served for me as an immediate means to express my exasperation. And because it was local, the reaction was always swift and strong. In Chicago, they don't stab you in the back, they fillet you from the belly. Now my salad days of ice cream are over. My precinct captain won't even speak to me.

The leap from local to national issues was a small one. Nepotism, greed and racism still prevail on the national scene as well, and some of the faces are the same. It's just on a wider screen.

In these days of canned pop-top logic and shop-worn cliché, the impact of an original, slashing cartoon can be devastating. Although the shelf life of a newspaper is short, the political cartoon has a second life on refrigerator doors, office bulletin boards and through syndication. In the muddle caused by the information glut, the cartoon is striking in its simplicity and poignance. All these qualities make the political cartoon more memorable and describable than the column, the editorial or the film at eleven.

Most of all, our medium is timeless. Just as Thomas Nast educated the illiterate immigrants, we today appeal to those sensory overloaded masses yearning to be free by Friday.

How successful I am is in the eye of the beholder. I don't kid myself by saying that a single political cartoon can change people's ways of thinking. But cartoonists are one influence that helps them shape their thoughts (or, for the uninformed, their prejudices). In a world of gray areas, in judgment and brain matter, we glow—we turn on a light bulb. That makes the work more memorable. With humor as honey to go with the medicine, we keep a hold on the readers. Some cartoonists are more serious than funny. Others are so funny that they're not taken seriously. The best have something to say, and do so with the versatility of an artist's quill: using the plume to tickle and the point to prick. And in a rare magical moment of inspiration, some even manage to dip a sledgehammer into the ink.

I've yet to find a politician who can wash out India ink.

—Jack Higgins
Chicago Sun-Times

HIGGINS
©1988 CHICAGO SUN-TIMES
WITH APOLOGIES TO ANDREW WYETH

HIGGINS
...WHY JUST MOMENTS AGO MY WORKERS HOISTED ME ON THEIR SHOULDERS
M

The Baby Jessica Story —An American Tale of a small, humble community that banded together and offered a hand to this bundle of joy...
$
MOVIE RIGHTS
HIGGINS

HOW ABOUT MORE BLACKS IN LEADERSHIP POSITIONS IN SPORTS AND SPORTS COVERAGE!
We'll burn that cross when we come to it!
Owners
HIGGINS

©1988 CHICAGO SUN-TIMES
HIGGINS
THEY'RE OFFENDED BY MY PICTURE... THE WAY I SHOW CHRIST ... MY DISPLAY OF WOMEN ... THE PARTIAL NUDITY ...
You're just ahead of your time...

©1988 CHICAGO SUN-TIMES
HIGGINS
Mind if I play through?
QUAYLE

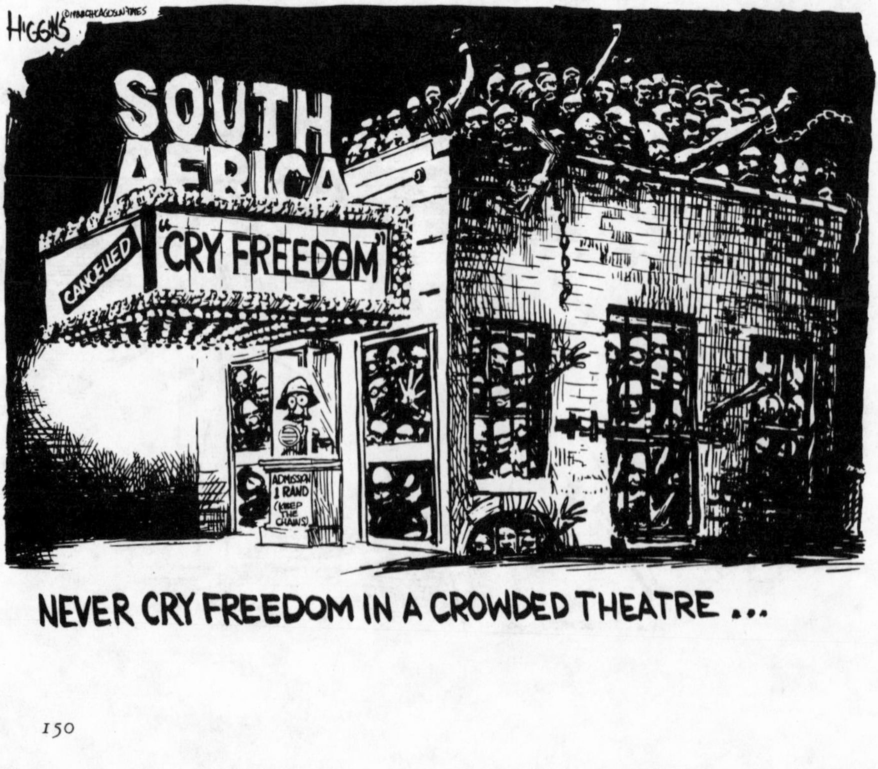

NEVER CRY FREEDOM IN A CROWDED THEATRE ...

HIGGINS

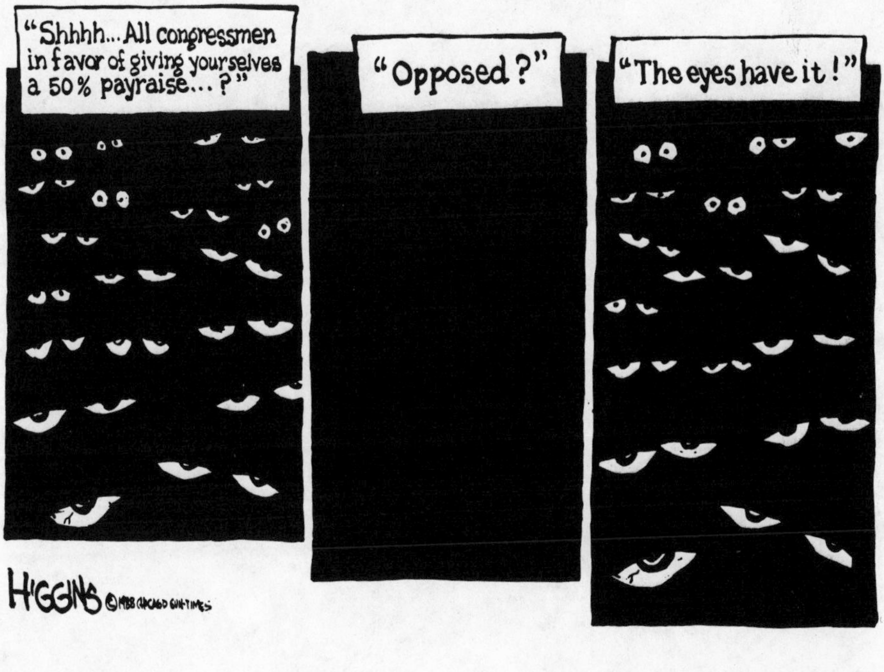
"Shhhh... All congressmen in favor of giving yourselves a 50% payraise...?"
"Opposed?"
"The eyes have it!"
HIGGINS

FIVE

THE GREAT TAX GIVEAWAY

1989 WINNER IN THE NATIONAL REPORTING CATEGORY

"For a distinguished example of reporting on national affairs . . ."

The Philadelphia Inquirer
Donald L. Barlett and
James B. Steele

Camouflaging tax breaks for key political supporters has become a fine art in Washington. After exhaustive research, the team of Barlett and Steele was able to crack the code. Here's how it's done and who benefits.

When it was enacted by Congress, the Tax Reform Act of 1986 was widely hailed as a stunning defeat for special interests and an unprecedented victory for ordinary taxpayers.

Senator Bob Packwood, the Oregon Republican who, as chairman of the Senate Finance Committee, was one of the measure's two principal architects, put it this way:

"The Jane and Joe (working) in an Oregon mill making $16,000 or $17,000 and paying $800 or $900 in taxes will no longer have to hear stories of unfairness. Those will be gone."

Representative Dan Rostenkowski, the Illinois Democrat who, as chairman of the House Ways and Means Committee, was the other prime mover behind the legislation, said:

"Tax reform's popular appeal and its political force is its promise of fairness to working families. No other theme could have gained the support of such a broad spectrum of taxpayers. It was not the hope of more tax cuts that stirred a doubting, often cynical nation—but the sense that the family down the street or the corporation across town can't beat the system any longer."

But a close reading of the new law, undertaken as a follow-up to articles written about the far-reaching overhaul of the Internal Revenue Code that summer, turned up another side of tax reform. It was a side that Packwood, Rostenkowski and other congressional leaders were intent on keeping secret.

Woven throughout the 925-page tax law and a pending technical corrections bill that would grow to nearly 1,000 additional pages were hundreds of mysterious paragraphs. Each was cryptically worded in language that was arcane even by tax-law standards.

The paragraphs all bore common traits. Each contained detailed information—such as the date a business was incorporated, the description of a project, the date of some unnamed person's birth or death—clearly intended to define a specific individual or company.

None of the paragraphs mentioned the individuals or businesses by name, although the purpose of each was to excuse that person or business from complying with certain provisions of the tax code.

Indeed, the paragraphs were so carefully phrased that if 10,000 individuals were in a similar situation, only one could qualify for the favored treatment. The pattern was the same for businesses.

The tax-writing committees further muddied the issue by releasing lists of purported beneficiaries of the tax breaks with entries that in many instances were as obscure as the tax law itself. There were, for example, the "620 Project," "Ormesa II," "Louisiana ESOPs," "Navy Ships," "Fertilizer Plant," "Mattress Factory," "An Estate" and—the ultimate—"Unknown."

A few newspapers focused on tax breaks in their areas.

Two national newspapers published the lists. But none systematically sought to identify the people who would profit from what amounted to their own private tax laws. (Members of the House and Senate who wrote the legislation, and their aides, refused to name the individual beneficiaries when asked about them.)

To begin the process, we created a computer data base to compare the official lists with the descriptions we found in the tax law of those who had been exempted. As a result of this comparison, we discovered that the tax-writing committees had omitted from their lists scores of projects and had concealed the identities of the beneficiaries.

What's more, the congressional taxwriters failed to name any of the actual individuals who ultimately would be granted immunity from the payment of certain taxes. And in some instances, they incorrectly identified the recipient of the tax favor.

One example was an entry labeled "Ireton Coal Corp." The provision in the new law that allegedly described "Ireton" was worded this way:

"A taxpayer is described in this clause if the taxpayer filed a title 11 case on December 8, 1981, filed a plan of reorganization on February 5, 1986, filed an amended plan on March 14, 1986, and received court approval for the amended plan and disclosure statement on April 16, 1986."

Days were spent trying to locate the Ireton Coal Corp. All the available electronic data bases and corporate registers were examined without success. Incorporation records in nearly two dozen states were checked by telephone. Again, no record of "Ireton Coal Corp." Interviews were conducted with officers of coal companies, union leaders and industry officials in major coal-producing states. None had ever heard of "Ireton Coal Corp."

Well into the second week of interviews and record checks it was determined that the "Ireton Coal Corp." entry was just one of many mistakes on the committee lists.

The company was not "Ireton Coal Corp." There was no such company. Rather, it was Ironton Coke Corp. in Ironton, Ohio.

And the real beneficiary was yet someone else, a New York lawyer, Stanley I. Deutsch, who had acquired a controlling interest in Ironton and who would reap the largest gain from a tax concession worth an estimated $18 million.

Other names on the congressional lists were even more difficult to decipher. Like the one entitled, "Personal holding companies." After days of electronic data base searches, the methodic combing of corporate records to match information in the tax code, and a constant cross-checking of documents, we identified the company as Cantor, Fitzgerald & Co., a securities dealer with offices in Beverly Hills and New York.

Once again, the real beneficiary was not the company but its principal owner—B. Gerald Cantor, a wealthy patron of the arts with many influential friends on Capitol Hill.

Even when it was possible to match a name on the lists with a provision in the tax law, there was still no clue as to who would escape payment of taxes.

Then there were those custom-tailored tax breaks that the congressional committees, for whatever reason, chose to exclude from the lists. These were picked up through a line-by-line reading of the tax bill and then comparing descriptions with information in our computer data base.

One of those provisions was crafted for an unnamed corporation that had taken advantage of a tax-shelter scheme in the U.S. Virgin Islands. The law described the company as a domestic corporation "actively engaged directly or through a subsidiary in the conduct of a trade or business in the Virgin Islands and such trade or business consists of business related to marine activities and . . . such corporation was incorporated on March 31, 1983, in Delaware."

From a series of court filings involving another business we secured a list of companies that had used the tax shelter to avoid payment of hundreds of millions of dollars in taxes. By identifying the background of each company on that list—a slow process, since most were private firms owned by a few stockholders or partners—we ultimately pinpointed the one for which the tax break had been written.

It was called Bizcap Inc., a Dallas-based company controlled by William H. Bowen, a wealthy Dallas supporter of conservative causes.

This identification procedure was repeated scores of times. The task was slowed considerably by the fact that in each case, a different approach had to be used to identify the beneficiary. Overall, records were obtained from dozens of local, state and federal agencies; state and federal courts; and private citizens in more than two dozen states.

The records included city council proceedings; limited partnership agreements; state insurance commission filings; affidavits for subpoenas; videotapes of public meetings taken by private citizens; election commission records; corporate franchise tax reports; bankruptcy, civil and criminal cases.

No one document was more important than another to the series. More often, what was helpful in decoding one provision was useless in unraveling another.

After "The Great Tax Giveaway" series was published, several colleagues told us they assumed that we had cultivated sources on the tax-writing committees, who put us on the trail of the breaks. In fact, not a single beneficiary was identified through tips. Nor could the story have been reported in that way. So secretive was the dispensing of the tax giveaways that many staff members were unaware of the true beneficiaries.

One of the more rewarding letters we received after the series was published came from a government attorney who had spent a year working on a case involving one of the companies that had been singled out for special tax treatment.

Until he read *The Inquirer* series, the attorney said, he had never known who the man was behind that company—the man for whom congressional tax writers had created the tax break.

—Donald L. Barlett
James B. Steele
The Philadelphia Inquirer

HOW THE INFLUENTIAL WIN BILLIONS IN SPECIAL TAX BREAKS

SUNDAY, APRIL 10, 1988

BY DONALD L. BARLETT AND JAMES B. STEELE

Imagine, if you will, that you are a tall, bald father of three living in a Northeast Philadelphia rowhouse and selling aluminum siding door-to-door for a living.

Imagine that you go to your congressman and ask him to insert a provision in the federal tax code that exempts tall, bald fathers of three living in Northeast Philadelphia and selling aluminum siding for a living from paying taxes on income from door-to-door sales.

Imagine further that your congressman cooperates, writes that exemption and inserts it into pending legislation. And that Congress then actually passes it into law.

Lots of luck.

The more than 80 million low- and middle-income individuals and families who pay federal taxes just don't get that kind of personal break. Nor for that matter do most upper-middle-class and affluent Americans.

But some people do.

Like Mrs. Joseph J. Ballard Jr., widow of a socially prominent Texas businessman. Geraldine Ballard lives in a $600,000 home in an exclusive Fort Worth enclave whose residents include Perry R. Bass, patriarch of the billionaire Bass oil and investments clan, and concert pianist Van Cliburn.

For her, tax writers have drafted the following paragraph that they intend to insert in tax legislation that Congress soon will take up:

For purposes of section 2656(b)(8) of the Internal Revenue Code of 1986, an individual who receives an interest in a charitable remainder unitrust shall be deemed to be the only noncharitable beneficiary of such trust if the interest in the trust passed to the individual under the will of a decedent who resided in Tarrant County, Texas, and died on October 28, 1983, at the age of 75, *with a gross estate not exceeding $12.5 million, and the individual is the decedent's surviving spouse.*

The paragraph will, if enacted into law, allow the estate of Geraldine Ballard's late husband to escape payment of an estimated $4 million in federal taxes that the Internal Revenue Service says the estate owes.

Tailored to meet the needs of a single taxpayer, the provision is just one of scores of similar special-interest deals awaiting congressional action.

Each would exempt a specific individual or corporation, or group of individuals and corporations—usually unnamed—from taxes that people and businesses in similar situations are obliged to pay.

When Geraldine Ballard was asked about the provision, she replied:

"I really just can't explain it because I don't understand it myself. . . . I have no earthly idea what they are doing. The Texas Bank of Commerce in Arlington handles it. It's a trust. I wish I could help you.

"I presume you are referring to the bill that Jim Wright was putting through?"

"Jim Wright" is the Fort Worth Democrat who is speaker of the House of Representatives.

When Congress passed the Tax Reform Act of 1986, radically overhauling the Internal Revenue Code, Rep. Dan Rostenkowski (D., Ill.), chairman of the tax-writing House Ways and Means Committee, hailed the effort as "a bill that reaches deep into our national sense of justice—and gives us back a trust in government that has slipped away in the maze of tax preferences for the rich and powerful."

In fact, Rostenkowski and other self-styled reformers created a new maze of unprecedented favoritism. Working in secret, they wove at least 650 exemptions—preferences, really, for the rich and powerful—through the legislation, most written in cryptic legal and tax jargon that conceals the identity of the beneficiaries.

When they were finished, thousands of wealthy individuals and hundreds of businesses were absolved from paying billions upon billions of dollars in federal income taxes. It was, an Inquirer investigation has established, the largest tax giveaway in the 75-year history of the federal income tax.

There were provisions that accorded special treatment not available under either old or new tax laws. There were provisions that excused taxpayers from complying with IRS or court decisions holding them liable for payment of taxes. And there were provisions that merely granted exemptions from the tax law—licenses, if you will, not to pay taxes.

The recipients were, among others, White House dinner guests, members of Forbes magazine's directory of the 400 wealthiest Americans, corporate executives, major campaign contributors, companies that have slashed the pension or health-care benefits of their retirees, foreign investors, corporate raiders, former officials of federal agencies, personal or business friends of members of Congress, and businesses and individuals who paid little or no tax in the past.

That was Round 1.

Now, Congress is preparing to do it all over again, this time adding the private tax provisions to a so-called technical-corrections bill to remedy defects in the Tax Reform Act of 1986.

The cost of the latest round of special deals—many of which are still being written—already is approaching the multibillion-dollar range.

Whatever the final figure, it will come on top of the $10.6 billion outlay for such concessions in 1986. That $10.6 billion, by the way, was Congress' official estimate; the ultimate price tag, Inquirer projections show, could run two to three times that amount.

Even the understated $10.6 billion cost was substantial. It exceeds every dollar paid in federal income tax for the next five years or more by low- and middle-income residents of Philadelphia.

As might be expected, congressional tax-writing committees prefer to shroud their work in secrecy, writing the private provisions in obscure language, as in the case of Geraldine Ballard. A sampling of exemptions from the 1986 act, and the beneficiaries of those exemptions as determined in an Inquirer investigation, illustrates the practice:

THE LAW. *In the case of any pre-1987 open year, the amendment made by section 1275(b) shall not apply to any domestic corporation if . . . during the fiscal year which ended May 31, 1986, such corporation was actively* *engaged directly or through a subsidiary in the conduct of a trade or business in the Virgin Islands and such trade or business consists of business related to marine activities and . . . such corporation was incorporated on March 31, 1983, in Delaware.*

THE BENEFICIARY. That paragraph describes Bizcap Inc., a Dallas firm whose principal stockholder—and thus the major beneficiary of the tax break—was William H. Bowen, a 71-year-old Dallas millionaire and supporter of conservative political candidates and causes.

Bizcap was in the category of corporations that a federal judge described as "the ultimate tax shelter," one that "was organized for the specific purpose of exploiting a gap" in federal law. It was incorporated in Delaware, established its headquarters on St. Thomas in the U.S. Virgin Islands, and generated most of its revenue from business interests in the United States.

Because it maintained an office in the Caribbean, Bizcap considered itself a foreign corporation for U.S. tax purposes and avoided payment of millions of dollars in income taxes on its U.S. investments. Tax authorities eventually caught on to the practice and issued a deficiency notice, claiming that Bizcap owed $5.1 million in unpaid income taxes for 1983 and 1984, and a negligence penalty of $767,554. The private tax law excused Bizcap from having to pay the taxes.

THE LAW. *The amendments made by section 201 shall not apply to any property placed in service pursuant to a master plan which is clearly identifiable as of March 1, 1986, for any project described in any of the following subparagraphs . . . such project involves a port terminal and oil pipeline extending generally from the area of Los Angeles, California, to the area of Midland, Texas, and . . . before September 26, 1985, there is a binding contract for dredging and channeling with respect thereto and a management contract with a construction manager for such project.*

THE BENEFICIARY. That paragraph describes a 1,032-mile, $1.7 billion pipeline that will carry Alaskan crude oil from tankers berthed in the Long Beach, Calif., harbor to Midland, Texas, where it will feed into an existing pipeline network leading to refineries along the Gulf Coast and in the Midwest. It is to be built by the Pacific & Texas Pipeline & Transportation Co. of Long Beach. The company is the creation of Cecil R. Owens, a promoter and real estate developer whose investment activities first caught the attention of the U.S. Securities and Exchange Commission in 1985.

In a lawsuit filed last September in federal court in Los Angeles, the SEC contended that Owens and his company made fraudulent claims in the sale of $2.1 million worth of unregistered Pacific & Texas stock. Investors, the SEC said, were promised a yearly return of 500 percent on their money. The SEC said the company also neglected to mention to potential investors that it had paid nearly a half-million dollars on Owens' behalf for "among other things, travel, living expenses, lobbying and entertainment, political contributions and various business expenses."

Without admitting or denying the government's allegations, Owens and his company consented to the issuance of a permanent injunction prohibiting both from engaging in unlawful securities practices.

Because of the pipeline exemption in the 1986 tax act, the company ultimately may avoid payment of about a half-billion dollars in federal income taxes. The project is to be financed in part with tax-exempt bonds and it will qualify for the investment tax credit and accelerated depreciation that have been canceled for ordinary businesses and investors.

THE LAW. *The amendments made by section 201 shall not apply to any property which is part of a project . . . which is certified by the Federal Energy Regulatory Commission before March 2, 1986, as a qualifying facility for purposes of the Public Utility Regulatory Policies Act of 1978 . . .*

THE BENEFICIARY. That paragraph describes hundreds of companies and individuals who are investors in alternative-energy facilities, including a cogeneration plant near Pottsville, Pa., that has just begun its test phase, producing electricity from coal refuse.

It will allow investors in the plant to avoid payment of an estimated $26 million in income taxes. The plant is a joint venture of subsidiaries, affiliates or companies that share common ownership with the

Bechtel Group Inc. of San Francisco, a global construction and engineering company; Pyropower Corp. of San Diego, a designer of cogeneration equipment, and the Gilberton Coal Co. of Pottsville.

The facility, known as the John B. Rich Memorial Power Station, is named in memory of one of Northeast Pennsylvania's most powerful coal barons, whose descendants own the Gilberton Coal Co. Rich was convicted in 1965 of federal charges that he and his Gilberton Coal Co. filed false and fraudulent tax returns and evaded individual and corporate income taxes. He and the company paid back taxes, fines and costs totaling one-third of a million dollars; a prison sentence was suspended and he was placed on probation for three years.

The Bechtel Group and its owners, the Bechtel family—whose holdings have been valued at close to $1 billion—have a direct or indirect stake in tax breaks worth tens of millions of dollars in the 1986 act.

THE LAW. *Treatment of certain partnerships. In the case of a partnership with a taxable year beginning May 1, 1986, if such partnership realized net capital gain during the period beginning on the first day of such taxable year and ending on May 29, 1986, pursuant to an indemnity agreement dated May 6, 1986, then such partnership may elect to treat each asset to which such net capital gain relates as having been distributed to the partners of such partnership in proportion to their distributive share of the capital gain or loss realized by the partnership with respect to each asset . . .*

THE BENEFICIARY. That paragraph describes the partnership that became Bear Stearns Cos. Inc., a Wall Street investment banking and brokerage firm and one of the dozen largest member-firms of the New York Stock Exchange. It will save Bear Stearns partners an estimated $8 million in taxes.

Among the partners are Alan C. Greenberg, chairman of the board and chief executive officer, whose $5.7 million in cash compensation in 1986 made him the highest-paid executive of a publicly owned Wall Street brokerage. Others include:

James E. Cayne and E. John Rosenwald Jr., both members of the office of the president, who each earned $3.9 million in 1986; Alvin H. Einbender, executive vice president and chief operating officer, who earned $3.7 million, and Thomas R. Anderson and Denis P. Coleman Jr., both executive vice presidents, who each earned $3.4 million.

THE LAW. *The amendments made by section 201 shall not apply to two new automobile carrier vessels which will cost approximately $47 million and will be constructed by a United States-flag carrier to operate, under the United States flag and with an American crew, to transport foreign automobiles to the United States, in a case where negotiations for such transportation arrangements commenced in April 1985, formal contract bids were submitted prior to the end of 1985, and definitive transportation contracts were awarded in May 1986.*

THE BENEFICIARY. That paragraph describes Central Gulf Lines, the principal subsidiary of International Shipholding Corp. in New Orleans. It will save the company an estimated $8 million in taxes by allowing it to claim the investment tax credit and accelerated depreciation that Congress terminated for most corporate taxpayers.

Millionaire brothers Niels W. Johnsen of Rumson, N.J., and Erik F. Johnsen of New Orleans own 40 percent of the stock of International Shipholding Corp.

The two ships given favored tax treatment were built in shipyards in Japan and will carry Japanese-manufactured autos to U.S. dealers. Each has a capacity for about 4,000 cars. The Green Lake made its maiden voyage last October, arriving in Baltimore with a load of Toyotas. The second vessel, the Green Bay, made its first voyage last November, arriving at Long Beach, Calif., with a load of Hondas.

□ □ □

On Capitol Hill, such tax concessions are known as transition rules. In the beginning, they were intended to cushion the impact of tax-law revisions.

Lawmakers reasoned that when individuals or corporations entered into business, investment or financial arrangements based on one law, it was unfair to abruptly alter the law.

Sen. Bob Packwood (R., Ore.), who as chairman of the Senate Finance Committee personally passed on the rules inserted in the 1986 act, explained at the time the rationale for the exceptions:

"Transition rules are designed to ease the passage from the present law to the new law. These are necessary because people had relied upon the law as it was. In those cases, they deserved a transition."

That was a definition that would have applied in the 1950s, a time when massive overhauls of the Internal Revenue Code were a rarity. In fact, the 1954 revision was the most far-reaching in decades.

But by the 1980s, when Congress took to revising the tax code every year or two, adding thousands of pages of new laws and regulations, the old reasoning made little sense.

Lawmakers rewrote the code in 1981, 1982, 1984, and 1986, and in two of those years, 1981 and 1986, the changes touched the daily lives of every taxpayer.

This meant that if Congress intended to be fair, it would have to enact transition rules for millions of taxpayers, or none. Instead, it chose to give relief to select individuals and corporations.

As a result, most transition rules became little more than grants of immunity to those whose power and influence gave them access to congressional tax writers.

It is in that context that Congress now is preparing for a replay of 1986.

Passage of a major tax bill customarily is followed by legislation to correct inevitable typographical, spelling, punctuation, capitalization and other errors.

In the case of the 1986 Tax Reform Act, there are errant commas to be removed, parentheses to be closed or opened, capital letters to be made lower case and paragraphs to be renumbered.

One section refers to "New Orleans" when it should be "Pensacola." Another refers to "real" when it should be "rail." "Spring cotton" should be "spray cotton." "Diversatch" should be "Diversatech." And "1935" should be "1985."

Then there is the transition rule written into the law to grant special treatment in connection with the issuance of tax-exempt bonds in an unnamed state.

The law says in part that "a bond is described in this paragraph if . . . such bond is issued before Jan. 1, 1993, by a state admitted to the Union on June 14, 1776 . . ."

The Union, of course, did not exist on June 14, 1776, a date three weeks before approval of the Declaration of Independence, and 11 years before Delaware became the first state. Such is the way that tax laws are written.

Legislation introduced last week by the House Ways and Means and Senate Finance Committees will rectify these and other mistakes. It will also do something else. It will serve as a vehicle for Round 2 of congressional tax giveaways.

Lobbyists, lawyers and lawmakers—many of whom missed out on the tax-preference windfall in 1986—are scurrying to include their clients and constituents in the second round.

Some are seeking remedies for businesses and individuals placed at a disadvantage when Congress indiscriminately penalized some taxpayers and rewarded others the last time. Some are seeking a fresh batch of tax favors. Some are seeking to correct what they perceive as legislative mistakes or oversights.

The drive to secure the breaks has become so intense that Congress may delay action on the technical-corrections legislation until after the November election.

The reason: Each new break adds to the federal deficit and encourages other members of Congress to seek similar, or additional, exemptions from a tax law that everyone else must comply with. In an election year—or, more accurately, in the months before an election—lawmakers would prefer to avoid publicity about arranging tax breaks for exclusive constituents. This leaves the tax-writing committees with four choices:

Enact a pure technical-corrections bill without any special breaks; drastically limit the number of such breaks to be included in the bill; postpone action on the legislation until after the election, when the bill can be loaded with concessions without incurring voter wrath, or enact a pure bill and, after the election, bury the breaks in other legislation.

Whatever happens, about all that can be said for certain, given Congress' record to date, is that the personal tax provisions will be cloaked in secrecy.

Members of the three tax-writing committees—the House Ways and Means Committee, Senate Finance Committee and Joint Committee on Taxation—have on occasion identified the beneficiaries of transition rules.

They also have concealed them.

It is possible, in a methodical reading of the more than three million words that make up the Internal Revenue Code—that's roughly the equivalent of five copies of *War and Peace*—to uncover some special-interest provisions.

But it is impossible to detect them all, since many are phrased in a way that disguises their true intent. Furthermore, others are slipped into the hundreds of bills that Congress enacts each year that are unrelated to the income tax.

These practices permit members of the tax-writing committees, when they choose to do so, to guarantee complete anonymity for those individuals and corporations excused from paying taxes.

With certain exceptions, lawmakers who request the private tax laws refuse to acknowledge their involvement, presumably for fear of antagonizing the mass of taxpaying voters who never receive preferential treatment.

Likewise, the tax-writing committees and their staffs refuse to identify those lawmakers, who, in the words of one congressman, dispense "favors to individuals the way royalty might do."

According to the official tabulation by the Senate Finance Committee and Joint Committee on Taxation, the 1986 Tax Reform Act contained about 650 provisions that they designated as transition rules.

The figure, like much of what the reformers had to say about their legislative handiwork, was both incorrect and misleading.

The tax-writing committees and their staffs misidentified the recipients of some tax gifts and omitted others—like Bizcap—from their tally.

An Inquirer investigation has established that the actual number of individuals who will profit from the special rules will run into the thousands. Most cannot be identified beyond their economic status—upper income.

The Senate Finance Committee staff also reported that the various concessions would result in a revenue loss of $10.6 billion, a figure that was certified by the Joint Committee on Taxation, the body with final responsibility for tax data. The estimate was as illusory as the reported number of tax dispensations.

The cost of one break was originally placed by the Joint Committee at $300 million. After passage of the legislation, the figure was adjusted upward to $7 billion.

That worked out to a 2,233 percent miscalculation, a mistake so large as to defy comprehension. It would be roughly akin to a family who bought a house expecting to pay $400 a month on its mortgage but who discovered, belatedly, the payments would actually be $9,332 a month.

It seems the tax writers intended to construct a law that only a small number of wealthy people could take advantage of. Instead, they wrote it in such a way that virtually all wealthy people could profit from it.

Congress responded as only Congress can do. It rephrased the provision to meet the original intent, inserted it in the federal budget bill enacted last December and promptly announced that the change constituted a tax increase that would generate billions of dollars in new revenue.

ESTIMATING THE COSTS

How do such errors come about?

When a member of a tax-writing committee suggests a specific tax break, a U.S. Treasury official explained, the committee staff makes an estimate based on the proposal.

But the "wording of the statute has not been finalized," he said, "and the people who are finalizing the language are not the ones who have been involved in making the estimate.

"So there's a misunderstanding between them that only becomes apparent after one sees the estimate by itself and also has the luxury of being able to see the wording of the statute."

Such blunders aside, even the understated $10.6 billion revenue-loss estimate from the 1986 tax bill represents a major drain when measured against the federal taxes that others must pay.

It exceeds the income taxes that will be paid by all low- and middle-income individuals and families in Vermont, South Dakota and Wyoming for the next five years.

It exceeds the telephone excise tax that will be paid through much of the 1990s by all low- and middle-income individuals and families—a regressive tax that was due to expire last December but that Congress retained in order to raise revenue to meet its budget goals.

It is the equivalent of the income tax that will be paid by 1 million families earning $25,000 annually for the next five years.

Indeed, ordinary taxpayers across the country must make up part of the lost revenue. They are the individuals and families who, under the 1986 Tax Reform Act, are being taxed for the first time on college fellowships, full unemployment compensation benefits and some unreimbursed employee business expenses, and who have lost all or part of their traditional deductions for medical expenses, sales taxes and consumer interest.

They are the individuals and families who, in many cases, will pay higher taxes this year as a result of Congress' decision to gut the progressive rate system and to place a single professional woman who earns $25,000 in the same top 28 percent tax bracket as an investor who earns $25 million.

They are the individuals and families who Jan. 1 began paying higher Social Security taxes—another levy borne disproportionately by low- and middle-income people—and who will see that tax go up again in 1990.

Congress' tax reformers, to be sure, downplay the cost of personal tax breaks and chide critics of them.

"In the overall scheme of events," said Bob Packwood just prior to enactment of the 1986 act, a few billion dollars in transition rules represents "a relatively minor part of the whole bill."

THE DEFICITS GROW

It was—and is—such an attitude that has contributed to the runaway federal deficits of the 1980s. And it explains why the 1988 deficit will be up, rather than down, as the reformers promised when they sold the 1986 tax act.

For the first five months of the current fiscal year that began last October, the government is running $89.7 billion in the red. That exceeds the $72.7 billion deficit posted for the entire year of 1980, when Ronald Reagan was campaigning for his first term.

It also surpasses the cumulative deficits for all of the 1950s and virtually all of the 1960s, thereby guaranteeing that more and more tax dollars will be diverted to interest payments on a $2.4 trillion—and fast growing—national debt.

With seven more months to go in the fiscal year, and a deficit already of $89.7 billion, Congress will not come close to meeting the goals set in the 1985 deficit reduction law that was to move the government into the black—permanently.

Dubbed Gramm-Rudman-Hollings for its three sponsors—Sens. Phil Gramm (R., Texas), Warren B. Rudman (R., N.H.) and Ernest F. Hollings (D., S.C.)—the law set a maximum deficit of $108 billion for 1988.

Congress recast the Gramm-Rudman-Hollings targets last year and fixed the new 1988 maximum at $144 billion, a figure that the government still may not meet.

All this notwithstanding the euphoric statements by congressional leaders last December when they pushed through federal budget and spending bills that were widely—and incorrectly—portrayed as deficit-cutting measures.

Sen. John F. Kerry (D., Mass.) described the legislation as "welcome relief from the distorted budgetary pattern of 1980 to 1987." It will, he said, "reduce the federal deficit by $80 billion within two years, by cutting $33.7 billion in 1988 and $46 billion in 1989."

Sen. Robert C. Byrd (D., W.Va.), Senate majority leader, applauded the measure as "the largest two-year legislative package of permanent deficit reduction. That is not a mouse. It is an achievement of which we can be proud."

What the legislation did was allow members of Congress seeking re-election, as well as those seeking their party's presidential nomination, to put off until some time after the November 1988 election the tough decisions that will have to be made on stiff tax increases and sharp spending cuts.

In the meantime, some lawmakers are quietly building support among their colleagues for enacting new taxes and raising existing ones. Among their favorites: a national sales tax, a value-added tax and a whopping increase in the gasoline tax.

Each of the taxes is regressive. Each would fall disproportionately on low- and middle-income individuals and families.

The value-added tax is especially appealing to certain members of Congress because it is a hidden levy. It is, in effect, a multiple sales tax built into the cost of consumer goods at different stages in the manufacturing process. As a result, consumers are unable to determine how much tax they are paying.

Whatever the economic cost of personal tax breaks, it is dwarfed by the cost in fairness.

In 1986, Congress extended preferential treatment to thousands of individual taxpayers and hundreds of companies at the expense of other individuals and companies in similar situations.

It gave tax breaks to urban development projects in some cities and withheld them in others. It gave tax breaks to some trucking companies and withheld them from others. It gave tax breaks to some insurance companies and withheld them from others. It gave tax breaks to some housing projects and withheld them from others. It gave tax breaks to some utilities and withheld them from others. It gave tax breaks to some universities and withheld them from others. It gave tax breaks to some communications companies and withheld them from others. It gave tax breaks to the steel industry and withheld them from the copper industry.

Without exception, Congress denied comparable breaks to middle-income taxpayers who shoulder the brunt of the overall federal tax burden. But this was in keeping with the way Congress has been making tax law since the late 1960s.

And it was typical of so many legislative revisions that have fueled a growing distrust of the tax system among middle-class taxpayers, an attitude that has been reflected in one public opinion poll after another.

That distrust—rooted in the belief that there is one set of rules for the ordinary citizen and another set for the privileged—surfaced in the 1970s and has led to steadily rising noncompliance by taxpayers seeking to avoid, or even evade, their taxes.

The 1986 tax act did nothing to dispel the belief that the system is riddled with inequities.

For example, Congress eliminated the deduction for interest payments on student loans for millions of middle-income taxpayers, but offered no special exemptions.

It eliminated the investment tax credit for family farmers who bought tractors, but offered no special exemptions.

It eliminated the investment tax credit for drivers who own their tractor-trailer rigs, but offered no special exemptions.

Congress did, however, grant a special exemption that lowered the tax rate on a millionaire securities dealer.

It did grant a special exemption that allowed a wealthy Chicago family to claim the investment tax credit on a warehouse.

And it did grant a special exemption that permits a large trucking company, whose principal owner is a major contributor to the Republican Party, to claim the investment tax credit on its trucks.

The disparate treatment was more evident when considering two specific groups of taxpayers and two specific changes in the law.

In 1984, the latest year for which complete figures are available, 11.7 million families with annual incomes of $20,000 to $40,000 claimed the working-couple deduction. It allowed them to avoid more than $1.5 billion in taxes.

Because Congress, in the 1986 tax act, eliminated that deduction—without any exceptions—all 11.7 million families lose it when they file returns this year, and many will pay higher taxes as a consequence.

Again during 1984, about 400,000 individuals and families with incomes above $100,000 claimed the investment tax credit. The writeoff allowed them to avoid $1.6 billion in taxes.

Like the working-couple deduction, the investment tax credit was eliminated. But not for everyone. Through personal tax breaks, Congress retained the credit for thousands of upper-income taxpayers.

All this helps explain why the House Ways and Means Committee and Senate Finance Committee have resolutely refused to name individual lawmakers who request tax-immunity provisions for constituents.

It helps explain why the provisions are couched in language that conceals the beneficiary's identity.

And it helps explain why the tax-writing committees decline to say how many people and companies are in situations similar to those of the beneficiaries, yet do not receive special consideration.

The entire legislative process surrounding tax indulgences is so dependent on congressional secrecy that most members of Congress are unaware of the provisions when they vote on tax legislation.

In 1986, congressional leaders withheld even a partial list of tax preferences from House members until after they voted in favor of the legislation.

The process has become so byzantine that, at times, key lawmakers involved in writing tax bills profess their ignorance about breaks that they personally approved.

Just before the Senate ratified the Tax Reform Act of 1986, Sen. Howard M. Metzenbaum (D., Ohio) questioned the Senate Finance Committee's Bob Packwood about one particular provision.

Referring to a vaguely worded clause that would permit anonymous dairy farmers, located mostly in California and Nebraska, to escape payment of $22 million in taxes, Metzenbaum asked:

"I think we have a right to know. Who are those persons? What do they have going for them? Are they small farmers? Are they large corporations? More importantly, maybe, are they American-owned? Are they foreign corporations? Are they foreign-owned corporations?"

Packwood, who with Dan Rostenkowski was responsible for approving or rejecting the custom-tailored tax breaks, replied:

"I have no idea who the individual or corporate beneficiaries are."

TAX CHAIRMEN FAIL TO RESPOND TO QUERIES

SUNDAY, APRIL 10, 1988

Last November, The Inquirer sent a letter to Sen. Bob Packwood (R., Ore.) asking two questions about a tax concession—for an unnamed business—that was buried in the Tax Reform Act of 1986.

Packwood, who was chairman of the Senate Finance Committee when the tax law was written and was one of its chief architects, never answered.

An identical letter was sent to Packwood's counterpart in the House, Rep. Dan Rostenkowski (D., Ill.), chairman of the Ways and Means Committee. It, too, went unanswered.

Letters with more detailed questions, sent to the staffs of the Senate Finance Committee, House Ways and Means Committee and the Joint Committee on Taxation, also brought no response.

Dozens of telephone calls placed over a period of months to the staffs of the tax-writing committees and to committee members resulted in either no response or a flat "no comment" to questions.

Virtually everyone associated with writing private tax laws that exempt select individuals and businesses from the payment of federal income taxes refused to identify beneficiaries, to provide estimates of the amount of taxes avoided or to name the members of Congress who sought the tax breaks.

With a few notable exceptions, businesses and individuals receiving—or seeking—tax breaks were only slightly more responsive.

Some confirmed the existence of their concessions. Some suggested that the tax savings were overstated by the Joint Committee on Taxation. Most declined to talk or refused to reply to written queries.

For example, a spokesman for Wheelabrator Technologies Inc.

of Hampton, N.H., who was asked about a provision in the Tax Reform Act of 1986 that allows the company to avoid paymentof millions of dollars in federal income taxes, said: "The company prefers not to comment."

A spokesman for CNA Insurance Cos. of Chicago was asked about a provision that has been drafted, is expected to be inserted in legislation that Congress will take up this year and that will allow the company to avoid payment of millions of dollars in federal income taxes. He said:

"No comment."

HOW BUSINESSES INFLUENCE THE TAX-WRITING PROCESS

TUESDAY, APRIL 12, 1988

BY DONALD L. BARLETT AND JAMES B. STEELE

When it comes to politics, special-interest tax breaks and the congressional committees that write the nation's tax laws, there are some remarkable coincidences.

Look at where the money flows—campaign contributions, speaking fees, retainers to well-connected law firms—and you're likely also to find tax favors.

This does not mean that those who grant tax favors are doing anything illegal. Nor does it mean that everybody who gives money is looking for a tax break.

But the money does provide access to the people who write the tax laws, a ticket, if you will, to get in the door to what in the 1980s has become an almost annual event on Capitol Hill—the rewriting of the Internal Revenue Code and the dispensing of tax benefits.

Once inside, the contributors have the opportunity to argue their cases in the most favorable light before legislation affecting them is passed by Congress—an opportunity not available to the overwhelming majority of ordinary taxpayers.

Consider, for a moment, speaking fees paid to members of the congressional tax-writing committees in 1986, and campaign contributions to those same members in 1985 and 1986, the two years during which the Tax Reform Act of 1986 was being written.

Item. Rep. Dan Rostenkowski (D., Ill.), who as chairman of the House Ways and Means Committee was one of two lawmakers who approved hundreds of special-interest provisions in the tax act, received a $5,000 speaking fee from Joseph E. Seagram & Sons Inc., the U.S. subsidiary of Seagram Co. Ltd., a Canadian distilling company controlled by the billionaire Bronfman brothers, Charles R. and Edgar M.

Rep. Thomas J. Downey (D., N.Y.), a member of the Ways and

Means Committee, and Sens. Max Baucus (D., Mont.), Bob Dole (R., Kan.) and John H. Chafee (R., R.I.), members of the Senate Finance Committee and supporters of the tax overhaul, each received $2,000 in speaking fees from Seagram.

Sen. Bob Packwood (R., Ore.), who as chairman of the Senate Finance Committee shared responsibility with Rostenkowski for approving hundreds of special-interest tax breaks, received a $1,000 campaign contribution from Edgar Bronfman. So, too, did Sen. Daniel Patrick Moynihan (D., N.Y.), a Finance Committee member and ardent advocate of the tax act. Dole and Downey each received $2,000 in campaign contributions from Edgar Bronfman.

Rostenkowski received a $1,000 campaign contribution from Samuel Bronfman 2d and $2,000 in contributions from the Joseph E. Seagram & Sons Inc. Political Action Committee (PAC). Rep. Charles B. Rangel (D., N.Y.), a member of the Ways and Means Committee, and Sen. Charles E. Grassley (R., Iowa), a member of the Finance Committee, each received $1,000 campaign contributions from the Seagram PAC.

Seagram received its own private, custom-tailored tax break from Congress in the 1986 act that allows it to avoid payment of perhaps as much as $40 million in taxes.

Item. Packwood received a total of $3,000 in campaign contributions from Jay, Selig and Cathy Zises. The Zises brothers, Jay and Selig, founded and run Integrated Resources Inc., a New York financial services company whose origins were rooted in the sale of tax shelters to wealthy investors seeking to escape payment of taxes.

Moynihan received a total of $2,000 in campaign contributions from Jay and Selig Zises, Grassley received $1,000 from another brother, Seymour, and Downey received a total of $3,000 from Jay, Selig and Seymour Zises.

Integrated Resources received its own private, custom-tailored tax break from Congress in 1986 that allows it to avoid payment of an estimated $43 million in taxes.

Item. Grassley received a $500 campaign contribution—the Republican Party and other GOP candidates received an additional

$4,400—from John Ruan, a wealthy Des Moines businessman, and his family.

A Ruan leasing company received its own private, custom-tailored tax break from Congress in 1986 that allows it to avoid payment of $8.5 million in taxes.

□□□

Speaking fees and campaign contributions, of course, are only two of the ways that businesses and individuals seek to exert influence on the tax-writing process.

Sometimes they use a more indirect route to win access. They hire former congressional staff members who have drafted the tax laws or who have served as tax advisers to individual lawmakers.

As part of a long-standing Washington tradition, the staff members serve a sort of apprenticeship writing tax laws for congressional committees, then head off to join law firms, lobbying organizations and corporations that are constantly pursuing preferential treatment under the tax laws.

Better than anyone else, these former staff members know which buttons to push—which lawmakers to approach for favors, when to make their pitch and, perhaps, when to back off.

None of this is to suggest that only those lawmakers who serve on the House Ways and Means and the Senate Finance Committees have enough influence to secure tax favors.

Sometimes concessions are parceled out to other lawmakers by the tax writers to assure their votes on a measure whose outcome may be in doubt. Some Capitol Hill critics contend that that was why the Tax Reform Act of 1986 was stuffed with favors.

Sometimes others in leadership positions enjoy the same privileges as those who are members on the tax-writing committees. And when a special-interest captures the attention of both the tax writers and other congressional leaders, a tax break is almost certain to follow.

Regardless of how a special tax break comes about, Congress' multimillion-dollar speechmaking and honorarium industry is, in the opinion of some in Washington, a potentially corrupting influence on the legislative process.

In a speech delivered in early March, Assistant Attorney General

William F. Weld, head of the Justice Department's criminal division, zeroed in on the situation.

Recalling an incident that occurred not long after he arrived at the Justice Department in 1986 after five years as U.S. attorney in Massachusetts, where he had built a reputation for political-corruption prosecutions, Weld said:

"Just after I came to Washington, I read that a group of federal legislators had toured the facilities of a commercial enterprise over which their committee had jurisdiction, and for this had each received expenses plus a $2,000 'fee'—not for their campaign treasuries, but for their personal bank accounts.

"This sounded to me, fresh in from the hinterlands, like a prima facie criminal violation. But when I went to the law books, I discovered to my surprise that in fact only members of the executive branch and the independent agencies are prohibited from supplementing their salaries with fees and honoraria for job-related activities.

"Thus, actions that would be illegal if committed by someone in the executive branch were perfectly all right if committed by a member of Congress. Congress has exempted itself from coverage of this law [the 1978 Ethics in Government Act]."

Weld added that "congressmen who expect the public to believe that large monetary donations do not affect their votes or their views, or their decisions about how they spend their time, underestimate the intelligence of the American people."

Weld has since left his post. He and five other Justice Department officials resigned on March 29 over the ongoing legal problems of Attorney General Edwin Meese 3d—essentially an issue of conflict of interest.

□ □ □

As Weld said, under federal law legislators may accept honorariums from individuals and businesses, even from those who are directly affected by legislation the members later enact.

The 20 members of the Sentate Finance Committee and the 36 members of the House Ways and Means Committee are, like all those in Congress, required by law to report speaking fees on their annual financial disclosure statements. The fees cited here were drawn from those records.

The campaign contributions cited here were drawn from reports filed with the Federal Election Commission (FEC). Because FEC records are so voluminous, and the agency maintains only partial indexes, the list may be far from complete.

Here is what some of the records show:

Item. Sen. Chafee received a $2,000 speaking fee from American International Group Inc. (AIG), a global insurance holding company. Rep. Richard A. Gephardt (D., Mo.), a Ways and Means Committee member and supporter of the tax act, received a $2,000 speaking fee from CIGNA Corp., another global insurance holding company.

AIG and CIGNA received their own private, custom-tailored joint tax break from Congress in 1986 that allows them to avoid payment of an estimated $20 million in taxes.

Item. Sen. David Durenberger (R., Minn.) and Sen. Steven D. Symms (R., Idaho), both Senate Finance Committee members, each received $2,000 speaking fees from Massachusetts Mutual Life Insurance Co.

Reps. Brian J. Donnelly (D., Mass.), Richard T. Schulze (R., Pa.), Guy Vander Jagt (R., Mich.), Ronnie G. Flippo (D., Ala.), Byron L. Dorgan (D., N.D.) and Sam M. Gibbons (D., Fla.), all members of the Ways and Means Committee and all supporters of the tax act, each received $2,000 speaking fees from Massachusetts Mutual Life Insurance Co.

Rep. Rostenkowski; Rep. Marty Russo (D., Ill.), a House Ways and Means Committee member, and Sen. Grassley each received $1,000 in campaign contributions from the Massachusetts Mutual PAC.

Massachusetts Mutual Life Insurance Co. received a custom-tailored tax break from Congress in 1986 that allows it to avoid payment of an estimated $11 million in taxes.

Item. Symms and Chafee each received $2,000 speaking fees from the Aetna Life Insurance Co. Rostenkowski received $3,000 in campaign contributions from Aetna's PAC, Grassley received $1,000.

The Aetna Life Insurance Co. received a custom-tailored tax break from Congress in 1986 that allows it to avoid payment of an estimated $15 million in taxes.

Item. Sen. William V. Roth Jr. (R., Del.), a Senate Finance Committee member, Sen. Dole and Rep. Gephardt each received $2,000 speaking fees from Merrill Lynch & Co., the New York-based securities dealer and investment banking firm.

Merrill Lynch received its own private, custom-tailored tax break from Congress in 1986 that allows it to avoid payment of an estimated $4 million in taxes.

Item. Rep. Barbara B. Kennelly (D., Conn.), a Ways and Means Committee member, received a $2,000 speaking fee from New England Mutual Life Insurance Co. Rostenkowski received $4,000 in speaking fees from New England Mutual.

New England Mutual Life Insurance Co. received a custom-tailored tax break from Congress in 1986 that allows it to avoid payment of more than $1 million in taxes.

Item. Sen. Moynihan received a $2,000 speaking fee from Morgan Guaranty Trust Co., a New York bank.

Morgan Guaranty received its own private, custom-tailored tax break from Congress in 1986 that allows it to avoid payment of an estimated $32 million in taxes.

Item. Rostenkowski received a $2,000 speaking fee from MCA Inc., the Hollywood entertainment conglomerate. Sen. Packwood received $2,000 in campaign contributions from MCA's chief executive officer and the officer's wife. Rostenkowski received a $1,000 campaign contribution from the head of the Walt Disney Co., and Grassley received a $1,000 contribution from the Disney Co. PAC.

MCA and the Walt Disney Co. received their own private, custom-tailored tax break in 1986 that allows them to avoid payment of an estimated $65 million in taxes.

In a few instances, individuals or corporations that obtained private tax laws ultimately were unable, due to unrelated circumstances, to make use of them.

For example, Drexel Burnham Lambert Inc., the New York-based securities dealer and investment-banking firm, obtained a provision that would have saved the firm an estimated $20 million in taxes.

But the tax break was tied to Drexel Burnham's move into a new headquarters building in New York City. When the firm decided to cancel the move, it could not take advantage of the concession.

In all, $13,000 in speaking fees were paid by Drexel Burnham to members of tax-writing committees. Rostenkowski got $5,000, Gephardt and Rep. Downey each received $2,000. Sen. Bill Bradley (D., N.J.), a Finance Committee member and an architect of the tax act, received $2,000, as did Dole.

□ □ □

The total 1986 speaking fees of Rostenkowski, the most powerful of the Capitol Hill tax writers through his chairmanship of the Ways and Means Committee, where all tax legislation must originate, eclipsed those paid to every other member of Ways and Means or the Senate Finance Committee.

For the full year of 1986, Rostenkowski collected $177,500 for delivering speeches, more than twice his House salary of $75,100.

In addition to speaking fees from businesses that obtained private tax laws, that figure includes tens of thousands of dollars in honorariums from other special interests that had a direct stake in the outcome of the tax legislation.

For example, Rostenkowski received $10,000 from the Chicago Board of Trade, $2,000 from the Midwest Stock Exchange, $2,000 from the American Horse Council Inc., $5,000 from the Municipal Issuers Service Corp., $5,000 from the Western Association of Equipment Lessors.

Of the tax writers, Sen. Dole placed a distant second in speaking fees in 1986, picking up $118,500. Sen. Moynihan came in third with $108,975.

They could not keep it all, though. Members of Congress are restricted in the amount of speaking fees and other earned income they may retain over and above their congressional salaries. For 1986, senators could keep $30,040 of such income, an amount equal to 40 percent of their salaries. Representatives could keep $22,530, an amount equal to 30 percent of their salaries.

In Rostenkowski's case, he reported keeping $22,000 as personal income and donating the remaining $155,500 to charitable organizations, as required by law.

As the financial disclosure statements of Rostenkowski, Dole, Moynihan and other lawmakers indicate, the congressional speech-making business has evolved into a multimillion-dollar cottage industry that not only provides income for members of Congress but pays political dividends as well.

A lawmaker who contributes thousands of dollars to charities in his home state builds good will among voters, making it more difficult for opponents to mount a successful challenge.

What charitable organizations did Rostenkowski contribute his $155,500 to?

He isn't talking.

"He doesn't release that," said an aide.

Is there some reason to keep the information secret?

"Between us chickens," said the aide, who asked to remain anonymous, "his feeling is that, you know, that releasing it will do nothing but yield additional solicitations from people asking him for money. I mean, it's just a little bit provocative in that regard."

Does that mean, perhaps, the contributions do not go to Illinois charities?

"A lot of it goes to Chicago and Illinois," said the aide, adding, "I haven't seen a list recently. But I would guess that probably, you know, it breaks more or less half and half, maybe a bit more toward Illinois."

Some lawmakers voluntarily disclose which charities they contribute to, although the law does not require it.

Similarly, while some lawmakers use the income from speeches to augment their congressional salaries to cover living expenses, and others to accumulate wealth, some of the most ardent advocates of preferential tax provisions have no need to do so.

Among the latter group is Sen. John Heinz (R., Pa.). One of the Senate's wealthiest members—his fortune grew out of family holdings in the H.J. Heinz Co.—Heinz championed some of the most costly tax breaks written into the 1986 act. A single concession was worth upward of $400 million to the country's largest steel companies.

The major steel producers obviously could appeal directly to Heinz because, even in the declining steel economy of Pennsylvania, the industry has retained its influence. The Pittsburgh lawmaker was a member of the Senate Finance Committee that helped write the tax law.

While the steel industry enjoyed direct access to Heinz's office, not all industries have such a ready friend. Instead, many businesses hire lawyers with tax expertise gained during years of working for Congress on tax legislation.

Keith D. Martin is a lawyer with the Washington office of the New York law firm, Chadbourne & Parke. Before entering private practice, Martin was legislative counsel to Daniel Patrick Moynihan on the Senate Finance Committee.

Chadbourne & Parke, with Martin, represented Catalyst Energy Development Corp.; ENESCO—the Energy Systems Company Inc.; Gilberton Power Co.; Independent Power Systems International Inc.; Applied Energy Services Inc.; PLM Power Co., and Oxbow Geothermal Corp. in 1986.

A tax break in the Tax Reform Act allows the seven companies to avoid payment of more than a quarter-billion dollars in taxes.

Robert E. Lighthizer is a lawyer in the Washington office of the New York law firm, Skadden, Arps, Slate, Meagher & Flom. From 1978 to 1981, Lighthizer was chief minority counsel for the Senate Finance Committee, and from 1981 to 1983 he was the committee's chief counsel and staff director.

In 1986, Skadden Arps, with Lighthizer, represented General Development Corp., a developer of planned Florida communities.

A tax break inserted in the Tax Reform Act allows General Development to avoid payment of an estimated $11 million in taxes.

Some companies that retained former Capitol Hill aides also paid honorariums or made campaign contributions.

Such was the case with Bear Stearns Cos. Inc., Integrated Resources Inc. and Joseph Seagram & Sons Inc., which received combined tax breaks totaling nearly $100 million.

Officials of the three companies contributed to the election campaigns of certain members of the tax-writing committees. Seagram also paid speaking fees to committee members.

And all three employed John J. Salmon, a lawyer in the Washington office of the New York law firm, Dewey, Ballantine, Bushby, Palmer & Wood, to look after their interests. Before entering private practice, Salmon was a legislative aide to Rostenkowski and chief counsel of Ways and Means.

It is an old Capitol Hill tradition that those who write the tax laws one year go to work the next year for those seeking to tailor the tax laws to their own desires. What is new is that the pace of the practice has accelerated since 1981, when Congress took to rewriting the massive Internal Revenue Code every year or two.

Lawmakers often cite the need for simplification as the reason for tax-code revisions. That was especially true when President Reagan began marshaling support for the tax-overhaul movement that led to the 1986 Tax Reform Act. Declaring the system was "too complicated," the President said that Americans "often resent complexity" because "they sense it is unfair—that complexity is the means by which some benefit while others do not."

When the President and Congress' self-styled reformers had finished, they hailed the result.

"A vastly simplified tax structure will be created for both individuals and corporations," Sen. Edward M. Kennedy (D., Mass.) proclaimed. "Americans may not be able to file tax returns on a form that fits on a postcard, but much of the needless complexity of the current law has been removed," Sen. Chafee said.

And Sen. Lloyd Bentsen (D., Texas), then a member of the Senate Finance Committee and now its chairman, trumpeted: "Is this bill simplification? Yes, major simplification. . . . Most taxpayers will not have to pay a fortune to an accountant or a tax lawyer to make out the return."

THE OUTCOME WAS DIFFERENT

Instead of simplifying the code, the reformers in 1986 actually rendered it the most complex ever, fueling what has become, in the 1980s, America's most explosive growth industry—the tax industry. As a result, more lawyers, accountants and tax specialists than ever are needed to interpret the law.

Who better to do that for businesses than the people responsible for writing the code in the first place?

In the 18 months since passage of the Tax Reform Act of 1986, one after another of those who helped write or fashion it have left Capitol Hill to join major law firms or corporations.

Among them was David H. Brockway, chief of staff of the Joint Committee on Taxation during the drafting of the tax act. Brockway, whose committee provided technical advice to legislators, knew more about the bill's contents than the elected members of Congress who are charged with the responsibility of writing the tax laws.

Repeatedly during congressional meetings, leaders of the tax-reform drive, Sen. Packwood and Rep. Gephardt among them, deferred to Brockway when questions were raised about the legislation.

In January 1988, Brockway joined Dewey, Ballantine, Bushby, Palmer & Wood, one of many law firms that seek to mold tax laws to fit the needs of their clients.

At the time the Tax Reform Act of 1986 was being written, according to lobbying reports filed with Congress, Dewey Ballantine's clients included Chrysler Corp., which received a $78 million tax break; Beneficial Corp., which received a $67 million tax break; Tobacco Row Associates, which received an $8 million tax break; Integrated Resources, which received a $43 million tax break; Bear Stearns, which received an $8 million tax break; and Joseph Seagram & Sons Inc., which received about a $40 million tax break.

Other Capitol Hill staff members went before, and after, Brockway.

William J. Wilkins was the minority chief of staff for the Senate Finance Committee when the 1986 act was written—Moynihan hailed him as "an exemplar of public service at every stage, providing insightful, direct and accurate analysis always."

Wilkins subsequently became the committee's staff director. In March, he announced his resignation to join Wilmer, Cutler & Pickering, a Washington law firm.

Maxine C. Champion, a member of the tax staff of the Ways and Means Committee for four years, resigned in January to become vice president for government relations for the LTV Corp. in its Washington office. LTV received a tax concession in the 1986 act.

Joseph K. Dowley, chief counsel of the House Ways and Means Committee, resigned in April 1987 to join Dewey Ballantine. Kenneth Kies, minority tax counsel for the Ways and Means Committee, resigned in January 1987 to join the Washington office of Baker & Hostetler, a Cleveland law firm.

THE ROLE OF STAFF MEMBERS

How important are the staff members on the tax-writing committees?

Not only do they draft the legislation, they also sometimes determine which individuals and businesses seeking preferential treatment will be rewarded.

During the legislative process leading to passage of the 1986 tax act, Packwood, who at the time was head of the Senate Finance Committee, said he was inundated with "roughly 1,000 requests from 94 senators" for transition rules—exemptions from the tax law. He explained what happened next:

"I did not sit down and go through all 1,000-plus requests one by one. . . . What we did is say to the staff, 'Here are the rules by which transitions are to be selected. Try to avoid violating those rules.' By and large, they were successful."

Sometimes, other lawmakers in critical leadership positions dictated the rules.

Thomas P. "Tip" O'Neill, the Massachusetts Democrat who retired last year as speaker of the House of Representatives, and certain unknown members of the tax-writing committees, were responsible for one of the more inequitable tax breaks in the 1986 act.

As a result of their combined influence, preferential treatment was accorded to 15 large life insurance companies, and denied to 1,800 other life insurance companies.

The tax break grew out of the insurance companies' investments in so-called market discount bonds, on which they were to pay the then-prevailing capital gains tax rate of 28 percent. When the tax writers proposed increasing the rate for corporations to 34 percent, the insurers appealed to Congress to guarantee them the old capital gains rate.

As the 1986 bill headed for passage, all life insurance companies selling market discount bonds were to be exempted from the increase in the tax rate, a move that was expected to result in a revenue loss of $120 million.

But then revenue estimates prepared by the staffs of the tax-writing committees indicated the cost of providing relief to all insurers would be much higher than originally thought.

When one proposal was made to scale back the relief for all companies, O'Neill objected, insisting that the John Hancock Co., in his native Boston, be fully exempted from the higher capital gains rate.

This forced the tax writers to pick and choose among insurers, rather than give a blanket exemption. In the end, they distributed the tax break to only 15 large firms.

A spokesman for one life insurance company left out by the bill explained: "I think a lot of congressmen were genuinely embarrassed when they saw the bill come out on the life insurance companies. The idea was never to pick out 15 people out of an industry of 1,800. But that's what the staff did. . . ."

What followed was inevitable. The rest of the industry mounted a lobbying campaign that produced a new provision, one extending the benefit to all life insurance companies. It is awaiting congressional action.

□ □ □

For the business or individual taxpayer in search of special treatment, persistence sometimes is as important as access. For the lawmaker seeking to accommodate that business or individual, imagination is sometimes as important as persistence.

Some special-interest tax breaks never make it into the printed bill, and others that do are deleted before final passage, all for a variety of reasons.

In some cases, the lawmakers pushing the preferential provisions lack the necessary clout in the all-important tax-writing committees. In other cases, opposition to a particular provision is too overwhelming.

DEVISING STRATEGIES

Whatever the reason, once colleagues refuse to incorporate a break into a tax bill, the lawmaker devises a new strategy.

Most often, he arranges to have the controversial provision inserted in another bill, often with a title that implies it is unrelated to the income tax, in the hope that it will escape the attention of opponents.

There was, for example, the Recreational Boating and Safety Act of 1980 that was to promote boating safety. But it also contained a provision that granted the investment tax credit to forest-product companies and landowners for planting trees.

There was the Black Lung Benefits Revenue Act of 1981. It was intended to bail out the financially strapped disability trust fund that paid benefits to about 200,000 disabled coal miners and their survivors.

But it also contained a provision that increased the unsubstantiated business-expense deduction from $3,000 to about $20,000 for members of Congress. This meant lawmakers could spend that sum for most any purpose and write it off on tax returns.

(When the details of the tax gimmick emerged after its passage, the public uproar was so great that lawmakers tripped over one another in a stampede to denounce the offending provision and the news media for focusing attention on it, although not necessarily in that order. It was subsequently repealed.)

And there was the Omnibus Budget Reconciliation Act of 1986. It was intended to pare the deficit through a combination of spending cuts and the sale of government assets.

But it also contained a provision that preserved the investment tax credit for an Iowa truck-leasing company, although the Tax Reform Act passed several weeks earlier had canceled that credit for most all other truck-leasing companies and businesses.

The story behind that provision attests to the persistence of both the taxpayer and the lawmakers who set out to win the tax break for him.

THE RUAN COMPANIES

From an office in Des Moines' 36-story Ruan Tower, the tallest building in Iowa, John Ruan directs a network of trucking, leasing, real estate, banking and insurance companies.

Not all has gone well in his mini-empire in recent years. Ruan's Carriers Insurance Co., which once provided liability coverage to the long-haul trucking industry, was ruled insolvent in 1985 by the Iowa Department of Insurance.

Policyholders and creditors filed claims amounting to $117 million. In a civil lawsuit, state insurance authorities accused Ruan and three associates on Carriers' board of "gross negligence" and "self-dealing."

The action, which was still pending in Iowa District Court, seeks to make Ruan and his associates in Carriers liable for $63 million in damages to policyholders and creditors.

The Iowa insurance commissioner contended that Carriers filed reports with state authorities indicating that the company was in sound financial condition, while, in fact, it was insolvent. Ruan denied the allegations in court papers.

During the same period that Ruan's Carriers Insurance Co. was collapsing, his truck-leasing company was embarking on an ambitious expansion plan.

Ruan had been developing a new generation of long-haul vehicles, called mega-trucks, that would travel up to a million miles with a minimum of maintenance. Orders for a new fleet were placed in 1985, but full delivery was not expected for two years.

Like hundreds of thousands of other corporate and individual taxpayers who made similar capital investments that year and early in 1986, Ruan based his decision on the existing income tax law, which allowed a 10 percent investment tax credit for the purchase of equipment.

When Congress rewrote the tax code in 1986, it not only repealed the investment tax credit, it did so retroactively to Jan. 1, 1986.

As a result, all those businesses and individuals who had ordered equipment based on one law, and did not receive it in a specified period, suddenly were confronted with an unexpected 10 percent increase in the cost of doing business.

For the majority, there was nothing they could do except absorb the costs.

But it was not the case for Ruan, who secured an exemption from the tax law, allowing his company to claim the investment tax credit denied to others.

As might be expected, other trucking companies were dismayed that Congress extended a tax break to Ruan, thereby providing the Iowa company with an economic advantage over its competitors.

Larry Miller, president of Ruan Transportation Systems Inc., defended the exemption.

"They [other trucking companies] had the same right to do exactly what we did, and apparently no one did to my knowledge. . . . It enabled us to get what we had coming to us when we ordered the trucks."

As pieced together from congressional documents and interviews with those involved, here is what happened:

Because Congress intended to repeal the credit retroactively to Jan.

1, 1986, anyone who had ordered trucks or equipment but had not taken delivery by a fixed date would be affected.

Enter Charles Grassley of Iowa, a Republican member of the Senate Finance Committee. Grassley asked those drafting the credit repeal to write in an exception for Ruan.

When the Senate tax-reform bill finally was printed in May 1986, the Ruan provision was missing. That was when Grassley enlisted the aid of Bob Dole, then Senate Majority leader. Helping get a tax break for an Iowa trucking company would be a plus for Dole, who was at the time a budding GOP presidential candidate looking for a good showing in the nation's first referendum for White House aspirants.

Then, too, the Ruan family was a major supporter of Republicans, having contributed more than $23,000 to various GOP candidates and committees in 1983 and 1984.

With Dole's backing, Grassley introduced an amendment—the Ruan exemption from the tax law—saying that the provision had been "inadvertently left out" of the bill. It was incorporated into the measure that passed the full Senate in June 1986.

A conference committee then was appointed to blend together the two versions of tax revision enacted separately by the House and Senate, each with its own array of special interest deals. When the bill emerged from the conference, the Ruan tax exemption once again was missing.

Dole and Grassley next inserted the errant Ruan clause into a resolution to correct bookkeeping mistakes—misspelled names, incorrect dates and misidentified sections—in the tax bill itself. Called an enrolling resolution, it was soon laced with a new round of tax favors.

Congress balked, refusing to pass the resolution.

Undaunted, Dole and Grassley next slipped the Ruan provision into an unrelated piece of legislation—the budget reconciliation bill, which Congress enacted in September 1986.

While the Dole-Grassley action stirred controversy in Iowa, where the Ruan provision was labeled "The Tax Break That Would Not Die" by local newspapers, it attracted little attention outside the state.

And so found buried in a bill that directed the sale of Conrail, reduced government payments for cataract surgery and increased the federal debt limit was this paragraph:

The amendments made by section 201 shall not apply to trucks, tractor units, and trailers which a privately held truck leasing company headquartered in Des Moines, Iowa, contracted to purchase in September 1985 . . .

That clause allows Ruan's company to escape payment of $8.5 million in taxes.

INTEGRATED RESOURCES

The brothers, Selig A. and Jay H. Zises, and a childhood friend, Arthur H. Goldberg, founded Integrated Resources Inc. in 1968 to sell tax shelters to wealthy investors looking for a way to reduce or eliminate their federal tax payments. (Goldberg is not the former U.S. Supreme Court justice.)

The company marketed a variety of shelters in real estate, equipment leasing, oil and gas ventures and deferred annuities, most structured in such a way as to generate paper losses that could be used to offset real taxable income.

As the company explained in its 1977 annual report:

"[Integrated's] privately offered real estate and equipment investment programs are attractive primarily to investors in high income brackets who are able to take advantage of current provisions of the U.S. Internal Revenue Code by utilizing losses and credits generated by such investments to offset income and tax liabilities arising from other sources."

In a typical real estate or equipment leasing transaction, Integrated would arrange for a corporation to sell its headquarters building or some other asset, such as its machinery or equipment, to private investors, who, in turn, would lease the building or equipment back to the corporation.

The deals offered a little something for everyone. Investors received generous tax writeoffs. The corporation received a cash infusion. Integrated received fees for arranging the sale and leaseback.

In some cases, the Zises brothers and other Integrated executives also received interests in the partnerships and tax writeoffs.

Integrated received a big boost from President Reagan's 1981 tax-cut plan, which liberalized depreciation writeoffs and made tax shelters, especially in real estate and equipment leasing, even more attractive.

The company's revenues soared from $120.9 million that year to

$322.5 million in 1983, prompting the Wall Street Journal to comment on the company's "dazzling profits" achieved through the sale of "tax shelter investments."

"Integrated Resources Inc. has become extremely successful," the newspaper reported, "by helping rich people—mainly doctors, dentists, corporate executives and small businessmen—avoid taxes."

Although Integrated's revenue reached $830.2 million in 1986, and it was publicly owned, the company remained very much a family affair of the Ziseses and Goldbergs.

In 1986, Jay Zises, chairman of the executive committee, received $1,036,882 in salary, fees, bonuses and other compensation. Selig Zises, chairman of the board and chief executive officer, received $1,008,595. Arthur Goldberg, president and chief operating officer, received $1,013 396.

Nancy Frankel, a first vice president who married Jay Zises in June 1986, received $404,000. Jeffrey Krauss, senior vice president of three of the company's life insurance subsidiaries, and a brother-in-law of Arthur Goldberg, received $270,926 that year.

Seymour Zises, a marketing executive and insurance agent for the company and a brother of Jay and Selig, received $250,095. Bernard Zises, who located properties for the firm's investment program and was the father of the three brothers, received $138,000.

Overall, the Zises and Goldberg family members collected $4.1 million in salaries, bonuses and other compensation. That was in addition to a variety of company-paid benefits.

In addition to profiting from the general boom in tax shelters through the 1970s and early 1980s, Integrated also benefited as a corporation from certain provisions in the tax code.

One of these was the ability to use an accounting method originally designed for family farmers and small businesses rather than enterprises the size of Integrated.

When the House approved its version of the tax-reform bill in December 1985, it took away the option of financial services companies like Integrated to use the favorable cash method of accounting.

In its 1986 annual report to the U.S. Securities and Exchange Commission (SEC), Integrated listed the adverse effects the change could have:

"This provision, if enacted in its current form, would require the company to switch to the accrual basis method of accounting for tax purposes, which would result in the acceleration of certain items of income and deduction. On balance, the company expects that such acceleration of income and deductions will, in the aggregate, adversely affect the Company's cash flow since certain tax obligations of the Company . . . would be currently payable."

When a similar provision appeared in the Senate Finance Committee's bill in 1986, Integrated sought its own private tax law to cushion it from the full force of the change.

The Tax Reform Act, finally approved by Congress in September 1986, contained this obscure section:

The amendments made by this section shall not apply to contracts for the acquisition or transfer of real property, and contracts for services related to the acquisition or development of real property, but only if such contracts were entered into before September 25, 1985, and the sole element of the contract which has not been performed as of September 25, 1985, is payment for such property or services.

While it makes no mention of Integrated, that paragraph will save the company an estimated $43 million in taxes—or three times the amount of taxes it paid in 1986. A study by Tax Analysts, a Washington organization that specializes in tax analyses, showed that Integrated paid taxes that year at a rate below 13 percent—about the same rate levied on individuals and families with incomes of $25,000 a year.

Like so many other special-interest clauses, the one applying to Integrated is worded in such a way that other companies might be able to take advantage of it as well. But it was clearly Integrated that sought the provision.

The company referred to its exemption in the fine print of a stock registration statement filed with the SEC in March 1987. After pointing out that the Tax Reform Act would require companies like Integrated to change the way they accounted for certain income and deductions, Integrated said:

"However, because of special relief provisions included in the 1986 act, the company expects that such acceleration of income and deductions will not adversely affect the company's cash flow."

It says much about how tax law is made that a company that

profited from helping others to avoid taxes received a tax break from lawmakers who said they were changing the law to prevent people from avoiding taxes.

THE SEAGRAM PARAGRAPH

Notwithstanding the amendments made by subtitle B of title III, gain with respect to installment payments received pursuant to notes issued in accordance with a note agreement dated as of August 29, 1980, where . . . such note agreement was executed pursuant to an agreement of purchase and sale dated April 25, 1980, more than one-half of the installment payments of the aggregate principal of such notes have been received by August 29, 1986, and the last installment payment of the principal of such notes is due August 29, 1989, shall be taxed at a rate of 28 percent.

That paragraph describes Joseph E. Seagram & Sons, Inc., the U.S. subsidiary of Seagram Co. Ltd., a Canadian company that is the world's largest producer of wine and distilled spirits. The billionaire Bronfman brothers own or control 33 percent of the parent company's stock.

Under Seagram's private tax law, the company is permitted to pay capital gains taxes on one transaction at the old corporate rate of 28 percent, rather than the new 34 percent tax rate levied on other companies by the 1986 Tax Reform Act.

While both congressional tax writers and Seagram officials declined to place a value on the break, an Inquirer analysis suggests it could range as high as $40 million.

The lower tax rate will be applied to income that Seagram is still receiving from the sale of an oil and gas subsidiary to the Sun Co. for $2.3 billion in 1981.

According to a study by Tax Analysts, Seagram—which also owns 23 percent of the Du Pont Co.—paid taxes on its worldwide income at a rate of 7 percent in 1986.

Internal Revenue Service statistics show that was below the rate paid by people who earned $15,000 a year.

When Congress prepared to vote on the 1986 act, the tax reformers glossed over the exemptions they engineered for companies like Seagram, and concentrated instead on glowing generalities about the overall benefits of their work.

"This tax-reform bill, and the process by which it is being enacted, represents a triumph of the individual, average American over the larger special interests," said Max Baucus, Democratic senator from Montana.

"The biggest beneficiaries of this bill are ordinary taxpayers who have no access to high-priced lawyers and lobbyists," said John Chafee, GOP senator from Rhode Island.

"We can be proud of this legislation and proud that we voted in favor of it. It is a tax bill that we can honestly describe to the American people as tax reform," said the Senate's Dole, a Kansas Republican.

Baucus, Chafee and Dole were all members of the Senate Finance Committee, all supporters of the tax act—and all received honorariums from Seagram.

GREENBRIER LEASING

Not everyone who received preferential tax treatment contributes to the campaigns of the tax writers or hires them to speak. On occasion, just being a constituent is sufficient to bring about the same result.

Consider the case of Greenbrier Leasing Co. in Lake Oswego, Ore., a Portland suburb.

Greenbrier leases rail cars and highway trailers. All told, the company owns and manages about 10,000 pieces of transportation equipment, according to the company president, William A. Furman.

Greenbrier embarked on a major expansion in 1985 to capture more of the market in specialized rail cars to transport cargo from West Coast ports to the East.

By early 1986, Greenbrier had placed orders for 1,200 new flat cars. Then, along came the tax-reform bill with its plan to scale back accelerated depreciation and repeal the investment tax credit, retroactive to Jan. 1, 1986. Furman, in an interview, explained the company's reaction:

"When the tax drafting came along, lo and behold we read it, and we saw that the date of the investment tax credit and several other benefits were changed, and they would apply to orders of equipment made only before Jan. 1, 1986. Obviously, we were concerned that we might get caught with our pants down."

Greenbrier's problem was that it would not take delivery on 1,000 of the cars on order until after the tax incentives had been repealed or cut back.

"We would be caught with an order we couldn't perform on," explained Furman, "because we had factored in the benefits of the tax laws as we understood them in 1985."

But unlike other companies in the same bind, Greenbrier had a solution unavailable to others. As an Oregon company, it had access to Bob Packwood, GOP senator from Oregon and chairman of the Senate Finance Committee.

"We just wrote a letter to the senator and explained it to him, and had a member of his staff contact us," Furman said. "We made a case to our senator that it wasn't fair, that we would lose the order because the economics were all changed. So we were successful in getting some protection.

"We were very fortunate that Sen. Packwood was willing to consider the particular problems of our company.

"I'll bet there are some transition rules that are not good ones. But, boy, I'll tell you this one—we're sure pleased that we got it."

DISGUISING THOSE WHO GET TAX BREAKS

WEDNESDAY, APRIL 13, 1988

BY DONALD L. BARLETT AND JAMES B. STEELE

Herewith a civics quiz.

As a result of efforts by Congress' tax reformers, the Internal Revenue Code contains a provision that will:

(A) Allow members of a socially prominent Chicago-area family, who have made the Forbes magazine list of the 400 richest Americans, to take tax writeoffs denied to most taxpayers.

(B) Permit a millionaire Beverly Hills stockbroker, who boasts the world's largest private collection of Rodin sculptures, to escape payment of taxes that others must pay.

(C) Benefit a New York lawyer, who has specialized in helping his clients avoid taxes, by allowing him to buy the losses of a defunct company and use them to reduce the taxes owed by a profitable company.

(D) Raise the taxes of several million low- and middle-income individuals and family members who are dealing with chronic diseases or unexpected and costly illnesses.

(E) All of the above.

If you answered (E), score yourself 100.

Each of those provisions was wrapped into the Tax Reform Act of 1986 that was so widely praised as a model of fairness by the lawmakers and others who engineered it.

You wouldn't know who had benefited, though, from reading the law. In virtually every instance, the provisions were written in such a way as to disguise the identity of those who gained from the tax breaks.

Now, Washington's tax writers are at it again. They have begun the preliminary, behind-the-scenes maneuvering that is expected to lead to a tax increase—and quite possibly a hefty one—next year for middle-income Americans.

And there are new custom-tailored tax provisions, to be inserted in pending legislation, excusing select individuals and businesses from payment of taxes.

Among those already written is one that, for tax purposes. calls an Erwin, Tenn., plant that fabricates nuclear-submarine fuel a nuclear power plant, thus qualifying it for a $5 million tax break.

Beneficiaries of the nuclear-fuel provision include the president and the chief financial officer of Coca-Cola Co.; the chairman of the board of the Robinson-Humphrey Co. Inc., an Atlanta-based brokerage firm; a tax-law specialist and member of the Atlanta law firm of Hansell & Post; and a New York venture capital specialist.

As in 1986, the new provisions are being written in such a way that they mask the identity of the real beneficiaries. Like the following:

Paragraph (4) of section 251(d) of the Tax Reform Act of 1986 . . . is amended by striking out 'and' at the end of sub-paragraph (RR), by striking out the period at the end of sub-paragraph (SS) and by adding at the end thereof the following . . .

(UU) A 173 room hotel for which a UDAG grant was preliminarily approved on February 2, 1986, and the rehabilitation of which was completed by April 16, 1987 . . .

That describes the Claridge Hotel at 1244 N. Dearborn St. in Chicago and, according to estimates by congressional tax writers, will save its investors $2 million in taxes.

The old hotel, once known as the Tuscany, was renovated by Centrum Properties Inc., a firm run by Arthur Slaven and Larry Ashkin, two Chicago real estate developers.

Other special-interest provisions waiting to be incorporated in pending legislation would cost taxpayers much more. One would allow Wells Fargo Bank in San Francisco, and other banks, to avoid payment of an estimated $80 million in taxes. Wells Fargo alone, by the bank's own estimate, would save $20 million.

To understand what is going on behind the scenes today on Capitol Hill, it is worth returning to 1986 and examining how lawmakers obscured the identities of those they rewarded with tax favors.

That was the year of the greatest tax giveaway in the 75-year history of the federal income tax. The official estimate: $10.6 billion. The real cost: $20 billion to $30 billion.

As Congress prepared to pass the Tax Reform Act, the Senate Finance Committee released a list of about 650 projects and businesses that would be exempted from specific provisions of the law.

An Inquirer investigation has established that the committee omitted certain names from the list. Of the names that were reported, in many instances the committee failed to disclose the real beneficiaries. In still other instances, it misidentified them.

□ □ □

In the latter category was the case of the New York lawyer who won a tax concession—referred to by lawmakers as a transition rule—for a defunct company.

In one of the hundreds upon hundreds of such paragraphs that run through the Internal Revenue Code, lawmakers wrote the following provision exempting an unnamed company from a specific section of the law:

A taxpayer is described in this clause if the taxpayer filed a title 11 case on December 8, 1981, filed a plan of reorganization on February 5, 1986, filed an amended plan on March 14, 1986, and received court approval for the amended plan and disclosure statement on April 16, 1986.

THE WRONG NAME

The Senate Finance Committee, headed in 1986 by Sen. Bob Packwood (R., Ore.), identified the recipient of that special-interest provision as the Ireton Coal Corp.

A search of major coal-producing states, as well as interviews with coal industry executives and union officials across the country, failed to turn up any company by that name.

There was, however, an Ironton Coke Corp. in Ironton, Ohio. And it happened to satisfy the four abstruse requirements spelled out in the new law.

Ironton Coke Corp. filed for reorganization under Chapter 11 of the Bankruptcy Act in U.S. Bankruptcy Court in Detroit on Dec. 8, 1981. It filed a reorganization plan on Feb. 5, 1986, an amended plan on March 14 of that year, and it received court approval of the amended plan on April 16, 1986.

As a result of the 1986 tax provision, Ironton Coke Corp. will enjoy a $20 million tax break.

But Ironton Coke ceased operations in 1981. It has no employees.

It has no physical assets. Indeed, the plant, which dates back to the turn of the century, is being dismantled.

So why would Congress give a $20 million tax break to a company that no longer exists?

Actually, in one of those quirky arrangements so peculiar to federal tax law—or, more accurately, to the avoidance of taxes—the real beneficiary is someone else.

He is Stanley I. Deutsch, a 44-year-old New York lawyer with offices on Park Avenue, who is described by one acquaintance as a "venture capitalist" rather than a practicing attorney.

How did a New York lawyer secure a tax concession in the name of an Ohio company that had been in bankruptcy court in Michigan for five years?

Deutsch said he does not know exactly how he got it.

"You'll have to understand," he said, "that the mechanical process of how the transition rule got in [the law] is unknown to me."

One of Deutsch's business associates, Menelaos D. Hassialis, a professor emeritus of mining at Columbia University, was more forthcoming.

RESEARCHING THE ISSUE

Hassialis said that Deutsch conferred with the staffs of congressional tax-writing committees and "spent a lot of his own time researching the question" of a transition rule (an exception to the law intended to ease the way from old law to new) for Ironton Coke. "In fact," he said, "it ended up inadvertently that [Deutsch] helped them structure part of the tax law."

However inadvertent it may have been—Congress never permits ordinary taxpayers to write their very own personal sections of the Internal Revenue Code—Deutsch also got some help from an accounting firm, Seidman & Seidman, in Chicago.

In court documents obtained by The Inquirer, Kenneth J. Malek, a Seidman & Seidman tax partner at the time, recounted conferences with staff members of the congressional committees that were writing the 1986 law.

"Our assistance to Mr. Deutsch," said Malek, "was an important element in his obtaining a special transitional rule."

While Deutsch and others were wresting a multimillion-dollar tax break from a dead business, former employees of that business were still waiting to collect the benefits they were owed. Some may never collect.

"I had been there 21 years, over 21," said Gary L. Blankenship, a former maintenance supervisor at the Ironton plant who now lives in Riverdale, N.D., and works at a coal gasification plant owned by the federal government.

"They owed me $13,351 in severance and vacation pay," Blankenship said, "and they paid me $1,191."

Other Ironton workers fared worse.

Ironton owed more than $1 million to the Pension Benefit Guaranty Corp. (PBGC), a quasi-government entity created to assure that workers receive at least part of their pension benefits in the event a company fails.

The company also owed another $1 million to workers like Blankenship whose benefits were not fully protected by the PBGC.

The decline of Ironton, which had been in operation since the early part of this century, began in the 1970s. It was known then as the Semet-Solvay Division of Allied Chemical Corp.

In 1977, Allied sold the plant to McLouth Steel Corp. in Detroit. McLouth, in turn, formed a new subsidiary, the Ironton Coke Corp.

McLouth already was in a precarious financial condition. The year before, the company had eked out an $11 million profit on record sales of $512 million.

Because McLouth was dependent on others for coke, and prices had nearly tripled since 1970, company executives had concluded that they could ease the financial strain if they acquired their own coke plant. The timing proved fatal.

McLouth's largest customer was the auto industry and its related suppliers. But production of cars and trucks in the United States began a downward spiral in 1979. By 1982, domestic output was little more than half its record 1978 level of 12.9 million vehicles.

Fewer cars obviously meant a reduced demand for steel. To aggravate matters, auto manufacturers were using less steel in cars that they were building. And McLouth could buy coke, which is used to make steel, cheaper on the open market than at its Ironton plant.

It was against this background that McLouth and Ironton filed for reorganization under the bankruptcy laws in 1981.

In Ironton's case, a series of failed rescue efforts followed, including a proposal by a local company that called for federal loans and price guarantees so that the plant could be converted to a synthetic fuel facility.

Robert S. Hertzberg, a Detroit lawyer who had been appointed trustee in the bankruptcy proceedings, began selling off Ironton's assets and collecting money that the company was owed.

By the time Hertzberg had sold Ironton's physical holdings, the company still possessed a piece of paper that represented a major asset, at least in the eyes of those who understand the labyrinthine ways of the federal tax system.

That was when Stanley Deutsch appeared on the scene.

Ironton Coke had run up $60 million in losses during its last years of operation. For $250, Deutsch secured a 45 percent interest in those losses. Why $250?

"Well, that's all you do," said Hertzberg. "You do just enough to meet the requirements of the Internal Revenue Code."

Under the right set of circumstances, the losses could be used to offset income taxes that otherwise profitable companies would be obliged to pay.

In other words, if a new Ironton Coke acquired the National Widget Co., which was making money and paying millions of dollars in taxes, the losses from the old coke plant would reduce the Widget Co.'s tax bills into the 1990s.

The arrangement has no parallel for individual taxpayers, but it would be roughly comparable to a person who, with an abundance of itemized deductions, reduced his own tax bill, then gave leftover deductions to a neighbor to allow that person to reduce his tax bill.

That, in part, explains why Congress moved to end such practices several years ago. If carried to their logical conclusion, corporations would no longer have to pay any income tax, and individuals would be obliged to make up the lost revenue.

To prevent profitable companies from acquiring failed enterprises just to use their losses, Congress enacted a series of stringent guidelines.

The guidelines applied to virtually every company except Ironton Coke Corp., which was exempted from them in the 1986 tax act.

As Hertzberg, the Ironton trustee, explained Deutsch's plan in papers filed in the bankruptcy proceedings:

"It is Ironton's intention to structure its investments so that, to the extent permitted by law, the earnings of the investment would be sheltered by Ironton's net operating loss carryovers."

Another lawyer took note of Deutsch's "creative tax proposal" during a bankruptcy court hearing and asked where he "learned all of this information about taxes." Deutsch replied:

"Virtually all of the principals of the companies that I [have worked with in the past]. . .. were non-resident aliens of the United States and it was my responsibility on their behalf to structure the business activities in such a way that would enhance the tax attributes of every one of those transactions. . . ."

During the hearing, Deutsch did not identify the "non-resident aliens" for whom he arranged favorable tax transactions. Documents filed in the bankruptcy case also make no mention of the firms for which he worked.

Rather, the documents say only that he ran an unidentified international shipping company, managed an unnamed business that provided computer systems to the shipping and offshore oil industry and managed investments in minerals for unnamed clients.

In the first of a series of interviews and an exchange of correspondence with an Inquirer reporter, Deutsch said there was nothing secretive about his past business relationships.

"My engagements in the [companies]," he said, "were also legal engagements. That means I ran the [companies]. I was also general counsel . . . so that I got involved in running these companies because I originally served as either business or legal adviser for the principals in those companies.

"There is no secret as to which those companies were. It's just that the names associated with the companies have a right to confidentiality. . . . They are not secret. And I have no need to hold them secret. If you want more about my background, I would be prepared to give you more information. I just don't see it's very relevant."

Nonetheless, Deutsch subsequently declined to name the companies. Asked why the same information had been excluded from Ironton bankruptcy records, he said:

"[Disclosure statements] generally don't go into a long rigamarole on resumes. It's really quite unusual. I think they were looking more for what my background was in terms of ethics and honorability, because it was important here that somebody like that be presented to the creditors committee."

Deutsch was equally vague about how the tax break ended up in the revenue code.

"Are you really asking me," he said, "do I have any unknown political influence or contacts? Let me assure you, none. Zero."

After explaining that his only contact with a congressional tax committee "was by written correspondence," Deutsch had this exchange with a reporter:

Reporter—What committees do you mean?

Deutsch—The Senate Finance Committee, Joint Committee on Taxation and the House Ways and Means Committee.

Reporter—You mean all three committees?

Deutsch—I was writing to whoever was working. You have to understand that I was involved in this process for a period of time. And depending on when I was involved . . . one week it was this committee, and then it was the next committee, and then it was the Joint Committee.

Deutsch reiterated that "I have no political influence. I have no relationships with the senators or the members of the House. I merely wrote letters and put my case before them and they found a favorable ear, I guess, only because what I was asking for had merit."

Was it possible that someone else secured the concession?

"I should speculate with you for a second," Deutsch said. "I even asked some of the major creditors to write letters to their [congressmen]. . . . And who knows whether or not—well, no, I was told actually that no one did. . . . So it's my letter writing."

And who might the major creditors be?

"You know, there, I'm under confidentiality," Deutsch said. "It's not in the best interests of the company to start discussing major creditors. . . . I would really be breaching whatever privacy these people want. It really wouldn't be right of me."

Others familiar with the custom-tailored tax break attribute it largely to Deutsch's lobbying efforts, although there is some disagreement on how and where the lobbying took place.

Richard M. Bank, a Washington lawyer who represented former Ironton workers in the bankruptcy, said that Deutsch had related this explanation:

"He [Deutsch] went down there [to Washington] and lobbied on it very hard. He went down to talk to the staff about it, and, you know, [he] told us that while he didn't have very much political leverage, in fact none, because he was on his own, that he was able to convince the staff that this was the right thing to do on the merits. That's his position. He's very proud of that."

The staffs of the three tax-writing committees all refused to discuss the Ironton provision, as they have all other tax favors.

A CORPORATION REBORN

Whatever the explanation, a company that has no employees and that ceased all operations years ago has been reborn under the 1986 tax law.

It has a new name, Rockcrest Corp. It has $60 million in old losses to offset the profits of some other going business—at a cost of $20 million to the U.S. Treasury. And it has a new chief executive, Stanley I. Deutsch, who owns nearly half the stock in the company.

Gary Blankenship, like other former Ironton workers who never collected their benefits, owns a small piece of Rockcrest.

"I got a [stock] certificate. I think it was for 76 shares of stock in Rockcrest Corp.," said Blankenship.

What was he told about the company?

"Nothing . . . The only thing they told us," he said, "was it was non-negotiable until I think 1990 or 1991. I just threw it in the drawer and let it lay."

As so often is the case with such tax breaks, one begets another, like this provision that a friendly tax writer hopes to insert into pending legislation:

Subsection (f) of section 621 of the Tax Reform Act of 1986 is amended by adding at the end thereof the following new paragraphs: (9) For purposes applying section 382(k)(6) of the Internal Revenue Code of 1986, preferred stock issued by an integrated steel manufacturer incorporated on November 9,

1982, and reincorporated on February 11, 1983, and having its principal place of business in Trenton, Michigan, and mentioned in a letter of intent dated July 10, 1987, signed by such manufacturer, shall not be treated as stock.

That refers to McLouth Steel Products Corp., an offshoot of the former parent of Ironton Coke Corp. If enacted into law, it will save McLouth an estimated $26 million in taxes in the next three years.

□□□

While the Senate Finance Committee failed to correctly identify the Ironton Coke Corp. as a beneficiary of Congress' preferential tax treatment in 1986, other names on its list were accurate but misleading. Such was the case of the North Pier Terminal in Chicago.

As part of the overhaul of the tax code, Congress eliminated the investment tax credit claimed by both businesses and individuals. The Finance Committee offered this rationale for the decision:

"As the world economies become increasingly competitive, it is most important that investment in our capital stock be determined by market forces rather than by tax considerations."

Once more, there were exceptions—this time thousands of individual taxpayers at the very top of the economic ladder. Needless to say, there is no hint as to who they are.

Rather, a friendly lawmaker inserted the following provision, which preserves the investment tax credit and other allowances:

The amendments made by this section and section 201 shall not apply to . . . the rehabilitation of 10 warehouse buildings built between 1906 and 1910 and purchased under a contract dated February 17, 1986.

Not by chance, 10 warehouse buildings erected between 1906 and 1910 formed an exhibition complex located near Chicago's lakefront. The facility later was converted to a warehouse and now is known as the North Pier Terminal.

Who arranged for the provision?

A spokesman for Sen. Paul Simon, the Illinois Democrat who recently suspended his campaign for his party's presidential nomination, said: "There were several of the [Illinois] delegation who worked on that—Simon and [Democratic Sen. Alan J.] Dixon and [Democratic Rep. Dan] Rostenkowski [chairman of the House Ways and Means Committee].

"Given Rostenkowski's central role in the bill, he might have played the most direct role. But several did provide help in that case."

A $12 MILLION BREAK

That "help" is worth an estimated $12 million to investors who are turning the warehouse into a commercial and retail complex.

The top four floors of the seven-story building "are being converted into loft office space," said Dona Laketek, vice president for marketing for Broadacre Development Co., the Chicago company overseeing the rehabilitation.

"The first three floors," Laketek said, "are being converted into specialty retail, restaurants, entertainment, kind of a festival market place."

There will be a waterfront promenade—the warehouse is located along a slip of the Chicago River—and a parking garage for those who come by car, moorings for those who arrive by boat. The first office tenants moved in last December and the retail section is scheduled to open this summer, Laketek said, with Bob Jani planning the grand opening ceremonies.

Jani produced President Reagan's second inaugural celebration, staged the opening and closing ceremonies for the 1984 Olympics in Los Angeles, produced the half-time show at the 1982 Super Bowl and orchestrated the 1976 Bicentennial extravaganza in New York Harbor.

But what about the tax break? Who will get the tax writeoffs for North Pier?

"The partnership that owns North Pier," Laketek said.

And who might the partners be?

"I think in total," she said, "there's about 35 limited partners. And, you know . . . that's the whole reason for partnerships. I guess people don't want that to be known. . . . We don't want to go out and just tell everyone who has ownership in this."

THE SEARLE FAMILY

According to records in the Cook County Recorder's Office, the partnership, North Pier Venture Ltd., is very much a family affair. The limited partners include a flock of Searles:

• Daniel Crow Searle, one of three great-grandchildren of Gideon D. Searle, founder of G.D. Searle & Co., the pharmaceutical manufacturer that developed and marketed the highly profitable artificial sweetener aspartame under the brand name NutraSweet. A former chairman of the drug company board, he is a member of the Forbes 400.

• William Louis Searle, second of the three great-grandchildren of Gideon D. Searle. He is a former director of the drug company, which the family sold in 1985 to Monsanto Co., the chemical manufacturer, for $2.8 billion. He also is a member of the Forbes 400.

• Suzanne Searle Dixon, third of the three great-grandchildren of Gideon D. Searle. She, too, served on the drug company board until its sale to Monsanto. And she, too, is a member of the Forbes 400. The magazine estimated that the three Searles share in trusts worth more that $750 million.

• Wesley M. Dixon Jr., husband of Suzanne Searle and former director of the drug company.

• Dain F. Searle, wife of Daniel C. Searle.

• Sally B. Searle, wife of William L. Seale.

• Katherine D. Thomson, Carolyn F. Dixon and John W. Dixon, the children of Suzanne Searle and Wesley Dixon.

• Marion S. Chandler, Louise C. Searle and Elizabeth S. Reichert, the children of William L. and Sally B. Searle.

• D. Gideon Searle, Michael D. Searle and Anne Searle Meers, the children of Daniel C. and Dain F. Searle.

• Robert Meers, husband of Anne Searle Meers.

The North Pier Terminal is not an exclusive Searle family tax break.

Other investors include Abra Prentice Anderson, one of the fourth-generation heirs to the Rockefeller fortune; Henry W. Meers, a millionaire Chicago investment banker, and James L. Dutt, former chairman and chief executive officer of the Beatrice Cos. Inc., who collected a nearly $4 million settlement when he was ousted from the food products company in 1985.

The partnership records in the Cook County Recorder's Office show that trusts representing the various Searles have invested more than $5 million in North Pier Venture Ltd.

In addition, Richard J. Ramsden, chief executive officer of the Earl

Kinship Capital Corp., has invested $4.3 million in the venture on behalf of yet another partnership.

Earl Kinship Capital, which has offices in Chicago and other cities, is a financial management firm that looks after the investments of the Searle and Dixon families.

And finally, Robert Meers is president of Broadacre Development Co., the company that is managing the restoration of the warehouse building.

Like many wealthy families, the Searles are not strangers to tax-avoidance opportunities, whether offered by historic-preservation projects or some other arcane tax-savings device.

The Internal Revenue Service issued a deficiency notice in 1985, stating that Daniel C. Searle and his wife owed additional taxes for the years 1979 and 1980.

The IRS disallowed part of the losses the Searles had claimed from a partnership set up to trade securities, U.S. government obligations, options and commodities futures contracts.

The agency maintained that the partnership, and thus the Searles, had overstated deductions by engaging in straddle transactions—a complex series of sale and purchase arrangements designed to create paper losses.

The Searles settled the claim last year, according to records filed in U.S. Tax Court in Washington. They agreed to pay $41,143 in back taxes and acknowledged that the underpayment had been due "to a tax-motivated transaction."

There were scores of entries on the Senate Finance Committee's 1986 list of 650 special-interest provisions that were similar to "North Pier Terminal."

Some were even more obscure, like the one labeled, "personal holding companies."

□ □ □

For Bernard Gerald Cantor, a securities dealer who shuttles between two prestigious addresses—a home in Beverly Hills and an apartment on New York's Park Avenue—1986 and 1987 were especially noteworthy years.

In April 1986, the Metropolitan Museum of Art opened the Iris and B. Gerald Cantor Exhibition Hall, a 10,000-square-foot gallery.

Cantor and his wife, Iris, donated the exhibit area, which was inaugurated with a display of 70 works by Rodin, including 31 sculptures that the Cantors had given to the museum.

In October 1986, President Reagan signed into law the Tax Reform Act of 1986, which contained a tax break for Cantor's securities firm, Cantor, Fitzgerald & Co. Inc. Cantor is reported to own 70 percent of the stock in the closely held firm and thus was the chief beneficiary of the concession.

In April 1987, the tax-exempt Iris and B. Gerald Cantor Foundation sponsored an Israeli art exhibit—"Treasures of the Holy Land: Ancient Art from the Israel Museum"—at the Los Angeles County Museum of Art. About 2,000 people from the West Coast's twin worlds of society and entertainment—Eva Gabor and Merv Griffin among the latter—attended a black-tie opening.

In September 1987, the Cantors celebrated the opening of the Cantor Gallery in the Brooklyn Museum, which houses more than 50 Rodin sculptures donated by the couple. For the occasion, they converted a floor of the museum into a replica of Coney Island in the early 1900s. Party-goers mingled with belly dancers and clowns and threw balls at stuffed cats to win prizes.

And in October 1987, Forbes magazine elevated Cantor to its most recent edition of "the 400 richest people in America." Forbes estimated his net worth at $225 million.

Of the five events, four attracted substantial public attention. The New York Times, the Los Angeles Times and other newspapers devoted several thousand words to chronicling the Cantors' art and social activities, and the guests at their parties.

The special tax provision, on the other hand, received scant mention —a sentence fragment in the New York Times, and that limited to a reference to Cantor's company rather than to him personally. The Senate Finance Committee made no mention of Cantor at all when it released its list of 1986 tax breaks.

The Cantor tax exemption, which appears in a section relating to taxes paid by personal holding companies, states:

Special Rules for Broker-Dealers—*In the case of a broker-dealer which is part of an affiliated group which files a consolidated Federal income tax return, the common parent of which was incorporated in Nevada on January*

27, 1972, the personal holding income (within the meaning of Section 543 of the Internal Revenue Code of 1986) of such broker-dealer, shall not include any interest received after the date of enactment of this Act with respect to . . .

Records on file with the Nevada Secretary of State indicate that Cantor, Fitzgerald & Co. Inc. was incorporated on Jan. 27, 1972.

The Senate Finance Committee, in addition to failing to identify Cantor's company as a beneficiary of the transition rule, also neglected to mention how much money the provision would cost the U.S. Treasury in lost tax revenue.

Efforts to interview Cantor were unsuccessful. Only Cantor and the IRS would know the value of the tax break, but tax-law specialists interviewed by The Inquirer said it could run into the millions of dollars.

Whatever the amount, the 70-year-old Cantor has done well in recent years, as evidenced by his membership in the exclusive Forbes 400.

A BROKER'S BROKER

His company, which has offices in Beverly Hills, New York, Boston, Chicago and Dallas, specializes in government securities and sometimes is referred to as a broker's broker.

According to Financial World, which monitors the salaries of Wall Street executives, Cantor earned $12.6 million in 1985 and $11.3 million in 1986.

Cantor's financial success has enabled him to indulge his passion for collecting fine art. Since World War II, he has assembled what many experts consider to be the world's largest private collection of pieces by the French sculptor Auguste Rodin.

Over the years, he has accumulated an estimated 700 pieces of Rodin sculpture and has donated about 400 of the artworks to museums and universities.

One recipient, Stanford University, which houses the B. Gerald Cantor Rodin Sculpture Garden, boasts the largest collection of the artist's sculpture outside the Rodin Museum in Paris.

As patrons of the arts, the Cantors travel in a rarefied circle of movers and shakers—people like Betsy Bloomingdale, the close personal friend and confidante of Nancy Reagan and member of the President's Committee on the Arts and Humanities; Ann and Gordon P. Getty of the Getty Oil fortune (he is a Forbes 400 member); Jennifer Jones, the Academy Award-winning actress *(The Song of Bernadette),* and her husband, Norton W. Simon, industrialist, art collector and another Forbes 400 member; and Jane and Michael D. Eisner (he is chairman and chief executive officer of the Walt Disney Co.).

(The world of tax-break recipients also is quite rarefied. Disney Co. received a private tax provision in 1986 which will enable the company, along with MCA Inc., to escape payment of an estimated $65 million in taxes.)

In the past, Cantor's gifts, which have resulted in substantial deductions on his personal tax returns, have piqued the interest of IRS auditors.

The agency issued a deficiency notice in 1980, claiming that Cantor and his first wife, who were divorced in 1976, owed an additional $64,925 in taxes on their 1973 return.

Among the disputed items was a $320,225 deduction for contributions. The IRS disallowed part of the writeoff, saying that "it has been determined that the claimed fair-market value of the pieces of art, sculpture, etc., you contributed to charitable institutions was excessive by $84,700."

The Cantors eventually settled the claim by paying an additional $33,000 in taxes.

For the year in dispute, the Cantors' total income placed them among the top one percent of all taxpayers. Yet the percentage of their income subject to tax was below that of many middle-income families.

MOYNIHAN'S ROLE

Who arranged for the Cantor tax concession in the 1986 reform act?

It was Daniel Patrick Moynihan, the Democratic senator from New York who has nurtured a reputation as a champion of minorities and the economically oppressed.

When the Tax Reform Act emerged from the Senate Finance Committee in the spring of 1986, Moynihan said that one of the bill's goals was to attack tax avoidance by upper-income taxpayers who used gimmicks and shelters to lower their tax bills.

Moynihan said that the thrust of numerous federal studies about tax avoidance could be summed up in six words: "The rich were not paying taxes."

Nevertheless, as a member of the Finance Committee, he inserted no fewer than a half-dozen exemptions—in effect, private loopholes—in the code, among them one for Cantor.

After the tax bill was sent to both houses for passage, Moynihan issued a brief press release listing the transition rules he had sponsored but gave no details about them.

Although he took note of the press release on the Senate floor on Sept. 27, he indicated that he would have no comment.

". . . There has been some discussion of transition rules," Moynihan said. "I would like to record that on the day the conference report on this legislation was filed, I released a statement of all the transition rules that I have been associated with, and have had no comment since."

Rather than talk about the individual tax breaks he had fathered, Moynihan chose instead to pay homage to the tax-reform bill itself, calling it "a profound statement concerning the requirements of citizenship and the ethical basis of the American Republic."

CONGRESS CAN'T ADD, SO THE TAXPAYER PAYS

THURSDAY, APRIL 14, 1988

BY DONALD L. BARLETT AND JAMES B. STEELE

When Congress passed what it called deficit-reduction measures last December, a number of tax favors for special interests were tucked away in the fine print.

Among them was a private tax law intended to help the Long Island Power Authority. The authority wants to buy—and shut down—the troubled Shoreham nuclear power plant.

Congress' Joint Committee on Taxation at first said that the Shoreham bailout would cost the U.S. Treasury—that means all taxpayers—$1 million from 1988 to 1990. A month later, the committee revised that figure upward to $241 million for the same period.

But that wasn't right either.

What the committee didn't say was that the Shoreham project would be financed through tax-exempt bonds that extend into the next century. So if the authority goes ahead with the buyout, it will cost the Treasury not just the $241 million for 1988 to 1990—but an added $3.5 billion to $4 billion by the time the bonds are paid off in the 21st century.

The costs beyond 1990 were ones that Congress chose not to count when it calculated the price of the tax breaks it granted.

Welcome to the new math as practiced on Capitol Hill.

But surely, you say, this is an aberration, that those who write the tax laws—and grant exemptions from them—are usually more precise.

Well, no, not really.

Not only can they not count dollars, they can't count power plants either.

When Congress was preparing to vote on the Tax Reform Act of 1986, these same tax-writing committees released what they said was a complete tabulation of all special-interest provisions inserted in the act. They identified by name fewer than 100 hydroelectric plants and cogeneration projects—facilities that generate two or more forms of energy from one fuel source—that qualified for special breaks.

In fact, more than 600 such installations—and thousands of affluent investors—qualify for the preferential tax treatment, an Inquirer analysis of records maintained by the Federal Energy Regulatory Commission shows.

Nobody on the tax-writing committees would talk with Inquirer reporters about the discrepancy.

All one can say for certain is that more than six times the number of companies listed can take advantage of the tax break.

The tax-writing committees also said the cost of the 1986 energy breaks would be less than $500 million.

In fact, the potential cost is several times that amount.

To be sure, not all of the facilities that qualify for the exemption actually will be built. (A blanket exemption was granted to alternative-energy ventures that had received federal certification by March 2, 1986.) Still, even if only a fraction are constructed, the taxes that investors will avoid paying will far exceed congressional estimates.

Those who write the nation's tax laws have indeed come up with a new math.

They count differently from the rest of us.

And the rest of us will be paying for that for years to come.

• The new math has fueled out-of-control budget deficits to the point where interest payments on the $2.4 trillion national debt now consume every dollar in income tax paid by low- and middle-income individuals and families for the first six months of each year.

Put another way, that means that every dollar in income tax paid by the average worker from January through June goes to wealthy investors in the United States and abroad, and to banks and other institutions that hold the debt.

• It has led to the gutting of the progressive tax system, so that now billionaires are in the same tax bracket as a family of three earning $45,000 a year, or a single person earning $25,000. Since Ronald Reagan moved into the White House in 1980, the top tax rate for individuals has fallen 42 percentage points, from 70 percent to 28 percent. The bottom rate has gone up—not down—one point from 14 percent to 15 percent.

The spread between the top and bottom tax rates now is at its narrowest since the mid-1920s. But in those years, the average worker paid no federal income tax. If the exemptions from the mid-1920s were in place today, the first $28,000 of income for a family of four would be tax-free.

• It also has inspired an entire new process by which tax-law changes are written. Each proposed tax revision that will result in a revenue loss must be offset by another provision that will produce a revenue gain. But since the estimates are so often faulty—and usually result in larger-than-projected losses—the deficit continues to grow.

That's an economic cost. The cost in fairness is greater, since the practice has spawned the largest number of private tax laws in U.S. history—franchises that allow select individuals and businesses to escape payment of some taxes.

Right now, congressional tax writers are preparing to weave scores of such breaks into a bill designed to correct typographical, spelling and other clerical errors in the Tax Reform Act of 1986.

Or, if the tax breaks become too controversial, lawmakers could bury the provisions in any number of other pieces of legislation, as they did with the tax concession granted to the Long Island Power Authority.

Beneficiaries of the new tax breaks range from banks to electric utilities, from wealthy individuals to telecommunications companies.

Consider how one industry—the alternative-energy industry—has benefited and will continue to benefit from those tax concessions.

□ □ □

Many tax breaks awarded by Congress contain hidden economic costs. Such is the case with government-subsidized alternative energy, one of those good ideas in theory that went bad in practice.

To understand how it happened, one needs a little background.

To a large extent, alternative-energy companies owe their existence to provisions in the Internal Revenue Code and federal energy incentives dating from the oil crises of the 1970s.

That was the decade marked by long lines of angry motorists at gas stations and spiraling prices of all fuels, triggered first by an Arab oil embargo and later by the shutoff of oil from Iran.

Congress responded by enacting an array of energy tax benefits, including the investment tax credit, to encourage conservation, stimulate production of alternative-energy sources and thereby ease dependence on foreign oil.

Then, to assure a market for the new energy facilities, Congress required utilities to purchase electricity produced by independent sources, which were not government-regulated the way utility companies are.

This meant that if someone built a windmill or tapped a garbage dump for its methane, the local utility was obligated to accept and pay for whatever power the owner wanted to sell.

What happened next was predictable. Tax-avoidance specialists who mine the Internal Revenue Code like the gold prospectors of another era formed partnerships to develop new energy supplies.

These investment advisers guaranteed their affluent clients that they could invest in energy projects that would yield large deductions which, in turn, would reduce their income tax bills.

Thousands of new companies and partnerships were formed to develop everything from wind farms to solar stations, from small hydroelectric plants to biomass facilities.

They were attracted by the potential of this new, unregulated market—with its captive buyers of alternative energy.

For while such major energy suppliers as public utilities were compelled to submit proposed rates to state or federal regulatory agencies for approval, these unregulated companies could operate outside that restrictive framework.

With that as background, let's jump forward to 1986, when congressional tax reformers reduced or eliminated accelerated depreciation and the investment tax credit—except for the lucky few who were specifically exempted.

□ □ □

When lawmakers granted concessions to energy projects in the Tax Reform Act of 1986, which was passed by Congress in September of that year, they provided a blanket exemption to all alternative-energy ventures that had received federal certification by March 2, 1986.

It is unknown why the March 2 date was settled on, since tax writers have refused to discuss any of the concessions in the act and how they were arrived at.

Scores of projects were announced or started after that March date. None of those could make use of the tax benefits that had existed prior to the 1986 act. None, that is, except for three projects that tax writers currently have singled out for new concessions. One is in Kern County, Calif.; another is in Decatur, Ill.; and the third is this one, masked in the customary legal jargon:

(a) Section 204(a) of the Tax Reform Act of 1986 is amended by adding at the end thereof:

(40) The amendments made by section 201 shall not apply to—

(F) $87,500,000 of property used in connection with a coal gasification project to be constructed in Summerset {sic} County, Pennsylvania.

That clause, if enacted into law, would save an estimated $7 million in taxes for a coal gasification plant that is to be built near Johnstown, about 60 miles southeast of Pittsburgh.

The project is a joint venture of affiliates of M. W. Kellogg Co. of Houston, an engineering and construction company, and the Bechtel Group Inc. The U.S. Department of Energy will provide about half the funds for the $175 million facility. The tax break will come on top of that.

The cryptic language of the Kellogg provision is typical of how tax writers have disguised the growing number of beneficiaries of tax breaks throughout the 1980s. This language explains in part why no one noticed in 1986 that instead of granting tax concessions to fewer than 100 energy projects, as the self-styled reformers claimed, the Tax Reform Act actually extended favored treatment to hundreds of such ventures.

What kind of projects received the tax favors? Who were some of the people who benefited from the largest tax-giveaway bonanza in history?

Item. John C. Brewer of Salt Lake City is president and guiding light of Garb Oil & Power Corp., which plans to build a plant in Rialto, Calif., about 50 miles east of Los Angeles, to generate electricity by burning up to 10 million old tires each year.

Area residents, local government officials and even the congressman for the district opposed the facility, contending that it would spew pollutants into the already-smoggy skies over the San Bernardino Valley. Nonetheless, Brewer had support elsewhere in Congress.

Back in June 1981, the company conducted a demonstration of its process for shredding and burning tires at a pilot plant in Seattle. (The byproduct of the burning at the Seattle facility was oil, not electricity.) Orrin G. Hatch, the Republican senator from Utah, flew in for the occasion at the company's expense. "I think Garb Oil has something really going here," said Hatch.

Through a tax break written into the 1986 Tax Reform Act, investors in Brewer's electricity-generating Rialto plant will be allowed to escape payment of an estimated $2 million or more in income taxes.

Although San Bernardino County sued to block construction, Brewer says he expects a favorable court ruling by summer. "Legally, the plant should be built," he says, and "everyone recognizes that."

Brewer criticized environmentalists, who he said first called attention to the tax break.

There were "apartment complexes and all kinds of projects that fell under the transition rule," he said, "but they picked on this one [the tire-burning plant] because it was one that they were opposed to. But you have this everywhere you go. . . . You've got some people who are just opposed to any kind of progress."

Item. James J. Lowrey, as chairman of the board and single largest stockholder of Catalyst Energy Corp. in New York, has profited from a series of energy projects in which investors will avoid payment of an estimated $187 million in taxes.

According to records filed with the U.S. Securities and Exchange Commission (SEC), Lowrey and his wife, Marianne, own around 20 percent of the company's stock, which is worth about $25 million even in a depressed market.

Investors in three Catalyst hydroelectric facilities in West Virginia, Louisiana and California will be able to claim the investment tax credit and accelerated depreciation that have been eliminated for most other taxpayers. One of the stock market's high-flying energy companies the last several years, Catalyst was founded in 1982 by Lowrey—a rising young star on Wall Street in the 1970s—and several associates.

Records filed with the SEC show that in 1984 and 1985, Lowrey's wife received 785,000 shares of Catalyst stock as gifts or through stock splits. Then, from August 1986 to July 1987, she sold 785,000 shares for prices ranging between $19.25 and $26.87—just under the all-time high of $29. In all, Marianne Lowrey received $17.5 million.

On a more personal level, Lowrey is contesting a claim by the Internal Revenue Service that he underpaid his income taxes in past years. Among the issues in dispute: His deductions of around $30,000 in 1977 and $29,000 in 1978 to have his fingernails manicured, his hair styled and his shoes shined. He also claimed a $24,000 deduction for parking his car. Lowrey considered all the writeoffs as business expenses.

Item. Three former officials of the U.S. Environmental Protection Agency (EPA), who now are officers of Long Lake Energy Corp. in New York, stand to profit from a series of hydroelectric projects the company is developing in New York State. Long Lake may avoid payment of $23 million or more in income taxes.

Paul J. Elston, who founded Long Lake in 1980 and is chairman of the board, president, treasurer and a director of the company, was the EPA's deputy assistant administrator for resources management. C. William Carter, a senior vice president and director of the company, also was an EPA deputy assistant administrator for resources management, and Donald E. Hamer, a senior vice president of the company, was EPA's comptroller.

Long Lake took note of the special tax provision in a report filed with the SEC, pointing out that it could continue to claim tax credits and depreciation schedules denied to other businesses.

How important was the tax break? Well, without it, the company said, "in certain cases, [the] construction [of plants] may become uneconomic."

Item. James J. Tedesco of Old Forge, Pa., is an officer and shareholder in a company that is building a power plant in Luzerne County, Pa., to generate electricity by burning coal refuse. Investors in the plant will avoid millions of dollars in taxes.

According to records of the Pennsylvania Department of Environmental Resources, Tedesco is president of Jeddo-Highland Coal Co.

and a stockholder in its parent company, Pagnotti Enterprises Inc. of Pittston, Pa. Pagnotti plans to build the cogeneration plant near Hazelton, Pa.

Tedesco pleaded no contest in 1977 to federal charges of conspiring to fix coal prices. A Tedesco company, Lehigh Valley Coal Sales Co., also pleaded no contest that same year to federal charges that for 13 years it had conspired with five other coal companies to rig the price of anthracite coal.

A 1980 report by the Pennsylvania Crime Commission said that Tedesco also had "participated in fixing coal prices in 1944 with Santo Volpe Sr. . . . who became the first boss in northeastern Pennsylvania of what is known today as the Bufalino Cosa Nostra family."

□ □ □

Some of the energy projects that mushroomed under the government's munificence were economically viable even without tax breaks and the mandatory purchase requirements that were imposed on utilities. But many others—perhaps most—were not, particularly after the price of world oil collapsed.

A California utility offers a model.

Confronted with the requirement that utilities buy any independently produced power, Pacific Gas & Electric Co. of San Francisco signed contracts for about 8,000 megawatts—the equivalent of the electrical output of eight Limerick power plants.

Many of the agreements were struck at a time when it was widely assumed by government and industry alike that energy prices would continue in one direction—up. Few were prepared for what happened next.

When conservation measures took hold worldwide, following the shortages of the 1970s, energy consumption went down, supplies went up, and the Organization of Petroleum Exporting Countries (OPEC), caught in the middle of the two forces, lost its control of world oil prices.

In 1981, Saudi Arabia, the world's largest producer, sold its crude oil for $34 a barrel. Today, it goes for $15.

Marilyn Beret, a spokeswoman for Pacific Gas & Electric, explains what it will mean if independent producers begin generating the 8,000 megawatts of electricity the utility is committed to buy:

"If only 38 percent of the projects that have not yet been built are, in fact, built, PG&E's more than four million electric customers will be paying about $857 million a year more than they would have to if PG&E were able to either produce the power themselves, or buy it from a more economic source."

The $857 million, she said, translates into "a 7 percent across-the-board rate increase" for consumers.

How is this possible?

"If you had a windmill in your back yard today," Beret said, "and you went to the California Public Utilities Commission and said you wanted one of these variable contracts, you would be offered about 3 cents a kilowatt hour for the electricity you produced.

"Now, the windmill operator of two years ago is today getting paid about 7.5 cents for that electricity because it was predicated on oil being a lot more expensive in 1987 than it actually is."

So a law that was intended to increase energy production at a time when energy was scarce ends up costing the consumer, in this example, an extra 4.5 cents per kilowatt hour.

But from the standpoint of the independent energy producer, it was a formula for success.

One need look no further than Catalyst Energy Corp., which describes itself as "the nation's leading independent power producer."

Among the company's nearly three dozen energy projects are three large hydroelectric plants either under construction or on the drawing boards in West Virginia, Louisiana and California.

Each plant when completed will generate and sell high-priced electricity to local utilities, and those utilities are required by federal law to buy it, even if they don't need it. The utilities will pass along the increased costs to consumers.

Investors in those plants, in turn, will reap the benefits of lower federal tax bills.

It was the potential of this new, unregulated market—with its captive buyer—that stirred the imagination of James Lowrey, Catalyst's chairman. The company concentrated, as Catalyst put it, on producing electricity "not subject to rate-of-return regulation."

In other words, while major energy suppliers like public utilities were compelled to submit proposed rates to state or federal regulatory agencies for approval, Catalyst and other such companies could operate outside that restrictive framework.

The first thing Catalyst did was build small energy-producing facilities—a 2.9 megawatt hydroelectric plant in Indian Valley, Calif.; a 6.2 megawatt cogeneration plant at San Jose State University in San Jose, Calif.; and a 5.7 megawatt alternative fuel project at North Powder, Ore.

Next came plans for three large-scale hydroelectric plants—a $100 million, 34-megawatt plant at New Martinsville, W. Va.; a $650 million, 118-megawatt facility in El Dorado County, Calif., and a $550 million, 192-megawatt plant in Vidalia, La.

Then the company moved into the steam-heating business, acquiring systems in St. Louis, Baltimore and Youngstown, Ohio. In January 1987, a subsidiary purchased from Philadelphia Electric Co. the steam system that heats office and commercial buildings in Center City and West Philadelphia.

By mid-1987, Catalyst reported that it had "30 facilities in operation or under construction in 20 states." In a report to stockholders, the company saw an even more promising future for unregulated energy:

"In our opinion the bulk of additional capacity in the 1990s will come from a new type of generating company that will construct both conventionally and unconventionally fired generating plants in a less regulated and more entrepreneurial environment."

By far the company's most ambitious undertakings are its three large hydroelectric plants. As required by law, the local utilities in the three states have signed contracts to buy electricity from the Catalyst facilities.

Yet even with the contracts, which virtually ensure that consumers will pay more than the prevailing market rate for the electricity, the evidence suggests that the Catalyst ventures were dependent on tax breaks.

A January 1985 study prepared by a California environmental foundation maintains that the profitability of Catalyst's hydroelectric project on the South Fork of the American River, about 75 miles west of Sacramento, is linked directly to tax concessions.

The Planning and Conservation League Foundation in Sacramento concluded that without the investment tax credit and accelerated depreciation, the annual profits forecast by supporters would "become annual losses in each of the project's first ten years of operation."

Would Catalyst build the hydroelectric plants without the tax incentives?

Lawrence S. Coben, the company's senior vice president, seemed uncertain in an interview with The Inquirer.

Reporter—Would the projects be viable without the tax breaks?

Coben—Yeah, but I'd say less so. I mean, obviously less so. Hydroelectric plants are generally viable. It's hard, well, I don't know quite how to—when you say viable, maybe I should ask you what you mean by viable before I answer your question.

Reporter—Would someone invest without the transition rule?

Coben—I would say, well, God, I don't know. I honestly don't know. I think they'd probably get done in a very different way by very different people, but—I really don't know how to answer that.

Catalyst will receive millions of dollars in fees for arranging the three deals. In addition, it has retained a 50 percent interest in the Vidalia, La., facility and therefore will derive the tax benefits from it.

Financing of the West Virginia plant has been completed and construction is well under way. When finished, the New Martinsville facility will sell its electricity to the local utility, the Monongahela Power & Light Co.

In turn, Monongahela Power, which has no present or foreseeable need for the electricity but still must buy it, will pass along the increased costs to consumers in West Virginia, the nation's second poorest state measured in per capita income.

Russ Lorince, a spokesman for the utility, said that under the contract with Catalyst "we will be paying 7.6 cents per kilowatt hour for the first 15 years." It would be possible, he added, to buy electricity from other utilities for "considerably less."

Much the same is true at Vidalia, where construction also is well under way. The plant is being built by Avondale Industries Inc., a long-time shipbuilder that is branching out into new construction fields.

Interestingly, Avondale received its own tax break under another section of the 1986 tax act. This means that a company that received preferential tax treatment is building a plant for a company that received preferential tax treatment.

While these projects may not seem to be such a good deal for consumers, who ultimately must pay the higher-than-necessary charges for electricity, or for taxpayers, who must make up the taxes avoided by investors, Catalyst and investors in its projects have fared rather well.

In 1985 and 1986, Catalyst recorded profits of $9 million. During the same two years, the company paid not a penny in federal income taxes.

This has created the not uncommon situation in which a company that pays no corporate income taxes is building projects for which investors will be able to avoid payment of individual income taxes.

Whose are those investors?

For the Louisiana plant, Catalyst and Dominion Capital Inc. have formed a partnership to share the profits, losses and tax benefits.

Dominion Capital is a subsidiary of Dominion Resources Inc., the holding company that owns the Virginia Electric & Power Co. (VEPCO), the Richmond utility that supplies electricity in most of Virginia and parts of North Carolina.

Concluding, apparently, that it cannot beat the independent power companies, VEPCO and several other utilities have decided to join them in developing unregulated power supplies.

They are doing so outside their home marketing areas, where it would be politically awkward to try to pass along the cost of higher-priced electricity to consumers.

In short, what VEPCO cannot do in Virginia it can do in Louisiana as an investor.

The New Martinsville hydroelectric plant also has been sold to private investors. But Catalyst is reluctant to identify them. Said Catalyst's Coben:

"I don't know that they want their names known."

SIX

THE PALESTINIAN UPRISING AND GORBACHEV'S GRAND PLAN

1989 WINNERS IN THE INTERNATIONAL REPORTING CATEGORY

"For a distinguished example of reporting on international affairs, including United Nations correspondence . . ."

The Washington Post
Glenn Frankel

The New York Times
Bill Keller

The Israeli army and West Bank and Gaza Strip Palestinians spent the year entangled in a bitter struggle over dreams as much as over territory. Glenn Frankel talked with members of both sides, who continue to choose conflict over dialogue.

To measure the distance we all have traveled since the Palestinian uprising began, I only have to look at my aging Fiat sedan. In December 1987 it was untarnished, and a fresh "Foreign Press" sticker was prominently displayed on the windshield. Now there are a half dozen or more small dents, nicks and rust spots from stones—and the foreign press sticker is hidden away in the glove compartment.

The press lost its privileged status as a neutral observer early on in the uprising, and we have yet to retrieve it. Palestinians, who are all too aware that plainclothes security men routinely pose as journalists, greet us with suspicion and sometimes with rocks. Israeli soldiers, who have been encouraged by their own officers and by Israel's political leaders to see us as enemy sympathizers, automatically evict us from virtually any place where trouble might occur. And so we have learned to skulk around the occupied West Bank and Gaza Strip in dented, unmarked cars, sifting for reportable truth among the flames and the ashes.

Perhaps it was inevitable that in a conflict in which both sides routinely invoke history, morality and religion for their cause, no one would be allowed to remain neutral for very long and that the press itself would be quickly perceived as a combatant. That is exactly what happened. I had always suspected that it would. I had come to Israel in 1986 after a three-year reporting stint in southern Africa, and I had watched the South African government gradually tighten the screws on press freedom during its own prolonged bout of uprising. When I first came to Israel, I had been amazed by the high amount of freedom and access we were allowed in the territories. But this would quickly change.

I came to the *intifada* knowing very little about Palestinians but a bit about the dynamics and implacable logic of uprisings. The tear gas smelled the same in Gaza City as it had in Soweto. But more importantly, I could see early on that this too would be a children's crusade, a war waged by teen-agers not only against the Israelis but against their own parents. I also knew that virtually everything the army did would feed the unrest.

The conflict would gradually suck in all of the possible actors—students, merchants, soldiers, settlers, politicians. Just about everything that could happen eventually did happen—Israelis too began to die, and we woke up one morning to find 15 Palestinians had been killed on a certain Saturday in April, and no one was very surprised or even shocked. The right question was not why the uprising was happening, but why it had taken 20 years of military occupation for it to begin.

It became clear early on that from my narrow perspective the only way to cover the chaos was to stay close to the ground, to write about individual places and people caught up in something large and terrible. I tried not to draw too many conclusions—not to overestimate the impact the uprising might have, nor to write it off. Eventually it would change everything, the way Palestinians and Israelis looked at each other, but also the way they looked at themselves. But I didn't know then, and I don't know now, whether what we were watching was the beginning of the end of the 100 Years War between Arabs and Jews, or maybe just the end of the beginning.

It was a tough year. Besides dodging rocks and soldiers, I also had to cope with working without official press accreditation for nearly a month when the Israeli government suspended my press card for defying military censorship in writing about Israel's assassination of Khalil Wazir, a senior Palestine Liberation Organization leader in Tunis.

But despite the restrictions, ultimately our access to those caught up in this drama was wide and deep. I could go from the modern office of Defense Minister Yitzhak Rabin in Tel Aviv on one afternoon to the bleak apartment of a bereaved Palestinian family in a Nablus slum the next. I could talk to people who could never talk to each other, could see the similarities in suffering and the invisible lines of grief that ran from one side to the other.

As in South Africa, I found myself becoming a regular funeral-goer. I went to many Palestinian ceremonies, drank the bitter coffee that is part of the ritual. More than 350 Palestinians were shot dead last year —about one a day—and as the deaths became cruelly routine, it became harder and harder for all of us to find new ways to describe the circumstances and the pain.

But the funeral I remember best was the burial of a young Israeli mother and her three children at the Mount of Olives in Jerusalem. They had been burned to death when someone had thrown a firebomb at the passenger bus they were riding in. They were to be buried in the same grave, and I recall thinking that the hole was far too small for all four. It seems to me that, like that sad hole, Israel and the territories are far too small to hold all of the restless dreams and nightmares of those who live there and of those of us who strove to capture their agony.

—Glenn Frankel
The Washington Post

GAZA MERCHANTS CAUGHT IN MIDDLE

PROTESTERS FORCE SHOPS TO CLOSE; SOLDIERS INSIST THEY STAY OPEN

THURSDAY, JANUARY 7, 1988

BY GLENN FRANKEL

GAZA CITY, Jan. 6—It was a cat-and-mouse day for Palestinian youths and Israeli soldiers in downtown Gaza City today, and the merchants of Omar el Mukhtar Street were the cheese.

When they arrived early this morning, the merchants were greeted by masked young men carrying stones who told them to keep their shops closed as part of a general strike. A few hours later, Israeli soldiers in purple berets and armed with automatic rifles ordered them to reopen. When the soldiers left, the Palestinian youths quickly returned and ordered them to close again.

"You tell me, what can I do?" said the glum-looking manager of the Dador Trading Center. He pointed to the scarred hinges on his sheet metal doors that soldiers had pried open with a crowbar, then to the fresh glass in a window that youths had smashed with a rock a few days before.

"I am twisted from all sides. Every day it's open and close, open and close. If everything is closed here, why does the Army tell me to open?"

In Jerusalem today, the government reacted with what officials called a "low key" statement of "regret and disappointment" to yesterday's U.S. vote in favor of a U.N. Security Council resolution condemning Israel's plan to expel nine Palestinian activists. Foreign Minister Shimon Peres said, however, that the vote was "a serious kind of deviation from the framework of our relations with the United States."

But here in the occupied Gaza Strip, where there were more incidents of stone throwing and tire burning for the fourth day following the announcement of the expulsions, the diplomatic maneuvers seemed distant.

Gaza these days is a land of angry youths and determined soldiers locked in a confrontation of Palestinian stones and gasoline bombs against Israeli tear gas, rubber bullets and, at times, live ammunition. At least 24 Palestinians have died here and in the West Bank and more than 180 have been wounded since the violence began Dec. 9.

But it is also a land of merchants and workers, of people trying to eke out a living in circumstances that even in the best of times are tough and unforgiving.

And these are not the best of times. Ever since trouble first exploded here four weeks ago, the shops have been closed almost continuously and for much of that time, the 50,000 Gazans who travel to jobs in Israel daily have been cut off from what for most of them is their only source of income.

Some Israeli officials contend that these Gazans and their counterparts on the West Bank form something of a silent majority that would simply like tranquility to return.

"The Arab population . . . wants to return to normalcy because it also sees that . . . disturbances, acts of incitement and rock throwing do not lead anywhere," Prime Minister Yitzhak Shamir told Israel radio earlier this week.

In fact, many older Palestinians said, their dilemma is more complex than Shamir's characterization. Many said they feel sympathy for the young men battling the Army. Most have had a run-in at one time or another with Israeli soldiers, incidents that can range from a minor humiliation at a military checkpoint to a jail sentence.

Everyone expressed grievances about conditions after 20 years of military occupation and many insisted they have no second thoughts about the work days and the money they have sacrificed.

But some, when interviewed in private away from other Palestinians, expressed reservations. For many, the first few days of last month's strike were voluntary, something they agreed with and got caught up with. But as the strike ground on, some grew tired but said they were compelled to stay away from work by youths with rocks and threats.

There have been days when "going to work has been like going to war," said Bahai Sofiri, a maintenance worker at the Erez Dayan clothing factory in an Israeli-owned industrial zone just inside the Gaza line. Sofiri said he has reported for work as often as he could during this past month.

"From an ideological point, I agree with the youths, but from a practical point there is no alternative" to working, he said. "I have a wife, I have three children. To continue living, I have to work."

For Arab merchants and workers, the war begins early each day. This morning in Palestine Square, the main commercial center of Gaza City, youths stoned workers lining up for the buses and taxis that take them to Israel. Many went home. At Erez Dayan, only 10 of the 60 workers made it.

Things had grown fairly quiet near the end of last week, merchants said, but then on Sunday Israel announced that it had issued expulsion orders to nine activists, four of whom live in the Gaza Strip, and a soldier killed an Arab woman in a Jerusalem suburb. By Sunday night, Gaza City was erupting again.

On Monday the youths turned their attention to the shopkeepers on Omar el Mukhtar, Gaza's main commercial strip.

The merchants close when they are told to, but they remain on the premises behind metal shutters or outside their shops waiting for the soldiers. They do so, they said, because if they do not open up when ordered, the soldiers either crack open their padlocks with crowbars or weld the doors shut.

Today a 10-man patrol of the crack Oivati brigade made its way down Omar el Mukhtar at about 1 p.m. after a police van with a loudspeaker cruised the street ordering everyone to open. Slowly doors were opened a crack at the Maju Hirat Huna and Lateef Ayyad jewelry stores, at the Ibn Sina pharmacy, the Faris Boutique, the Abu Rahma appliance shop and the El Falugy sewing shop. Some merchants objected, saying they feared protesters would break their windows, but the soldiers ignored them.

The Army said it forces the shops open for the welfare of the merchants and the public.

"We know the main reason these shopkeepers are closing is because they are threatened by other people," said a senior Army commander, who asked not to be named, in an interview before the violence intensified. "And in most cases we learned that what they prefer is for us to push them. It gives them an excuse to open, which is what most of them want to do."

The merchants dismiss such explanations. "We do not want to open but they force us to," said one of the jewelry shop owners. Like most of the other merchants, he refused to give his name for fear of reprisals. "When they leave, I will close again. This is the crazy life we are living."

After the 10-man patrol left Omar el Mukhtar Street this afternoon, it headed down a side street toward a corner where someone had managed to hang a small flag of the outlawed Palestine Liberation Organization from an electricity wire. The soldiers stood for several minutes pondering the limp banner, then ordered two boys to bring a wooden ladder from a nearby mosque.

The ladder was too short to reach the flag, but then the patrol stopped a blue van and ordered one youth to climb atop it. Standing on a small stool on the roof of the van, he swung at the flag with a broom handle. The soldiers laughed as the boy, age 16, swung and missed three times and almost lost his balance. On the fourth swing he succeeded and the flag fell to the road, where the patrol leader picked it up.

But while the patrol was lingering on the side street, the stone throwers returned to Omar el Mukhtar. They pulled shelves and merchandise from one shop into the street, blocked the road and pelted passing cars with rocks. Like turtles receding into their shells, the shopkeepers quickly shuttered their stores again and the streets emptied.

For the workers at the Erez Dayan factory, working in Gaza contains its own special set of contradictions. The company's prime product is military gear produced by Palestinians who said they hold the Army in fear and contempt.

"It's work, it's nothing," said a worker who gave his name as Samer as he sewed Army jackets. "Look, all Palestinians working are helping Israel whether we do it for the Army or for civilians."

Samer said he broke the general strike and came to work today because he had participated in recent demonstrations and wanted to be able to claim the alibi that he was working when the police come.

A worker who said his name is Mohammed said he had returned because, "I had enough. People can't last a month or more without work."

NEWS ANALYSIS

ISRAEL HAUNTED BY COMPARISON WITH SOUTH AFRICA

ANALOGY BETWEEN COUNTRIES ELICITS BITTER RESPONSE IN JERUSALEM

MONDAY, JANUARY 25, 1988

BY GLENN FRANKEL

JERUSALEM, Jan. 24—Shlomo Avineri, a prominent Hebrew University political scientist close to Foreign Minister Shimon Peres, was recently discussing the six weeks of Palestinian protest in the occupied West Bank and Gaza Strip when he raised a specter that sends shivers down the spines of many Israeli Jews.

Israel is strong enough militarily to hold on to the territories indefinitely despite Arab resistance, Avineri said. But if it chose to do so, he warned, "the next 15 years will look more like the last weeks . . . and by the year 2000 we will look into the mirror and we will see South Africa."

There are critics who claim that Avineri's vision of the future has come to pass already on the streets of Gaza. The rise of a new generation of angry young men challenging the might of an army with stones and bottles, the shootings and the beatings, the increasing restrictions on press coverage—all of it, they contend, eerily echoes similar scenes in the black townships of South Africa.

So, too, does the image of a government that has resorted to a hard-line security stance to quell widespread civil disorder because it is unwilling, or unable, to take the risk of seeking a political solution.

Of all the charges leveled during the recent violence, none has stung the Israeli government more or produced more bitter reaction than the claim that Israel is becoming the South Africa of the Middle East. It is an analogy that, in the eyes of Israeli officials, not only equates this nation with a country that they find morally repugnant—although they have had close ties with it in the past—but also challenges the very right of the Jewish state to exist.

Israeli officials see the claim as part of a propaganda war waged by Israel's Arab enemies and abetted to some extent by the western news media. ABC News, for example, in two recent programs drew the comparison with film showing striking resemblances between scenes of fighting in South Africa and here and between the hard-line rhetoric of South African President Pieter W. Botha and that of Israeli Prime Minister Yitzhak Shamir.

The aim of such analogies, officials here contend, is to resurrect the concept first given voice in the 1975 U.N. General Assembly resolution equating Zionism with racism—that Israel, like South Africa, is a pariah state outside the comity of nations and that it should be quarantined and delegitimized. Such isolation is especially feared here because, unlike South Africa, Israel is a small state, relatively bereft of natural resources and mineral wealth, that cannot stand alone.

"It's a disgusting and unfair comparison," said a senior Foreign Ministry official, "and there is more than a little anti-Semitism behind it. It's made by people who sit behind their desks in London and Washington smiling at our distress."

To help dispel the analogy, Israel last year cut back on longstanding close commercial and diplomatic ties with South Africa. More recently, the Foreign Ministry issued a confidential guidance paper to its embassies and consulates abroad outlining what it sees as the main differences between the two countries.

To assess the similarities and differences between South Africa and Israel is to step into a mine field of politics, history and emotion. "South Africa is a state of mind," said Israeli social scientist Meron Benvenisti, suggesting that the facts do not matter as much as the feeling that the two countries are becoming more alike.

Nonetheless, the question lingers, and it has become a topic of increasing controversy here. Among those drawn into the debate are government officials, academics and journalists—including this reporter, who between 1983 and 1986 was The Washington Post's southern Africa correspondent.

Both nations came of age in 1948, when Israel gained its independence as a Jewish state and South Africa saw the triumph of Afrikaner nationalism in a watershed parliamentary election. But there, most Israelis argue, the similarities of history abruptly end.

While Jews were building a democratic state based on Zionist principles, the Afrikaners were constructing a system of white domination known as apartheid. It was a complete ideology, a total system that attempted to justify white-minority rule on economic, political, religious and even moral grounds.

South Africa's blacks were disenfranchised, confined to bleak rural homelands or overcrowded townships and ultimately denied citizenship in the land of their birth. Meanwhile, Israel's Arab minority had parliamentary representation and full civil rights, at least on paper. Arabic is an official language of the parliament, alongside Hebrew.

Then came June 1967 and Israel's triumph in the Six Day War, when it fought for its very existence after Syria, Iraq, Jordan and Saudi Arabia moved forces toward its border and Egypt sent thousands of troops into the Sinai. To maintain a crucial margin of security against future invasions, Israel occupied the West Bank and Gaza Strip with its 1.2 million Arab residents. It was to be temporary. But 20 years have passed, and Egypt is the only Arab country to have made peace with Israel. The occupation remained, and its Palestinian subjects have only the limited rights that military rule bestows.

The result, critics say, bears more than a surface resemblance to South Africa. Both governments operate under sweeping security regulations that give them broad powers against opponents far beyond those generally accepted in western democracies. Both nations maintain elaborate security police forces and networks of informers. Allegations of torture, secret files and other trappings of a police state can be found in both states despite the fact that they both boast a tradition of an independent judiciary.

"The lesson is that when one people controls another people, regardless of the reasons—and our reasons are very different from those of the South Africans—you end up doing the same things," said Dan Sagir, a journalist for the newspaper Haaretz who was based in South Africa until he was expelled by the Pretoria government in 1986.

Israelis argue that the reasons for the occupation—the continuing state of war between Israel and the Arabs, the ongoing threat to Israel's survival—explain and justify their actions in the occupied areas in ways that apartheid cannot be justified. South African blacks do not seek to destroy the state, the Israelis contend, but to become equal partners in it, and they have shown no desire to drive whites into the sea.

Palestinians, by contrast, do not want to become part of Israel but rather seek their own state, one that Israelis believe threatens Israel's existence and certainly its Jewish character.

But white Afrikaners argue that their survival, too, is under threat. Black rule, they contend, could destroy the country's economic system and mean the end of democracy for the whites who presently enjoy it. They say it also could mean cultural suicide for Afrikaners who fear that once they lose political control, they would forfeit control over institutions such as schools, churches and businesses.

Ultimately, for Afrikaners as well as Jews, it is their ethnic identity and their homeland that they believe is at stake. Neither will talk to his enemy—Pretoria refuses to negotiate with the African National Congress, Jerusalem shuns the Palestine Liberation Organization.

Both employ the peoples they rule over as pools of cheap labor to do their most menial tasks. In Israel's case, Palestinian workers comprise only 6 percent of its work force, whereas South Africa's entire economy is built upon the prevalence and use of black labor.

But as Jerusalem Post reporter Hirsh Goodman, himself a South African émigré, points out, the squalid black townships of South Africa were built by the white government to serve as reservoirs of cheap labor, whereas the equally squalid refugee camps of Gaza were constructed by Egypt and other Arab states unwilling to absorb the Palestinians who poured out of Israel in 1948.

Perhaps most important, Palestinians say they experience under occupation the same sense of powerlessness and humiliation that black South Africans must live with. "Any young soldier at a checkpoint from Ramallah to Jerusalem can order me to stop and humiliate me in front of my family," says Ibrahim Karaeen, owner of the Palestine Press Service, the pronationalist news agency based in East Jerusalem.

Now the unrest has created new similarities. As in South Africa, a new generation of disenfranchised Palestinians, believing that they lack any other means to express grievances and fulfill aspirations, disaffected with their old leaders, has taken to the streets in mass protest with a vehemence that has surprised their rulers and even their parents.

Tear gas has the same effect whether it is fired in Soweto or Gaza. But statistics suggest that Israel has a long way to go to catch up to South Africa in the ferocity of either the violence or the suppression of it.

According to the South African Institute of Race Relations, more than 2,300 persons died in South Africa in violence between September 1984 and February 1987—although many of these were blacks killed by other blacks. During one three-month period between March and June 1986, blacks were being killed at the rate of more than six per day. By contrast, the official death toll here is 38 Palestinians over a 45-day period—fewer than one per day. Given the discrepancies in population, the death rates are not dissimilar, but the critical difference is that South Africa sustained a high rate for more than two years.

Pretoria detained nearly 12,000 people in 1985 and as many as 30,000 in 1986, according to figures from the government and the Detainees' Parents Support Committee. The committee says about 32,000 of the two-year total were arrested under emergency regulations and could be held without charge or trial for as long as the emergency continued.

By contrast, about 2,000 Palestinians have been arrested in the past 45 days, and most have either been released or tried and sentenced by military courts. Critics have mocked the trials as summary and unfair—but at least the sentences that they hand out are of fixed duration.

There is also the contrast between the armies of the two nations. Both had trouble responding in early days to the unrest, and both found that a hard response provoked violent reactions while a soft response was seen by activists as weakness. But analysts say South African police units appeared better trained and better equipped to deal with rioters than Israeli soldiers.

After the early violence, South African police seldom patrolled on foot, moving instead in armored personnel carriers. By contrast, Israeli soldiers patrolled on foot in small units, refusing to wear helmets and often lacking antiriot gear. The financially strapped Israeli Army had chosen not to purchase water cannon and other sophisticated equipment. When trapped, soldiers sometimes felt they had little choice but to open fire with live ammunition.

Both governments have pursued a hard line in response to the violence, and both are led by stolid nationalists in their 70s. But there the political similarities end.

South Africa has been ruled for 40 years by the National Party, which maintains a massive majority in Parliament and suffocates dissent. There are debates and dissenting views within the ruling party, but the face that it shows to the outside world has but one determined expression.

Israel's government, on the other hand, is an uneasy coalition between Prime Minister Shamir's Likud and the more dovish Labor Party of Foreign Minister Peres. The political atmosphere here is loud, impulsive, untidy, disruptive, full of dissonance and dissension—the tumultuous noise of a functional democracy, even critics concede.

Many here, such as Avineri and Benvenisti, fear for Israel's future. The violence, they say, is helping to solidify the Israeli right while causing turmoil in the Labor Party, whose ideology is much more fuzzy than that of the Likud. The end of the road could be the collapse of Labor and the triumph of the right similar to the collapse of the centrist Union Party in South Africa in the late 1940s and early 1950s.

At the same time, these academics contend, demographics are slowly but steadily leading to an Arab majority population in Israel proper and the territories combined. Israel ultimately will have to surrender the territories to maintain its Jewish character or else deny democracy to an Arab majority. The latter is seen as the "South Africa option."

It is a gloomy scenario and one not accepted by many here. They contend that Israel's essentially democratic character will assert itself and prevent an Israeli version of apartheid from gaining a foothold.

There was a time not long ago when Israeli officials greeted new arrivals from South Africa with a smile and noted that they had come from the one place that had more intractable problems than Israel itself faced.

But South Africa is a broad land with great wealth whose people share a birthright, though not a political vision. Israel has no such wealth to share among its fractious population and no clearcut solutions. And its officials are no longer smiling.

PALESTINIAN CHILDREN OF THE STONES

YOUNG ARABS HURL ROCKS FOR THRILL AND 'TO GET BACK OUR LAND'

SUNDAY, FEBRUARY 7, 1988

BY GLENN FRANKEL

DEHAISHE, Feb. 6—Theirs is a gray world of stone—stone fences, stone houses, stone gardens. The soil is hard and unforgiving, the sun bright and punishing. Vegetation is scarce. Stone is the most available resource, the easiest thing for children to see and touch. In a place where playthings are scarce, it is their toy.

Meet Mohammed, a 10-year-old with a runny nose and a smudged face, dressed in frayed blue jeans and a tattered blue sweater. In one of his pockets is a home-made slingshot—a small patch of leather inside a large rubber band—that he uses to shoot pebbles and marbles at cars and buses.

On his left shin is a perfectly round, bluish-red bruise he got Tuesday from an Israeli rubber bullet when soldiers fired at stone throwers in this refugee camp on the occupied West Bank. "It hurt a little bit but I didn't cry," he says proudly.

Then there is Farid, age 12. Every morning when he starts out for school he packs a few stones in his book bag. He likes to throw the stones at Israeli soldiers and at the Jewish vehicles passing near his home. It's fun, he says, and besides, "We hope that by throwing stones we will get back our rights and our land."

And there is Thaer, age 7, wearing plaid bedroom slippers with no socks, a brown sweater, a green scarf and a wide grin yesterday morning. His parents tell him not to throw stones but "I don't listen," he says. "I want to be like the rest of the kids." He says his heroes are Yasser Arafat—and Lenin.

These are the children of the stones, the youngest warriors in a wave of civil unrest that started more than eight weeks ago in the occupied West Bank and Gaza Strip. They live in the Dehaishe refugee camp, a bleak, overcrowded ghetto of perhaps 10,000 Palestinians whose concrete houses cling to the side of a rocky slope just south of Bethlehem in the West Bank.

Dehaishe is located to the east of the Jerusalem-Hebron road, a main highway that has become the newest battleground in the violence. Jewish settlers use this road to travel to their homes in places like Efrat and Kiryat Arba. The highway has become a shooting gallery, and their cars and buses are targets for stones, bottles and molotov cocktails. So are the soldiers assigned to protect them.

It is, increasingly, a children's war. Motorists and soldiers say they usually do not get a good look at the stone throwers who dart out from behind the shops that line the highway, fling their rocks and then dash back in retreat. But those that do often express surprise at the youth of their assailants.

Most Israelis who have seen these children from refugee camps believe the children throw stones for excitement, or because they are ordered to do so by their older brothers and sisters. "They are so young, I don't think they hate us," said an Army officer in Tulkarm, a refugee camp in the north. "It's just a game to them."

But like Farid, most of the dozen or so young stone throwers interviewed yesterday say they throw rocks not just for fun but because they believe they are harming their enemies. And even the youngest among them, such as six-year-old Said, knows who the enemy is. "It is the Jews," he says with a shy smile.

Dehaishe, like every refugee camp in this region, has its own bitter history. Most of the residents came here in 1948, fleeing from 39 villages around the central Israeli towns of Lod and Ramle and from Jerusalem. Some were expelled by Israeli forces during the 1948 independence war, while others left on their own because of fear or because their leaders ordered them out.

Dehaishe was supposed to be a temporary stopover on the way back to their homes and fields. Instead it has become a permanent address and, for many residents, a cage. The caged feeling is exacerbated by the 20-foot-high chain-link fence the Army has erected between the camp and the highway to block the stones, and by the barricades of concrete-filled oil drums and barbed wire that seal off all but one entrance to the road.

The children here are very young, but already they are well-versed in the abiding grievances of their people. Many have fathers, uncles or brothers who have been arrested and jailed by the Israelis.

As they grow up, they see scenes that fit the stories they hear, such as the razor wire blocking off the local youth center. The center was boarded up five years ago by the authorities, who claimed it was a planning ground for violent demonstrations. Some have been awakened after midnight by shouts and screams when soldiers entered the camp to make arrests. They have also seen settlers, infuriated by stone throwers, invade the camp grounds brandishing weapons and shooting out windows of houses, or seizing young suspects and hauling them to the nearby military headquarters.

"They have very strong feelings about what's going on," said an Arab child psychologist in the southern city of Hebron who asked not to be identified. "They see their brothers throw stones and they want to do it too.

"I have a niece who is 2½. When she sees soldiers, she runs away shouting, 'They want to shoot me.' She's developing the same characteristics and fears of her parents and her brothers."

And so, indoctrinated in their cause by both their families and their enemies, the children of Dehaishe have joined the war. "They have broken a lot of our glass, so we have to get our glass back," says Farid about the Israelis. "But we also want to injure them because they have injured us and killed our people."

The children say the best time for stone throwing is just before school, at around 8 a.m., when Jewish commuters head toward Jerusalem, or around dusk when the light fades and it is hard to catch a child in Dehaishe's maze of winding dirt roads. The best targets are the red-and-white Egged (pronounced Egg-ed) public buses, because they are big and have many windows. The best place is near the shops, where there is a long gap in the preventive fence.

Since he is 12, Farid is in the pivotal age group between the very young and the teen-agers. "Sometimes I lead the younger kids and sometimes I follow the older kids," he says.

Sometimes the young work for their older brothers, Mohammed says, piling up stones at strategic locations and bringing buckets of water to help ward off the effects of tear gas. The youngest also serve as scouts, standing watch on the low ground and scampering up the hill to warn their brothers when the soldiers arrive.

Like good quarterbacks, the children quickly learn to throw ahead of a speeding car so the stone arrives at the same time as the vehicle. They can distinguish between the dull sound of rubber bullets and the sharper report of live ammunition. They know there is only one unit of soldiers guarding the road after dark and they know where those soldiers are posted.

They collect spent cartridges and tear gas canisters as souvenirs, and have songs that celebrate the stones as their weapons.

Faced with this kind of enthusiasm, the soldiers have few tools to fight back. They can round up the youngsters and hold them temporarily, but the Army says it imprisons no one under 14. While slapping a curfew on a camp inhibits the adults, it appears to have little impact on the children.

Sometimes the soldiers get angry and some of the older children say they have been caught and slapped around.

Wael, 12, says he was on his way to his grandfather's house Thursday when soldiers grabbed him and beat him on the back and then broke his arm, now tightly wrapped in splints. His father, Zahail, a van driver, is deeply angry.

"After what happened to my kid, I'm ready to lead a demonstration myself," Zahail says. "They broke his arm for nothing. It's crazy for the Army to respond to little kids. The reaction is much worse than the action. The Army should just leave."

Mohammed says his parents do not approve of his stone-throwing and beat him once when they found out he had been involved. Other parents seem ambivalent and some seem wrapped to tightly in their own web of anger that they offer vocal or tacit approval even though they know their children risk physical injury.

Halima, a mother of six, listened to her 10-year-old son, Ghassam, describe his involvement in the stone-throwing. Asked if she approves, she replies, "We are afraid for our kids but all our people have to resist the occupation. Even if he's injured, we are used to it now. Of course we are affected, but other people's kids are killed. So we don't stop them."

And what about the occupants of the cars they hit, some of whom are children also? "Any mother is pained when a child is hurt because a child is not responsible," replies Halima. "It's the adults who should be blamed. We hurt the Jews and they hurt us. They are provoking us. They don't stop their soldiers, so we don't stop our kids."

Shmuel Ben Yishai is a Jewish settler from Kiryat Arba who started packing a gun and riding the highway with other vigilantes after the cars of his neighbors were smashed by stones. He has been inside Dehaishe many times in the past year and he hates the Arabs as much as they hate him. The young stone throwers do not surprise him.

"Maybe I'll teach my kids to throw stones at Arab cars," he says. "Look, this is a war. My kids are their enemy and their kids are my enemy. It's as simple as that."

ARAB UPRISING: DRAWING THE POPULATIONS INTO WAR

SUNDAY, MARCH 20, 1988

BY GLENN FRANKEL

BIREH, WEST BANK—The yellow Israeli bulldozer rumbled methodically through the backyard of Ahmed Abdul Aziz on a crisp spring morning last week. It buried his vegetable garden, then assaulted his grove of 25 almond, olive and mulberry trees, ripping each one out of the earth and shoving it aside while Aziz and his family looked on in gaping silence.

Four days earlier, someone had hidden in the grove, which lies next to the main highway 10 miles north of Jerusalem, and had thrown a gasoline bomb at a passing school bus filled with Jewish children. The children escaped unharmed, but the bus caught fire and burned spectacularly.

And now the Army was retaliating. The target was not the bomb thrower, however, but the land and those who live on it.

The Palestinian uprising in the occupied West Bank and Gaza Strip reached the age of 100 days this past week and at the same time it turned a corner. What began as a confrontation between stone-throwing teen-agers and young soldiers has now taken on an air of permanence, blossoming into a full-scale intercommunal struggle between Arab and Jew—"a war of populations," in the words of Israeli journalist Joel Greenberg.

"You may not be interested in war, but war is interested in you," wrote Leon Trotsky. He was referring to the vortex that war inevitably creates, sucking in whole communities and individuals who have thought of themselves as neutrals or noncombatants.

So it was with the uprising this past week. Arab policemen who had stood on the sidelines, still working for the Israeli administration but shunning political and security cases, were forced to resign after receiving a threatening directive from Palestinian activists.

Farmers and merchants who sell their produce and wares in the markets that dot the West Bank were cut off and sent home by an Army determined to raise the economic stakes of the challenge to Israeli rule. Families like the Azizes found themselves bewildered victims in a struggle they barely understood.

The two sides seem locked in a test of will that is both logical and chaotic at the same time. The Palestinians appear to be aiming at decimating the system that has administered the occupation for 21 years, while the Israelis are seeking to puncture the sense of euphoria and triumph that so far has marked the uprising for the Palestinians.

Each side appears determined to inflict the maximum pain on the other. Palestinians burn a school bus and so Israelis bulldoze trees. Arabs stone cars of Jewish settlers and so settlers vandalize Arab cars. Someone throws a molotov cocktail at a fuel tanker and so the Army cuts off gasoline supplies. Arab police resign and so the Army restricts travel, closes markets and cuts off international phone lines.

Defense Minister Yitzhak Rabin has compared this contest to the "war of attrition" that Israel fought with Egypt in artillery duels and air raids across the Suez Canal in the late 1960s. Each side is seeking to wear down the other, he told the Israeli Cabinet recently, adding, "I can assure you, the Army will not be the first to tire."

But the Palestinians do not sound tired either. "We have never felt so close, never felt this sense of identity or pride or this feeling of oneness," said Saeb Erakat, a West Bank political scientist. "What the Israelis are doing now will not bring us to surrender. Four months ago we were ignored by everyone, and now we have moved the world.

"We didn't plan or anticipate this uprising. But now people really feel that if we stop and look back, we'll be lost like Lot's wife. The only alternative is to go forward."

Erakat's family home is in Jericho, a sleepy West Bank town that illustrates just how wide the uprising has spread. Jericho is a farming and tourist center and traditionally a tranquil oasis where Arabs and Israelis both come for long lunches and languid afternoons under palm trees.

While the rest of the West Bank was burning, Jericho stayed calm. But three weeks ago someone threw a molotov cocktail at soldiers, someone stoned a tourist bus here and a few days later someone else killed an Arab policeman in a refugee camp on the outskirts of town.

The Army then swung into action, sealing off the area for several days and detaining several dozen alleged activists.

This past week, the Army's net spread much farther. The military governor decreed that shops and the central farmers' market would only be allowed to open in the afternoon—the time when the Palestine Liberation Organization decreed they should be closed during the partial commercial strike it has conducted throughout the territories. Soldiers patrolled the marketplace and stopped wholesalers' trucks coming to buy produce.

"They just want to tell us that they control the streets," said Munther Arekat, whose family grows vegetables and watermelons on a 200-acre spread east of town. "They want to break our spirit by making us lose money."

If so, that aspect of the ban is working. Crates of tomatoes that normally wholesale for up to $20 this time of year are now going for $3.50, says Arekat, because customers have all but vanished.

But the restrictions are politicizing the generally conservative farmers and turning them into smugglers. They sell directly from the fields, with one eye scanning the horizon for Army patrols, cutting deals with those wholesalers brave enough to run the risk of being stopped and arrested for having a vanload of produce.

The verdict is still out on whether the new crackdown will succeed, but some activists welcome it.

"Collective punishment at this time is good for us," Mubarak Awad, an advocate of nonviolent resistance to the occupation, told The Jerusalem Post. "The cut-off of electricity, phones, fuel and perhaps even water means Israel is doing the job of separation for us. Collective punishment strengthens us morally, spiritually and unites us. It is our water and our spirit."

The defense establishment, made cautious by the international alarm that arose when Rabin announced previous strategies, has kept public silence on the new economic sanctions. But Brig. Gen. Yaacov Orr, the military commander of Gaza, acknowledged the limits of the Army's strategy in an interview.

"The question we always ask ourselves is who is controlling the area," he said. "Most of the people, they don't love the situation, they don't love Israel. In fact, you can say they may hate us. But I think we are now in a new phase where people maybe are a little tired and they feel they can't achieve anything more with demonstrations."

Orr has been a professional soldier for 24 of his 42 years and he is a restrained, methodical commander. He believes he and his men have succeeded in limiting the war on the ground between soldiers and stone throwers, but expresses less confidence in the effectiveness of collective sanctions.

"We prefer that the economic steps be very pinpointed against those arrested or involved in any violence," he said. Otherwise, "it won't work. It might even hurt more."

The Army has 10 times as many troops in Gaza and the West Bank as it had before the uprising began in early December, according to Orr, who noted with pride that as of Wednesday, only one Gazan had been shot dead by soldiers since Jan. 15. Two others died from beatings in incidents still under Army investigation.

"I can say we have stopped violent demonstrations with aggressiveness and with force, but not with shooting," he says. "But the situation is not back to normal. It's far from it."

Indeed, on Friday, two days after Orr spoke, a new wave of riots hit Gaza. Soldiers opened fire, killing one man and wounding at least a dozen others.

Orr understands the limits of his firepower in Gaza, but sometimes he daydreams about how quickly he could suppress this revolt if he had the same tools that the Syrian government used in killing up to 20,000 rebels and bystanders in the city of Hama six years ago.

"There are very nice techniques," he said with a small smile. "You could bring a tank here and fire, and everything would be fine very quickly. But you can't do it."

Instead, Israel's high-tech Army is turning the clock back. Rather than concentrate on designing computerized weaponry for the electronic battlefield, researchers are developing fiberglass clubs to replace the wooden ones that splintered too quickly on the streets. A cannon that shoots gravel at demonstrators was unveiled two weeks ago.

And there is the bulldozer, another symbol of the Army's new look. Bulldozers lately have been used to seal off main roads in recalcitrant Arab villages and neighborhoods. One was involved in a notorious incident last month in which four Palestinians were briefly buried alive. And one came to the Aziz homestead in Bireh Thursday to take revenge for the bus firebombing.

For two hours it worked its way through the yard until finally it came to the last survivor, a slender tree clinging to the hillside beyond the reach of its steel jaw. Soldiers swung a noose of cable around the slim trunk and for 20 minutes the machine tugged and grunted, bending the tree but not breaking it.

Finally it snapped with a loud crack. Mission accomplished, the soldiers scrambled back up the hill to their jeeps, the bulldozer pulled away. Another small skirmish was over in a bitter, prolonged struggle.

NIGHTMARE ON THE WEST BANK

MISUNDERSTANDINGS, FEAR BLAMED IN CLASH THAT KILLED 3

THURSDAY, APRIL 14, 1988

BY GLENN FRANKEL

BEITA, WEST BANK—Perhaps the saddest part of the story, as each side tells it, is that no one set out to kill anyone. The young Jewish settlers were taking advantage of a warm spring morning for a holiday hike through hills and valleys they consider their birthright. The Arab villagers were tending their fields and, ultimately, defending land they consider theirs.

Yet when it was all over last Wednesday afternoon, two young Arab men and a 15-year-old Israeli girl lay dead, and another Israeli lay battered into unconsciousness.

Each side was confronted by its own worst nightmare that morning. For the Palestinians, it was a Jewish settler, a warm M16 in his hands, stalking into their village after killing one of their young men. For the Israelis, it was the sight of hundreds of angry Arabs, some throwing stones, others brandishing knives, gathering on rooftops and in the streets in a growing fury.

It was all "a misunderstanding," Gen. Dan Shomron, the Israeli Army's chief of staff, told reporters later.

The Israeli girl, Tirzah Porat, was the first Israeli civilian to be killed since the Palestinian uprising began more than four months ago. But what happened at Beita—and why—was not so much a watershed as an illustration of the fear, hatred and misunderstanding that are elemental forces in the conflict.

Despite its attempt to defuse the situation, the Army appears to have compounded the misunderstanding. Shomron and other officials first said Porat had been stoned to death by the villagers. They then withheld, until after her politically charged funeral, autopsy results indicating she had actually been shot in the head with the M16 of one of the settler guards.

The Army says it is still determining whether the bullet was fired by one of the guards accidentally or by a villager who seized the gun.

After the deaths, the Army sealed off Beita, rounded up all males between ages 15 and 60, demolished 14 houses and bulldozed seven acres of olive trees. Six of those allegedly involved have been ordered expelled.

The Army took these actions without trying or convicting anyone and, in the case of the house demolitions and the uprooting of the trees, allowing no time for legal appeal. Soldiers also shot and killed a 19-year-old man who they said ignored their orders to halt while fleeing the village.

In blowing up the houses, Army sappers caused visible, sometimes extensive, damage to at least a dozen nearby houses. And in one case, the Army concedes, it destroyed the house of a family who had helped the Jewish youngsters.

The men in that family, Hafez Bani Shamseh, 70, and three of his sons, sat on a neighbor's porch this week and discussed what had happened last Wednesday and why. In the distance they could see the collapsed rubble of their house, which they said had been in the family for nearly a century.

Some of them were angry, some resigned. "That's the way of the world," said Nizzam Bani Shamseh, 28, who works for a construction firm in Israel. "There's a war between Jews and Arabs and we were in the middle trying to help people."

The following account is taken from members of Hafez Bani Shamseh's family who said they witnessed the incident, from the Israeli teen-agers who appeared at a press conference in Jerusalem Sunday, and from military officials who insisted on anonymity.

There are a few facts not in dispute about that morning when 16 Israeli teen-agers, most from the nearby settlement of Elon Moreh, and two armed guards started a nature hike through the winding trails east of the village. They had stopped for a break in a dry river bed when youngsters from the area began throwing rocks at them. Some of the Arabs said they had heard that the settlers roughed up a young shepherd. The teen-agers denied this.

One of the Israeli guards was Romam Aldubi, 26, a religious militant who had been banned from the West Bank city of Nablus for six months last year by the Army for his involvement in several shooting incidents. The other, Menachem Ilan, 55, had been convicted in 1984 of destroying evidence and obstructing justice in connection with the killing of an 11-year-old Arab girl by another Elon Moreh settler.

According to Army investigators, the two escorts took only one magazine of bullets each for their automatic weapons and a walkie-talkie tuned only to an Elon Moreh frequency and unusable in the valley around Beita.

When the stones began to fly, Aldubi fired into the air, the Jewish teen-agers said. Then a young Arab man approached the group. Some of the Israelis contended that the man tried to grab Aldubi's M16. Arab witnesses said the man merely sought to persuade the group to leave the area quietly. In any case, Aldubi shot the man at close range, killing him.

Villagers came out to retrieve the victim and rushed him to a Nablus hospital. Hundreds of villagers arrived from nearby fields and from Beita, many wielding farm tools.

Some of the villagers contended that the settlers could have fled east or north. But the teen-agers said they were surrounded and compelled by the Arabs to walk to Beita.

Upper Beita is built on the side of a hill, its houses crammed together along narrow, winding pathways. It is easy to sense the claustrophobia both groups must have felt when the settlers arrived with the villagers in their wake, choking the streets and climbing atop roofs.

"People saw him [Aldubi] coming in with his gun," recalled Taysir Bani Shamseh, brother-in-law of the dead man. "He already had killed someone outside, and when we saw him coming we thought he was coming to kill us."

Rami Hoffman, 17, one of the Jewish teen-agers, said villagers were shouting, "Kill the Jews!" When they got near the village, he said, "the women and children began to come out, with axes, pruning hooks and metal tools. . . . They constantly tried to get to Romam and grab his gun. We saw their eyes on the rifle, and they were trying all the time to push in and get to it."

The villagers were divided about what to do, according to Azzam Bani Shamseh, 26. "Some people wanted to wave them through and get them out of the village, some people wanted to hit them. Some wanted to take them to the mosque so that the Army could come and arrest them."

The mob halted the teen-agers, who formed a tight ring around Aldubi, outside the Bani Shamseh house. Azzam Bani Shamseh said he pushed into the crowd and tried, with a few older residents, to escort the Jewish teen-agers out of the area. But meanwhile, he said, a car returned to the village with the dead man's body.

At that point, Azzam Bani Shamseh said, "the whole village became agitated." Rocks began flying again, people began closing in on the group. Someone grabbed one Israeli teen-ager and hit him, pulling the camera from around his neck and smashing it. The mother and sister of the dead man moved around behind Aldubi, investigators say, and smashed him on the head with rocks.

The Jewish settlers contend Aldubi fired only once in the air at this point. But Azzam Bani Shamseh said he saw Aldubi firing blindly and heard four or five shots. At least two Palestinians were hit, and one of them later died. Tirzah Porat also fell wounded, he said.

Other Arabs continued to batter Aldubi with rocks and sticks. Someone apparently threw an explosive device that scattered shrapnel around the area, wounding some of the teen-agers. Then most of the attackers fled. Two men took Aldubi's and Ilan's weapons, which were later smashed. Army investigators said they have no evidence that an Arab fired either gun.

When first interviewed after the incident, the Israeli teen-agers said they thought Porat had been killed by stones. But three days later, after long discussions with their parents and settlement leaders, some of the youngsters told a press conference that they had seen a masked Arab fire a Kalashnikov assault rifle from a roof.

The villagers said there was no Kalashnikov, and Army investigators said the bullet that killed Porat entered her head from below at close range and exited through the top of her skull, making it impossible that she was shot from a roof.

Rami Hoffman said he and other youngsters tried to revive Porat with mouth-to-mouth resuscitation. Azzam Bani Shamseh pushed on her chest to try to revive her heartbeat. Other members of his family brought water to some of the Israeli teen-agers to wash blood from wounds. Another family took three girls to their house and hid them.

"People were not after the kids," said Azzam Bani Shamseh. "People were after the guard. If they had wanted to they could have killed them all."

But when the Army came, Bani Shamseh, like hundreds of other young men, fled Beita. Some returned after helicopters dropped leaflets warning that they and those sheltering them would be punished.

Azzam Bani Shamseh came back Friday to find the army had already demolished his house. Hafez Bani Shamseh said he tried to explain to an Army captain that his sons had aided the youngsters, but, "he said I was lying."

Azzam was held for a day, tied up and blindfolded with dozens of other young men. His photo was shown to some of the Israeli teenagers, who identified him as one who had tried to help them. He was then released, and the military governor of Nablus apologized for the destruction of his house and promised compensation.

Shomron said the houses were destroyed and other punitive measures taken so that both Arabs and Israelis would see immediate results.

Azzam Bani Shamseh called the Army's action "a crime." But he and many villagers expressed no anger that soldiers have kept Beita sealed off. They fear the settlers more than the Army, they said. And when the Army leaves, many expect the settlers to return.

HIGH BACKING SEEN FOR ASSASSINATION

TOP ISRAELIS REPORTEDLY APPROVED SLAYING OF PLO AIDE WAZIR

THURSDAY, APRIL 21, 1988

BY GLENN FRANKEL

JERUSALEM, April 20—Khalil Wazir, number two leader of the Palestine Liberation Organization, was gunned down by an Israeli commando squad after the assassination was approved by Israel's policy-making inner cabinet, according to informed sources here.

Israel has lowered a curtain of official secrecy over the operation. But with information compiled from a Tunisian investigation and from Israeli sources, it is possible to assemble some of the key pieces in the secret story of how the raid was planned.

The operation was planned and carried out by a combined team from the Mossad spy agency, the Army, Navy and Air Force, but the actual assassination early Saturday morning in Tunis was carried out by a special Army commando unit known in Hebrew as the Sayeret Matkal, sources said. The name translates as "reconnaissance party of the general staff."

The raid was overseen by several senior military commanders in a specially equipped Boeing 707 who were in constant radio contact with the squad on the ground.

The 10-member inner cabinet discussed the assassination twice before approving it, once immediately after last month's terrorist bus hijacking in the Negev desert in which three Israeli civilians were killed and again last Wednesday. No formal vote was taken at the second session, but the only dissenting voice was that of Ezer Weizman, a former defense minister.

Foreign Minister Shimon Peres, who raised objections at the previous session, was silent at the Wednesday meeting, the sources said.

Education Minister Yitzhak Navon, who also had objected to the plan, was overseas and did not attend.

Despite the fact that Israel has not publicly acknowledged ordering and carrying out the killing, the assassination has caused widespread elation here and boosted morale both among the public and in the Army, which had been worn down and disheartened by several recent incidents and the grinding rigors of fighting the four-month-long Palestinian uprising in the occupied territories.

Israelis have pointed to the careful planning, efficiency and "humaneness" of the attack—the fact that only Wazir and three of his bodyguards were killed, while his wife and child were spared—as proof that when it comes to such operations, Israel is still the world leader.

But the early jubilation, shared by both the liberal left and far right, over the killing of a man branded as a senior Palestinian terrorist, has begun to fade. Some Israelis have warned that the assassination is an artificial quick fix that, on the eve of Israel's troubled 40th anniversary, illustrates the country's inability to find a political solution to the problem of coping with the Palestinians both within and outside its borders.

Such an operation, wrote Yoel Marcus, columnist for the Hebrew daily Haaretz, "is good for our egos, but doesn't deal with the serious problems facing our country." Israel, he warned, is reverting to "the same methods and tools that were appropriate 20, 30, 40 years ago. The Abu Jihad assassination is a symbol of what is happening to us."

At best, these critics contend, the assassination will be a serious short-term blow to the already fragile Middle East peace process. At worst, it could reignite the secret war in which dozens of Palestinian operatives, Israeli diplomats and innocent civilians were gunned down in the 1970s.

For several days, Israel's official silence, enforced by military censorship, was effective in concealing the government's role, even though the modus operandi clearly was Israeli. While the PLO, the Arab states and the Israeli public all knew who had committed the act, the official silence allowed Israel to dodge international condemnation.

But the silence has frayed. Weizman has spoken out against the operation, tacitly acknowledging Israel's role by noting that until last week, Israel for several years had adhered to an unwritten agreement not to attack PLO leaders. "The fact is that we have never done so—why now?" Weizman asked.

Asked by reporters whether Israel ordered the killing, Weizman replied, "Guess for yourselves."

Even Prime Minister Yitzhak Shamir, while condemning Weizman's comments, has not been able to restrain himself from broad hints. At a memorial ceremony for Israeli war dead last night, Shamir said, "Let's hope that our enemies will realize and understand that Israel knows how to wage war, and that all those who hurt us will be hurt manifold."

Shamir's only reported direct comment on the assassination came on Sunday when, Israeli radio said, he told Cabinet members at their weekly meeting, "I heard about it on the radio, just like you."

Security officials reportedly have discussed assassinating Wazir for many years, but the operation gained new impetus after the March 7 Negev bus attack, for which Wazir's Fatah military organization claimed responsibility.

The inner cabinet, made up of five senior ministers each from the rival Labor and Likud political blocs in the coalition government, first discussed the issue on the day after the bus hijacking. Security forces were given a yellow light to prepare an attack, sources said, but the final decision was postponed.

Last Wednesday's inner-cabinet discussion took only 30 minutes, sources said. Yossi Ben-Aharon and Yossi Beilin, the senior aides to Shamir and Peres respectively, were asked to leave the room. Weizman raised his objection while Peres reportedly remained silent. "Based on the previous discussion, it was understood he was not crazy about the idea," a source said of Peres.

Those who had originally opposed the plan—Weizman, Peres and Navon—are all members of the Labor Party, the more dovish half of Israel's shaky coalition. The other two Labor ministers in the inner cabinet, Defense Minister Yitzhak Rabin and Police Minister Haim Bar-Lev, both supported the assassination, according to sources. Shamir, in keeping with past practice on sensitive security matters, did not ask for a show of hands.

The mission had several objectives, sources contend. One was to punish the PLO for the bus attack and send a warning that no Palestinian leader—even the heavily guarded, security-conscious Wazir—was safe from retaliation. The other was to deflate the uprising, which had begun spontaneously last December but in which Israeli officials believed Wazir played a major coordinating role in recent months.

The Army was also in need of a boost to its morale and self-image after last November's hang-glider attack in which a lone Palestinian commando killed six Israeli soldiers and injured a dozen others before he was killed.

The Army's image suffered further damage in the March bus attack because the hijackers, after infiltrating into Israel, drove to the site in an Army sedan they seized from three army officers they ambushed. The officers, on their way to a track meet, were out of uniform and unarmed and fled. They were later severely disciplined.

Three of the Army's top commanders have experience with raids such as the one against Wazir. The chief of staff, Gen. Dan Shomron, led the raid on the Entebbe, Uganda, airport in 1976 that freed a hijacked jetliner. His deputy, Maj. Gen. Ehud Barak, led a 30-member commando squad that killed three major PLO leaders and dozens of Palestinian guerrillas in Beirut in 1973. The commander of that operation, Gen. Amnon Shahak, is now head of military intelligence.

Analysts say the assassination especially fits the strategic thinking of Barak, a commander who favors swift, limited strikes over grand-scale operations.

As in the Beirut raid, a three-man Arabic-speaking Mossad advance team entered Tunis using false Lebanese passports, reconnoitered the area and arranged for rental vehicles for use by the hit team. Some 30 to 40 commandos were ferried to an isolated seashore site in rubber dinghies launched from a missile boat manned by the Navy's seaborne commando force.

Some reports said the attackers were wearing uniforms of the Tunisian National Guard, although this could not be confirmed here.

While the raiders were approaching their target, a Boeing 707 equipped like an American airborne warning and control system aircraft, with sophisticated electronic gear, was flying over the Mediterranean just outside Tunisian air space. The plane was used not only to jam telephone communications around Wazir's home, as Tunisian investigators have charged, but also to monitor and coordinate the entire operation.

Senior military commanders were aboard the plane and a source whose account cannot be confirmed said among those present were Barak, Air Force Commander Avihu Bin-Nun and, possibly, Shahak. The operational commander on the ground has not been identified.

Tunisian officials said the Boeing used a civilian radio signal designated as 4X. According to an account in Haaretz today, that signal is used by Israeli military aircraft and indicates the plane was on Flight Path Blue 21, a route between Sicily and northern Tunisia that is under supervision of Italy's aviation authority, not Tunisia's. Thus the plane could have remained in the area without Tunisian knowledge.

A similar Boeing, painted over to look like a civilian El Al airliner, served as operations center during the Entebbe raid. Those aboard included one of Barak's predecessors, Maj. Gen. Yekutiel Adam, and the then-commander of the Air Force, Maj. Gen. Benny Peled.

The actual attack on Wazir's house took only minutes. The three guards were killed by silenced weapons and Wazir was mowed down when he emerged from his study with a pistol.

In the 1973 Beirut operation, a number of innocent bystanders were killed, including the wife of one of the targeted PLO officials, along with two Israeli commandos. This time, sources say, the only Israeli casualty was one wounded commando.

A senior military officer, who refused to confirm or deny the above account, nonetheless said the operation would boost Army morale. "Here's one of the top terrorist leaders and planners and he gets hit in his home thousands of miles from Israel," said the official. "That has to restore some of the deterrent factor that may have been lost after the hang-glider attack."

It has also restored the confidence of many Israelis. Israeli television last Saturday night carried part of an interview from Tunis with Wazir's teen-aged daughter, in which she described to foreign reporters the terrifying scene when she and her mother stepped out of their bedrooms to find her father lying in a pool of blood and armed strangers standing around his body.

Her mother turned her back and put her head against the wall, awaiting an executioner's bullet, the daughter recalled. But instead, she said, one of the men, speaking Arabic with a heavy Hebrew accent, told the girl, "Go tend to your mother." And with that the men left —and the assassination of Abu Jihad entered into Israeli legend.

ISRAEL TURNS TO DETENTIONS AS WEAPON AGAINST UPRISING

CRITICS SAY SYSTEM IS HARSH AND ARBITRARY

FRIDAY, MAY 13, 1988

BY GLENN FRANKEL

RAMALLAH, WEST BANK—It was just after midnight when a dozen Israeli soldiers and two plainclothesmen came for Walid Abdul Salaam.

"You are going on a long journey," Abdul Salaam said one of the agents told him, as they pulled him from the room where his wife and two children were sleeping. "Please hurry, you are the first."

He said he dressed quickly while they waited. Then they bound his hands behind his back, blindfolded him and guided him to a bus that served as a makeshift paddywagon. Throughout the night it rumbled through the occupied West Bank, plucking Palestinian activists from their beds.

Abdul Salaam, 32, spent the next 18 days as a prisoner in Israel's crowded, chaotic and, by Arab accounts, often brutal military prison system.

He was never charged with a crime, never tried, never even interrogated by the authorities—but he considered himself lucky. While he was granted an early release, hundreds of other Palestinians have remained imprisoned under regulations that allow the authorities to hold them for at least six months without charge or trial.

As the Israelis have sought to throttle the five-month-old Palestinian uprising, they have turned to a form of arrest that they call "administrative detention" as one of their prime weapons. Until December, Israel generally held about 50 Arabs under these regulations. Now Israeli officials say the number is at least 1,700, more than one-third of the total 5,000 Palestinians currently imprisoned for alleged involvement in the revolt.

To hold these new inmates, Israel has opened or converted five additional prison camps, including a massive facility in the Negev desert where prisoners say water supplies are short and conditions rugged. To make it easier to hold them, the Army has abolished the requirement that each case be subject to judicial review and has given senior military officers the power to order detentions. New restrictions have also been put on family visits.

The result, according to critics, including defense lawyers, human rights activists and diplomats, is an arbitrary and harsh system of secret justice that has few discernible rules or standards and that offers its victims no workable appeal.

"In the past the Israelis always had some standards," said a western diplomat who monitors the process. "They needed enough evidence to at least satisfy their own consciences. Now the standards have been swept away."

[In Washington, the State Department said on Thursday it opposed administrative detention. "Those detained should be accorded judicial due process," said spokeswoman Phyllis Oakley.]

Israeli officials contend that administrative detention has helped stem the uprising, in which at least 176 Palestinians and two Israeli Jews have been killed.

"I do not believe that one measure constitutes a magic formula," Defense Minister Yitzhak Rabin said on Israeli television last week. "No one measure alone will extinguish the violence . . . [but] administrative detentions have made it easier for us to arrest the inciting organizers in a wide sweep."

The net is a wide one. It encompasses activists, alleged instigators and a significant segment of the Palestinian elite. Sometimes, the Army in its roundups seems to be working off lists of names of those previously arrested or convicted of security crimes. At other times, the detentions and the reasons for them appear more arbitrary.

"They don't inform the family, they don't even inform the person himself," says Mona Rishmawi, a Palestinian lawyer.

Among those being held are doctors, lawyers, union leaders, university officials and students, including many student council chairmen. At least 20 journalists are in detention, including five of the nine officers of the Arab Journalists Association, according to a tally by western diplomats. Four of the five full-time field workers of Law in the Service of Man, the Ramallah-based legal rights organization that Rishmawi works for, are also on the list of prisoners.

These people comprise much of the local Palestinian leadership in the occupied territories, precisely the kind of people that Israeli officials, including Rabin, say they want to negotiate with over the future of the West Bank and Gaza. Ironically, they are being held under the same kind of regulations that the British used during the days of their rule of Palestine to detain such future Israeli leaders as Golda Meir, Moshe Dayan and Rabin.

One of the most prominent prisoners is Nabil Jabari, 42, who is chairman of the board of trustees of Hebron University, a British-trained dental surgeon in East Jerusalem and the head of a charitable society. He was called in to the Shin Bet internal security service's office in Hebron on March 10 and has been held ever since.

A senior military official said Jabari is in detention because he allegedly maintained "very close connections with senior Palestine Liberation Organization activists in the territories and abroad" and received "instructions" on how to advance the organization's aims. The PLO is outlawed in Israel and the occupied territories, which Israel captured in the 1967 Arab-Israeli war.

Jabari also is accused of distributing PLO money to elements involved in the uprising and helping organize public disturbances at the university, according to the official.

None of these charges has been made in court, and Jabari has not been officially notified of them. They are part of a secret file he and his lawyers are not allowed to examine. The reason, the senior Israeli official said, is that the file contains clues to the identity of confidential informers and agents that might place their lives in danger.

"If we know for sure that disclosing information in public will endanger someone's life, we have no alternative except to use administrative detention," said the official.

But friends and western diplomats described Jabari very differently from the portrait in the file. "It's like Alice in Wonderland," said a diplomat who knows Jabari well. "He is very realistic, very moderate, not a real leader or collaborator, and he kept the university open. The charges about him organizing disturbances are totally false."

Until last month, prisoners had to be brought before a military judge within 96 hours of their arrest, and an appeals board would automatically review the case within three months. Both those safeguards have been dropped, and only those who request an appeal get a review. Jabari's lawyer has filed an appeal, but there is such a backlog that it may take weeks or months to be heard.

In the meantime, Jabari and his family say they pay a human price. His American-born wife, Carol, and his three children are allowed a 30-minute visit every two weeks. Last Monday, Carol Jabari said, she and her children waited three hours outside Jeneid prison in Nablus for their turn to stand in a small room with 10 other families and speak to her husband standing on the other side of a wire-mesh barrier.

"My daughter Suzanne [age 8] broke down, she was devastated," said Carol Jabari. "My son Talal [age 10] is just filled with hate now. Well, that's understandable, isn't it?

"You can't just sit there and cry," she added. "You have to get on with it. You have to cope with your children, you have to cope with your life."

Last weekend, however, the family's plight grew worse. Nabil Jabari was transferred along with dozens of other prisoners from nearby Jeneid to remote Ketziot, the new Negev desert detention center southwest of Beersheba, near the Egyptian border. It houses about 2,300 prisoners, nearly half of them under administrative detention, and the number is expected to grow to at least 4,000.

Conditions there are grim, according to Abdul Salaam, who spent 11 days of his detention there, and according to Israeli journalists who were taken on an Army tour of the facility two weeks ago. Inmates live in canvas tents, water supplies are limited, toilet facilities are primitive. The climate is scorching hot in daytime and cold at night.

But even worse than the physical conditions, said Abdul Salaam, is the sense of isolation inmates feel at the facility, which they have nicknamed "Ansar III," after the prison camp the Israelis maintained until 1985 in southern Lebanon. No one has a name there but rather a number—Abdul Salaam's was 1,101—which they must call out four times daily during roll calls while they sit in long rows cross-legged with their hands behind their backs and their heads down.

Abdul Salaam said his 18th day was the hardest because he knew that, under Israeli law, if he were held any longer he would automatically become a six-month prisoner. But at nightfall, he recalled, an official came to his tent and told him he could leave.

He and four other released prisoners were driven to the crossroads outside the desert town of Arad, where they were put out and told to make their own way, he said. They walked for miles in the starry desert night before an Arab driver stopped and gave them a ride to Hebron.

Abdul Salaam makes his living composing songs that he sings while playing the oud, a traditional Arab stringed instrument similar to a lute. In recent months he has composed many songs about the Palestinian uprising—but none yet about his time in Ansar III. It was, he said, too wrenching to sing about.

"In that place you feel you are at the end of the world," he recalled, "and if they do anything to you, nobody knows and nobody's heard of you. In that situation I was really afraid."

GORBACHEV'S GRAND PLAN

Mikhail Gorbachev's recasting of the Soviet Union's social contract has received mixed reviews at home and abroad. Yet each day the revolutionary changes bring new surprises. Bill Keller checks the pulse of perestroika and glasnost.

This is one of those rare moments when an exceptional reporter fastens onto an exceptional story and does what no one else has really been able to do before; in this case, find his way through the barriers that have prevented direct access by Western reporters to Soviet life for nearly as long as the Soviet Union has existed.

Mr. Keller's extraordinary output in 1988, touching every facet of Soviet life from rock music to corruption in Uzbekistan, from ideology to the ethnic challenges erupting in Armenia and the Baltics, contains articles of the highest caliber. His achievement wasn't simply to cover two superpower summit meetings, a leader's seemingly perilous struggle with his own Communist Party, or the century's most destructive earthquake: topics of that magnitude came with the territory for all Moscow-based correspondents. It was the way Mr. Keller covered them and, even more, the way he kept pressing beyond the obvious big events to get close to the gritty underlying realities. Never facile, always down to earth, he seized the new opportunities that are suddenly—and still fitfully—available to foreign correspondents in the Soviet Union to engage his readers in the drama of Gorbachev's challenge to a backward and recalcitrant society.

If there was a zenith of this reporter's year, it was his coverage of the tragic aftermath of the earthquake. An experienced backpacker, Mr. Keller several times hitchhiked his way around a 160-mile circuit of the earthquake zone as he shuttled from Yerevan, the Armenian capital, to the flattened towns of Leninakan and Spitak. He wrote of local citizens "who have become experts in the logistics of sudden death," of the stench of death clinging to the clothes and hair of rescue workers. He wrote of hollow-eyed families imagining they heard the cries of trapped children, as they squatted by the ruins of their homes. Then, reaching beyond grisly detail, he wrote of the drama of a compulsively secretive society opening itself to the succor and view of outsiders.

The melding of telling detail to large themes was what Mr. Keller's readers had learned to expect. He was the first correspondent to get to know initimately the Soviet youth scene and the new environmental and other citizens action groups that were suddenly developing outside the party; the first correspondent to establish contact with returning veterans of the war in Afghanistan. He negotiated a survey of Muscovite opinion with a Moscow polling institute. And he traveled the country tirelessly—to Magnitogorsk, to report on conditions in the Soviet rustbelt; to Zagorsk, to explore budding entrepreneurship in the new co-ops; to Ilyichevsk, for an article that showed how Gorbachev's drive for profits and efficiency was being translated into layoffs and resistance; to Khiva, to trace the political and environmental exploitation of Soviet Central Asia; to Sumgait and Yerevan, the first Western reporter to report from the scene in Armenia after the communal strife there.

In all this coverage, there was a fascinating work in progress, Mr. Keller's portrait of Gorbachev himself as both a creature of the system and the fomenter of a "revolution from the top." After the party conference, he wrote of the Gorbachev who "was on display as a master of political balance, a man of overpowering self-confidence and sometimes chilling arrogance." After the Politburo was reshuffled, Mr. Keller underscored the paradox of a leader who accumulates personal power but still lacks "real political power, the support of constituencies who understand what he has set out to do." Would the leader's commitment to openness survive the frustration of his modernization schemes? No one posed that central question more clearly or weighed the evidence more sensitively.

—The Editors
The New York Times

IN THE GANTLET OF DEMOCRACY, A SOVIET EDITOR TAKES KNOCKS

SATURDAY, JUNE 18, 1988

BY BILL KELLER

MOSCOW, June 17—When local newspapers announced the names of Moscow delegates to the coming national Communist Party conference, many residents of the Kirov district were distressed to learn that one of the Communists representing them would be Anatoly S. Ivanov, a conservative editor.

The other day they told him so, in a cathartic two-hour hectoring at the Znamya factory club that left the portly Mr. Ivanov mopping his brow and, perhaps, puzzling over this strange new contact sport they call democracy.

'TORTURING THE MAN'

"Comrades, you are just torturing the man," a woman in the fifth row finally implored in Mr. Ivanov's behalf, as the public interrogated its delegate on his views of politics and literature, prices and permissiveness, party secrecy and especially, relentlessly, the specter of history.

Citizens' meetings have traditionally been one of the soporific duties of membership in Soviet society. Under glasnost, and especially with the approach of a party conference dedicated to the general proposition of greater democracy, they have become a chance to exercise new-found vocal cords.

ON THE SPOT

But few of the 5,000 delegates to the conference this month have been quite so put upon as Mr. Ivanov, a man vilified by the perestroika vanguard as a remnant of the disreputable past.

He is the chief editor of Molodaya Gvardiya (Young Guard), a Communist Youth League monthly that, against the grain of glasnost, still appeals to the popular nostalgia for patriotic verities.

"Molodaya Gvardiya is an anti-perestroika magazine," declared Otto R. Latsis, deputy editor of the authoritative party magazine Kommunist. Mr. Latsis is also a conference delegate and a prominent partisan of perestroika, as Mikhail S. Gorbachev calls his campaign to remake Soviet society.

Ogonyok, the adventuresome weekly magazine, asserted that Mr. Ivanov had been foisted on the residents of the Kirov district in a secretive and anti-democratic cabal, a charge the audience was fully prepared to believe.

Mr. Ivanov responded that much the same could be said of Ogonyok's editor, Vitaly A. Korotich, who is a delegate from a city in the Ukraine where he no longer lives.

However he was chosen, Mr. Ivanov speaks for a significant category of Soviet citizens—he might call them the silenced majority—who are offended at seeing their history so mercilessly raked over by an aggressive press.

That, Mr. Ivanov said from the stage of the factory club Wednesday afternoon, would be his message to the party conference.

"I am not against change," the delegate said. "I am against the blackening of our history. I am the enemy of all these distortions."

"You said that you are against the blackening of our history!" a middle-aged woman shouted a bit later. "But maybe the fact is that our history is really black?"

"No, dear friends, if it was really black we would not have accomplished the great things—collectivization, industrialization. There were many good, beautiful things in our history."

"So, concretely, what do you mean by the blackening of history?" someone else pressed.

"When somebody says we built the wrong kind of socialism, or that we paid too high a price to build socialism and that we have nothing to be proud of, how can they say such things?"

"But Stalin killed millions of people!" came an angry cry from the balcony. "Millions were killed!"

"Correct," Mr. Ivanov conceded. "But we don't praise Stalin for killing millions of people. The party has condemned his mistakes and crimes. At the same time, I think that this man was not just a one-sided figure, as people write so often these days."

Sometimes the questions were passed to the stage on slips of paper, sometimes yelled out from the crowd of about 150, most of whom appeared to be workers from nearby factories and offices, but some of whom evidently came from the editorial staffs of rival magazines to beleaguer Molodaya Gvardiya's chief.

What about the xenophobic Russian nationalist group Pamyat, whose views sometimes find their way into his magazine, Mr. Ivanov was asked. (In the past it showed unhealthy anti-Semitic tendencies, he explained, but "Now it is being cleaned of extremist leaders.")

As a member of the national legislature representing Tashkent, in Soviet Uzbekistan, could Mr. Ivanov claim he knew nothing about the vast official corruption in Uzbekistan that is now being exposed in the Soviet press? (That was before his time.)

Why is a 59-year-old man editing a youth magazine, anyway? ("I am near retirement. Don't worry.")

Mr. Ivanov was challenged hard for his role in one of the unforgiven literary scandals of the Brezhnev years, the purge of the pioneering editor Aleksandr Tvardovsky. In 1969 Mr. Ivanov signed a famous public letter condemning the liberal works published in Mr. Tvardovsky's journal, Novy Mir.

"We did not decide the fate of Novy Mir," Mr. Ivanov retorted defensively. "We wrote about the tendency to replace our ideological values with lies."

On economic issues, Mr. Ivanov was scornful of the views of the market-oriented economists who advise Mr. Gorbachev. The proliferation of free enterprise, he said, has "opened the hatches" for shameless money-grubbing. Private businesses should have their prices controlled, he said.

Afterward Mr. Ivanov mingled with a few residents, then turned his back brusquely on an American reporter and escaped from the griddle of democracy in his black Volga sedan.

Konstantin Ivanov, a 63-year-old worker from a nearby auto repair shop, shook his head in awe at the spectacle he had witnessed.

"You know," he said with a broad grin, "after such a meeting in the Stalin period, half of them would have gone. . . . " He whistled in the direction of Siberia.

SOVIET CHANGE VS. THE WORKER'S SECURITY

TUESDAY, MAY 10, 1988

BY BILL KELLER

ILYICHEVSK, U.S.S.R.—Mikhail S. Gorbachev's new economic reality visited this Black Sea port city last year, passing like an unexpected tremor through the rock-stable lives of longshoremen, crane operators, mechanics and clerks.

Early in the year port executives informed the workers that, in keeping with the new drive for profit and efficiency, 634 of them would be laid off or retrained for different jobs, or pushed into retirement.

Anxious rumbles swept through this city not far from Odessa. So this was the bright future Mr. Gorbachev called perestroika, or restructuring. No vodka, no meat, and now, no jobs.

"It was so unexpected," said Mikhail Matiyets, a truck driver, who took a pay cut. "It was a shock, really."

Serafima Gorozhankina, a technical librarian who found her library organized out of existence, said: "Everybody was afraid. Nobody knew who would be on the list."

The port personnel director, Pyotr G. Sibalo, recounting the anxieties of a work force raised to think of the employer as a lenient parent, said, "In some cases I was close to tears myself."

But in the end, what many feared would be a painful upheaval was almost an anticlimax. For this was a Soviet-style layoff, in which cold-blooded economic sense gave way to the realities of a longstanding social contract.

EVERYONE GOT ANOTHER JOB

Everyone displaced was offered another job, with no loss of benefits. The few workers who complained about their new places were given jobs more to their liking. Yulian Serebrisky, offended at losing his job as a mechanic, sued in the local court to get his place back, and won.

The workers who stayed in their old jobs were given new promises of job security.

Profit took a back seat to labor peace: for every ruble the port saved by the cutbacks, it spent four rubles on generous pay raises designed to keep the work force contented.

Mr. Gorbachev's economists tell him that he if is to lift this backward country to a modern standard of living and make it competitive in the world, the Soviet Union will have to begin loosening the safety net of cheap prices, job guarantees and cradle-to-grave entitlements that stifle initiative.

In principle, Mr. Gorbachev agrees. He argues that people should be rewarded for their work and for their initiative, not for simply showing up—and that society should not coddle those who refuse to pull their weight.

But the ruthlessness of the marketplace violates the sense of justice and equality reinforced by 70 years of Soviet rule.

Perhaps more than any of the obstacles looming before Mr. Gorbachev—the intractable bureaucracy, the degraded state of technology, the legions of managers who have never been taught to manage, the legacy of corruption, the entrenched interests of those who have privileges and cling to them—it is this social contract that presents the most serious challenge.

The Soviet people expect, as a matter of basic right, something most economists believe is impossible: that perestroika should bring them a better life without risk, without discomfort.

The Soviet economy is run along the lines of an Appalachian coal company town. The company—in this case the state—is the source from which all material blessings flow. That is critical to understanding why ordinary citizens find Mr. Gorbachev's program so disturbing.

In Ilyichevsk, a city thrown up haphazardly around a new cargo port in the 1950's, the company is the Ministry of the Merchant Marine Fleet, known as Morflot. Those who do not work for the port itself work for something related—the maritime technical school, the ship repair yard, the electronics plant built to provide jobs for port wives.

Because of the imported goods the sailors bring in, and because of the gentle Black Sea climate, life is somewhat better than in other places. It is immeasurably better than the grinding poverty of most of the nation's villages, where it is still common to find housing—and even hospitals—without hot water. But the average American would find little to envy in the living standards of Ilyichevsk's 70,000 residents.

ALL THINGS FLOW FROM STATE: IN GOOD TIME, OF COURSE

As in much of the country, newcomers must wait 10 to 15 years for a separate apartment. In the meantime they live in shabby hostels where single workers double up and share communal kitchens and showers, and a family of five occupies a 10-by-15 room.

Meat and fruit are scarce, except in the unregulated farmers' markets, where a chicken or a slab of stewing beef costs several times the official price, and where a precious lemon sells for up to $5 in late spring.

Perestroika has done little so far to brighten the life of consumers. The latest national economic report, for the first quarter of 1988, is a litany of shortages: meat, dairy products, shoes, clothing—even that bulwark of the Soviet diet, potatoes.

Ilyichevsk has one of the new cooperative cafes that have sprung up under recent laws permitting private enterprise, and there are several more in nearby Odessa, but "you know what the prices are in those places," said Lyudmila Matiyets, a warehouse clerk, who has enough trouble keeping two growing daughters in clothes.

But if life in Ilyichevsk is not luxurious, it is at least heavily subsidized and relatively secure, assuring most residents a basic level of comfort with little regard for an individual's talent or effort. The necessities of life are provided as perks accumulated on the job.

Serafima Gorozhankina, who has worked at the port for 25 of her 53 years, recited the benefits that have accrued to her and her husband, a seaman, as a result of this system.

Their apartment, two cozy rooms in the port complex, takes only 27 rubles of their monthly 350 rubles in combined income, including rent, all utilities, and a telephone. The apartment is small, but it is theirs for life unless they move away.

The couple's basic medical care in the port clinic is free, as are the nursery schools and kindergartens their son and daughter attended. They can ride to work on port buses—transportation throughout the country is heavily subsidized—and vacation in port-owned homes or on travel vouchers provided at discount prices by their trade union.

When Mrs. Gorozhankina needed a new refrigerator, she borrowed 300 rubles from the port, interest-free. When the state stores are empty of meat and fish, she can often buy a chicken or piece of fish through the port cafeteria, "not the fish I would like, but fish all the same." Soon she will have a garden plot to grow her own vegetables —another perk from the port.

"There are little things you are so accustomed to you don't even notice them," she said. For example, she subscribes to all her newspapers and magazines through the port, because that way she can pay on the installment plan.

The port plays an almost parental role in the life of its workers.

If Mrs. Gorozhankina, who has traveled to Bulgaria and Rumania, wants to go abroad again, it is the Communist Party committee at her workplace that certifies she is trustworthy to be let out of the country.

"If they agree that I have no reprimands, that I don't drink and that I am a good mother, then I can go," she said.

"You see why we were so concerned" when word of the layoffs spread last year, Mrs. Gorozhankina added, as she poured cups of strong tea for visitors. "We receive practically everything from the port."

PAVLOV REVISITED: MONEY FOR WORK, NOT FOR BLUE EYES

In such a system, more money is not necessarily the key to a dramatically higher standard of living. It cannot usually buy a better apartment—only patience or privilege can bring better housing.

It cannot buy a car, because there are not enough cars to go around. The Government newspaper Izvestia reported last year that if the shortage of cars were suddenly eliminated, a million people in the Russian republic alone would turn up at sales outlets ready to pay cash. The right to buy a car, like housing, is bestowed on workers as a reward for patience or a senior position.

Money is, to be sure, an essential lubricant in the Soviet system of bribery and "blat," or pull. A hospital patient expects to pay the nurse a few rubles for an extra blanket, and someone languishing on an apartment waiting list may advance his position with a well-placed gift.

But for most workers, what counts is not so much a higher paycheck as staying put and hanging on.

This is the boat Mr. Gorbachev has started to rock.

Mr. Gorbachev's strategy is to reduce the subsidies and perks, while giving people more money and more good things to spend it on. In time, he hopes, people will begin to understand the connection between harder work and a better quality of life.

One approach is to reorganize the pay system in each workplace so the eager worker is not limited by arbitrary wage norms set by a ministry in Moscow and the lazy worker pays a price.

Some workers clearly relish the new opportunity, but many are wary.

As Stanislav S. Mikhailyuk, the Ilyichevsk port director, says, they are still accustomed to the old system, by which "we paid people, to a certain extent, for their blue eyes."

"The hardest thing of all is to make changes in the head," he said, "to teach people that there is a difference between receiving money and earning it."

When Soviet officials talk of tampering with this system of entitlements, they risk the charge that they are straying from basic socialist doctrine. In Soviet parlance, the phrase "human rights" does not mean freedom of speech or emigration; it means guarantees of housing, job security, medical care and so forth.

During a meeting with port officials, Boris Kondratsky, a young official of the local county executive committee, raised an obvious question: how can a worker really learn the value of a ruble when most of his necessities are seen as gifts bestowed by the state?

"True, to a certain extent it spoils people," the port director replied. "But it's also one of our advantages," allowing the port to hold on to good workers.

But suppose, Mr. Kondratsky suggested, that the worker got more cash in his pocket, and he had to pay the real value of his housing, his medical care, his children's kindergarten?

"Then it would be not socialism, but capitalism," the director replied without hesitation.

The reluctance to take on greater risk and responsibility is compounded by a wide-spread suspicion, reinforced by decades of unfulfilled promises, that things will not really get better after they get worse.

Perhaps when Mr. Gorbachev talks of the illogic of price controls —where bread is so cheap, he says, you sometimes see children using a loaf as a football—people get his point. But when he vows that ending subsidies will be painless, because everyone will get compensatory pay increases, they are skeptical. They already see prices creeping up as a result of a partial deregulation of farming.

Mr. Gorbachev's initial calls last year for "radical price reform" caused a panicky public reaction, hoarding and anxious letters to the press, so the Soviet leader agreed that state controls on consumer prices would not be lifted before 1990, despite the advice of his economists that price controls hamper other aspects of his economic program.

SPECTER OF UNEMPLOYMENT: IT'S NOT NICE TO BE A PARASITE

Nothing frightens Soviet workers quite so much as the sepecter of unemployment, and not just because it means being cut off from a reliable source of material benefits. This is, after all, a country where the best-selling newspaper is called "work," where a job is not only guaranteed by law but required, where someone without work is officially a "parasite."

Soviet officials insist that unemployment of any significant scale is not an immediate danger in the Soviet Union.

The country has a chronic manpower shortage exaggerated by the vicious cycle of the welfare state: workers have had little reason to exert themselves because they could not be dismissed, so that factories needed more workers to do the same job, so that even lazy workers became indispensable, encouraging them to perform badly.

Even if the average Soviet worker began to produce at Western levels, the country has many underutilized factories that could be run on two or three shifts, many working women who would be happier to stay home and tend their children, and a desperate need for people to provide basic services.

But repairing the economy will require dislocations. Soviet economists predict that 16 million people will have to be relocated or retrained by the year 2000, as the country tries to trim the fat from its factory work forces and create a service industry.

At Ilyichevsk, the layoffs last year entailed a six-month process of meetings, job placement, hand-holding and negotiations.

Port officials prepared the lists of which sections must be cut, and sent them to meetings of the "worker collectives" at each division of the port, where the workers themselves were told to choose who would go and who would stay.

THE UNEMPLOYMENT SHUFFLE: MUSICAL CHAIRS, SOVIET STYLE

For the most part, the layoff was carried out according to the rules of the social contract, keeping the people who needed the jobs, not those the company needed most.

"In our collective, first they took into account who has enough money, who is better off," recalled Fyodor Lobadrov, 63, who worked as a tallyman keeping track of cargo on the docks. "Second, those of pension age were asked to go. If a person had only a year or two until pension, of course he stayed. If someone had two or three children, he stayed. Or if a person could not learn another trade, he stayed."

A third of the tallymen had to be eliminated, so Mr. Lobadrov took a less demanding job supervising a boiler room.

Some workers say the cutbacks gave the remaining workers a new attitude toward their jobs, at least for now. The pay increases, workers say, had much less to do with this than the whiff of expendability.

"You can feel it," Mrs. Gorozhankina said. "People are more diligent in their jobs and they don't try to evade work. Maybe people are more afraid, afraid they will be fired if another cutback happens."

This disturbs Nikolai M. Grishin, the director's assistant, who feels people should be working better not out of fear but out of a sense that it will bring them a better life. At Ilyichevsk, he said, the jury is still out on this fundamental question.

"People are still thinking about whether it is advantageous to work harder," he conceded, adding, "When they develop a taste for money, perhaps that will be a decisive factor."

Since the layoffs at Ilyichevsk, employers have been given somewhat greater freedom, under new economic laws, to lay off unneeded workers. Job training and job placement centers are being upgraded, and laid-off workers are being encouraged to look for work in cooperatives or other private business ventures.

So far the new thinking has produced widespread anxiety, but little real change in the economic landscape.

In Moscow, for example, thousands of workers have been laid off as government ministries were abolished or merged in a shuffle intended to break the bureaucratic habits of an economy dictated from Moscow.

At the recently dismembered Ministry of Machine-Building for light and food industries and household appliances, which supervised the production of machines for food processing and other consumer industries, the corridors are dim and ghostly as the last workers clean out their desks.

Where have the 495 workers gone? How are they coping with the adjustment to less prestigious jobs, or to life away from the cultural and material attractions of Moscow?

"No one was forced to leave Moscow," said Anatoly M. Yershov, a Deputy Minister and chairman of the liquidation committee, in an interview at the office he will occupy for a few more weeks. "We cannot just tell a person he has to move. Nothing like that has happened."

In fact, most of the workers were simply, as one Moscow newspaper put it, "shifted from one armchair to another," shuffled to other Government offices, or to the administrations of Moscow industrial enterprises and research institutes previously overseen by the abolished ministry.

This attitude has slowed the growth of private business, which is a critical component of Mr. Gorbachev's economic strategy. Private business is supposed to quickly satisfy the public craving for better goods and services, while providing employment for many of the surplus workers in industry.

Private enterprise now employs some 400,000 people, according to the State Committee on Statistics, including those who moonlight doing repairs and driving taxis, and those who work in cooperative cafes, construction companies, beauty parlors and other businesses.

The new law has already spawned a small, energetic entrepreneurial class, mostly young people who have the appetite for Western-quality consumer goods and some exposure to Western ideas of commerce.

Here, too, economic change runs up against a prodigious sense of fair play.

In the Soviet Union, Horatio Alger would be called a "money-grubber," Donald J. Trump a "speculator." Americans believe the early bird gets the worm. Russians say the sunflower that grows tallest is the first to have its head lopped off.

Those who venture into private business recall from their history books the last great Soviet experiment of this kind, the so-called New Economic Policy that began in 1921, legalizing private trade. By the end of the decade, the private traders had been crushed, many of the "nepmen" arrested and put on trains for Siberia, often with the enthusiastic support of a public who despised them even as they patronized their shops.

Today the Soviet leadership is beginning to portray NEP in a more favorable light, but the basic bias against the "money-grubber" remains, evident in letters to the press and the complaints and personal slights often directed at new entrepreneurs.

"Some people don't understand," said Konstantin Kadtsi, who converted a warehouse in Odessa into a cafe offering cherry dumplings and Western videos. "Some people are very cautious. Some people are unhappy about the higher prices. Some expect real magic. It's not part of our everyday life yet."

'WORKING LIKE A DOG' GIVES WAY TO OLD LETHARGY

"The most serious obstacle to the cooperative movement is not bureaucratic, it is psychological," said Vladimir Y. Yakovlev, a 28-year-old former journalist, who runs Moscow's only consulting service for new entrepreneurs.

"A person starts working in a cooperative, and at first he works like a dog," Mr. Yakovlev said. "Because he's begun to make a lot of money, he works very hard—for the first two months. Then he gets used to the money, and automatically starts trying to work as little as he would in a state enterprise."

"The person is used to the idea that there's this enormous state, in which he is just a tiny cog, and the state pays for his every step, his trips, his health care and so on. And bankruptcy, or millions in profits—that's not his concern, that's the concern of the state."

A few blocks away from Mr. Kadtsi's cafe, Arkady and Tatyana Sakhnevich have found another niche in the new economic thinking. Under a contract with the state, the family operates a simple grocery store.

The store is unassuming, offering only a half dozen kinds of vegetables and a small fruit juice bar. But on closer inspection it is a step up from ordinary state stores.

The produce is picked clean of rotten leaves and scrubbed. Customers can pick out their own and weigh it on electronic scales to avoid cheating. The sales clerks smile and say good day, which is enough to draw double-takes in any Soviet enterprise. Prices are set daily according to quality and demand, and while they are a bit higher than state stores they are below the farmers' markets.

The Sakhneviches, a cheerful and industrious couple who employ much of their family in the shop, say customers are enthusiastic. And yet, many react as if this family venture had fallen to earth from another planet. They scratch their heads at the sight of the store director unloading trucks or clerks scrubbing the floor.

"Yes, there are some people who envy, who do not understand, who try to interfere," said 77-year-old Arkady Shvarts, a family friend who serves as a consultant to the store.

The family is convinced, however, that a proliferation of private ventures will bring down prices and win converts. A recent poll by Leningrad sociologists found that in Tallinn, the Estonian capital, which has one of the largest concentrations of cooperatives, popular approval is much higher than in Leningrad, where cooperatives are few. Younger people support them more than the older generation by a wide margin.

The people who have ventured into this alien world so far are hopeful. Mr. Shvarts, who lived through the New Economic Policy, says this time it will be different because customers are fed up with the old way of doing business.

He had heard all the talk about the intractability of the Soviet system, the pampered Russian worker, but when he runs up against a farm director who refuses to sell his vegetables to a small businessman, or hires a a 20-year-old worker who quits after a few days of washing potatoes because it smacks of real work, he thinks of the famed Russian circus trainer, Vladimir Durov.

"If Durov can teach bears to dance," he said with an impish laugh, "why can't we learn perestroika?"

IN STALIN'S CITY OF STEEL, CHANGE CONFRONTS INERTIA

TUESDAY, AUGUST 16, 1988

BY BILL KELLER

MAGNITOGORSK, U.S.S.R—Day and night, the smokestacks of the Magnitogorsk Metallurgical Kombinat heave their plumes of orange, black and white into the perpetually hazy sky.

This sight once inspired Soviet poets to pen heroic couplets about the city—"Eternal city! Iron city!"—built in the first fever of Stalin's industrialization campaign and still reckoned the world's largest steel producer in the days of Mikhail S. Gorbachev, the Soviet leader.

Today Stalin's city of steel is Mr. Gorbachev's heritage, a decrepit giant coughing its poisons into the air of the Ural Mountains and defying the economic good intentions of perestroika.

Here in the Russian rust belt, a visitor fresh from the heady political circus of Moscow finds a sobering dose of the realities Mr. Gorbachev is up against in his attempts to revive the torpid Soviet economy.

To be sure, Mr. Gorbachev's policies have meant startling changes for this working-class city of 430,000.

The city newspaper has grown bolder, writing about fatal accidents in the steel plant and about the local history of Stalin's terror, subjects that were untouchable not long ago.

There is a daring bit of nudity in the play about prostitutes on the stage of the Metalworkers' House of Culture, a surge of anti-Stalinism in the movie theaters.

People can now buy $2.80 pork kebabs or $650 custom-chiseled marble tombstones from independent vendors, a product of Mr. Gorbachev's move to open the way to private enterprise.

IN A BLEAK LANDSCAPE, STIRRINGS OF CHANGE

A more striking symptom of the Gorbachev revolution is an independent political group that gathers each Thursday night at the corner of Marx and Gagarin Streets to rally for cleaner air by way of cutbacks in production at the local steel mill.

The group is grudgingly tolerated by local officials.

But so far, the citizens of Magnitogorsk say they have seen more glasnost than perestroika, more openness than economic revival. Life is more interesting, but not more satisfying.

Meat, sausage, butter, sugar and vodka are rationed. Nearly a quarter of the city's population languishes on a waiting list to get into the monotonous concrete apartment blocks that line the outskirts of the city.

Worst of all, the steel mill itself, like much of the musclebound Soviet industrial economy, has become an albatross. The local iron ore is depleted, the technology outmoded, and the public increasingly alarmed by pollution and disease rates that, thanks to glasnost, are listed monthly in the newspaper.

"Pittsburgh 20 years ago," was the verdict of Robert Barry, deputy director of Voice of America, who grew up in Pittsburgh, when he visited Magnitogorsk for the opening of an American technology exhibit last month.

The city was flung up on an empty steppe in the 1930's, a crash project of Stalin's first five-year plan.

The site where the eastern slope of the Ural Mountains levels out, literally on the divide between Europe and Asia, was chosen because of a rich lode of iron ore—the Magnetic Mountain that gave the city its name—and because it was far from any threat of invasion.

INDUSTRIALIZATION ON THE GRAND SCALE

They built the plant big, in the prevailing spirit of gigantism that has only recently come into question. Today the plant's output of 16 million metric tons of steel a year is equal to the output of America's three largest steel mills.

John Scott, an American who worked as a welder on the project, recalled the primitive conditions of the city's birth in a book called "Behind the Urals."

"Money was spent like water, men froze, hungered and suffered, but the construction work went on with a disregard for individuals and mass heroism seldom parallelled in history," he wrote in late 1941.

But among the workers of Magnitogorsk the consoling memory of a time when things were much worse, the pride in shared sacrifice, is increasingly less vivid.

"It's been our place in history to build a new country, to build a new society, and we always worked without thinking of ourselves," said Valery N. Kucher, editor of the daily Magnitogorsk Worker. "But a time came when it was right to start thinking about ourselves."

Like many cities outside Moscow and Leningrad, Magnitogorsk issues monthly ration coupons for staples: 2.2 pounds of meat per person, 2.2 pounds of sausage, 6.6 pounds of sugar, 1.1 pounds of butter, and, since the vodka distillery was converted to a mayonnaise factory at the start of Mr. Gorbachev's anti-drinking campaign, one pint of vodka. Cheese is so scarce the authorities do not bother to ration it.

Residents resent the shortages, but they say that under the rationing system, at least the need is shared fairly.

Housing is a more bitter complaint. The wait for an apartment is typically 10 years, and city officials estimate that 100,000 people are on the list. At least half of them now live in communal housing with other families.

"Life here is no fountain," said Vladimir N. Lupachev, 27 years old, who graduated from the city metallurgical institute with an engineering degree but decided instead to seek his fortune selling tombstones.

He makes up to $1,280 a month, and his enterprise makes him a de facto part of the Gorbachev restoration. Only, he says, there is not much to spend it on.

The romance of the steel plant has also waned.

GIANT STEEL MILL: A TARNISHED SYMBOL

Before Rima Dyshalenkova, a feisty local poet, became disgusted by the pollution and moved 150 miles away to Chelyabinsk, she wrote of the noxious domain of coke ovens and blast furnaces as "our provider and destroyer." It is a common sentiment.

Someone in almost every family works at the plant, and virtually everything else in town exists to serve the factory and its work force.

The aging, open-hearth furnaces that made the steel for every second tank and every third shell sent to the front in World War II now produce steel of such low quality, one plant official says, that it is no longer suitable for the armaments industry. Most goes to make autos and agricultural machinery.

The plant is clearly inefficient, requiring 60,000 workers to turn out its 16 million tons. The most modern American steel mill, according to industry experts, produces 8 million tons with only 7,000 workers.

Industrial accidents killed 14 people last year, according to Tamara V. Popeta, the deputy chief doctor at the medical clinic serving the factory. The fatality rate is about double that in the American steel industry.

The plant's colorful, malodorous emissions are the first thing residents apologize for when meeting visitors.

THE DEADLY AIR: HIGH DISEASE RATES

The Magnitogorsk Worker periodically publishes a table of air quality statistics, and they are grim. This summer the air has contained nine times the legal maximum level of benzene and three to five times the legal maximum for sulphur compounds.

The rates of heart, lung and respiratory diseases are far above the national averages, especially among children—and the data are said to show things are getting worse, not better.

Local environmentalists say they have seen official data showing the life expectancy in Magnitogorsk is only 52 years, far below the national average of 69. Officials in Moscow declined to make their figures public.

At the steel plant, Polish and Soviet workers are now installing a modern electric converter to replace the open hearths that are still used in 60 percent of Soviet steel mills. A second converter is to be completed by 1995.

"By the year 2000, you won't see this smoke," said the mayor, Mikhail M. Lysenko, a blunt-spoken former steelworker, waving a hand at the fumes visible, and smellable, through his office window a mile from the plant.

But a group of American steel experts who toured the plant Aug. 2 were skeptical that Magnitogorsk's salvation is at hand.

Even with the new technology, the vast plant will still employ so many coke ovens and furnaces to make the raw pig-iron for the converters that, barring enormous investment in cleanup technology, the worst of the pollution will continue, the Americans said. And they questioned whether the plant would ever make economic sense.

Magnetic Mountain is almost wholly depleted and the plant now imports ore from Kazakhstan, 300 miles away.

"They're in a remote location, 1,200 miles from the sea," said Robert D. Pehlke, a professor of engineering at University of Michigan, who toured the plant last week. "So how are they going to be competitive? You have to wonder if this is economical."

The bookkeeping of a planned economy in which energy, raw materials and transportation are heavily subsidized, makes it virtually impossible to answer that question.

The new political group, Forward Movement of Perestroika, argues for cutting steel production by 25 percent, closing the least efficient and worst polluting ovens, and slowing the pace of work to improve quality. It contends that this can be done without layoffs.

The local newspaper, initially sympathetic, has lately disparaged the group as impractical and demagogic. A cut in steel production, the newspaper scoffs, will lead to social disruptions still unthinkable in this society.

OBSTACLE TO CHANGE: BUREAUCRACY'S NEEDS

Any notion of cutting output also will run up against the Ministry of Ferrous Metals, which, despite a pretense of decentralization, still runs the plant through state steel contracts amounting to 98 percent of its business.

The Soviet Procurator-General, Aleksandr Y. Sukharev, who is responsible for enforcing environmental laws, complained in an interview in the weekly tabloid Nedelya that even his own attempts to shut down offensive coke ovens in polluted cities have met the ministry's fierce resistance.

"There is no way out," said Viktor M. Svistunov, a plant official. "This is a planned system, and we've got to provide other enterprises with raw material."

One hears approximately the same sense of resignation, but with a more cynical edge, at a tavern across town from the factory, the kind of bar where workers order pints of murky beer four at a time and down them quickly.

"We had some Japanese here," said Vadim, who works in the rolling mill at the plant. "We said, 'Tell us, how far behind are we?' They said, 'Forever. You're behind us forever.' "

Asked about Mr. Gorbachev's calls for more democracy and local autonomy, workers smirk and roll their eyes.

"Listen," confides Aleksandr, a driver. "You have a Mafia. We have a system of princes."

Passivity, bewilderment and pessimism about the economy abound.

Citizens interviewed in their homes and workplaces during a five-day visit were more likely to predict economic stupor than success for Mr. Gorbachev.

This attitude—perhaps as much a legacy of Stalin as the steel mill—annoys Mr. Kucher, the editor, who sees in it perestroika's real enemy.

"Everybody is still waiting," he said, "to get their orders."

ARMENIAN CAPITAL IS ROUSED BY CALLS FOR NEW FREEDOMS

POLITICAL RALLIES SPREAD NATIONALISTS WIDEN DEMANDS TO INCLUDE SOME SELF-RULE—STRIKES THREATENED

MONDAY, SEPTEMBER 5, 1988

BY BILL KELLER

YEREVAN, U.S.S.R., Sept. 4—Two nights ago, more than 100,000 Armenians, defying an official ban and a heavy police cordon, streamed into the square in front of this city's imposing stone opera house for a town meeting.

The vast crowd in the southern republic's capital was reminiscent of those in the heady days last February when Armenians began their campaign to claim the territory of Nagorno-Karabakh, ruled by Azerbaijan. But there are two important differences.

The placards displaying the face of Mikhail S. Gorbachev, the Soviet leader, and his slogans of change have disappeared, replaced by an outspoken disenchantment with the Kremlin chief.

A POLITICAL MOVEMENT

And the campaign for Nagorno-Karabakh has grown into something bigger. The movement began as a campaign for the return of the small region, an enclave with a mostly Armenian population that is surrounded and governed by Azerbaijan, yet claimed by both Soviet republics for cultural and historical reasons. But the campaign has become a broad and ambitious political movement that appears to be headed for a direct confrontation with the Communist Party.

Recent developments in Armenia have gone unreported in the Soviet press, which now portrays Yerevan as a city back to normal.

But a visit by this correspondent to the Armenian capital, the first since officials lifted a six-month ban on travel here by Western reporters, tells another story.

It is true that the general strikes that periodically paralyzed Yerevan earlier this year have ended, but no one seems to doubt that they will return. The uniformed troops that once patrolled the city, sometimes carying automatic rifles and truncheons, are not in sight, but there is evidence that those same soldiers now walk the streets disguised in police uniforms.

And the mass demonstrations that first drew the world's attention to this region are now a weekly event, with a new sense of political purpose.

At the rally on Friday, the 11-member Karabakh Committee, a group of intellectuals recognized by many Armenians as their de facto leaders, read the detailed manifesto of the new Armenian National Movement. The committee described the group's plan to press its demands through electoral politics, backed by the threat of civil disobedience.

"We are very serious about this," said Galstyan Ambartsum, an ethnographer and a member of the Karabakh Committee, in an interview today at an outdoor cafe. "They gave us a little bit of liberalization, but we are now well beyond that."

DEMANDS AND TENSIONS

The beginning of a national movement resembles the people's fronts that have been organized recently in the Baltic republics to promote greater economic, political and cultural independence. Many of the goals of the Armenian group are similar, including a measure of Armenian economic sovereignty, and priority for the Armenian language in schools and in public affairs.

But in Armenia, the relationship between the new movement and the officials of the Communist Party has been tense.

At the Opera Square on Friday, a member of the Karabakh Committee demanded that the second-ranking party official in the republic, a Russian, be dismissed because of insensitivity to Armenians.

In turn, committee members have been attacked in the local press as extremists.

POLICE OR SOLDIERS?

The authorities have not broken up the mass demonstrations that take place each Friday night, but the latest gathering was reportedly surrounded by thousands of men in police uniforms.

Karabakh Committee members said the police onlookers were in fact Russian soldiers wearing militia uniforms. The troops were reportedly called in because the local authorities did not trust the native police force to take action.

That assertion appeared to have substance. Near the Dinamo Sports Hall, busloads of non-Armenian men in police outfits came and went today from a camp guarded by uniformed army personnel.

The goals laid out in the new Armenian manifesto stopped short of the call for complete Armenian independence advocated by some student firebrands, but the goals are enough to cause concern in the Kremlin.

The Armenians insist on veto power over all federal projects built in the republic, a demand intended to stop a new chemical plant and a nuclear power station.

FLAG AND LANGUAGE

Other demands include the freedom to fly the flag used during Armenia's brief independence, from 1918 until 1920, when the Armenian Republic came under Soviet rule; the right to open consulates in countries with large Armenian populations, and the creation of an Armenian army detachment so that young men from the republic can perform their military service on home soil, using their own language.

Unification of Armenia with Nagorno-Karabakh, rejected by the Soviet Government in July, is still regarded as an overriding goal. Karabakh Committee members said they have gathered more than 400,000 signatures on a petition demanding that the Armenian Legislature defy Moscow by unilaterally declaring the disputed territory part of Armenia.

The Legislature is scheduled to meet in October, and committee members say they may call a general strike to dramatize their demand.

"We plan to do everything according to the Soviet Constitution," said Babken Ararktyan, a member of the Karabakh Committee and the head of the mathematics department at the University of Yerevan. "Our Constitution says nothing that prohibits strikes."

'TAKE UP OUR ISSUES'

The committee has also begun organizing for next year's legislative elections, which Moscow has promised will, for the first time, be open to a wide range of competing candidates.

"If we can elect even a few dozen deputies out of the 340 in the Armenian Legislature, that will be enough to force authorities to take up our issues," Mr. Ararktyan said.

Judging from interviews in Yerevan and in nearby Echmiadzin, the seat of the Armenian Orthodox Church, the committee has broad public support and respect, not only among intellectuals and students but among ordinary working families and even Communist Party members.

SOURING ON GORBACHEV

The committee's weekly town meetings draw 100,000 to 200,000 of Yerevan's 1.4 million residents, participants say.

Armenians say that while Mr. Gorbachev's promises of greater democracy and openness originally gave heart to their efforts, the public turned sharply against the Soviet leader after two events in July.

One event was a clash between Soviet troops and Armenian strikers at Yerevan's Zvartnots Airport. A 22-year-old Armenian was killed during the chaos, and dozens of people were injured. This was followed on July 18 by Moscow's decision to leave Nagorno-Karabakh under Azerbaijani jurisdiction.

On Opera Square, where a few hundred people assemble each evening to debate current events, the mention of the Soviet leader's name sets off a hostile murmur.

'A SCORPION'

"He's a scorpion," said one young man Saturday night.

"Gorbachev killed our trust," shouted an older man at the same meeting.

Other Armenians are somewhat more sympathetic to Mr. Gorbachev, pointing out that he feared an uprising in Azerbaijan if he yielded to the Armenian demands, and that conservatives in the Kremlin might seize on any concession as a sign of weakness.

But the sense of disappointment is deep and freely expressed.

"Glasnost, perestroika, since July 5 we don't use those words," said Mr. Ambartsum. "After all that's happened, those words are discredited here."

GORBACHEV'S GRAND PLAN: IS IT REAL OR A PIPE DREAM?

MONDAY, DECEMBER 5, 1988

BY BILL KELLER

When Mikhail S. Gorbachev first visited the United States one year ago this week, the biggest question in most Western minds was whether he was the reformer he claimed to be, or simply a totalitarian with style.

As the Soviet leader prepares for his second trip to America, Western curiosity and skepticism seem to have shifted from his intentions to his prospects: not "Does he mean it?" but "Can he pull it off?"

Mr. Gorbachev is scheduled to arrive tomorrow in New York, bearing, one Soviet official promised today, "very interesting new ideas" to be disclosed on Wednesday in a speech at the United Nations and a lunch with President Reagan and President-elect Bush.

'WEIMAR RUSSIA'

In this astonishingly eventful year of Kremlin intrigues, nationalist eruptions and economic discontents, Westerners and Soviet citizens alike—and probably Mr. Gorbachev himself—have come to grasp better the magnitude of what the Soviet leader is up to, and what he is up against.

Only half in jest, Stephen Sestanovich, director of Soviet Studies at the Center for Strategic and International Studies in Washington, calls Mr. Gorbachev's perilous situation "Weimar Russia," alluding to the period of political moderation and economic crisis in Germany that gave way to the Third Reich.

The joke would evoke dark laughter in the parlors of Moscow intellectuals. For many of Mr. Gorbachev's admirers, euophoria has given way to pessimism.

And yet this has also been a year in which Mr. Gorbachev's program has begun, in small but unmistakable ways, to take hold where it matters most, in the thinking and behavior of ordinary Soviet people.

Few imagine that Mr. Gorbachev's revolution-from-the-top is now widely popular, let alone irreversible. But Soviet citizens seem increasingly convinced that the genie is not going back in the bottle.

Mr. Gorbachev's aim is to preserve his country's status as a major power by stopping its steady economic decline relative to the West.

The problem, as he has recognized from early on, is only partly the cruel, corrupt and inefficient system he inherited from Josef Stalin and Leonid I. Brezhnev.

It also lies in a popular psychology that has changed little since the czars ruled peasant Russia. It is a conservative mentality, accustomed to complying with strong central authority, egalitarian in the extreme, deeply respectful of tradition and intolerant of rival opinions.

The Western concept of citizenship, with its respect for individual rights and responsibilities, never took root in Russia.

To these instincts, seven decades of Soviet power have added a strong streak of cynicism and apathy.

SWITCHING TO FAST FORWARD

Mr. Gorbachev, therefore, is trying to fast-forward Russia through the Renaissance and the Enlightenment, and build a political culture that prizes initiative, individual responsibility and law over forced discipline and mindless equality.

The past year has made it dramatically clear that the Soviet leader faces dangerous opposition on both flanks.

The conservative resistance includes comfortable bureaucrats loath to give up their power and privileges. It includes the more active opposition of dogmatic Marxists in the party apparatus, who would prefer to modernize the economy without the discomforts of a more aggressive press or greater democracy. And it includes a public fearful of change, as demonstrated by the open resentment directed at the new class of private entrepreneurs, and by the apparent revival of brooding, xenophobic Russian nationalism.

GORBACHEV COUNTEROFFENSIVE

Mr. Gorbachev now acknowledges that he underestimated the strength of these conservative forces. This year he mounted a strong counteroffensive. He purged or weakened conservative rivals in the

Kremlin, sending holdovers from the Brezhnev era into retirement and isolating his putative chief rival, Yegor K. Ligachev, in the thankless job of running agriculture.

He has given the press even greater license to rake up the sins of Stalin and Brezhnev, and opened the debate on the future of socialism to longtime outcasts such as the human rights advocate Andrei D. Sakharov and the dissident historian Roy Medvedev.

He has grown steadily more radical in his prescriptions for the economy, embracing more private farming, worker ownership of industry, and greater integration with the outside world.

He has pushed through a far-reaching redesign of the political system aimed, he says, at shifting greater power to elected legislators and independent courts and rendering the course of change "irreversible."

All of this has demonstrated Mr. Gorbachev's nimbleness as a politician, his toughness, and his capacity for compromise. But in consolidating his own position, he has also reminded his supporters how much the drama of change in the Soviet Union depends on this one compelling but mortal figure.

It may be that Mr. Gorbachev cannot decentralize power until he controls it, but his steady accumulation of authority has somehow left him appearing both lonely and imperial.

DANGER OF IMPATIENCE

Armenia and Estonia have taught the world this year that conservative resistance is just one of Mr. Gorbachev's worries. Impatience is another immediate peril.

Mr. Gorbachev's liberalization has set loose bitter grievances that have simmered since Stalin's time in many of the 14 non-Russian republics.

The hatred between neighboring Armenians and Azerbaijanis, focused on the disputed territory of Nagorno-Karabakh, has left dozens dead in both republics and forced the Soviet leader to put the region under military supervision.

Yearnings for independence in the Baltic republics of Lithuania, Latvia and Estonia have given birth to huge, popular movements that seem to be seriously competing with the Communist Party for political control.

The Soviet leader has failed so far to find any unifying ideology—a new patriotism or Soviet pride—to counteract the divisive stresses of many nationalisms.

And unless Mr. Gorbachev can satisfy public demands for a quick improvement in the standard of living, he faces the danger of similar uprisings from angry consumers and workers.

But the disorders in his domain are also signs that people have begun to take Mr. Gorbachev at his word—faster than he reckoned.

'A NEW WAY OF THINKING'

In Armenia and Azerbaijan, the result seems dangerously intractable, an explosive situation that Mr. Gorbachev's more authoritarian critics can cite to prove the dangers of liberty.

But in the Baltic region, Mr. Gorbachev seems convinced that compromise and restraint will prevail over impatience and anti-Russian feeling. If he is right, the potential reward is a Baltic economic success that becomes an example for other regions of the country.

"This is not disorder," a prominent Soviet editor said recently, discussing the bold popular demands for greater autonomy in the Baltic republics of Lithuania, Latvia and Estonia. "It is a new way of thinking about order."

Ed A. Hewett, an economist at the Brookings Institution in Washington, often tells Soviet colleagues that more turmoil in the economy would be cause for celebration, not alarm. Mr. Hewett says he will believe economic change is serious when he sees bankruptcies and strikes, the natural upheavals of an economy adjusting to reality.

The same is true in the political realm. Democracy is messy. How much of it the system—or Mr. Gorbachev himself—is willing to tolerate is still unknown, but it has already tolerated more than anyone thought possible a year ago.

Mr. Gorbachev's supporters can already point to other hopeful portents for the survival of perestroika, or restructuring.

A LOWER LEVEL OF FEAR

Perhaps most striking is the general reduction in the level of fear, as ordinary citizens begin to say in the press and on the streets what they once said only around their kitchen tables. Even though Mr. Gorbachev has not yet delivered on his promise of new laws to safeguard individual rights of expression, people have begun to accept those rights as their own.

Another sign is the birth of genuine interest groups to defend the promised changes. These include not only the popular fronts in Baltic and other republics, but associations of private entrepreneurs organized to protect their new niche in the Soviet economy.

There are also fitful flickers of faith in the system, startling in a population that has grown so cynical about such official institutions as the courts, the legislature and elections.

Proposals for new laws and constitutional amendments now provoke the kind of heated debate that suggests the public believes the outcome makes a difference.

Dissenters who once might have turned to the underground press now turn to the long discredited court system.

A few months ago, Boris Kagarlitsky, an organizer of a small independent leftist group in Moscow, sued the official newspaper Komsomolskaya Pravda for maligning his name, and—to his own amazement—won. This fall a lawyer from the Ukraine went to court to defend the name of Stalin, and lost.

EAGER WESTERN BUSINESSES

In Armenia, a nationalist campaigner entered a special election to the republic's legislature and won, defeating the Armenian Minister of Internal Affairs. The Communist Party voided the election, but accepted the outcome when the challenger won a rematch.

Even the rubber-stamp national legislature, the Supreme Soviet, has seen its first dissenting votes in decades.

In recent months, even as Western Kremlinologists have been calculating Mr. Gorbachev's political life expectancy, bankers and businesses in Western Europe have slowly begun to gamble on Mr. Gorbachev, with loans and joint business ventures.

When Chancellor Helmut Kohl of West Germany and President François Mitterrand of France visited last month, their jets were packed with eager businessmen, searching out ventures in the Soviet Union.

This is a small vote of confidence, and one that could help Mr. Gorbachev deliver some satisfaction for his consumers.

If success is defined as catching up with the West, few, even among

Mr. Gorbachev's admirers, can quite imagine it. The leap across a chasm of psychology is so vast.

If success is defined more generously, as continuing at some pace on the path toward a more normal Soviet Union, then the question—Can he pull it off?—is still very much an open one.

FROM SOVIET QUAKE, ECHOES WIDEN

SUNDAY, DECEMBER 18, 1988

BY BILL KELLER

SPITAK, U.S.S.R., Dec. 16—Last Tuesday rescue leaders from a half dozen countries convened in the green army tent that is now Spitak's Communist Party headquarters for a tense diplomatic faceoff in the middle of the most staggering misery any of them had ever seen.

The Soviets announced that after six days of pulling Armenian children from collapsed kindergarten buildings and picking half-alive victims from flattened nine-story apartment blocks, it was time to give up, shoo away the grief-stricken survivors and level what little remained of the city.

British, French, Austrian, Italian and other Western relief workers objected. Reports were still coming in that faint cries for help were audible in the debris. They made clear that if the bulldozers came in too soon, what had been an unparalleled exercise in East-West emergency cooperation could become an international embarrassment for Moscow.

"I thought at one time they were trying to use the rescue teams to say that no one was left alive and they could go in to begin demolishing and clearing," said Norman F. Roundell, a London fire inspector who led the opposition. "We let them know in very strong terms that they were wrong."

The Soviets yielded and the gruesome dig went on until, on Thursday, the foreign contingent in Spitak met again and agreed that it was time to start packing up.

These days of death and diplomacy have exposed backwardness and inflexibility in the Soviet system that are certain to provoke months of official recriminations. But they have also seen a society long secretive about domestic tragedies and ashamed of soliciting foreign help, open itself to the world's pity—and defer to outside advice—as never before.

OFFICIAL TOLL IS STILL AT 55,000

As the emergency rescue effort gives way to evacuation, refugee relief, demolition and rebuilding, many participants in the rescue believe this painful time has also marked an important turning point in official Soviet attitudes to the outside world.

The spectacle in the earthquake zone is nauseating and numbing, both in the scale of the quake and in individual vignettes of loss. Each tortured city and village in the quake zone has its own special character of suffering. The official death toll is still put at 55,000, but many estimates are much higher.

Spitak, a regional center once known for its sugar factory and elevator plant, was barely recognizable as a city. In 200 seconds on Dec. 7, it was pounded flat by the three massive jolts of the quake.

The stench of thousands of corpses was so intense that some foreign workers smeared Vicks Vaporub on their chests to hide it. Reporters returned to their hotels in Yerevan, the Armenian capital, with the smell of death clinging to their clothes and hair.

Narband, a sheepherding village west of here, looked today as if it had been crisscrossed by a colossal plow. The grade school fell in a heap, killing 500 students and teachers, sparing only a group of eighth graders playing outside. The children in two kindergartens were also fatally engulfed in concrete and volcanic stone.

"In Narband, there are no children," said Gryant A. Mangasaryan, 57-year-old worker on a state livestock farm.

About half the population of 5,000 was believed dead, villagers said, and those who have not fled to relatives are camped in tents amid the ruins.

Mr. Mangasaryan took a visitor along a path through the ruins, past a litter of demolished houses, a gutted television set and campfires surrounded by shell-shocked survivors.

On Thursday, where his house once stood, he built from scrap a tiny dirtfloored shack where he and his wife can retreat from the freezing weather and grieve for their three daughters and the grandson who were found crushed to death.

"If they rebuild Narband, we will live here," Mr. Mangasaryan said. "If they build in another place, we will live there. We'll wait until they tell us."

AN ILLUSION OF LUCK: BRITTLE BUILDINGS STAND

Stepanavan, a city the same size as Spitak at the northern edge of the damage zone, presented an illusory picture of miraculous good luck. Most of the buildings remain standing; only one of 1,000 children was killed when the shock rattled the grade school. But the tremors left the surviving structures as brittle as eggshells.

"We will have to knock down 99 percent of the buildings," said Lieut. Col. Anatoly V. Khludnev, commander of an army unit that was initially sent to Stepanavan last month to enforce a state of emergency after clashes between ethnic Armenians and Azerbaijanis. "Even a mild earthquake now could bring these buildings down."

City residents sleep in tents or shepherds' yurts outside the hazardous buildings, awaiting evacuation. A contingent of West Germans was already demolishing buildings that threatened to tumble.

Leninakan, a city of more than 300,000 people, was an urban nightmare, with just enough tottering shells left standing to convey the outlines of a bustling city. There is an eerie, voyeuristic quality about buildings with walls sheered away, exposing living rooms and kitchens. Tonight, work crews with cranes and shovels picked over the debris by floodlight, ghostly figures wandered the streets and campfires flickered in the rubble.

"It's totally outside my experience," said Peter Wilson, a London fireman who was part of the last foreign rescue team still camped tonight at the Leninakan airport.

"As a fire professional, it's a very interesting technical problem," Mr. Wilson added, as his companions spooned up canned beans heated over a wood stove. "But as an individual, I wouldn't want to see anything like this again. It gives a very good impression, I suppose, of what the Second World War must have been like."

SEEMING WHIMSY TO PATH OF DESTRUCTION

Throughout this spectacular but hardscrabble wheat and cattle region of the Transcaucasus, the quake picked and chose with cruel whimsy.

Barns and pinkish stone houses in the village of Dzhamushlyu slumped to the ground, while a few miles down the road in Tsilkar farmers were peacefully pitching hay and doing farm chores, largely unscathed.

Especially in the first few days, rescue and relief efforts were plagued by confusion and inefficiency, according to relief workers and residents interviewed throughout the region.

Foreigners said they were frequently frustrated by a bureaucracy that still awaits orders from the top. A British rescue team had to go all the way to the commanding general to get clearance to use an army truck, and then had to negotiate for diesel fuel to run it.

Mr. Wilson, a divisional officer from the Kent Fire Brigade, said it took him a full day of arguing against strong resistance—evidently from the K.G.B.—before he was allowed to set up a satellite dish in Leninakan for direct communications with London.

Relief crews arrived at the Moscow airport, only to find that the authorities had no idea where to send them. It took several days to muster translators for the rescuers.

"Thousands of people came here of their free will, and sat for two or three days at the airport in Moscow," said a Latvian journalist who had spent days with an Italian team. Foreign doctors complained that Soviet physicians often refused to let them treat patients with the sophisticated medical equipment they had brought in.

SOLDIERS AT THE READY, BUT MOSTLY AS GUARDS

By chance, thousands of Soviet troops were already in the region to enforce a state of emergency imposed after ethnic conflicts that broke out last month, the latest outbursts in a 10-month territorial dispute with Azerbaijan. But as of midweek the military seemed to view its role as maintaining order rather than taking part directly in the rescue.

In the first two or three days, most of those pulled alive from the debris were rescued by local citizens using picks, shovels and bare hands. Later, the rescue was largely handed over to the more than 2,000 foreign specialists who came with training and equipment not available here.

Except for construction brigades sent to work on repairing rail and water lines, the soldiers in Spitak and Leninakan seemed to be doing little but controlling access to the damaged areas, chasing looters and standing around campfires.

Later, when the civilian bureaucracy proved inadequate and occasionally obstructive, the army also stepped in to organize the distribution of hot food, drugs and tents and to generally supervise the deployment of men and vehicles. But not until the end of the week was there any systematic distribution of food to the smaller villages.

The military is expected to play the major role in razing the cities. Hundreds of army tents and rows of earthmoving equipment have been deployed outsider Spitak and Leninakan.

OFFICIALS 'OVERWHELMED' BY SCOPE OF CALAMITY

Foreigners working here tended to be more forgiving than the Soviet press, which has railed against bureaucratic snags and ill-prepared local officials—though not against the military.

"I think the scale of it overwhelmed the local officials," said Mr. Roundell, the senior British aid representative sent to Armenia. "But this improved enormously as time went on."

Western rescuers said the recovery was severely hampered by the breadth of the quake. Unlike the 1985 quake that devastated parts of Mexico City, for example, the Armenian quake cut a wide swath, simultaneously crippling communications and transportation necessary to begin saving lives.

Railroads were twisted or blocked by upended boxcars, boulders tumbled into country roads and fractured roads tumbled into ravines. On the roads around Spitak, traffic was backed up for hours, a bottleneck of buses, ambulances, bulldozers and hay trucks.

Although the official death toll remains at 55,000, extensive travel through the zone of destruction lends credence to the view of many foreign specialists that it was perhaps three times that number. A French doctor this week estimated that 100,000 had died in Leninakan alone. In Spitak today, an Italian team that was packing to leave estimated that 30,000 had perished in this region of 50,000 people.

THE SOVIET OPENNESS REAPS A RICH REWARD

For the foreigners working in Armenia, the most impressive thing was that they were allowed in at all.

The Soviets have given free access to the foreign press and the monitors from foreign governments to make sure the aid was delivered.

On the day of the quake, while Mikhail S. Gorbachev was preparing to cut short a visit to New York and fly home, Foreign Minister Eduard A. Shevardnadze was asked repeatedly about Soviet interest in foreign aid, and he seemed slightly offended at the suggestion that the Soviet Union could not handle its own catastrophe.

But after initial hesitation, the Soviets embraced the contributions enthusiastically, including an estimated $6.6 million in Government and private aid from the United States and loads of medical equipment from Israel, with which Moscow has no relations.

"These people had to have been pretty shocked by what happened to allow this level of foreign assistance," said one senior Western diplomat. "Frankly I think they were overwhelmed by the generosity from Western countries. I don't think they expected to be treated this well by us."

The Soviet press has played up the Western donations as the greatest example of East-West comity since Soviet and American troops met at the Elbe River in 1945.

Nightly features on the television news and daily articles in the newspapers have doted on French, American, German and even Israeli contributions, often stressing the superior mobility and readiness of Western teams.

Julia Taft, director of the United States Office of Foreign Disaster Assistance, said Thursday after a tour of the quake zone, "It seems to reflect a change in official attitude."

Although foreign rescue workers were departing this weekend, there is a fresh influx of Western specialists to help with demolition and reconstruction, seismic studies and medical care.

AFTER CHERNOBYL, A 'TOTAL' DIFFERENCE

"It is a big transformation since Chernobyl," acknowledged Colonel Khludnev, the commander in Stepanavan, recalling the nuclear disaster two years ago. "After Chernobyl, they allowed foreigners to participate in the investigation of why it happened, but that was it. This time, we are asking for concrete help."

Although foreign rescuers found the Soviets overly impatient to end the search for individual survivors and begin erasing the mess, they were impressed that Soviet officials relented, mindful that they would be seen as insensitive, and perhaps swayed by the argument that prolonging the rescue work as long as possible would make it easier to deal with reluctant evacuees.

"It's not the number of lives you save, but the hope you give to the people that in fact you're making an effort to try to find their relatives," Ms. Taft said. "If you find that there is no hope for life after the people say 'Well, I think I heard voices,' and you tell the person that and you hug them and say you're sorry, they're so relieved because they can make the break."

Under the agreement reached at the end of the week, the Soviets are to forestall the wholesale bulldozing for a few more days, removing rubble systematically in hopes of uncovering survivors. The more time-consuming search with dogs, heat-seeking devices and sound detectors would be abandoned.

In the next few days, there is likely to be a separation of thousands of traumatized survivors from their cities and villages. Although many Armenians interviewed in the region said they did not want to go, foreign specialists agreed that this process is necessary.

"At some point you have to stop," Ms. Taft said. "At some point you have to say, 'These people are going to catch pneumonia if they stay out there.' The survivors then become the victims of the disaster because they have no place to go and no shelter."

Mr. Roundell, the British fire official, noted the emotional drain of unearthing dead bodies. "There's a limit," he said, "to how much more you can do before you crack up."

SEVEN

RESCUE ATTEMPT

1989 WINNER IN THE SPOT NEWS PHOTOGRAPHY CATEGORY

"For a distinguished example of spot news photography in black and white or color . . ."

St. Louis Post-Dispatch
Ron Olshwanger

A photographer has little time to think in the chaos of an emergency. When Ron Olshwanger arrived on the scene of a fire in St. Louis, his reactive instincts quickly took over.

I have long been interested in both photography and firefighting, but, reluctantly, I put aside my camera equipment after college to devote more time to family matters, business and volunteer work.

For 20 years, I was assistant chief of the Bi-State American Red Cross Disaster Service. My wife, Sally, our son, Steve, and I all volunteered many long hours for the Red Cross. But after I left the organization about five years ago, I grew restless and missed working with the fire departments in the St. Louis area. It was then that I revived my interest in photography. My wife bought me a good camera for a Christmas present, and I was soon regularly back at the fire scenes, but now I was practicing my hobby of photography.

At about seven in the morning on December 30, 1988, our son, Steve, a captain of the University City Fire Department, called me from his firehouse and told me the St. Louis Fire Department was responding to a five-alarm fire. I told him I would pick him up as he was getting off work, and we would get some photos of the fire.

We spent about 30 minutes at the fire scene, and as we were heading home, we picked up a one-alarm call on the fire radio scanner in my car. This fire was only two blocks away, so we were quickly on the scene.

On our arrival, I started to take shots of the firefighters in action. I saw a man standing in front of the building holding a cat in his arms. I assumed the animal had been rescued from the fire, and I turned to take a picture. As I focused my camera, I realized that it was just a bystander who was holding the cat. I then turned and aimed the camera at the front door of the apartment where four firefighters were about to enter the burning building. Suddenly, someone shouted and the four men backed away. Firefighter Adam Long ran down the stairs out of the building. He was carrying a small, limp child. Adam had thrown off his mask and helmet and was administering mouth-to-mouth resuscitation to the girl as he raced toward an ambulance. I focused on him as he moved and took a shot.

Long placed the girl, Patricia Pettus, in the ambulance beside her mother, who had also been badly burned before escaping from the building. (Another four-year-old daughter had already been taken to the hospital.) My son joined the ambulance crew on the ride to the hospital, and I returned to my car to put a new roll of film in my camera.

A photographer for the *St. Louis Post-Dispatch* approached and asked if I had gotten any good pictures. He had been at the five-alarm fire and missed this one. I told him I thought I had a couple of good shots but couldn't be sure until they were developed. He asked me to call him if I felt the photos turned out well.

I picked up my son at the hospital, took him home and then went to a photo studio. I waited an hour while the film was being developed, and when I saw what I had, I just stared at it for a long time. I took the picture home and showed it to my wife. She cried when she saw it.

I called the *Post-Dispatch* photographer, and when he saw the photo, he too was moved. He thanked me, said I would hear from the paper and left.

The photo appeared on the front page of the *Post-Dispatch* the next day, and our lives have not been the same since. Patricia died a few days later. My hope is that her death was not in vain. If just one person's life is saved because the photo inspired people to install smoke detectors in their homes or to make sure the detectors' batteries are working, then this photo will have done some good.

—Ron Olshwanger
St. Louis Post-Dispatch

1989 WINNER IN THE SPOT NEWS PHOTOGRAPHY CATEGORY

St. Louis firefighter Adam Long administering mouth-to-mouth resuscitation to Patricia Pettus as he carries her to an awaiting ambulance.

1989 WINNER IN THE FEATURE PHOTOGRAPHY CATEGORY

John Jerome, a junior, tries to scale a wall to give a note to junior Tina Curmi as sophomore Nancy Sutton looks on. Southwestern High School is a 72-year-old learning institution of brick and mortar in a rundown but historically rich community in Detroit.

Rebecca Yates joins other freshmen in the auditorium during the first day of classes. She later transferred. Last year, 129 freshmen transferred. Southwestern High School ranks third academically in the Detroit Public School system—a system in which 40 percent of incoming freshmen never make it to their senior year.

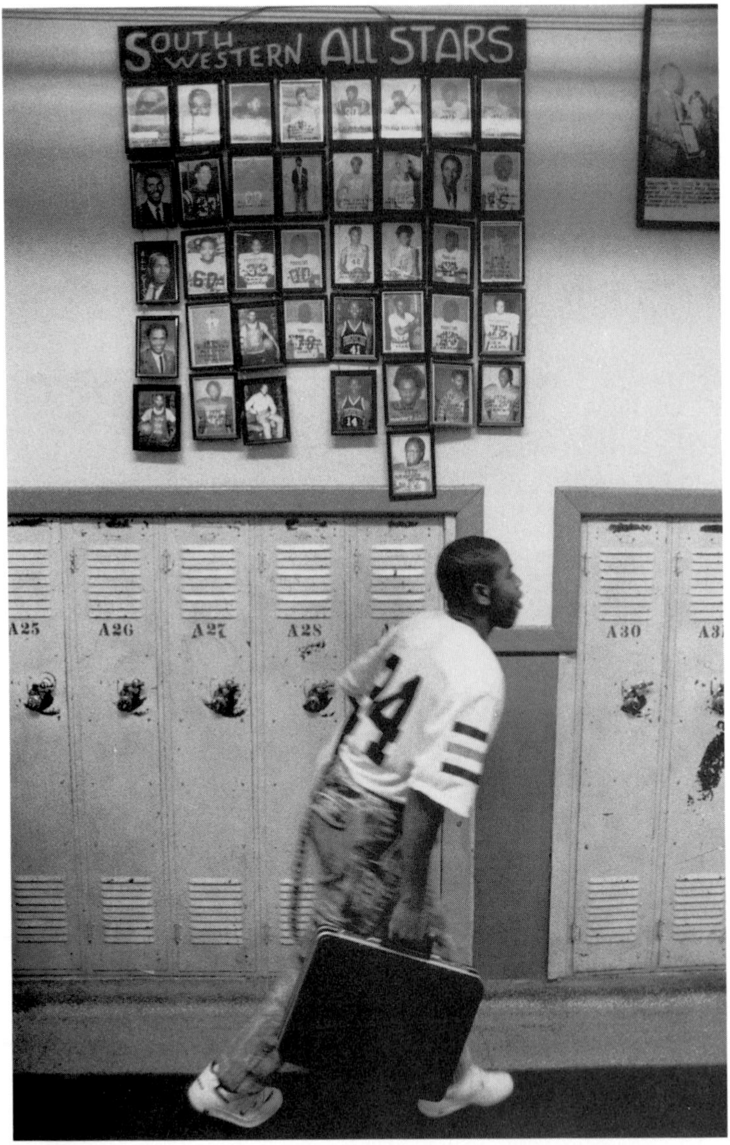

Briefcase in hand, football player Andray Garrett heads to class. The choice lockers are on the first floor near the office. Handwritten in marker on the wall above each set of lockers are "football," "basketball," "NHS" (National Honor Society) and "cheerleaders."

Tina Bussell watches for teachers or security guards while she and friends smoke in the girls' lavatory. The five-minute break between classes is enough time for one cigarette.

Students hold hands and sing "We Shall Overcome" during Black History Month celebrations in the school gym.

Early in the school year, freshman Romeo Pellrin cries after Dean of Students Earl Bryant suspended him for stealing a jacket. "I was just upset," he said months later. "The dean said he was going to kick me out for possession of a stolen item. I thought, 'Oh no, my dad is going to kill me.' But my dad was not so much mad as just disappointed."

A team of social workers counseled students about the trauma and guilt they felt over the suicide of a classmate who had been jeered at about the contents of her diary. Freshman Patricia Dalton, 13, shot herself at home several hours after pages of her diary were circulated throughout the school and she was taunted about sexual references in it.

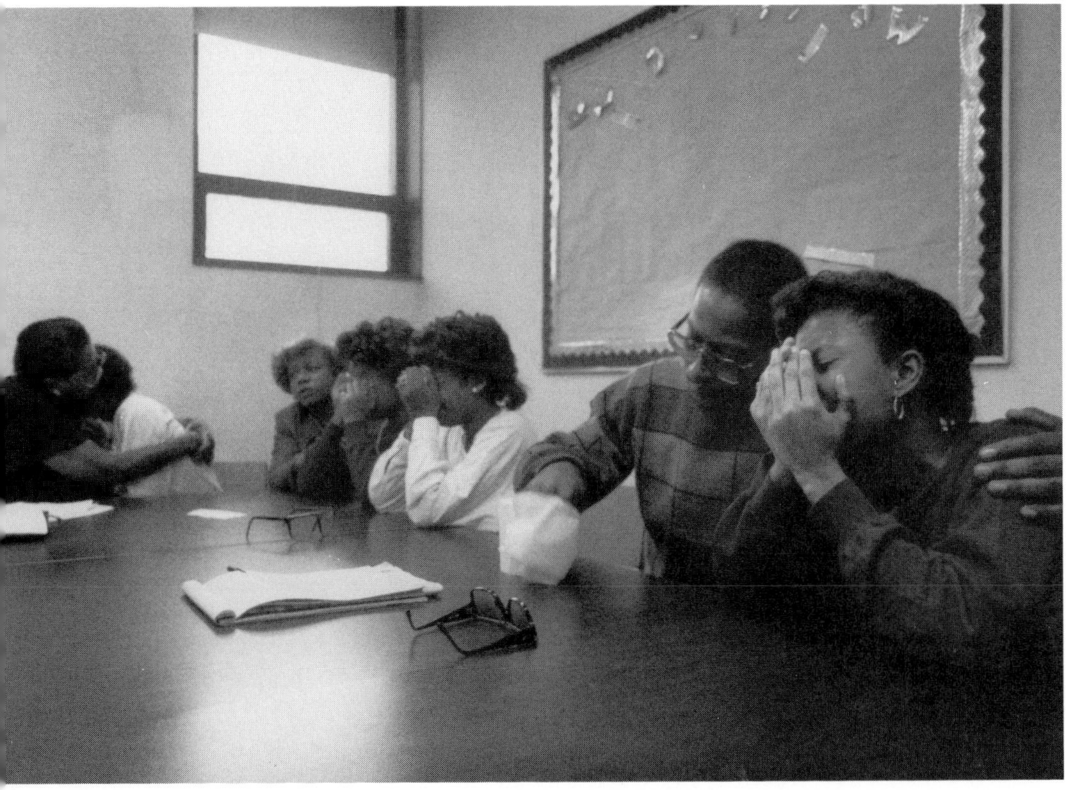

Senior Ray Ponder heads to the prom. "My auntie stressed it and I stressed it my own self that I wasn't going to be like the rest of the kids, dropouts or on the streets," he says. "It was my goal to do all that I can. I did good in football. I've maintained my 3.5 grade point average. I won scholarships. I am getting a lot of recognition."

Junior Brad Weaver and some friends smoke while hanging around outside the school. "Sometimes we will hang out outside the school, sometimes we will go to the park, other times we will go over by the garage," says Weaver, who later dropped out.

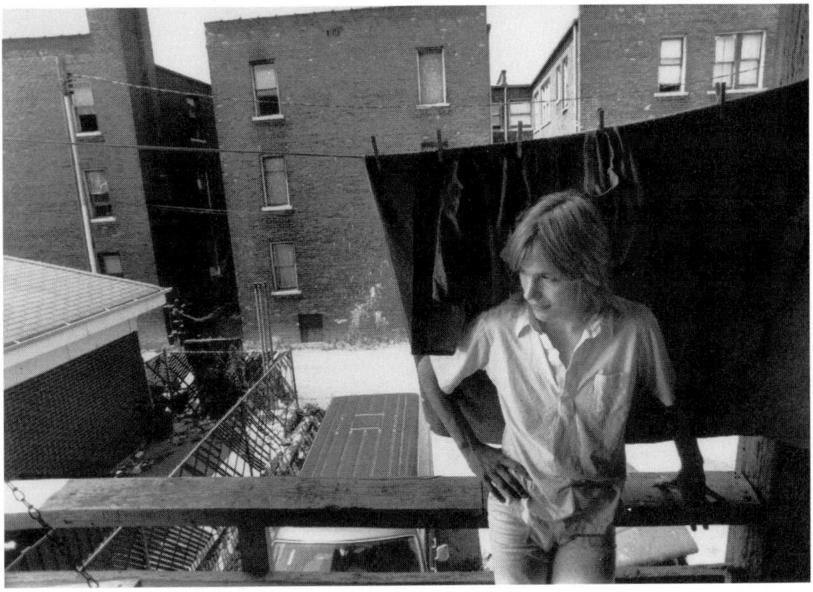

Brad Weaver spends a school day at home. He was a junior at Southwestern High School before he dropped out. "I just decided to quit school," Weaver said.

Brad Weaver and some friends head to downtown Detroit for the Motown Hoedown. From left: John Jerome, Dawn Glabosky, Weaver and Darren Carnes. All dropped out of high school except for Jerome.

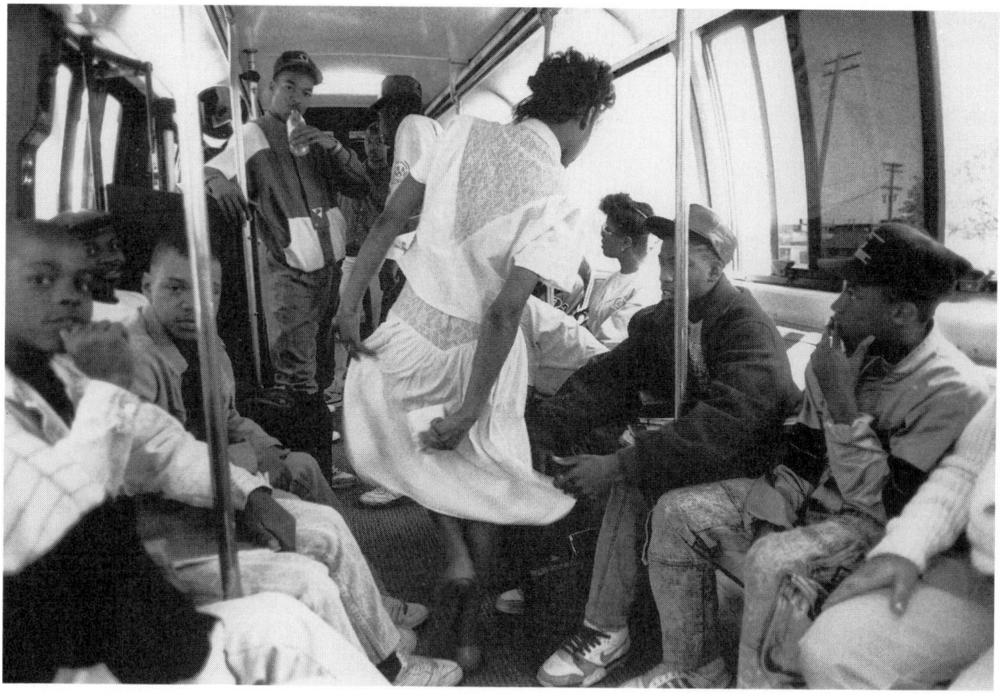

Freshman Tracy Shannon slaps away advances and stares in one of the buses that picks up students on Fort Street.

Romeo Pellrin, 14, kisses his girlfriend, Rebecca Yates, 14, before math class. The two, both freshmen, broke up when Rebecca transferred to another school. "We are in-between in the relationship," said Romeo. "We were in love. We still talk to each other, but there are a couple of things we need to straighten out."

Junior Angie Delgado, eight months pregnant, spent most of her school year carrying a child. "I didn't know whether to keep it or just go on and get rid of it. But I didn't want to get rid of it—I felt abortion was killing it, so I didn't want to do it. So I ended up keeping it, and I wanted the baby."

Angie Delgado and her boyfriend, Juaquine Botello, take Lamaze classes at Henry Ford Hospital. Nurse Diane Diab talks to them about what to expect after the birth. "I wanted it, so I'm going to take care of it the right way," says Angie. "My sister had two little babies and I like watching them and I always wanted one for myself so I can have the little baby and talk about it and take pictures, take him to the ball game."

Students drink at a neighborhood birthday party. Said senior Steve York: "All the people that came just came for the beer and the party and the dancing. Most of the people go to drink, to dance, to laugh, to listen to the music and maybe get lucky."

Students pitch quarters in the boys' locker room. The quarter closest to the wall wins. From left are Terrell Jackson, Ed Moore, Dwight Trammer, Steve York and Alfonzo Sharpe.

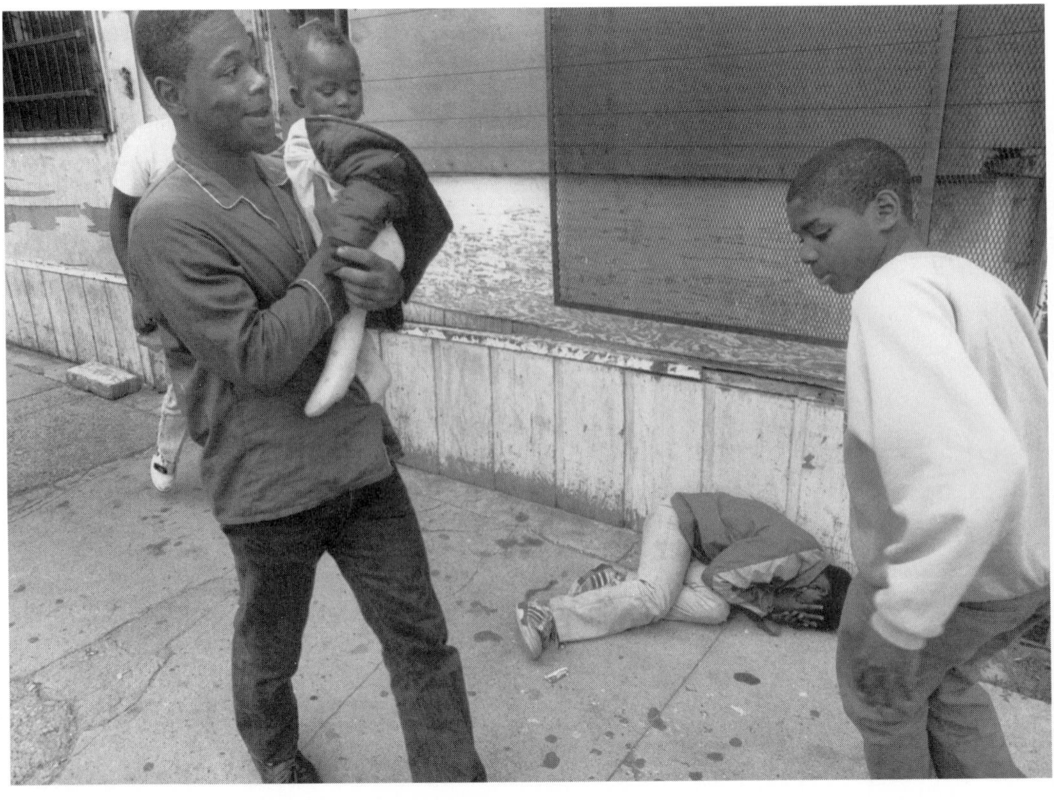

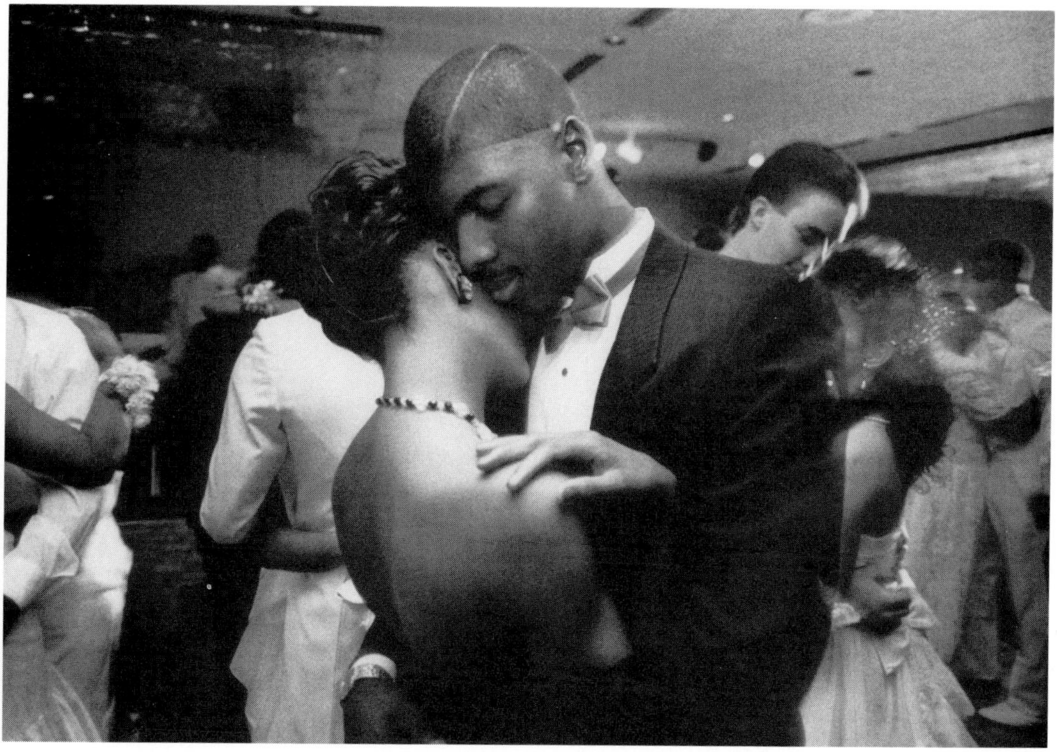

Senior Jerome Cochran dances with his date, Honey Gibbs. "I am trying to get her to be my girlfriend," Cochran said. "I met her at a track meet and my friends just hooked us up."

Lamar Benson, a freshman, says he's doing well at school, with a 2.0 grade point average, but he fears his neighborhood, Delray. "There is a lot of abandoned houses. There's a lot of drugs, drug addicts, too. Every time you walk up the streets, somebody asks you, do you want to sell some for them. It's not worth it."

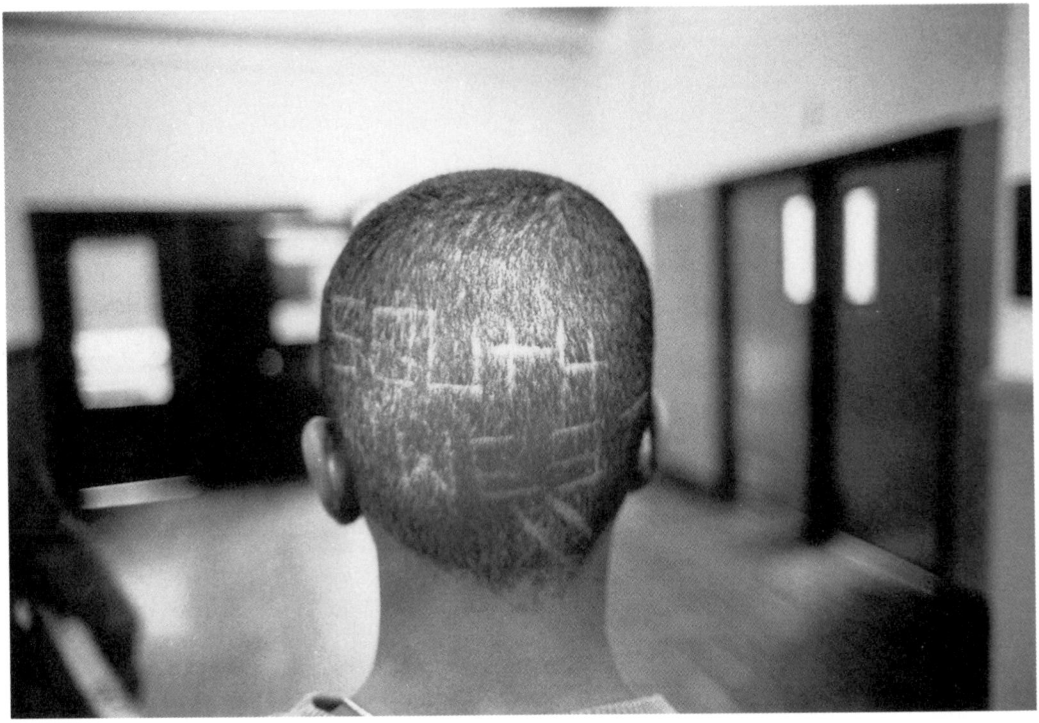

Sophomore Jermaine Bates expresses his loyalty to his school. Bates and several of his friends occasionally make statements with their hairstyles.

EIGHT

A CLASS ACT

1989 WINNER IN THE FEATURE PHOTOGRAPHY CATEGORY

"For a distinguished example of feature photography in black and white or color . . ."

Detroit Free Press
Manny Crisostomo

Daily life in our nation's high schools receives little attention, except for coverage of sports events or elements about Johnny's learning problems. Manny Crisostomo spent a year at a public school in Detroit and offers some thoughtful photographic insights.

SUNDAY, JUNE 6, 1988

In August 1987, I wrote to Detroit Schools Superintendent Arthur Jefferson, outlining a plan to document a full school year at Southwestern High School. The letter said, in part:

"I'd like to photograph the things that make a high school tick—classes, students, teachers, athletics, as well as the socioeconomic factors away from the classroom that have an impact on students. With this kind of time and commitment, I hope to capture the special character of high school life. While the time seems a bit long, I hope it will enable me to really understand the student life and get me beyond the misunderstood stereotypes."

With the superintendent's approval, I entered Southwestern's halls and was swept up in a sea of new faces. Many of those strangers are now friends.

I have photographed the students, faculty and staff, and listened to them. I have been in their classrooms and lunch rooms and hangouts. I have cheered them on at games and cried with them at a funeral. I have played basketball with them in the gym and danced with them in the cafeteria. I saw the fashions and haircuts change with the season and time. I have seen them when they were bad and when they were good. I have followed them home and seen how they lived and how they partied. We talked, laughed and argued about the city and the world. I saw a lot of them mature and come to grips with impending adulthood.

Some of what I learned speaks to the enduring tradition of high school—homecoming, proms, sports, classroom antics, flirting, romance, parties, breaking small rules and just being kids. But it was impossible to deny the negative side, reflecting the problems of the world outside Southwestern's dirty-red brick walls:

Smart kids dropping out, football players selling drugs, children having babies, teenagers feeling rejected or unloved or unwanted by their parents, youngsters victimized by violence at home and on the streets, promising lives ending by suicide and by accident.

If it is said that our schools mirror our society, then these images and words should be of concern.

Southwestern is a 72-year-old institution of brick and mortar in a rundown but historically rich community south and west of downtown. Its neighborhood is bordered by the Detroit River and the richly ethnic Vernor Highway area. Its neighbors include the Ambassador Bridge, Zug Island and the old, empty dinosaur of an auto plant—Fleetwood—that once was the proud home of the Cadillac.

It is a school whose staff's aspirations far outweigh its resources. It is a school that ranks third academically in the Detroit Public School system—a system in which 40 percent of incoming freshmen never make it to their senior year. It is a school whose more than 200 graduating seniors will receive close to $400,000 in scholarships. It is a school with a rich ethnic diversity in which blacks, Hispanics, Arabs and other whites share and work together, as their parents and grandparents did in many cases. It is a school whose community is a tough, working class neighborhood with too much unemployment, crime and poverty.

I hope these words and pictures provide useful insights rather than harsh interpretation. This section is not an indictment of our school system, but a call to our society, to our mothers and fathers, to our civic and church leaders. It is a call to work together for this new generation. Those bright students who are driven and motivated will always shine, and we should not ignore them. But let's keep an eye on those with less, those who teeter on the edge, those whose stories have the potential to warm our hearts . . . or break our hearts.

They are, after all, our children.

—Manny Crisostomo
Detroit Free Press

NINE

CITY GOVERNMENT'S FOLLY AND FRAUD

1989 WINNER IN THE EDITORIAL WRITING CATEGORY

"For distinguished editorial writing, the test of excellence being clearness of style, moral purpose, sound reasoning, and power to influence public opinion in what the writer conceives to be the right direction . . ."

Chicago Tribune
Lois Wille

Lois Wille doesn't tolerate nonsense. And she sees heaps of it in the daily workings of Chicago's "hidebound, stubborn, selfish politicians." Her remedies are refreshingly blunt.

No question. If Lois Wille were running Chicago, it would be a better place. Fairer, more decent, more honest, more demanding and more giving, preserving the best of its past, while reaching out eagerly to make even more of its future—for all of its people.

Her editorial voice is so strong, so clear, so persistent and invariably so right that, in a real way, she does have a hand in how this town is run. Mayors, aldermen, county officials, governors, all the political ins and outs, ignore her penetrating wit and wisdom at their own risk.

And they know that. Most of them see her as a mythic figure of Justice, weighing their transgressions in unforgiving scales. Fair enough. But the really sharp ones will have noticed that Lois Wille, unlike Justice, wears no blindfold. She sees their follies and their frauds with unparalleled clarity. Then dissects them in print with stinging accuracy.

Here are some fragments, as examples:

On attempts to block a mayoral election: "Chicago has endured more than its share of political corruption and irresponsibility in its 150 years. But this is the first time it has been burdened with a set of politicians of both parties arrogant enough to try to swindle the city out of an election."

On twisting requirements to fit bids: "Writing a bid to suit a pet contractor is an old City Hall tradition. Manipulating affirmative action contracts to suit pet contractors is a new City Hall tradition born out of a reform movement. Who says Chicago can't handle reform?"

On accounting for aldermanic expenses: "But until aldermen are required to give an accounting of what they do with the money, there is no way of knowing if they are breaking the law. City taxpayers can only assume the probable."

That's a start. There's more, much more, in this presentation of her editorials.

—The Editors
Chicago Tribune

DON'T MUZZLE ALDERMANIC STUPIDITY

FRIDAY, NOVEMBER 18, 1988

BY LOIS WILLE

Some Chicago aldermen are unhappy about a new city council resolution asking them to refrain in committee hearings from insulting witnesses because of gender, religion, race or ethnic background. Their feelings are understandable. Being offensive is as basic to their nature as the wink and the nod.

Chicago taxpayers should be unhappy with the resolution, too. It infringes on free speech, but that isn't the only problem. If all council members complied with this request, it would be impossible to measure the depth and breadth of aldermanic ignorance.

The Chicago City Council is the most expensive municipal legislative body in the nation, probably the world. This year it will spend $268,000 for each of the 50 aldermen, nincompoop or not. Next year it will spend $270,640. The city's taxpaying homeowners and businesses have a right to know if they are giving all that money to fools. The best way to find out how stupid some of them are is to let all have their say.

It was wonderful, for example, to hear Aldermen Robert Shaw and Ernest Jones complain that the resolution interferes with their freedom of speech. They didn't mind trampling on 1st Amendment rights when they stormed the Art Institute and tore down a painting insulting to the late Mayor Harold Washington.

Ald. Jones, for one, swears he will never "surrender his freedom of speech." Good. His insults are too hilarious to be muzzled. Who can forget his complaints about female police officers' "minister periods"? Would you have wanted that memorable instant lost to Chicago political history?

Ald. George Hagopian was offensive, no doubt about it, when he turned to city council visitors during a debate on gay rights and bellowed that they were "animals." It was the way he slobbered when he said it that made the moment too precious to forgo.

Ald. Burton Natarus is another who laments this attempt to restrict aldermanic speech. "If we aren't given the widest range to express our view," he said, "the people are lost." Yes, where would Chicago be today without the likes of him in the council? A few weeks ago he helped kill building code reforms that would have cut the price of a new home by $10,000 to $15,000, and he bragged that Chicago may be the only city in the world with such a restrictive code.

Let Aldermen Shaw and Jones and Hagopian and Natarus sound as stupid as they want, as often as they want. It may be the only hope that someday their constituents will be sufficiently fed up to rid the city council of their presence.

ANOTHER GOOD IDEA TO CUSS OUT

FRIDAY, FEBRUARY 19, 1988

BY LOIS WILLE

Chicago has spent a lot of creative energy recently to block plans that would boost its economy and help its poor. It would be nice for a change if those energies were used to promote growth instead of discourage it.

Let an individual or an institution or a civic group step forward with a promising idea and, within hours, the Coalition United to Stop Something will announce its opposition. It doesn't really matter what the proposal is or where it would go or who would pay for it, or how many new jobs or new homes or new tax dollars it would produce. If someone offers to do it, you can be sure there is a CUSS on the horizon that will stall it and work hard to kill it.

Navy Pier is on the verge of rotting into Lake Michigan because a few people think commercial and recreational development will soil its empty purity and a few others don't want the competition from shops and restaurants on the pier. As a result, the city forfeits hundreds of new jobs and millions in tax dollars.

Vast areas of the West Side look like the bombed-out ruins that scarred Europe after World War II. But, unlike their European counterparts, they may remain rubble forever because redevelopment plans are instantly attacked as plots to throw the poor into the street and give their homesteads to the rich. From the start, promoters of a new West Side sports complex have pledged that low-cost houses for all displaced families are an integral part of their plan. But the panic peddlers got to work, slandering community leaders who want to cooperate in the development and robbing poor people of better homes and jobs.

They're busy on the Mid-South Side, too, churning out propaganda to block a restoration project that would help hundreds of homeowners spruce up their property and fill vacant lots with residences for low- and middle-income families. The plan calls for demolishing rundown high-rise public housing and providing new homes for all the uprooted families, but the panic peddlers are spreading the lie that most of the families will be permanently locked out.

The forces against change—any change, no matter how healthy—are preventing construction of affordable homes by blocking revisions in the city building code. They are preventing expansion of new jobs and the tax base by blocking revisions in the city zoning code.

And now, just watch, they will regroup to block the expansion of the University of Illinois–Chicago.

A few days ago university officials talked about building dormitories and laboratories on vacant fields south of Roosevelt Road. It's difficult to think of any development that would do more to shore up a struggling area that needs new investment. Yet the first reaction from city officials was negative: This will take land that we have reserved for commercial growth. It's been "reserved" for commercial growth for 20 years, and there have been no takers.

The first reaction from community groups was also negative: This could be a battle between the "haves" and the "have nots." But if the "haves" are permitted to invest their money, new jobs will be created for the "have nots," who then can join the "haves."

Isn't that supposed to be the ultimate goal of city government and of community groups? Everywhere, it seems, but in Chicago.

HOW TO GET LOW-COST HOMES IN THE CITY

TUESDAY, MARCH 22, 1988

BY LOIS WILLE

Another high-priced housing development will be rising west of Chicago's Loop early next year, this one financed by investors based in Seattle. That's great news for taxpayers, and not just those in Chicago.

The extra property tax revenue generated by the $180 million Riverbend project will help city government, Cook County government, city schools and city parks. The 2,000 or so well-off people expected to fill the new apartments presumably will want to spend some of their money nearby, creating new retail jobs and sales tax revenue that will find its way into the state's threadbare treasury and its school aid fund.

And this new development, sitting on railroad tracks at the junction of the north and south branches of the Chicago River, is bound to lure other investors to the expanding downtown, just as the pioneering Presidential Towers apartments lured Riverbend's investors.

The necessary city approvals are coming along promptly and smoothly, more good news. The architects, Harry Weese and Associates, worked with a civic group, Friends of the River, to design a beautiful waterfront esplanade. Still more good news. And of course it's gratifying to see all that West Coast money pouring into this old Rust Belt town.

□ □ □

So much for the bright side. Now it's time to ask if, in the midst of this wonderful boom in costly housing that is spreading south and west of Chicago's Loop, there is any good news in sight for the people who can't afford to pay $600 a month for a place to live, let alone $1,600.

The answer, unhappily, is no.

What's worse, Chicago's government could easily reverse that reply into a resounding yes, but it has refused to take any action that will help create decent, low-cost homes for the thousands of Chicago families stuck in rundown, unlivable dumps.

The necessary steps are well known. They work in other cities. But Chicago's hidebound, stubborn, selfish politicians are too caught up in their endless factional wars and too easily cowed by narrow special interests to do anything about the city's dwindling supply of low-cost homes. Mayor Sawyer has made a few proposals that would help, but has done nothing to push them through the city council. Ald. Tim Evans is too busy proclaiming himself the heir to Harold Washington's progressive poor people's movement to actually do anything progressive for poor people. Ald. Dorothy Tillman, chairman of the council's Housing Committee, squandered a big chunk of her budget to hire Evans loyalist Jacky Grimshaw, who spends all her time trying to undercut the mayor instead of trying to get better housing for poor people.

Meanwhile, most of the white aldermen are having too much fun watching the blacks fight to spoil it with a little work on such things as housing.

If Chicago had a strong, responsible city administration and city council, here is what they would do to help low-income families get decent homes:

- Modernize Chicago's rigid building code.

The building trades unions have long used their political clout to protect provisions that require expensive, labor-intensive materials and procedures. Builders estimate that if the Chicago code conformed to industry-approved models used around the country, the price of new housing would fall by almost a third. Jack McNeil, chairman of the nonprofit Metropolitan Housing and Development Corp., says a house in the suburbs can be built for $32 to $38 a square foot, but "in the city you can't go under $50."

- Create a housing fund from new tax revenue.

When high-cost developments such as Presidential Towers and Riverbend start to produce property tax money, set aside a portion for building or restoring low-cost housing. Some of Mayor Washington's key supporters wanted to slap an extra tax on downtown projects to create this fund, but that so-called "linked development" would backfire, dampening downtown resurgence and its potential for enriching the entire city. Chicago will be better off if it puts out a welcome mat for all types of investors, stashing away part of the extra tax revenue for neighborhood renewal.

• Use federal "paybacks" for low-cost housing.

Over the next seven years the city will get about $50 million in repayments of low-interest loans awarded under the federal Urban Development Action Grant program. This money should be recycled into low-interest loans for the construction or repair of low-priced housing.

• Spur housing restoration with a tax break.

The Cook County Board should pass Assessor Thomas Hynes' proposal for a temporary cut in property taxes for owners who repair rundown apartment buildings in low-income neighborhoods and scale the rents to low- or moderate-income families.

• Cooperate with developers who want to build low-cost housing.

The fact that this last point must be made at all shows the rampant incompetence and irresponsibility in City Hall. A plan to build 3,000 units of low- to moderate-cost housing on the Mid-South Side, including 450 units of scattered public housing, is stalled because the area's alderman, Tim Evans, and the Chicago Housing Authority Board won't cooperate. It could be a prototype for restoration of other destitute neighborhoods, but Chicago's ranking politicians prefer controllable destitution to uncontrollable renewal.

ELECTION BOARD CAVES IN TO A SWINDLE

THURSDAY, APRIL 7, 1988

BY LOIS WILLE

Just when it seems that some Chicago public official has sunk to the very limits of disgusting behavior, another one or two or three prove there are still new depths to be plumbed.

What, for example, could be worse than Ald. Timothy Evans blocking construction in his ward of 900 units of scattered low-rise public housing to replace 900 units in rundown high-rise buildings that are miserable places to live, but popular with politicians who think it's easier to control votes when they're stacked in concentration-camp settings?

What could be worse than Ald. William Henry stamping out job-creating development opportunities in his desperately poor North Lawndale ward because he wanted to be part of the deals?

Difficult as it may seem to surpass such foul deeds, Chicago's Board of Election Commissioners has managed to do it.

□ □ □

The three commissioners are supposed to make certain Chicago elections are run honestly and fairly. Does it have to be spelled out to them in big, easy-to-read letters that they also are supposed to make certain the city has elections in the first place? Apparently so. This trio, bending under pressures from various political masters and their own spinelessness, decided on Tuesday that they can't decide whether Chicago must have a mayoral election in the spring of 1989.

The state law, they said, simply doesn't give them enough guidance.

That's garbage. The law is abundantly clear. Its newfound "ambiguity" is so obviously phony it's amazing that Gov. James Thompson and Sheriff James O'Grady and House Speaker Michael Madigan and Cook County Board President George Dunne and the crew propping up Mayor Eugene Sawyer think they can get away with mouthing it.

Didn't it ever occur to them that some people might actually look up the state law and see with it says?

The relevant passage in the Illinois Cities and Villages Act—the only passage relevant to Chicago's mayoral situation—states that "if a vacancy occurs in the office of the mayor of a city with a 4-year term, and there remains an unexpired portion of the term of at least 28 months, and the vacancy occurs at least 130 days before the general municipal election next scheduled under the general election law, the vacancy shall be filled at that general municipal election."

Mayor Harold Washington died with at least 28 months remaining in his term, and at least 130 days before the state's next general municipal election. Those elections, as the Illinois election code specifies, occur "in odd-numbered years . . . on the first Tuesday in April."

A general municipal election is scheduled in Illinois on April 4, 1989, as the law provides. A city that normally would not elect a mayor until the 1991 general municipal election is required, by Illinois law, to elect one on April 4, 1989, if its mayor died as early in his term as did Harold Washington.

If Gov. Thompson, Mike Madigan, George Dunne and the rest of the "ambiguity" crowd are correct, the law can be interpreted to mean that a city can stick to its own election cycle no matter when its mayor departed. Then why even bother to have a law concerning mayoral vacancies? According to the newly minted interpretation by Thompson et. al., no vacant mayoral term ever would be filled by voters. A mayor could die the hour after taking the oath and not be replaced with a duly elected mayor for another four years.

The ambiguity boys know the state law was never intended to be interpreted that way. Each of them has another reason for not wanting the people of Chicago to elect a mayor for several more years.

- Speaker Madigan wants no distractions, particularly in fundraising, from his own campaign for County Board chairman in 1990.
- Gov. Thompson wants anything that Mike Madigan wants, if that is the price for the speaker's support of a state tax increase.
- Sheriff O'Grady and his Republican backers want time to build an O'Grady mayoral campaign, and the longer Eugene Sawyer is in office embarrassing himself and his supporters, the better for them.

• George Dunne wants what he thinks the committeemen who reinstated him as county Democratic chairman want, and right now the majority of Chicago's Democratic committeemen are too gleeful about the prospects of cleaning up under Eugene Sawyer to risk giving it up next spring.

• As for Acting Mayor Sawyer, the people who run him saw what happened to a few of their crowd in last month's primary. They were chopped down. They are not about to let their meal ticket go before the voters if there is any way they can prevent it.

□ □ □

With heavies from both parties pushing at them to abrogate their responsibility to schedule a mayoral election next spring, the three Chicago election commissioners obligingly caved in.

Michael Hamblet, a Democrat, said don't look at me, it's up to the city clerk to set the next election. Utter nonsense. James Nolan, a Republican, said gee, I don't know what to do; it's up to the state election commissioners to advise me. Nikki Zollar, a Democrat, thought the Nolan copout sounded good to her and seconded it.

Chicago has endured more than its share of political corruption and irresponsibility in its 150 years. But this is the first time it has been burdened with a set of politicians—of both parties—arrogant enough to try to swindle the city out of an election.

ONE HIT, THEN BETRAYAL IN SPRINGFIELD

SUNDAY, JULY 3, 1988

BY LOIS WILLE

Next time, the University of Illinois will know what to do to get a fair shake from the state legislature: threaten to move its sports programs to Florida.

What sick old people or abused children can do remains a problem. Their athletic abilities are generally not impressive.

For them, the highlight of the spring session of the 85th General Assembly of the State of Illinois came shortly before midnight on Thursday when Rep. John Dunn, a Democrat from Decatur, rose up and yelled:

"What in the name of heaven are we doing at this hour with every top-ranking politician in this state standing on the floor of this chamber to take care of the White Sox when we can't take care of the children, we can't take care of the poor and we can't take care of the people who need our help?"

Of course the legislature did the right thing when it voted to build a new stadium and provide ongoing subsidies that will keep the White Sox in Chicago. A professional baseball franchise is well worth coveting for its economic impact alone, and even more so for the zest it adds to city life. The Sox subsidy will come almost entirely from a hotel tax levied only in Chicago, so legislators did not rob schools or mental hospitals or Downstate interests when they approved it.

No, there is nothing wrong with the White Sox bill and the way it was pushed, pulled and strong-armed through the General Assembly. What was so disgusting about the entire session is that the miserable conditions in Chicago schools, deteriorating health services, poor prison security and the welfare of the state's most vulnerable people mattered so little to its political leadership in comparison with a baseball team.

□□□

This legislative session had three major pieces of business: pass a tax increase to reverse years of decline in state services, impose airtight reform on the Chicago school system and keep the White Sox. It collapsed in a quivering heap on the first two. And for all the joy over the Sox decision, there's no question which should have ranked third in priorities.

Education did get a little more money—so little that the University of Illinois will lose some of its prized professors to states that value higher education. Its out-of-date equipment will continue to deteriorate. And its students, slapped with a 20 percent tuition increase last year, may face another 20 percent hike.

Most state agencies will get less than they need to maintain their already inadequate level of services. The Department of Corrections will provide a little less security at state prisons and a much-needed new prison will be scrapped. Departments that care for homeless children and elderly invalids once again will shelve their hopes of expanding into first-class agencies.

Sure, Illinois can skate by without a tax increase. But the price is another year of eroding services, and ultimately its economy will pay dearly for that.

□ □ □

The failure to pass a tax increase, painful as that will be for the old and the sick and the poor, turned out to be only a prologue to the craven act of betrayal that concluded this legislative session.

All the bold talk of forcing reform onto the Chicago school system faded into a few whimpers. The Chicago Teachers Union emerged with barely a nick in its obstructionist powers. Its leaders easily turned around the ever-fearful Mayor Eugene Sawyer, whipped black legislators into line with threatening talk about racial unity and sent the white Democratic leadership—including the little dictator himself, House Speaker Michael Madigan—cowering into a neutral corner.

In the face of that combination, Republicans gave up their fight to create a school oversight authority with genuine power. The union and black legislators insisted on giving the mayor of Chicago the majority of appointments to the authority, and they stripped from an earlier bill its power to withhold school funds if the Board of Education reneges on a reform agenda.

The oversight body apparently will have some ability to block provisions in new union contracts that are inconsistent with reform, but the language is so muddy and vague that it's difficult to know whether it will have any real impact.

Other steps to break the union's ironclad control over Chicago classrooms, including an end to the abuses of the seniority system, were scrapped.

It's possible that if the oversight authority is dominated by strong, influential people dedicated to change and willing to stand fast in face of political pressure and even a long strike, it will be able to make some structural improvements in the school system. But however committed it may be, neither the authority nor the new local school councils can do much to help children most in danger of failing. When Speaker Madigan killed the tax increase, he also killed the most effective way to improve education in Chicago: early learning classes for disadvantaged children.

HOW CITY HALL COPES WITH REFORM

TUESDAY, NOVEMBER 22, 1988

BY LOIS WILLE

It's not true that Chicago government isn't ready for reform. It's been ready a long time—ready to take any alleged reform measure and twist it into a new and more intricate way to bilk the public.

If all that creativity had been used to improve schools and housing and public health services, Chicago today would be the garden spot of the nation.

The case of the amazing ash-hauling contract is the latest example of City Hall's rare talent for squeezing the worst out of change.

Last week, Tribune reporter Joel Kaplan revealed that Mayor Sawyer's administration passed up the low bidder when it awarded a one-year contract worth as much as $10 million to haul ash from the city's incinerator. The winner was Fred Barbara, nephew of 1st Ward Ald. Fred Roti. The loser, despite his lower bid, was Odis Reams, a black West Sider.

On the surface, that looks as if Roti's once-fearsome 1st Ward organization is wielding clout the way it used to in the pre–Harold Washington days, and that minority contractors are again out in the cold. Not at all, says the mayor's people. Barbara Trucking Co. got the contract because Odis Reams' Big "O" Movers and Storage Co. failed to meet bid requirements.

Odis Reams says those requirements were written specifically to fit Barbara's bid, but he too can meet them if given the chance. It wouldn't be the first time City Hall tailored bids to favor a favored contractor, but the Sawyer administration insists that wasn't the case. Why, it's own Office of Municipal Investigations checked and found the award was absolutely clean.

What went into that finding, however, is unknown. Officials of the mayor's Office of Municipal Investigation say their report is confidential, and we'll all just have to take their word that everything is okay.

A government investigative agency that issues only verdicts with no documentation to back them up is worse than worthless. It can become a co-conspirator in deceiving the public.

If the possibility of a steered bid were the only problem with the ash-hauling contract, it would be bad enough. But as often happens with Chicago's government, the deeper you dig, the more rot you find.

One of the changes Mayor Washington brought to City Hall is a requirement that minority-owned firms get 25 percent of city contracts and female-owned firms get 5 percent. A lot of odd deals have crept into city purchasing under the guise of that rule, but none more inventive than the ash-hauling arrangement.

Barbara's minority partner turned out to be a small trucking company financially controlled by the versatile Howard Medley, board member of the Chicago Transit Authority, owner of a moving company that has profited from city business, big supporter of Mayor Sawyer and a partner with Sawyer in a real estate venture. He is presently spending his days in federal court, where he is on trial charged with taking a $22,500 bribe in connection with a CTA contract.

Medley got control over the small trucking company's business decisions in return for selling it some of his trucks in a bargain deal. It is, for all practical purposes, Medley's company, using Medley's trucks.

And where did Barbara find his female business partner? Right in his own office, what a coincidence. He picked a company called Karen's Kartage. Its owner was Barbara's secretary and its address is a Gold Coast condominium owned by Barbara.

Writing a bid to suit a pet contractor is an old City Hall tradition. Manipulating affirmative action contracts to suit pet contractors is a new City Hall tradition born out of a reform movement. Who says Chicago can't handle reform?

MUST CITY ALDERMEN OBEY THE LAW?

FRIDAY, NOVEMBER 25, 1988

If the Chicago City Council doesn't act soon to require its members to account for what they do with their $18,000-a-year apiece in expense money, it's time for a taxpayers' suit demanding the accounting.

The possibility that a majority of aldermen will order themselves to do this is so remote that somebody may as well start work on the lawsuit.

Other working men and women in this country, whether in government or private business, have to give their bosses some kind of accounting of what they do with their expense money. But not the 50 members of the Chicago City Council. Each gets $18,000 a year for "contingent expenses," no questions asked. Each also gets $40,000 in annual salary, $95,000 a year for office staff and $5,280 for travel expenses. Thirty have committee positions that give them still more tax dollars for staff and extraneous expenses.

In all, Chicago's taxpaying homeowners and businesses will spend an average of $268,000 this year on each member of the city council, the nation's most expensive municipal legislature.

In return, wouldn't you think that taxpayers have a right to know if their aldermen are using a tiny part of that money—the $18,000 a year in expenses—in accordance with the law?

In a series on the city council published last year, The Tribune reported that some aldermen treat their expense money as part of their salary, spending it as they please. Some use it for private business matters.

Ald. David Orr introduced a package of ordinances that would require aldermen to disclose how they are spending the $18,000. Another of his proposals would specify that car phones, office furniture, personal computers and other equipment bought by aldermen with their expense money or their committee funds belongs to the city, not to them personally. Orr also wants to stop aldermen from claiming that their part-time staff members are full-time so the part-timers and their families can get the city's generous health benefits.

Ald. Orr's colleagues reacted in expected fashion. They kicked him out of his job as vice mayor.

Now he has strong legal reinforcement for at least one of his measures. Judson Miner, the city corporation counsel, informed Orr that aldermen can spend expense money only on official council business. If they use it for other purposes, they are illegally converting public funds and subject to criminal prosecution—even if they pay income tax on the money they pocketed. But until aldermen are required to give an accounting of what they do with the money, there is no way of knowing if they are breaking the law.

City taxpayers can only assume the probable.

TEN

LITERARY HEROES AND "CREATIVE WRITING"

1989 WINNER IN THE CRITICISM CATEGORY

"For distinguished criticism . . ."

The Raleigh News and Observer
Michael Skube

From his post in Raleigh, North Carolina, Michael Skube keeps tabs on the latest offerings from the nation's publishing houses. His praise and his criticism both find their mark.

It was James Atlas who alerted me to the silliness of it all, although I don't believe Mr. Atlas thought it silly in the least. He had written a piece last year in *The New York Times* Sunday Magazine on the English Department at Duke University. The point of the piece, as I remember it, was to portray the daring and élan of a department that was acquiring a reputation in some circles for being very much with-it. Under the chairmanship of Professor Stanley Fish, Duke had recruited some of the hottest names in academic literary theory, paying some of them football coaches' salaries, and down from New York came Mr. Atlas to take a look.

I don't know much about the care and feeding of English professors, but I like to think I can spot the kind of pretentiousness that passes for serious scholarship—I too spent a few years in graduate school. So I read Mr. Atlas' piece mildly interested in what all the excitement at Duke was about. There was a corollary reason: James Atlas was a writer I had admired since reading his biography of Delmore Schwartz 10 years ago. I admire him still. But in this piece, it seemed to me, his critical sense had gone off for a snooze, and he had become a bit of a fan. I thought his piece faintly fawned over a subject that begged no little skepticism. Thus the column entitled "Western Lit from Milton to Zane Grey (and Others)," which tries to find the ridiculous in the overspecialization of the humanities and of English departments in particular.

My column, modest through it was, dismayed some and heartened others in the Raleigh-Durham-Chapel Hill area's large academic community. Along with a subsequent column on a related subject, it fostered among some English professors the unwarranted notion that I harbor against them some deep and unresolved grievance. One prominent literary theorist soberly proposed in an address to the Modern

Language Association that newspapers give reporters advanced training so that they would be up to covering the goings-on in the nation's English departments. Newspapers hire specialists these days to cover science and medicine and business, so why not literary theory as well?

All this is by way of suggesting a point of view, or rather an attitude, that underlay some of the following articles. These pieces tend, for better or worse, to be doubting, skeptical, resistant to fashion and to local heroes. The article on creative writing—coming at the English departments from another angle—is another such piece. It had occurred to me that everyone seemed to be taking "creative writing" today, and my suspicion was that an awful lot of these courses were what used to be called Mickey Mouse courses. Along with this notion, I held (and still hold) the view that one of the sorrier things to have happened to American fiction had been its institutionalization by the English departments: Where young writers once set out to experience the world, today they get their Master's of Fine Arts degree and hole up in the university. Hence the sterility and uniform dullness of so much contemporary fiction.

The piece on Southern writers got its impetus from a press release announcing the formation of something called the Fellowship of Southern Writers. No doubt the project had intentions noble and good, but I caught a whiff of the provincial and self-congratulatory about it, too. It sounded like the Fellowship of Christian Athletes. If the impulse behind the piece was lighthearted, a stronger motive began to take hold as I wrote it—the belief that the field was becoming crowded with "professional Southerners." It seemed to me that we were up to our galluses in a kind of fiction that was self-consciously "country," cute little novels that had little relation to the South as most of us know it. In any case, the column elicited a whiny telephone call from a young Southern novelist, a few testy letters to the editor and a grumpy polemic from Prof. Louis D. Rubin Jr., estimable critic, president of Algonquin Books of Chapel Hill and godfather to a handful of young novelists.

I realized I had blasphemed local deities, but I knew also—because I had been dismayed to see the raw copy of some of these same novelists—that they might consider taking a refresher course in English composition. If it outrages some to hear this, I can only advise those souls that in publishing as in journalism an editor's work goes unseen and unsuspected.

Among the other pieces presented here, one, my review of the letters of the composer and music critic Virgil Thomson, originated from writerly admiration. Virgil Thomson is a writer any critic ought to try to emulate—pungent in his prose, pointed in his opinions, uncompromising in his standards of what is good and what is shoddy.

Three other pieces in the entry suggest the range that a book page in a medium-size city must try to cover. A James Michener novel is an automatic best seller. Many such books it seems pointless to review, but book editors for metropolitan newspapers cannot blithely ignore a new Michener as they might a new Sidney Sheldon or Danielle Steel. I reviewed the Michener wondering if I could actually read one—make it, that is, from cover to cover. Having done so, I haven't the energy to try it again. The review intends to say all the usual things about Michener while also giving him due—and perhaps having fun, too.

T. S. Eliot is obviously a very different undertaking from Michener. I reviewed Lyndall Gordon's biography for the purest of reasons—to learn what Eliot the man was like. I suspect this is why many general readers open biographies of large figures whom they know only for their poetry or their novels or their political careers. And, of course, a biography of T. S. Eliot is a book that ought to be reviewed by a newspaper that serves as educated a readership as ours does.

Somewhere between Michener and T. S. Eliot, perhaps, falls a figure like Larry McMurtry—popular but hardly lowbrow, literary by training and instinct but not belletristic. Over the years I had marveled at the seeming ease with which he wrote intelligent novels that drew their characters and setting from the Old West, and yet I knew he had for years been prodding Western-born writers to give up the old cowboy myth and write fiction rooted in the urban reality of the present. The review is of Mr. McMurtry's novel *Anything for Billy,* but takes as its point of departure an article he wrote several years ago in a Texas newspaper. In that article, if I understand him right, he is saying we've written enough novels like *Anything for Billy.* I'm not sure that I agree, but then, we don't have many Larry McMurtrys to write them.

Which is another way of saying that whatever merit these pieces have, it lies as much with the subject as the writer.

—Michael Skube
The News and Observer

SHOULDERING THE BURDEN OF THE SOUTHERN WRITER

SUNDAY, FEBRUARY 21, 1988

BY MICHAEL SKUBE

The burden of Southern history, to appropriate C. Vann Woodward's hallowed phrase, just gets heavier with the passing years. The backs of the region's writers are bowed to the breaking point under the weight of something one of them has called "the awful responsibility of Time." We all have our crosses to bear, but my, that does sound like quite a load.

In recognition of the Southern writer's Sisyphean lot, 21 of the most distinguished of their number have gathered at the altar of Faulkner to worship and, while they're at it, pat a few of those bone-tired backs. Specifically, they intend to form the Fellowship of Southern Writers, which may vaguely suggest the Fellowship of Christian Athletes but in fact would be a regional version of the American Academy of Arts and Letters. The group would be limited to 36 novelists, poets, critics and historians with what would amount to lifetime appointments. The estimable Cleanth Brooks already has been named "chancellor."

Precisely what function these presbyters will carry out is not at all clear, but the group has taken upon itself one practical task: raising funds from publishers, foundations, state commissions for the humanities and the like in order to offer fellowships and prizes to younger Southern writers.

In fiction, at least, I haven't noticed any dearth of Southern writers—good ones, yes, but let that pass for the moment. Let me instead, with as little pomp as possible, introduce these 19 gentlemen and two fine ladies who are founding fellows: Brooks, the noted critic; Fred Chappell, poet and novelist; George Core, editor of the Sewanee Review; James Dickey, novelist and poet; Shelby Foote, novelist and historian; John Hope Franklin, Duke University historian; Ernest Gaines, novelist; George Garrett, novelist and poet; Blyden Jackson, critic; Andrew Lytle, novelist; Walker Percy, novelist; Reynolds Price, novelist; Louis D. Rubin Jr., critic and novelist; Lewis P. Simpson, critic; Elizabeth Spencer, novelist; Walter Sullivan, critic and novelist; William Styron, novelist; Peter Taylor, novelist; Robert Penn Warren, poet and novelist; Eudora Welty, novelist; Woodward, historian.

FULL CITIZENSHIP

This is as august a group of Southerners as has gathered in living memory, and my admiration for many of them—Fred Chappell, Vann Woodward, to name two—is deep and genuine. But I beg to quibble, even so. There was a time—and it seems to me it was yesterday—when Southern writers were asking full citizenship in the larger society of American letters. No more of the subtle patronization implied by the term "Southern writer." Southern writers, with some exceptions, didn't want to be regional writers; they wanted to be writers, period. And well they should.

"Regional," Ms. Welty said, "is an outsider's term. It has no meaning for the insider who is doing the writing, because as he knows he is simply writing about life. Jane Austen, Emily Brontë, Thomas Hardy, Cervantes, Turgenev, the authors of the books of the Old Testament, all confined themselves to regions, great or small—but are they regional?"

No, they are not, and for the very good reason that they are not self-consciously English or Russian or Spanish or anything else so constraining. Which is not to say, obviously, that they did not draw heavily from their native soil, wherever it might have been.

If the same can be said for the ink swell of "Southern" fiction of late, it has entirely escaped my notice. There are exceptions, like Anderson Ferrell's exceptional first novel "Where She Was," set in Eastern North Carolina but concerned with larger themes than daft grandparents and nutty uncles. Indeed, Ferrell's is one novel with a Southern setting that attempts to explore some deeper aspect of our existence.

For many of the rest, the writer's attention is not so much on Time as trivia. In the South, mama and daddy and gran no sooner step onto the venerable old front porch that the trapdoor of recollection flies open again, letting free the stale air of myth and memory and all the rest of the Southern literary inheritance. The thing needs to be hermetically sealed for at least a generation. From it pour forth stories that ramble on in a contrived baby-talk just as Southern as sorghum, hon, and a whole lot more cloying.

CRITICAL CONFECTIONS

It is not only the molasses of fiction. It is much of the critical writing as well. When Southerners write about Southerners, they don't merely scratch backs—they give bear hugs. George Core, one of the 19 founders of the fellowship, reviewed Reynolds Price's collection of essays, "A Common Room," in The Washington Post last week and delivered of himself this lumpy confection: "Among the diverse strands that bind the book into a thick hawser of flexible strength and long reach are the distinct voice of its maker, the suppleness of his prose, and penetration of his critical judgments, and the repetition as well as the breadth of his interests and commitments."

That is as unctuous, as embarrassingly *bad,* a sentence as I have read since last fall when Deacon Core genuflected before another book with a Southern theme. Mix the swampy rhetoric native to the region with all-purpose reviewers' jargon and you can come up with some unlovely mongrel effects (or at least George Core can).

Am I an ungracious guest? (I've lived in the South, and happily, for 24 years now.) I hope not. But I hope, too, that there's more to commend new work to our attention than the mere fact that it's Southern. Let it be good as well.

This, I think, matters less to the Southern literati than it ought. I wonder, with malice toward none and charity to all, if a Fellowship of Southern Writers might not set as its aim the fostering of more writing that is simply vital and good and less that merely advertises its roots in the pea patch. If so, the nature of its business will have to be artistic more than geographic. That alone would take a burden off us all.

WESTERN LIT FROM MILTON TO ZANE GREY (AND OTHERS)

SUNDAY, JUNE 12, 1988

BY MICHAEL SKUBE

Jane Tompkins of the Duke University English Department is evidently an expert on Westerns and a professor besides, so I should be sheepish about betraying my naïveté. But I have read some Zane Grey in my brief time—not just as a fifth grader but one frivolous night last month—and I missed the deep stuff altogether. Mostly there were horses and and cowboys, a sheriff or two and enough desert dust to do a Ph.D. dissertation proud. But not a lot of Significance, unless I mistook it for sagebrush.

One should never be surprised to hear what's in style in the English departments, but when I read last week that Zane Grey was *au courant* (Louis L'Amour, too!), I thought I was back in the Sixties. In fact, I was, although the foment for social change back then overlooked the writers of the purple sage. It pretty much contented itself with the "people" and the pigs, and let it go at that.

That's why James Atlas' fawning article in The New York Times Magazine—an excerpt of which was carried in The News and Observer—peeled the scales from my eyes. In the furor over what is afoot in the humanities these days, it had escaped me what was at issue: not just the racist-sexist West but the Wild West with it, and anything else a professor can stake his tenure to. Overspecialization has drained the great wells of Western literature dry. The humanities, a skeptical Walter Jackson Bate of Harvard told Atlas, are in "their worst state of crisis since the modern university was formed a century ago." Bate, distinguished biographer of Keats and Samuel Johnson, said of the new enthusiasms, "They're looking for things to write. You can't write the 40th book on the structure of 'Paradise Lost.' "

So the English departments—long a burial ground for anyone wishing to become a writer—now become excavation sites. Hidden meanings are found where none had been suspected; forgotten masterpieces are exhumed; neglected writers are canonized, literally and figuratively.

All this is well and good. There ought to be more to literature than the short row of marble busts extending from Homer to T.S. Eliot—dead white men, as the insurgents are wont to say. But as usual in academia, proportion is lost, and what is peripheral to literature's enduring concerns becomes someone's career. Prof. Tompkins teaches a course titled "Home on the Range" (and, as Prof. Tompkins is a feminist, you may be sure the range is not the one in the kitchen); she also teaches courses on the novels of 19th century American writers who would be flattered to be called even minor.

Why, though, do courses need to be taught on these writers? Walter Jackson Bate's answer—that young professors are scavenging around looking for something, anything, to write about—only gets at part of the truth. More to the point, as Atlas reports, the curriculum has come to be seen as an instrument for social and political change. And the change is to the left. As Marjorie Garber, director of English graduate studies at Harvard, instructs us: "It wasn't only women we'd neglected. It was the whole third world."

A SONGFEST AT STANFORD

Whatever is eventually unearthed from those lost libraries of Khartoum, I wonder whether it is worth it to torch everything else. We see, at any rate, what the songfest was about at Stanford last year, when the Rev. Jesse Jackson played pied piper and the little girls and boys tagged along chanting "Hey, hey, ho, ho, Western culture's got to go." Those were English majors, I will wager—why, they may have been English *professors.* They call to mind Bazarov in Turgenev's "Fathers and Sons," the perfect embodiment of 19th century nihilism, who would destroy for the sake of destroying.

Well, let's not call them nihilists. They're simply students and professors going about with cliches and jargon pasted to their foreheads like bumper stickers. Western literature is Eurocentric, it's phallocentric, it's logocentric. One would like to think it was once heliocentric as well, young minds turning like buttercups toward the light of reason.

But let's don't haul out the platitudes. Perhaps it was all a sham.

Perhaps there's more to literature than what is universal in human experience. In the canon-busting that's going on at Duke, Stanford and elsewhere, there is also a large measure of campy politics, and it is the politics more than the literature that counts. "Gynocriticism"—the study of women in literature, for you simpletons who didn't know—is everywhere. At Harvard, Marjorie Garber is doing something to Sherlock Holmes called "cross-dressing" that doesn't sound good, and at Duke, Prof. Frank Lentricchia is hard at work feminizing Wallace Stevens' image. I don't know what will become of the Jane Austens and the Brontës and the Willa Cathers who have long been a part of the literary tradition of the English-speaking world, but the professors are shuffling the rankings. Even in the provinces, from N.C. State to Quaker State, the humanities are in ferment.

I suppose I am out of touch on this as on much else, but "Paradise Lost" I always took to be the story of man's fall from grace. I never stopped to think that Milton was male and white, only that "Paradise Lost" was not, as they say, a fast read ("No one ever wished it longer," Dr. Johnson rued). Neither did I, one night last month, interrupt "The Thundering Herd" to ponder the deeper meaning of it all. I took Zane Grey at face value, just as I did when I was kid, and let him put me safely to sleep. Naïve me.

NORTH TO ALASKA WITH JAMES MICHENER

SUNDAY, JULY 3, 1988

BY MICHAEL SKUBE

James Michener's new cinderblock of a book, "Alaska," is 868 pages long, and I think I began reading it sometime toward the end of the last Ice Age. I have been chipping away at it, in any case, for what seems an awfully long time. "Alaska" (Random House) is not a book to be read so much as got through. Events move along at glacial speed, an inch at a time, until the dinosaurs are gone and the oceans have receded and the landmasses have emerged and at last something we might recognize as Alaska comes dimly into view. When you've not read one in a while, you forget just how long a book James Michener can write.

Everyone knows, of course, about Michener. He writes woodenly, he appeals to people who move their lips when they read and his books sell by the truckload, like so many boxes of bran flakes. It is all true and it is also shooting fish in a barrel to assert it every two years when Michener sits atop the best seller list. Maybe a little snobbish, too. This is a plump and tough old tuna, and he has taken many a shell from his more literary detractors.

There's little point, then, in a critic's making a pre-emptive strike when the trucks dock outside the book stores, freighted with spanking new Micheners. They will sell anyway. "Alaska," which arrived in the stores less than two weeks ago, has made its first appearance on The New York Times best seller list and is immediately No. 1. It will remain at the top or near it for a long while, in hardback and then in paperback. Michener's readers don't care what any reviewer thinks, and who knows that they are not the wiser for it?

More to the point, the reviewer doesn't set himself up to sell or not sell books. He offers unsolicited opinions about them, among other things. In Michener's case, the temptation is always strong to fire a few well-aimed BBs at the barn door and knock off for the day. I wondered, though, what it is that readers find in novels heavier than the dictionary and shapeless as a sack of potatoes. I kept thinking of what two writer-friends—both of them people I respect—happened to say recently. One was talking about Michener's energy: "Say what you want about his style, his writing, all of that. Here's a man 81 years old doing a hell of a lot of research and writing books that people want to read."

The other friend confessed to having read Michener's "Covenant," his South Africa saga: "All I knew about South Africa from papers and TV was that its crazy government wouldn't let black people have the vote, so violence and strikes persist. Because the book started with events that happened something like 300 years ago, I understand better how South Africa got that way."

HISTORY AS FICTION

So it's "history," is it? Or at least the feeling of history. With Michener, fact and fiction are never far apart; indeed, one wonders if he does not write something we should call "faction." Regardless, his appeal is for many readers the feeling of real events, of history done up in fictional dress and on the march. "At least when I read Michener," I've heard people say, "I feel like I'm learning something." You might grit your teeth, as I did mine, but it's worth considering why intelligent people know so emphatically what they like.

Equally, it's worth considering that the line between fiction and nonfiction is not so inviolate as we sometimes think. Since the appearance more than 20 years ago of Truman Capote's "In Cold Blood," fiction and nonfiction have borrowed from one another with scant regard for veracity or authenticity. E. L. Doctorow, in "Ragtime," "World's Fair" and other novels, places historical figures in situations that could not have existed. Robert Coover, in "The Public Burning," has a narrator named Richard M. Nixon (he makes an appearance in Kurt Vonnegut's "Jailbird," too). Joseph Heller's "Good as Gold" has a character who could only be Henry Kissinger. Gore Vidal not only puts his own words into Lincoln's mouth but gives him, in a manner of speaking, syphilis.

The reverse of this occurs at least as frequently—applying the storytelling techniques of fiction to journalism or history. Bob Woodward and Scott Armstrong's book about the Supreme Court, "The Brethren," rests heavily on conversations the authors could not have overheard. Likewise Norman Mailer's "true-life novel" about the convicted murderer Gary Gilmore, "The Executioner's Song."

"For many novelists," says the critic Michael Wood, "there comes a point when you think, 'I don't want to write another book about me and my divorce. My next work should be *significant.*' And so you go out hunting for historical material."

He was not speaking of James Michener. Historical matter is Michener's meat and he serves it up like hamburger. In "Alaska" (once we've made it out of the Bronze age) we follow the Dutch navigator Vitus Bering, on commission from Peter the Great, tracking the vast emptiness east of Siberia. There are more cossacks than Mikhail Sholokhov could ever have imagined, Aleuts and Eskimo chiefs, whale and walrus and an old wise woman called the Ancient One, the Gold Rush and, if you make it that far, the Alcan Highway. And all this in a novel. There are people who say things like, "Son, if you take that route, you and me is gonna cross swords," and thoughts for the day like, "A man's character reveals itself on an ice pack or a mountain slope." There's a sex scene—I guess that's what it was—that made me think of two sawhorses.

Not to put too fine a point on it, this is not minimalist fiction. It is not a wan story about wan little people in which nothing happens. And that is precisely why Random House manufactured 750,000 copies of "Alaska" for first printing, and has already gone into second printing. Its octogenarian author, a publicist at Random House tells me, is on location in Miami researching a new docudrama—Caribbean. Don't hold me to it, but I predict he will take us from roughly 1 million years ago to the Age of Fidel and Jimmy Buffett. And he will weigh in at just under 1,000 pages. When this man turns on the faucet, he lets it run.

A MOST EXCELLENT MAN, ON THE FACE OF IT

SUNDAY, JULY 17, 1988

BY MICHAEL SKUBE

At 50, Orwell wrote, everyone has the face he deserves. No one deserves a face like Virgil Thomson's. No one has earned a face like that. Look at it: homely as a cantaloupe and hard as a coconut, and ready at a flash to put fools in their place. At 91, Virgil Thomson has the face he deserves, and let us applaud him for it.

Unless you have more than a nodding acquaintance with American music, the name may ring a bell, but only faintly. Virgil Thomson—composer, critic, Francophile from Kansas City—is one of the last survivors of the Lost Generation of American artists who went to Paris in the 1920s and '30s. His collaboration with Gertrude Stein—in "The Mother of Us All" and "Four Saints in Three Acts"—revitalized American opera ("Gertrude was not very musical, and I didn't write poetry, so that kept us out of each other's professional hair"). Practically the entire American expatriate crowd in Paris he knew—Hemingway, Fitzgerald, the Murphys, Sherwood Anderson and all the rest. Through Sylvia Beach he met James Joyce ("at her flat, I think"). He spent enough time around Picasso to remember him not just as a genius but also as "a bastard and an SOB."

But all this, for me at least, is incidental. Paris was yesterday if not the day before, and, anyway, I know nothing about musical composition and am happily ignorant of the opera. Crotchets I know something about. These Thomson had plenty of and he did not wait for anyone's permission to express them. He hated German music, and he hated more the slavish pedantry of the German-influenced American music schools; he called Vladimir Horowitz a "master of musical distortion" (reviewing a Horowitz recital, he wrote: "He made [Chopin's] Funeral March sound like a Russian boat song"); and he felt not the slightest hesitation in calling a performance by the New York Philharmonic a disaster.

From 1940 to 1954, as music critic of the New York Herald Tribune, Virgil Thomson wrote some of the best-informed and most pungent criticism our century has seen. He was more than a critic among musicians and a musician among critics; he was Virgil Thomson, and people paid attention. Seven years ago, Dutton published in paperback "A Virgil Thomson Reader," a rich collection of his pieces over half a century. Now Summit has published "The Selected Letters of Virgil Thomson" (edited by Tim Page and Vanessa Weeks Page, $24.95).

The great critic was also one of our great letter writers. He answered one reader:

"I thank you for the charming letter. German music has been smelling bad for a long time. It is largely from this fact that I conclude it must be dead. It will take a little time, however, to get it buried."

To a musician incredulous that he could have called the first movement of Beethoven's "Eroica" a "dud," he answered with what amounted almost to a review in itself—ordered paragraphs comparing the first movement with the second and the work as a whole to the Fifth, Sixth, and Eighth symphonies. He paid his dues to genius ("I assure you I do not hold any controversial opinions about Beethoven"), and held to his convictions: "A beautiful work it is, yes, a very beautiful work, but far more often than not a well-known putter-to-sleep of audiences."

WAITING FOR A WATCH

He flattered readers he had never met by taking the time to write even while he jousted with them (in this regard and others, he was much like H. L. Mencken). But many of Thomson's best letters had nothing to do with music or art. Two of these he wrote to the Hamilton Watch Company. The first asked that his watch be repaired ("Please make it work for me. I miss it"). A month later, he reminded the company that he had sent the watch as registered mail No. 415534, had soon thereafter paid a repair bill of $22.95 including New York City sales tax, and still no watch. He would appreciate "a letter stating the nature of the repair done and, if this included a cleaning, how long I may expect the watch to remain in service before it will need a further cleaning." And while the company was at it, it might also provide him "an explanation of the charge for New York sales tax or return of the amount erroneously so charged."

But above all he wanted that watch back. "Your silence," his letter closed, "gets me down."

The pleasures of Thomson's letters are the pleasures of his published prose. He combines a sophisticate's wit with a Missourian's frankness, and the sound that results is authentically American. As a critic, he had no use for congealed opinion; he would make up his own mind. Answering criticism of an unflattering review of Jascha Heifetz, he once wrote: "I could not then, cannot now, regret having told what I thought the truth about an artist whom I believed to be overestimated. To all such reputations, in fact, I was sales resistant, like William James, who had boasted, 'I am against greatness and bigness in all their forms.'"

This is not always a universally appreciated trait. Thomson, when he first began writing music criticism for the Herald Tribune, heard important names in New York demanding that the newspaper fire him for an inadequate piety toward the Metropolitan Opera and the Philharmonic (the truth was that his reviews of their performances were generally favorable). The newspaper, to its great credit, resisted unprincipled pressure. Thomson, to his credit equally, remained a critic and not a fan. If some of us look into the mirrow and wonder if justice has been done, Virgil Thomson can look into it and know that it's been done and done very well.

T. S. ELIOT'S SOLITARY SEARCH FOR SALVATION

SUNDAY, NOVEMBER 6, 1988

BY MICHAEL SKUBE

> **ELIOT'S NEW LIFE**
> By Lyndall Gordon, (Farrar Straus Giroux)

"Nothing but a brilliant future behind me," T. S. Eliot said in 1934. He was 45 years old, the most revered figure in modern poetry, a man who with a single poem—"The Waste Land"—had given voice to an age. His triumphs were public and historic, his failures were private and hellish. It is these latter—the long shadows in T. S. Eliot's solitary existence as a man—that Lyndall Gordon explores in this second volume of her masterly biography. With its predecessor, "Eliot's Early Years," it penetrates better than any previous biography to the skull beneath the skin (to borrow Eliot's famous words), and it does so in a manner that is as sympathetic as it is judiciously critical.

It has not always been easy to accord T.S. Eliot a measure of human sympathy. He was not a man whose feeling for others exactly bubbled over. His look was cold, severe, wrathful. The poet and essayist Donald Hall, in his fine book "Remembering Poets," recalls first meeting him when Mr. Hall was editor of the Harvard Advocate, the campus poetry magazine: "His face was pale as baker's bread. He stooped as he sat at his desk, and when he stood he slouched like the witch in the gingerbread house. His head shook forward slightly, from time to time, almost as if he nodded toward sleep. He smoked, and between inhalations he hacked a dry, deathly, smoker's hack. His speech—while precise, exact, perfect—was slow to move, as if he stood behind the boulder of each word, pushing it into view. Eliot was *cadaverous*, in 1951."

T. S. Eliot died in 1965, about the time his star went into full eclipse. We're apt to overlook in 1988, on the centenary of his birth, how supremely Eliot shone in the firmament only half a century ago.

The Cambridge History of English Literature assigns to three writers alone the custody of entire periods of poetry and prose. In the Cambridge History, there is no Age of Milton, no Age of Dickens, not even an Age of Shakespeare. But there is an Age of Dryden and an Age of Johnson. And there is an Age of Eliot.

THE PRIVATE ELIOT

Lyndall Gordon—a lecturer in American and English literature at Oxford—doesn't waste her time or ours arguing Eliot's place in literature, although her incidental judgments strike me as sharp and discerning. Her real subject is Eliot as ambitious poet, unhappy husband, searcher for spiritual salvation, monk *manque.* The outward facts of his life are well-known: He grew up in St. Louis, went to Harvard, then to England after graduating. His interests were originally in philosophy—he finished a doctoral dissertation on F. H. Bradley—but he had written verse in his Harvard years. In Europe, he was befriended by Ezra Pound, who suggested he cut here and recast there a poem Eliot showed him. The poem, published in 1915, was "The Love Song of J. Alfred Prufrock."

In June of the same year, Eliot married a woman he had known less than three months, Vivienne Haigh-Wood. The marriage was a disaster, for both ("The awful daring of a moment's surrender/which an age of prudence can never retract"). It is one of Ms. Gordon's central points that "The Waste Land" was a reflection not only of the cultural disintegration of the postwar years, but also of Eliot's precarious sanity. The Eliots separated in 1933, Vivienne half-sane and half not, her husband saved only by his conversion to the Anglican Church.

Eliot embraced the faith in 1927. The same year he renewed his friendship with Emily Hale, a woman he had been in love with before he sailed for Europe 12 years earlier. Emily Hale, in Lyndall Gordon's telling of the story, was the woman Eliot should have married and did not. She was the woman Eliot could have married once he and his wife separated, and still did not. "Emily Hale," Ms. Gordon writes, "never claimed, like Vivienne, to have been Eliot's muse. She was concerned more with the man than the poet. . . . Of the latent monk, and the heights of a destiny that would exclude any close human contact until it was fulfilled, she saw perhaps not enough."

AN ETHEREAL LOVE

To a deeply unhappy T. S. Eliot, Emily Hale represented an idealization of love—she was pure and, for Eliot, inviolable. Eliot, whose bloodline was New England Puritan, had never been entirely comfortable with the sordid rushes of the flesh, and he never forgot his wife's adultery with Bertrand Russell, his onetime benefactor. In Emily Hale, Eliot saw "the material of religious poetry," Ms. Gordon writes. "And when his poetic searching of the soul came to an end, so too did his interest in her."

The notion is magnificently Eliotic, and maybe a little idiotic as well. In any event, "what Eliot needed was not love in the usual sense, passion or care, but love's transforming power, the idea of a momentous drama, partly on the model of Dante and Beatrice, partly a Jamesian drama of buried sensibilities." Eliot was not the first to ask more of love than love can give. By the time of his religious conversion, the pre-eminent poet of modernism was prepared to renounce love for salvation. Miraculously, he would find both. In 1957, eight years before he died, he married his 30-year-old secretary, Valerie Fletcher.

"Marriage," Ms. Gordon writes, "brought out a sense of fun that was always there, in the child on a St. Louis street corner, smiling mischievously at his nurse, Annie Dunne; in the middle-aged Eliot who had entertained Janet Adam Smith's children with readings from 'Uncle Remus.' " He had won the Nobel nine years earlier; now the impulse to write poetry was fading. Now he exchanged fan letters with Groucho Marx (hanging his picture on his mantelpiece alongside Yeats). He permitted himself domesticity, discussing cake shops and greengrocers: "He liked to play the humorous pet, like one of his cats who represent, in caricature, some aspects of Eliot himself. Macavity, the monster of depravity, vanished in this period, but Gus the theatre cat remained, and Jennyanydots, the domestic purrer."

The peace of which T. S. Eliot wrote in the years of his celebrity—the "still point in a turning world"—he found where he had never before looked. It is not the least of Lyndall Gordon's gifts as a biographer that she somehow portrays this most saintly and rarefied man as a man after all.

LARRY McMURTRY STILL THE BEST IN THE WEST

SUNDAY, NOVEMBER 13, 1988

BY MICHAEL SKUBE

ANYTHING FOR BILLY
By Larry McMurtry, (Simon and Schuster)

Seven years ago, Larry McMurtry issued an encyclical of sorts on what might apologetically be called the state of letters in his native Texas. It was a remarkable document, fiercely intelligent, opinionated and hardly imaginable in any other state. He surveyed the roll of Texas writers and found just one, maybe two, who repaid a reader's time. The Bureau of Census neglects to tabulate these things, but it's a reasonable guess that there are more writers in that rowdy republic than in any principality outside New York City. None of them stands so prominently in contemporary American fiction as Larry McMurtry, a part-time resident these days of Washington, D.C., California and the Texas ranch on which he grew up.

The gist of his criticism was that the fiction being written by Texas writers still slavered to a rural-cowboy myth: "Not only are there few readable city books, but many of the country books are filled with explicit anti-urbanism. Writer after writer strains to reaffirm his or her rural credentials. . . . Why are there still cows to be milked and chickens to be fed in every other Texas book that comes along? When is enough going to be enough?" We have, he said, too many bucolics; "what we need is a Balzac, a Dickens, even a Dreiser."

I bring this up for two reasons. One is that it suggests an argument that could be made in many another state that looks nostalgically to its rural past even though it has been predominantly urban for decades. But my more immediate interest is in the luck of Larry McMurtry, whose 12th novel, "Anything for Billy," was a best seller almost as soon as it arrived in book stores.

No modern writer, surely, has resisted his own advice more successfully than Larry McMurtry has. When his article appeared in the pages of The Texas Observer in 1981, "The Last Picture Show" and "Horseman, Pass By" (the movie version settled for a less literary "Hud") were more than 10 years behind him. He had moved on, to paraphrase the title of another of his books. "Terms of Endearment," an affectingly beautiful novel that explored the bonds of familial love, was set in modern Houston; that was 1975. Other novels followed, one set in Las Vegas, another in Washington, still another in Hollywood; all of them were funny, none of them stayed long in one's memory.

Then—four years after his call for an end to the myth of the cowboy—came "Lonesome Dove." It won Mr. McMurtry the Pultizer Prize, it secured him a huge new following and, not incidentally, it established itself as a Western idyll. Never before had the Old West, cowboys and all, been rendered so lyrically, made to permanently alive. Mr. McMurtry followed "Lonesome Dove" with another, lesser Western novel. "Texasville" was a contrived sequel to "The Last Picture Show" whose high humor could not mask the thinness of its imagination.

To come, then, upon "Anything for Billy" is as much a puzzle as it is a pleasure. If Mr. McMurtry believes "the death of the cowboy and the ending of the rural way of life [have] been sufficiently lamented," he no longer is in any great hurry to write about something else. "Anything for Billy" puts on display many of the things Mr. McMurtry has been doing well for more than 20 years now. It is often very funny, and sometimes very sad; it is a burlesque of Billy the Kid without being a novel "about" him. The Kid, in fact, is not the pitable Henry McCarty, who changed his name to Bill Bonney and lived a short, violent life that would be transmuted into romantic myth.

For that matter, Billy is not even the central character. From its lovely first sentence—"The first time I saw Billy he came walking out of a cloud"—to its somewhat anti-climactic finish in Philadelphia, "Anything for Billy" is the story of Ben Sippy, a not-very-good dime-novel writer. Sippy wearies of his wife Dora and their nine daughters, leaves Philadelphia for the Wild West and meets up in New Mexico with bucktoothed Billy Bone and Joe Lovelady, a quiet man who deserves better than he gets.

ROBBING THE TRAINS

Sippy's got it in his head he can write dime novels better than the hacks cranking out the adventures of Mustang Merle and the Kansas Kitten, and he means to learn something of the West first hand. What follows is a succession of improbable adventures in which Old West legend is put at the service of Mr. McMurtry's gift for comedy. Not infrequently the comedy is a little stagey, but it's a funny spoof just the same of all those Western movies. Sippy, for example, sets out to rob a train on an Easterner's naive belief that "if you showed up on the tracks with the proper hardware it would stop and let itself be robbed."

The first train Sippy tries to rob sends him diving off the embankment for his life. He tries again: "Rosy [his horse] and I raced up beside the engine and I shot off my pistol a few more times, thinking that the engineer would soon realize a robbery was in progress and shut things down." The engineer "just laughed and waved his cap at me and kept on engineering." Our determined train robber races alongside for several miles, firing shots into the air before dropping his pistol trying to reload on the run.

Nothing in "Anything for Billy" bears comparison with "Lonesome Dove," but there's no reason why it should. McMurtry has written an "entertainment," a book of modest ambitions and modest achievement. It's not giving too much away to report that the beguiling Billy is shot in the end, only it's not by Sheriff Pat Garrett.

What matters a good deal more is that Mr. McMurtry somehow sustains our interest with what seems the flimsiest of materials—a hoked-up Western legend, a finely drawn character or two and a cast of stage props, a narrative line spindly as a colt's legs. His prose is occasionally careless, his humor sometimes forced—so is Dickens', so is Balzac's. But there is a sweet poignancy in this most ordinary tale that few writers could achieve. That Mr. McMurtry should make of this unpromising material a novel as engaging as "Anything for Billy" only shows how adept a writer he is. Whatever he may advise others to do, he still writes the best Westerns in the land.

'CREATIVE WRITING' AND THE ENGLISH DEPARTMENT

SUNDAY, DECEMBER 11, 1988

BY MICHAEL SKUBE

Three days every week Pete Dexter writes a column for The Sacramento Bee. He recalls taking a few "creative writing" courses in college, back at the University of South Dakota, but he didn't get his education as a writer in any classroom. Mr. Dexter, whose novel "Paris Trout' won the National Book Award last week, feeds on raw life around him. "If you only listen to your own voice," he says, "it just gets narrower and narrower. I'm the kind of writer who's got to get out there and talk to people." Vision, structure, the imaginative process—all those things are fine to maunder on about in class, but writing is another thing entirely.

Obvious though this is, "creative writing"—I will put the quotation marks away—is a growth industry in the English departments these days. Enrollment in English as an undergraduate major has declined almost to the vanishing point, but creative writing is everywhere. Unpublished, of course. Readings and workshops dot the calendar like federal holidays. Baggage claim at the airports is bustling with Famous Writers, fresh from one conference and off to another.

I have my doubts about this, if you have not guessed, and they're the same ones I had about the Charles Atlas ads I used to read when I was still a 97-pound weakling. They promised too much, and preyed on the innocent. They did not very often deliver, either, and this is something else Charles Atlas and Famous Writer have in common. In my own disillusioning experience, I have seen the copy of too many graduates of so-called writing programs, some of them published authors. I don't know what they learned in creative writing class, but they certainly didn't learn to write well.

Pete Dexter, for one, questions whether creative writing can be taught at all. This is not to say that college students could not be taught to write better than they do—to write adequately, let us optimistically say. But then, teaching writing is not the business of the English department anymore, once freshman composition is out of the way. "You don't major in English to learn how to write," a professor recently told me. "You major in it to learn how other people write."

WRITERS AS TEACHERS

There are, as ever, splendid exceptions—underappreciated instructors in composition and writers who are known to excel as teachers. Of these latter, three come to mind immediately: Lee Smith of N.C. State; Doris Betts of the University of North Carolina at Chapel Hill, and Fred Chappel of UNC–Greensboro.

But there remains the question of creative writing as a thing apart. Tom Wolfe urges young fiction writers to do more reporting—more observing of the people and the world around them—and less communing with their muses. "From [personal experience], you get one book. You use up the first 25 years of your life in your first novel," he told Rebecca Freligh of the Cleveland Plain Dealer last month. Anyone who reads much contemporary fiction of the kind popular in the universities notices its remoteness from tangible, breathing human life. One of the reasons is the notion that writing fiction is a kind of holy experience. A North Carolina writer who defected from a graduate program several years ago talks about the literary life in the cloister:

"I got increasingly frustrated with what I think is the prevailing mood in graduate English departments, that literature is a precious substance somehow removed from its audience. The work they were developing, the attitudes they were cultivating, seemed too precious, too self-absorbed. I was certain they would be able to win the acclaim of other writers trained in similar programs, but unsure whether anything they wrote would have any real value."

Over the past 25 years, nothing has changed American fiction more than its institutionalization by the English department. Long gone is the day when a young writer headed off to Europe, unpublished but wanting to experience the world. Now he will enroll at the Iowa Writers Workshop, or one of the dozens of programs like it, and he will sit in seminars with a Famous Writer and the class will talk solemnly about the Theory of the Novel and they will listen to one another read. Our student might find some grant money, perhaps spend two weeks up at Bread Loaf/Yaddo/McDowell. He may write a collection of short stories to fulfill his requirements for the Master of Fine Arts, a degree no more indicative of achievement than the label on one's underwear.

WRITING FOR ROGER

But the fiction that has been coming out of these nurseries is hot stuff, albeit passionless, in the English departments. It is fiction emulative of the likes of Ann Beattie, Bobbie Jo Mason, Donald Barthelme, Raymond Carver and a dozen other dullards. It is sometimes polished in structure and other times impoverished in vocabulary. And it is almost always self-conscious, as though the writer were writing for Roger Angell at The New Yorker.

The editor Ted Solotaroff has been handmaiden to many of the best fiction writers of our time. Like the North Carolina free-lancer I quoted above, Mr. Solotaroff senses an insularity that does no writer much good. "At a respectable professional level," he says, "writing for publication makes one into someone who writes rather than, in Robert Louis Stevenson's distinction, someone who wants to have written. Writing without publishing gets to be like loving someone from afar—delicious for fantasies but thin gruel for living. That is why, to my mind, a strongly written review, a profile, a piece of reportage in a regional magazine—the Village Voice, or Texas Monthly, or Seattle Magazine—is worth three 'Try us again's' from The New Yorker."

He touches, without holding up for public view, on one of the reasons for the low standing of so-called literary fiction outside the English departments. The proliferation of creative writing schools has fostered the notion that writing fiction is a private reverie, with the result that any sensible reader soon gets bored and moves on to someone who has a real story to tell.

ELEVEN

THE PEOPLE'S REPUBLIC OF CHICAGO

1989 WINNER IN THE COMMENTARY CATEGORY

"For distinguished commentary . . ."

Chicago Tribune
Clarence Page

Clarence Page developed the watchful eye of a journalist at an early age. He still doesn't always like what he sees on the political and social landscape, and when he detects injustice, he flags it.

Am I a black American journalist or a journalist who happens to be a black American? Some people think the question is rude. For me, at least, I think it has some merit.

I would be lying if I said I was not profoundly influenced to this day by the bitter experience of being told at the age of six that I could not go to a nearby amusement park because "Little colored children ain't allowed in that park." It is an experience just about every black American has to confront at some time in their formative years. It made me sensitive to the feelings of others and to the plight of underdogs. It also made me sensitive to leaders who were true statesmen as well as those who were full of hot air. Such sensitivity is an important quality for journalists to have.

I decided when I was 16 years old that I would like to make my living as a journalist. The decision was closely linked with the history that was unfolding daily in the headlines. It was 1964. There were civil rights demonstrators risking their lives in the South. Anti-war demonstrators were just beginning to churn up on a few campuses. The nation still reeled from the shock of President John F. Kennedy's assassination. Barry Goldwater was promoting a countermovement of hard-core conservatism. A quartet of British mop-topped musicians called the Beatles was sending shock waves through Western civilization. History was happening. I wanted to be an eyewitness to it, perhaps even a part of it. It was a decision I might have reached had I not been black. But it would have been for a different set of reasons.

Born in the baby-boom years just after World War II, I grew up in the days when racial segregation was still the law of the land in many states and a matter of rigidly followed custom in others, including southern Ohio where I grew up. Watching the journalists who covered the civil rights demonstrations in the South had a profound impact on me as I worked on my high school newspaper in the North. Media exposure was crucial to the success of the movement in building public sympathy and political support. The power of the media to do good or support evil was vividly apparent to me.

For example, "The Mayor Stands by His Man—And Looks Like a Heel," resulted from outrage I felt at the sluggish way Chicago's second black mayor was responding to bigotry and anti-Semitism in his own administration in a scandal known nationwide as "the Steve Cokely affair." The column was a last-minute decision—written in about an hour—as Mayor Eugene Sawyer vacillated for what turned out to be almost a week over whether to keep Cokely in his administration. As fragile inter-ethnic coalitions crumbled, no black elected officials spoke out. I received calls from several people asking me to say something. In the absence of other voices during those tense days (Cokely finally was fired the day after my column appeared), I became what many called a badly needed voice of reason. It is, in my view, the most important role a columnist can have.

In composing "Tawana Brawley, Twice a Victim," I considered the central controversy regarding whether Brawley was raped as she claimed and whether it was being properly investigated, but I was stricken by how another, separate tragedy appeared to be happening to this young woman in the middle of the public spotlight. Perhaps my own experience made it seem particularly painful to me that this time the exploitation was the fault of blacks who called themselves leaders.

In composing "Dr. King's Legacy: The Way Is Clear, the Will Is Uncertain," I was dismayed by the way Reagan-era conservatives so freely invoked Dr. King's name in their attempts to roll back civil rights reforms that Dr. King supported. The anniversary of his assassination seemed an appropriate time to give a little history lesson.

By contrast, "A Deplorable Effort to Help Dentists Shun AIDS Victims," is an example of a Page column that has no racial angle but tries to take a moral stand that tries to help us all strike a delicate balance of human rights and freedoms in the face of a nightmarish health crisis. Again, I tried to interject a calm voice of reason into the middle of a highly emotional, often shrill debate.

Enough. Good columns should explain themselves. I'll let you, dear reader, be the judge. I offer all of this background to say that I hope my personal experience gives me a point of view that brings something fresh and important to the table of public opinion, whether readers agree with everything I say or not.

A final note: Except for my family, my work is my life. It became my dream as a junior in high school to become a newspaper columnist. So, as I tell young people these days, be patient; It took me only 20 years to become an "overnight success."

—Clarence Page
Chicago Tribune

THE PEOPLE'S REPUBLIC OF CHICAGO

SUNDAY, JUNE 26, 1988

BY CLARENCE PAGE

If you ever needed an example of how politics can be, in the words of Ambrose Bierce, a strife of interests masquerading as a contest of principles, just look at the fight some Chicago aldermen are waging with the American Civil Liberties Union.

The ACLU has filed a $100,000 federal civil rights lawsuit on behalf of an art student whose controversial painting of the late Mayor Harold Washington was seized from display at a student exhibit in the School of the Art Institute of Chicago by nine aldermen and various police officers on May 11.

The suspect painting, a thoroughly tasteless rendering of Washington in women's underwear, was eventually released from custody after apparently being roughed up (a hole was slashed across its face) and is still at large. So, unfortunately, are the aldermen.

Artist David K. Nelson, 23, says he meant no harm, that he was moved to make "an anti-deistic statement" when he saw a poster that portrayed Washington as something of a deity. Oh, really?

Nelson showed a reckless disregard for taste and civility in a town treacherously polarized along racial lines. Washington's memory is so highly regarded by blacks here that an attack on him is interpreted by many as an attack on the black community. If Nelson did not know that, he is more than a fun-loving goof. He's pretty stupid.

But even if Nelson were a fire-breathing racist, he deserves to win this case. His right to free expression deserves to be protected as much as the Picasso statue at the Daley Civic Center should be protected from the likes of one former alderman who once called for replacing it with a statue of ex-Cub Ernie Banks.

Attacks on anyone's civil rights, no matter how loathsome that person's expressions may be, can come back to bite you. One extreme example, Ald. Robert Shaw, who seldom lets facts get in the way of a narrow pitch to his constituency, accused ACLU lawyers of always taking "the white side" in black-white disputes. Say, what? Where was he during the ACLU's countless cases of defending the rights of minorities, like its victory for Dick Gregory's campaign to march through the late Mayor Richard J. Daley's all-white Bridgeport neighborhood in 1969?

And how about Ald. Bobby Rush, who as a Black Panther leader in the turmoil of Chicago in the '60s was helped many times by the ACLU? Now, as a party named in the Art Institute suit, Rush called the suit "frivolous and impetuous" and accused the ACLU of having political or publicity-seeking motives.

Well, as a black Chicagoan who has waited all of his adult life to see black political empowerment in a city where old power elites had held blacks back for decades, I am thoroughly disappointed by this episode. After seeing, under Harold Washington, a black leadership emerge as the very embodiment of Rev. Martin Luther King Jr.'s progressive dream, I have watched it deteriorate since his death in November to the likes of Idi Amin or "Baby Doc" Duvalier. Welcome to the People's Republic of Chicago.

Of course, with the 20th anniversary of Chicago's disastrous 1968 Democratic convention approaching, it is sobering to note how, at their worst, the city's emerging black political powers are only repeating the flagrant disregard for civil liberties their predecessors sometimes showed.

It is ironic to see aldermanic storm troopers, some of them lukewarm in their support for Washington during his life, become thundering zealots after his death, threatening the Art Institute with physical harm and compelling the police to order the painting imprisoned to avoid a riot. Sorry. Court precedents that support the duty of the police to control the mob, not the person whose expression is inciting it, run long and deep.

But the bigger irony is that Washington was a bold supporter of civil liberties. He probably would have laughed the painting off. "We're not in the business of censorship," he said when his aldermanic enemies bashed his administrator for a black poet's controversial poem on the city Department of Fine Arts' novel "Dial-A-Poem" service. "If you scratch one word, where does it stop?"

I am sure Washington would have had the good sense to have avoided making a major issue out of a silly drawing. Such good sense would have denied it the publicity it has enjoyed as it is flashed constantly on the local evening news as this issue drags on.

Frankly, I wonder how the aldermen found out about the painting. They are less likely to be associated with the fine arts than with, say, crayons and coloring books. Perhaps the artist told them. Maybe Nelson wanted what in the '60s we used to call a "happening" and today is called a media event. Whether that is what he wanted, it is precisely what he got.

"In the city of Chicago, the liberty of free expression is gravely ill," civil libertarian Nat Hentoff wrote in New York's Village Voice. So, it appears, is the sobering influence of good leadership.

THANKS FOR BEING HONEST, JIMMY 'THE GREEK'—TOO HONEST

WEDNESDAY, JANUARY 20, 1988

BY CLARENCE PAGE

Thank you, Jimmy "the Greek" Snyder. Your remarks about black athletes help confirm what many of us have been saying about the entertainment industry known as professional sports.

Patterns of racial discrimination run so deeply through professional sports, as through the rest of our society, that even a savvy 70-year-old oddsmaker like yourself can lose track of what is acceptable and what is just plain goofy to say on television.

You goofed after being asked by a TV reporter in a Washington restaurant for your comments on black athletes as part of a story observing Rev. Martin Luther King Jr.'s birthday.

Most folks know how to finesse such moments, even to the point of outright hypocrisy. President Reagan, who fought King while the civil rights leader was alive, lavishes him with tributes now that he is dead—even while opposing reforms King's movement brought about.

But you didn't play that game, Jimmy. You said what was on your mind and your mind had some pretty oddball notions about black athletes: "They've got everything. If they take over coaching like everybody wants them to, there's not going to be anything left for the white people. . . . I mean, all the players are black; I mean, the only thing that the whites control is the coaching jobs."

Yeah, you really stepped in it with that, Jimmy.

"The black is a better athlete to begin with," you said. "Because he's been bred to be that way, because of his high thighs and big thighs that go up into his back and they can jump higher and run faster because of their bigger thighs, you see. . . ."

"This goes back all the way to the Civil War when . . . the slave owner would breed his big black to his big woman so that he could have a big black kid. . . ."

I believe you when you say you were trying to praise, not demean, black athletes. You just had a peculiar way of doing it that reminded everyone of how a seemingly intelligent guy like you can harbor some pretty ridiculous notions about race.

It also reminded a lot of us how often the sentiments you expressed must be passed around in backrooms and boardrooms, in and out of sports.

Your "big thighs" sentiments were essentially like those of sports broadcasters who, in the heat of play-by-play analysis, attribute skill in white players to "intelligence" but in black players to "natural" talent.

And although your remark, perhaps offered in jest, that "there's not going to be anything left for the white people" was compared to last year's gaffe by former Los Angeles Dodgers vice president Al Campanis when he said blacks do not have the "necessities" to manage, it differs little from positions respected conservatives offer in complete seriousness.

"What a court adds to one person's constitutional rights, it subtracts from the rights of others," said Judge Robert Bork. Was he not saying, in effect, that if we continue to give rights to blacks and other minorities there will not be anything left for whites?

Sen. Paul Simon thought so. When he asked the judge to clarify his statement before the Senate Judiciary Committee, Bork did not back down. "I think it's a matter of plain arithmetic," he said.

When Bork says it he gets praise from conservatives and begrudging admiration from moderates. When you say it, Jimmy, you get the ax.

Sometimes it is not what you say but how you say it. Your mistake was to articulate your sentiments in the words of common folk.

Of course, there is another way of looking at it that could have kept you out of trouble. As Simon told Bork, "I have long thought it to be fundamental in our society that when you expand the liberty of any of us, you expand the liberty of all of us."

Judge Anthony M. Kennedy, no liberal, agreed. "Our constitutional history is replete with examples," said the current Supreme Court nominee. "As a result, all of our freedoms have been enhanced."

I hope your experience has taught some folks a valuable lesson, Jimmy. You do not have to show the race hatred of a Ku Klux Klansman or the racial fear of Bernhard Goetz to be a racist. You can have many black friends and still qualify, just by showing the racial ignorance of, say, an Al Campanis.

Now, like him, you're the fall guy. Some of us are willing to forgive you, Jimmy. The entertainment industry known as professional sports won't.

TAWANA BRAWLEY, TWICE A VICTIM

SUNDAY, JUNE 19, 1988

BY CLARENCE PAGE

When elephants fight, according to an ancient proverb of the East African Kikuyu people, it is the grass that suffers. So it is with the peculiar case of Tawana Brawley, a black schoolgirl who, whether or not she was the victim of a racially motivated abduction and rape as she says, appears to have become lost in the struggle between her "friends."

Last November, police found Brawley, then 15, of Wappinger Falls, N.Y., smeared with dog excrement and wrapped in a garbage bag, racial epithets written on her body in charcoal. She said she had been sexually abused over four days by six white men, one of whom showed a police-type badge and holster.

The case shocked the nation. Bill Cosby and a black publisher offered a $25,000 reward. Boxer Mike Tyson offered to pay for her college education. Black leaders challenged politicians and the media to explain why the bizarre case was not receiving more attention. That is not its problem today.

It has received the world as an audience via the media, including "Donahue" and "Nightline," with one question constantly raised: Can a black get justice in America's criminal justice system? Unfortunately, the case has turned into too much of a media circus and a mud-wrestling match for political opportunists to be a good one on which to judge that question.

The Brawley family brought in three controversial heat-seeking black activists, Rev. Al Sharpton and lawyers Alton Maddox Jr. and C. Vernon Mason, all of New York City and all of whom achieved national fame for forcing the Howard Beach case to a special prosecutor. In that case, one black man was killed and another badly beaten by white youths in Queens.

Brawley's hive of advisers pressured Gov. Mario Cuomo to appoint New York State Atty. Gen. Robert Abrams as special prosecutor in her case. Then they added to its bizarre nature with their bizarre behavior. Dissatisfied with Abrams because he has never tried a criminal case, they have refused to let her or her family cooperate with police or talk to reporters.

They are not impressed with the teams of seasoned prosecutors Abrams has under his command and the resources the state of New York has committed to Brawley's case. Instead, they have accused the state of a cover-up in which they also suggested, while offering no evidence, that the Mafia, the Ku Klux Klan and the Irish Republican Army are involved.

Unfortunately for Brawley's hive of advisers, her story has fallen apart. Medical tests showed no evidence of injury, sexual assault or lack of food. Police and reporters have found nothing to back up her account but quite a bit that contradicts it.

For example, some of her school chums and neighbors saw her at a party and elsewhere in the housing complex where she formerly lived during the four days she was missing and presumably held captive. Two neighbors say they called police after seeing her acting strangely and crawling into a garbage bag. Other witnesses say they heard voices and activity in the Brawleys' former apartment, then supposedly empty. Police later found dog feces and discarded charcoal in the courtyard and some of Brawley's clothing in the apartment.

Then last week Perry McKinnon, a private investigator and former aide to Sharpton, said on TV that Brawley's advisers had doubted her story all along but were keeping the charade going to enhance their own stature and fund-raising abilities. "There was no case, only a media show," he told WCBS-TV.

Sharpton and the lawyers called McKinnon a liar, but their credibility, already shaken, is crumbling. Abrams has subpoenaed McKinnon and the advisers may be on the verge of becoming defendants.

Sharpton, Mason and Maddox are men who would be "King"—Martin Luther King. They look more like clowns. As a black American, I see no reason to laugh. If they have been using Brawley's misfortune to squeeze an unsuspecting public of money and support under false pretenses, the joke may be on me.

And what about the central question: What really happened to Tawana Brawley?

Whatever happened, her misfortune has been compounded by sharpies like Sharpton and the rest who have not allowed her to go before a grand jury and let justice take its course. They are elephants of activism wrestling with elephants of the state while Brawley and the rest of us down here in the grass try to keep our heads down.

DR. KING'S LEGACY: THE WAY IS CLEAR, THE WILL IS UNCERTAIN

WEDNESDAY, APRIL 6, 1988

BY CLARENCE PAGE

It is always dangerous to play the game of "What if . . .?" But I cannot help but think Rev. Martin Luther King Jr., who was assassinated 20 years ago this month, would be amused to see what some people have done to his memory.

I think he would be amused to see his status exalted in some quarters to that of a saint. Ol' "Doc," as his associates called him, didn't even want long eulogies at his funeral. He said he just wanted somebody to say that "Dr. King tried to love somebody." He wanted to be remembered only as "a drum major for justice."

But if Dr. King would be amused by what others have done to his memory, he would be thoroughly bemused to see what has happened to his movement.

The broad coalition of students, laborers, sharecroppers, politicians, clergy and ethnic leaders he pulled together has split many separate ways. The moral clarity of his campaign against America's legal apartheid has become so muddled that even conservatives like Ronald Reagan, who opposed both the Civil Rights Act of 1964 and the Voting Rights Act of 1965, speak as if they know more about the civil rights movement than those who led it.

In fact, that's the justification Mr. Reagan has used to battle affirmative action and other modest efforts designed to open opportunities for women and minorities; he labels them "preferential treatment."

Maybe. No fair-minded person is comfortable with the idea of quotas.

But conservatives do not do Dr. King justice if they think "affirmative action" is an idea that popped up after his death. As he pointed out during the last Sunday sermon of his life, the first people to benefit from preferential treatment were not black. They were the people who settled the West and the Midwest in the years after the Civil War under an act of Congress that gave away millions of acres of land to encourage expansion and settlement of the Western frontier and, as he said, "to undergird its white peasants from Europe with an economic floor."

"But not only did [the government] give the land, it built land-grant colleges to teach them how to farm. Not only that, it provided county agents to further their expertise in farming. Not only that, as the years unfolded it provided low interest rates so that they could mechanize their farms. And to this day thousands of these very persons are receiving millions of dollars in federal subsidies every year not to farm. And these are so often the very people who tell Negroes that they must lift themselves by their own bootstraps."

At the same time, Dr. King noted, the Emancipation Proclamation freed the slaves without so much as a pot to put their porridge in.

"It's all right to tell a man to lift himself by his own bootstraps, but it is cruel jest to say to a bootless man that he ought to lift himself by his own bootstraps," he said.

Twenty years after Dr. King's death, most black Americans are enjoying the benefits of his work, in one way or another. Legal segregation is a thing of the past, blacks are in positions of visibility and authority that would have been hard to imagine 20 years ago and, depending on whose statistics you believe, a half to two-thirds of black Americans can be called "middle class."

But that leaves about 30 percent of black America still living under poverty, with life worse in many ways. When opportunities opened up, the most upwardly mobile blacks were the first to leave urban ghettos, leaving the hard-core unemployed more socially isolated than ever. With street gangs, drug dealers, teen pregnancy and inferior schools, many are locked into a seemingly permanent "underclass."

The biggest problems facing black Americans today are economic. They are not likely to be solved with civil rights remedies, but they could be relieved with public and private action to encourage economic redevelopment and rebirth in our inner city ghettos, just as government incentives played a key role in helping pioneers develop the Old West.

American ingenuity is expected to create millions of new private sector jobs by the end of this century. Yet millions of our young people will not be able to fill those jobs unless we reform our schools, break the welfare cycle and encourage new businesses to open in the communities of the people who need them most, especially when they can be owned and managed by some of those same people.

The government has no more land to give away, but it can invest in a new generation of urban pioneers. As Dr. King once said, "We now have the techniques and resources to get rid of poverty. The real question is whether we have the will."

A BREACH IN TV'S CYCLE OF IGNORANCE ABOUT BLACK LIFE

WEDNESDAY, FEBRUARY 24, 1988

BY CLARENCE PAGE

Long before "The Cosby Show" made its debut in the fall of 1983, Bill Cosby had to argue with writers, producers and network executives who questioned whether the program's middle-class Huxtable family was "typical" of black family life.

And after it hit the air, some critics ridiculed it as "a white show." One New York City critic went so far as to say Cosby was "so white he didn't even qualify to be an Uncle Tom."

This was foolish talk, of course. The middle-class Huxtables represent values to be found in far more black American households than the goofy clowns Hollywood usually passes off as typical black folks.

And Cosby got the last laugh. Black and white households across the nation welcomed the program as a respite from the narrow view of black family life put forth by such past efforts as "Amos 'n' Andy," "Beulah," "Amen" and "The Jeffersons." Now in its fourth season, "Cosby" remains firmly perched at the top of the ratings and in the nation's hearts.

Still, it is curious that the skeptics, almost all of them white, are so firmly convinced that they know more about black life than the black people who live it.

"Whenever someone starts talking about a 'typical' black family," said Dr. Alvin Poussaint, an associate dean at Harvard Medical School and a consultant to the program, "I ask them where they got their image of black family life. Usually it turns out that they got it from watching television."

Speaking as part of a panel discussion I moderated last week at the University of Illinois at Chicago, Poussaint asked the members of the predominately black audience to imagine what they would do if they were asked to write a story about life in an Asian-American household.

The statement brought a laugh. Except for the few Asian-American students in attendance, none of us claimed to have the background (the "cultural context," as Poussaint calls it) to know enough about Asian-American home life—at least not without doing a lot of research.

Yet the entertainment industry known as prime-time television routinely allows writers from middle-class and suburban white backgrounds to create inner-city minority characters without bothering to find out how minorities really think or behave. The results often are a perpetuation of stereotypes from the "Amos 'n' Andy" days that are so removed from everyday reality that they harm the view whites have of minorities and the view minorities have of themselves.

And the more they are shown, the more they are believed. That's how institutional racism works. It is not the racism that wears white sheets or burns crosses. In all likelihood, the writers, producers and other creative types mean no harm. This is not the racism of hate or fear. It is the racism of habit. It is the racism of ignorance that feeds upon itself and becomes institutionalized into a tradition that over time allows myth to be mistaken for truth.

Cosby, to his credit, has tried to break that cycle of ignorance. Unlike "All in the Family," which Cosby felt only made viewers more comfortable with their prejudices, he vowed to avoid drawing cheap laughs from race, sex, obesity or old age. He hired Poussaint to help screen out subtle stereotypical images and to insert subtle but positive information about black American life.

As a result, a girlfriend of young Theo Huxtable was rewritten so she would admire his scholarship as much as his basketball skills. A Norman Mailer novel assigned to Theo as homework was changed to "Invisible Man," a classic by black writer Ralph Ellison. Mentions of institutions like Harvard or Yale were changed to prominent black universities like Howard, Morehouse or Central State.

Poussaint has been criticized by some as sort of an in-house censor. That's a bum rap. As a consultant, he help keep the show honest, but he does not have the final word. If real doctors can consult "St. Elsewhere" and real lawyers can consult "L.A. Law," it only makes sense to give real black people a voice in shows about blacks. Better yet, we should look forward to the day when real black people have more of a voice in all areas of management.

Of course, the industry's copycat syndrome is not limited to matters of race. New ideas always have a tough time in television, at least until they make their first $1 million in profits.

But perhaps the success of "The Cosby Show" will open enough minds to make it easier for television to show a little more authentic black life in dramatic shows as well as in comedies.

The media, like other industries, only hurt themselves by remaining too firmly rooted in their misguided past. We need to wake up. It's not just a good deed. It's good business.

THE MAYOR STANDS BY HIS MAN—AND LOOKS LIKE A HEEL

WEDNESDAY, MAY 4, 1988

BY CLARENCE PAGE

It is an enduring curiosity of politics that so many leaders are brought down not by the exposure of their foolish acts but by foolish attempts to downplay their significance.

President Richard Nixon might have completed his time in office had his administration dealt in a straightforward manner with the Watergate affair, instead of dismissing it as a "third-rate burglary."

Jesse Jackson's presidential campaign was ruined four years ago not so much by the report that he had called Jews "Hymies" and New York City "Hymietown" as by his clumsy attempts to deny it for almost two weeks before he finally apologized.

Now here in Chicago, a town whose politics have never been for the squeamish, acting Mayor Eugene Sawyer is in danger of being brought down by foolish attempts to downplay his association with a key adviser whose fanatical views make Louis Farrakhan and Lyndon LaRouche sound like George Bush.

The top aide, Steve Cokely, has become famous in recent days for saying, in taped lectures for followers of Nation of Islam leader Farrakhan, that he believes Jews are part of an international conspiracy to rule the world, a conspiracy that includes Jewish doctors who are injecting AIDS into black children.

In his tapes, sold by Farrakhan followers, Cokely shows himself to be an equal-opportunity bigot.

He criticizes Jesse Jackson and the late Mayor Harold Washington for their association with Jews and recounts a speech he gave to students at Xavier University in Cincinnati in which he covered a crucifix with some of his literature and called it a "symbol of white supremacy."

Sawyer should have expected trouble when, as an alderman, he hired Cokely in 1985 after his previous employer, former Ald. Marian

Humes, fired Cokely for criticizing Columbus Day as a "racist holiday."

Of course, Sawyer jettisoned this loony right away, right? Wrong. Instead, he said he was asking Cokely to "tone down" his rhetoric, said that he was "reviewing" the situation, cited his own support for Jewish causes and called for sympathy for Cokely's need to have a job.

Okay. But does he have to have a $35,568 job as a "coordinator of special projects"?

Even if Sawyer's "review" leads to Cokely's removal, the damage of the delay will have been done.

Of course, Cokely then resigned swiftly to save his boss further embarrassment, right? Wrong. Cokely was about as enthusiastic about leaving as Ed Meese or Manuel Noriega—and twice as embarrassing. All he did was say he was sorry if his statements offended anyone.

Of course, Chicago's black leadership, which has been so forthright in criticizing Al Campanis, Earl Butz, Jimmy "the Greek" Snyder and every other white person who has said anything even mildly racist, immediately called for this embarrassment to resign, right? Wrong.

Remember, this is Chicago, the only town that associated St. Valentine's Day with a massacre, a town whose resentments run deeper than its deep-dish pizza.

City Hall insiders say Sawyer is afraid of black backlash. Ever since a coalition of white ethnic alderman—fierce foes of Harold Washington—and a few black alderman voted Sawyer into the mayor's seat in an all-night city council session last November, he has been trying his best to endear himself to Washington supporters, who view him with obvious skepticism.

Insiders say Sawyer is trying to buy time before edging Cokely into a less sensitive position. But Sawyer's failure to dismiss Cokely immediately only aggravates public outrage and exposes the deadly indecisiveness Sawyer showed on his historic election night, when he wavered so much over whether to accept the draft of a mostly white group that he appeared to faint from the strain.

Interestingly, Sawyer's black critics have been taking heat from Sawyer's white supporters of a sort that may be about to end. Washington's foes, who always tried to paint Washington's battle against Chicago's old-time political machine as a simple battle of black vs.

white, have been pushing Sawyer as a great healer ever since they put him in power. What's the matter, they would say to Sawyer's critics, can't you deal with a black mayor who gets along with white people?

Well, Sawyer's not getting along with white people so well these days. With his reluctance to offend even the most fanatical segments of his city's black community, Sawyer looks less like a healer than a heel.

It must be comforting for traditionalists to note that business goes on as usual in Chicago, a city never mistaken for a haven of brotherly love.

A DEPLORABLE EFFORT TO HELP DENTISTS SHUN AIDS VICTIMS

WEDNESDAY, JUNE 15, 1988

BY CLARENCE PAGE

A Chicago man notified his dentist of 10 years that he had the AIDS virus. For his courtesy, he was told never to come back to the dentist's office. The patient has sued. Now the Illinois General Assembly, in the apparent belief that no good deed should go unpunished, is considering a bill that would make such discriminatory conduct legal for all the state's dentists.

By allowing dentists to refer any "person with an infectious disease within 10 working days to another dentist" with "facilities or training equal to or better than the referring dentist," the law would free dentists to dump patients on other dentists, not because the patient needs special care but because the first dentist does not want to be bothered.

In a sense, the sponsors of this deplorable legislation, which whisked through a committee by a 13-4 vote after only a few minutes of testimony were allowed, are the moral equivalent of the vandals who burned an Acadia, Fla., family out of their home simply because their three hemophiliac children have the AIDS virus. What looks at first glance like a nice way to protect dentists from possible exposure to a deadly virus is really a reckless response to a serious public health dilemma, a feeble attempt to separate the feared from the fearful without educating anyone.

Although it violates ethical standards established by national medical societies that call for disciplinary action against medical personnel who refuse to treat AIDS victims, the proposed law has the backing of the Illinois State Dental Society, which argues that dentists do not want any government telling them whom they should treat.

Although that response sounds reasonable at first, it raises the wrong question. Since authorities believe as many as 1.5 million people are infected with the AIDS virus and that more than 90 percent do not know it yet, all dentists, as well as other medical workers, should be following the guidelines established by the federal Centers for Disease Control with all patients, rather than depending on the patients to tell them they have the virus—especially when states are considering legislation that will make AIDS victims even less likely to reveal their condition.

That means dentists should wear surgical gloves and masks when working in contact with body fluids. Unfortunately, many dentists would rather not bother to "glove up," whether for reasons of vanity, convenience or fear of unsettling patient confidence. That, in itself, is a shame, since the risk of catching herpes, hepatitis or a similar communicable disease probably is greater than that of catching AIDS. Of course, a dentist has as much right to behave foolishly as anyone else. Even so, legislation designed to help him or her discriminate will hardly help.

Besides, the legislation itself could be life-threatening to patients. The 10-working-day limit, dangerous for most patients who have, say, a gum infection, could be fatal to someone whose immune system has been thrown haywire by AIDS.

Then there are those within the profession who think dentistry is demeaned by laws that allow dentists to cop out on their fellow medical professionals, like surgeons and paramedics who face greater daily risk of AIDS exposure.

"The medical community is going to say once again that dentists are not really doctors," said Dr. John Davis, dentistry specialist at the University of Chicago's Zoller Clinic. "Or that we are not really ethical. That bothers me as a professional."

"A soldier can't decide in the heat of battle that it's too cold, there's too many bullets and I want to go home," said Dr. Stuart Levin, infectious disease expert at Rush–Presbyterian–St. Luke's Medical Center. "To do so would be a dereliction of duty, a cowardly act. If a dentist does not want to act as a professional, he should not expect to be called 'doctor.' "

Sadly, now that the public has more education and fewer irrational fears than ever about AIDS, legislation to protect discrimination against its victims revives the notion that carriers of the virus or victims of the full-blown disease should be regarded as civilly as lepers in the Middle Ages.

And that poses long-term danger. Even the Reagan administration, as hard-nosed as they come about protecting the rights of majorities against aggressive civil libertarians, has come around to the position that it is better to encourage those who are in high-risk lifestyles (particularly the three H's: homosexuals, hemophiliacs and hypodermic needle-using drug addicts) to be tested and, if found "positive," to be candid with those who should know about their condition.

If patients with AIDS know it could result in the loss of their chosen health care provider, they simply will be less candid with their dentists and with anyone else who has a need to know. Unless politicians begin to show some responsible leadership on this issue, the battle against AIDS, as one expert put it, will be won in the laboratories but lost in the streets.

TWELVE

BEING BLACK IN SOUTH AFRICA

1989 WINNER IN THE FEATURE WRITING CATEGORY

"For a distinguished example of feature writing giving prime consideration to high literary quality and originality . . ."

The Philadelphia Inquirer
David Zucchino

Daily life for a black man or woman trying to survive within the constraints of South Africa's system of apartheid is anything but predictable. David Zucchino's profiles give sharp dimension to the quiet, but ongoing, struggles there.

As a state of emergency entered its third year in South Africa in 1988, there was plenty of compelling news, but not much of it was coming from the black townships. The emergency decree prohibited all but the most superficial reporting of the very events that defined and controlled black lives—detentions, disappearances, security force sweeps, bannings and crackdowns on anti-apartheid protests. Like most other foreign correspondents, I was covering the townships on the run, chasing breaking stories, grabbing a couple of interviews and rushing home to "white" Johannesburg to file.

Robert Rosenthal, *The Philadelphia Inquirer's* foreign editor, thought something important was being missed. He had reported from South Africa during the height of the great township revolt in 1986. Now it appeared to him that the townships had disappeared. As far as American journalists and readers were concerned, they had been smothered by emergency rule. It had become illegal to describe what was really happening to three out of every four South Africans. We decided to lift the veil.

For three months, *The Inquirer* allowed me to bypass all but the most pressing daily news coverage and spend my days—and sometimes my nights—in the townships. I knew from many previous visits that virtually every black in South Africa had a painful and very personal story to tell about being black in a white-ruled world. I knew, too, that it was ordinary blacks—not just the handful of black leaders already well known to American readers—who had the most to fear and thus the most to tell. Of the 20-some blacks I eventually interviewed in depth for this series, only two had ever been interviewed before.

Through friends—both black and white—I had made in the anti-apartheid movement during two years of covering South Africa, I was able to spend time with blacks from across the political spectrum. A black friend from the South African Council of Churches (who has since fled the country for fear of arrest) introduced me to a fellow field worker who agreed to let me travel the townships with him on his daily rounds, secretly funneling money to detainee families and dodging the notorious Special Branch of the South African police. A friend at the black domestic workers' union let me listen for three days to dozens of black maids and gardeners who poured out tales of abuse and deprivation to her. A white anti-apartheid lawyer told me about a black laborer's activist son who had been killed by black township cops. Then he helped me locate the dead youth's parents and friends. A friend at the Detainees Parents Support Committee, a restricted group that assists detainees, told me of a black mother whose sons were in detention.

Not a single black person I approached refused to be interviewed. Yet each took enormous risks. It was not wise to talk too much in the townships, especially to strange white men asking questions. The security police had infiltrators everywhere. In South Africa, black people sometimes disappear after being caught in the wrong place with the wrong people. If they're lucky, the worst that happens is a few weeks of detention. (Two of the people I talked to ended up in jail later for reasons that, as usual, were never explained.) Even after I made initial contact with interview subjects, apartheid made it difficult to maintain normal personal relationships. They lived in the townships; I lived in an all-white suburb. We were separated by distance and culture and language. Even if the blacks had phones, talking was difficult. My phone was tapped, and some of their phones probably were, too. We sometimes used pre-arranged code words to set meetings times and places.

At least once to my knowledge, we were videotaped by a police camera unit. At one point, I was thrown out of a police station in Soweto by an Afrikaner police commander for trying to interview a black cop. The commander said he didn't want me "confusing the boy" with my silly questions. At a police roadblock in another township, I was stopped while driving with Peter Magubane, a black photographer whose assistance was invaluable during the reporting of four stories in this series. Ignoring me, a white security agent pawed through Magubane's personal papers for 10 minutes, copying down names and phone numbers from his address book. Ignoring Magubane —who had once served months in solitary confinement for the crime of committing journalism—the cop then apologized to me for the delay, telling me, "Have a nice day, sir."

Avoiding the security forces was easy enough. What proved far more difficult was threading my way past the emergency restrictions on reporting. Correspondents could not, for instance, report on detentions, "unrest," or security force actions. But the restrictions were capriciously applied. Just as there are "gray areas" in some neighborhoods despite legislated segregation, there are also gray areas in reporting under the emergency. I was able to cover the young activist's funeral, for instance, only because the family's lawyer had taken the case to court, alleging that the young man had been murdered by police; when the authorities responded to the allegations with their own version of the killing, I was free to write about the case. Detailing the detentions of the sons of the Soweto mother was another matter. But like most reporters, I bent the regulations when I felt I had to. Apartheid laws are enforced selectively; the fear of repercussions is often as effective a tool of control as actual enforcement. This time, as on many previous occasions, nothing happened.

Compared to the suffering of the people I was writing about, the risks I took were negligible. The worst that could happen to me was to be thrown out of the country. Some of the people I was spending time with woke up each day with the knowledge that all they owned —no matter how meager—could be taken from them. Yet I was surprised at their lack of bitterness and hatred towards whites. They detested apartheid, but rarely their fellow countrymen. Not one of them had given up hope. I asked each of the people interviewed if they believed their children's lives would be better than their own. Each one answered without hesitation: "Of course."

—David Zucchino
The Philadephia Inquirer

OUT OF CHALLENGE CAME DEATH

SUNDAY, DECEMBER 11, 1988

BY DAVID ZUCCHINO

TUMAHOLE, SOUTH AFRICA—It was not done the proper way, the old man said. The burial of his son had been spoiled, and it pained him that his final memory of the young man was so stained by discontent.

The damp dirt of his son's grave stuck to the shoes of Joseph Nakedi. His clothes smelled of tear gas. His wife was weeping. He could hear the rumble of police armored vehicles along the dirt path outside his shack.

Johannes Lefu Nakedi had just been buried on Oct. 10 in the windswept veld of the Orange Free State, his funeral watched from a safe distance by a crush of security police with shotguns and bulletproof vests. The mourners had been tear-gassed. The priests had been bundled into a riot vehicle. "Hippos"—troop carriers—roared up and down the roads, scattering and panicking the black children of Tumahole township.

The confrontation seemed to define the short life of Lefu Nakedi, an activist who had challenged the system and was ultimately killed by it. He was just 23, fresh from another stretch of detention, when he was shot dead by the Green Beans—killed one midnight by the black township police in their distinctive green uniforms.

To the South African police, Nakedi was a terrorist. They said he had attacked a Green Bean with a knife and was shot dead to prevent the officer's murder. They said, too, that the young blacks of the Tumahole Youth Congress, which Nakedi had led, had supplied fellow blacks with hand grenades for use against the authorities.

But Joseph Nakedi believes his son was murdered. The police could not break or silence him even after 15 months in detention, the old man thought, so they lured him into a trap and killed him.

Now Nakedi, a common laborer, totaled up the many ways that "the system"—as blacks call white rule—had encroached on his life. Long before Lefu was killed, there were regular visits by the security police in the dead of night. His shack was watched, photos were taken.

Lefu was detained for 13 months, then for two months. Another son, Benedict, was detained for 13 months. It seemed to Joseph Nakedi that the police lived at his place.

And the infringements did not end even with the claiming of his son's life by the system. It claimed his funeral, too.

Since June 1986, South Africa's black townships have been smothered by a state of emergency that now intrudes on the most prosaic aspects of daily life. The emergency dictates whether a book may be read, a pamphlet distributed, a meeting held, a speech delivered, a detainee visited, a funeral held. People may be detained without charge or trial or access to a lawyer. Police need no warrant to break in and search a home. Sometimes an activist is taken away and simply disappears.

Tens of thousands of black families in South Africa have suffered somehow because of emergency rule. About 32,000 people have been detained, and civil rights groups say at least 1,200 of them are still in custody. Countless others live in fear that they or someone they know will be detained, questioned, restricted, banned, informed upon, wounded or killed.

'TOTAL ONSLAUGHT'

The government says emergency rule is necessary to protect the majority of the country's 26 million blacks from intimidation and death at the hands of black revolutionaries bent on a "total onslaught" against law and order. No government, it says, would fail to take the same action against terrorists who openly seek to overthrow the state. Ordinary laws are not sufficient to deal with these radicals, Pretoria says, but law-abiding blacks need not fear detention or harassment.

Joseph Nakedi has broken no laws. Nor had his son, he insists, but what happened to them happens often to black activists who challenge the state.

Lefu worked at an advice office run by the Tumahole Civic Association, an affiliate of the restricted United Democratic Front. The office supplies legal advice and small sums of money for families of detainees and others affected by apartheid laws or emergency rule. The government portrays such offices as instigators of unrest.

SUSPICIOUS

The authorities are particularly suspicious of Tumahole. In 1984, the township, about 75 miles south of Johannesburg, was the first in South Africa to resist rent increases, thus helping to trigger the great township revolt of 1984 to 1986. It is still known as a "hot" township. At least 60 local activists have been detained, and 10 more have been shot dead by the police in the last four years.

Four weeks after Nakedi was killed, another Tumahole Youth Congress leader was shot dead by the Green Beans. The Civic Association released a statement the next day: "We perceive a concerted effort by agents of the system to break the resistance of the people by systematically eliminating activists."

A police spokesman in Pretoria declined to discuss the specifics of either killing beyond brief police statements already released. He said anyone who felt abused by the police could file a formal complaint.

Through the Civic Association, Joseph Nakedi has been provided a Johannesburg lawyer who intends to challenge the police in court. Nakedi said Lefu had been harassed by the Green Beans, who would stop him on the street, search him and threaten to kill him. He said that the night Lefu was killed, he was asked by a young woman to accompany him to a *shebeen*—a nightclub. The woman, Nakedi alleged, is a police informer.

At the *shebeen,* Lefu was shot in the eye, the back and the right arm. He died instantly.

"From that day on, the police have interfered in every single thing we have done," Nakedi said, speaking in the southern Sotho dialect of the area. "We did not have the right to bury our son in our own private way. We were not allowed even to mourn him in the proper way."

NIGHT VIGIL

The family tried to have a night vigil—the all-night venting of grief at the home of the deceased. The police imposed a time limit and restricted the number of mourners to 80. The Johannesburg lawyer, Priscilla Jana, managed to have the restrictions eased.

The funeral itself was even more heavily restricted. Because of bloody confrontations between mourners and police at highly politicized funerals during the 1984–1986 uprisings, the authorities severely restrict burials. In Nakedi's case, they even restricted access to the corpse at the funeral home. The family was permitted to see Lefu's body only after the lawyer intervened.

The police sent Nakedi a series of letters that quoted at length from the complex emergency laws. There were to be no more than 300 mourners. The memorial and burial could last no more than three hours, from 10 a.m. to 1 p.m. Only an ordained minister could speak. And "no ceremonial gathering, insofar as it takes the form of a memorial service for Johannes Lefu Nakedi . . . shall be held out of doors."

Nakedi was issued 300 slips of white paper. Each contained a number from 1 to 300—one "ticket" for each guest—and the words *Funeral* and *The late Lefu NAKEDI.* They were stamped with something that offended Nakedi: the official blue stamp of the Suid-Afrikaanse Polisie, the police. Nakedi could not insult his friends and family with these things. He refused to hand them out.

On the day of the funeral, the police surrounded Nakedi's corrugated metal shack and ordered the mourners to disperse. Some of the *amaqabane*—the young men who call themselves "comrades"—began the *toyi-toyi*, the rhythmic chanting and dancing that so antagonizes the police. Tear gas was fired, and three young men were arrested.

The two priests were dragged into a riot vehicle and taken to St. John the Baptist Catholic Church at the edge of the township. There, a rushed memorial service began.

A white Dominican priest, the Rev. Jan Jansen, compared Lefu's work to the work of Jesus. "He sought the liberation of his own oppressed people," he said of Lefu, speaking in Southern Sotho. Though it was illegal, a few comrades stood up and said the revolution would continue in Lefu's name, that the "racist regime" would be toppled.

Across the street outside, police commanders stood in a drizzle, bored, and swung imaginary cricket bats at imaginary balls. An officer with a gun on his hip filmed the service with a video camera so that informers could later identify people in the crowd.

When the mourners emerged from the church, an officer told Father Jansen that no one would be allowed to walk to the gravesite. They would have to take vehicles. But no one had a car; it was a small township.

A nun tugged at Father Jansen's arm. "Can't you talk to them?" she said of the police.

"No, I have tried," the priest said. "It's like Germany before the war. Orders are orders."

Soon some taxis were arranged and everyone piled in, some mourners standing on the bumpers. A few fell off and had to roll quickly out of the street to avoid the huge wheels of the armored vehicles that followed the procession. One Hippo had the words *Kiss Me* painted on the front.

The burial was a brief and chaotic affair held in an open field next to other graves in a pasture where cows grazed in the chilly spring air. The police watched through binoculars from atop their Hippos as Father Jansen said a few words and Lefu's damp-eyed mother, Lydia, wrapped in a wool blanket and supported by two women, tossed a handful of dirt on her son's coffin.

Sharp whistles and shouting broke out, like a sudden stiff wind. There were screams of *"Amandla!"* "power!"—and *"Voetsek!"*—an expression used to shoo away a dog. It was directed at the police, who stiffened at the sound but kept their distance.

Then it was over, and the taxis and the Hippos roared back to Nakedi's little shack. A funeral tent had been attached to the shack. Inside, guests ate a mourning meal of pap and mince—corn meal and ground meat—and tried to talk over the roar of the Hippos on the pathway outside.

In a burlap bag inside the shack were kept the dead man's clothes. Someone pulled them out. There was a scarlet shirt with a gunshot hole in the arm and a nylon ski jacket stained brown with dried blood.

Joseph Nakedi sat down in a heap. He was worn out. Everything had gone wrong. This was a miserable way to say goodbye to his son.

He knew this was not the end of it. Just two nights earlier, he said, the Green Beans had roused him from his sleep and told him they would rip down his shack if he caused any trouble. He did not consider himself a man easily cowed—a sign in his yard said "Beware of the owner—never mind the dog"—but he feared for himself and his family.

There was a living activist son to worry about: Benedict, just 18, but already familiar with a detention cell. The old man mentioned something the Green Beans had done the other night. They had pointed to Benedict and said: "Careful—maybe he's next."

A BOND OF NECESSITY FOR BLACK AND WHITE

MONDAY, DECEMBER 12, 1988

BY DAVID ZUCCHINO

JOHANNESBURG—The madam insisted that Mary stay up with the baby that night. Mary was weary. She wanted a break between housekeeping and baby-sitting.

By the next morning, Mary Thrusi had been fired. After 13 years of working as a maid and a baby sitter for the madam, she was back on the street. She had until the weekend to clear out her meager possessions from the servants' quarters in the garden behind the madam's well-tended home.

Well, that's it, Mary thought: 60 years old, black, uneducated and no more job.

It was just another working day in the South African suburbs. With four million blacks working in white homes as domestics and gardeners—"house girls" and "garden boys" as they are called by the madam and the *baas*—somebody gets fired somewhere every day of the week, Sundays and holidays included.

Behind the security walls of almost every middle-class white home, there are silent black figures toiling at menial tasks for token pay. They care little about unrest and riots and black revolution, for that is the stuff of the townships, not the serene white suburbs. Mostly, they care about finding a job and keeping it, about not offending the madam, about receiving the pay envelope at the end of the month.

Some have dared to organize themselves, despite resistance by a suspicious white government. The South African Domestic Workers' Union had been organized for just over a year when a bomb blew up its office in May 1987. Its current coffice is raided regularly by the security police, who have detained several organizers without charge. The police say the union people are encouraging unrest among naive black folks, spreading propaganda, undermining the security of the republic.

The week after she was fired, Mary Thusi took a bus down to the dim and shabby union offices. She told her story to Roseline Naapo, a big, robust union organizer who did something that surprised Mary: She picked up the phone and called the madam.

Lisa Thompson, a 34-year-old white employee of the state-run television network, listened politely as Naapo said she wanted to hear her side of the story. Thompson even agreed to Naapo's suggestion that she speak with Mary right then.

Mary knitted nervously at a scarf in her lap as Naapo handed her the receiever. She shook her head furiously.

"No!" she shouted, loud enough for her madam to hear over the phone. "Did you ever hear of a prisoner going back to jail to see the warden?"

Naapo shrugged. She handles 60 of these cases a month. She got back on the phone and persuaded Thompson to let her and Mary discuss the problem at Thompson's home the following week.

The meeting would reveal a delicate and paternalistic relationship between white boss and black servant. Mary would call her madam "my little girl," for she had been with Thompson since the white woman was 21 and just out of school. Thompson would call Mary "a member of my family." The two woman would say they loved each other, though in a contrived and distant way.

There is a symbiotic cord that binds black domestics to white suburbanites in South Africa. After three centuries of dominance, many middle-class whites have become dependent on household help. Millions of unskilled, poorly educated blacks have come to depend on domestic work as their only reliable and enduring means of support—as well as a bed in the safe white suburbs, away from the turmoil of the townships.

The domestics union accepts the relationship and even many of its most condescending and demeaning traits. What it demands is not an overthrow of the entrenched domestic system, but better pay, security and working conditions.

The domestics union was founded in early 1986. Its founders knew all too well the fears and insecurities of both master and servant. The blacks are victimized, exploited, degraded, beaten. They can be fired for no reason other than madam is having a bad day.

The whites point to shoddy work, drunkenness, petty theft and murders by fired gardeners or the boyfriends of fired maids, which occur with a regularity that terrorizes the white suburbs. It is rarely a political thing, just a grudge gone violent. (Some black revolutionaries, however, have suggested that every maid in town poison the baas' tea.)

The typical domestic worker in South Africa is paid 150 rand ($63) a month. In Johannesburg, the average pay for a domestic is higher, about 200 rand ($81) a month. The union is seeking a national guaranteed minimum of 200 rand a month, with hopes of eventually raising the minimum to 300 rand.

The union also hopes to guarantee a 5½-day workweek, three meals a day, maternity leave, pension plans and a three-day weekend off each month. Many employers already provide those benefits, but not uniformly. And thousands of servants get benefits for a while, then find they are suddenly withdrawn without explanation.

Even these meager conditions are better than virtually anywhere else in Africa. Servants in Kenya, Zambia and Zimbabawe—who work for expatriates as well as Africans and Asians—earn roughly half as much as those in South Africa, with fewer benefits. Unions—except those controlled by the state—are anathema to black-ruled governments, too.

It has been difficult to persuade South African servants to join the union, union officials said. Some fear they will be fired. Others are suspicious of anything that smells of politics.

The union has 66,000 members. The union believes there are four million domestic workers in the country—or 31 percent of the 13 million blacks who live in "white" South Africa rather than the all-black "homelands." That is nearly one servant for every one of South Africa's whites, plus a relative handful of well-to-do black employers.

□ □ □

Early one morning, Mary and Naapo drove to see Thompson. On the way, Naapo took the old woman's case history:

Began scrubbing floors for a white woman at age 13. Family "chucked out"—forcibly removed—from its home by the white authorities in the 1950s. A long series of madams: Mrs. Bryant, Mrs. Cadman, Mrs. Stephens, Mrs. Mitchell . . . Earned 200 rand a month from Mrs. Thompson, plus food, lodging, TV set, pension plan.

For Naapo, it was a familiar story. She had been a domestic herself for 17 years, on and off. Now she had transformed herself into the sort of figure the authorities regarded with suspicion—a formerly docile worker turned political activist.

Naapo had once been a policewoman. She resigned the day the bloody riots broke out in Soweto on June 16, 1976, in which security forces killed 176 blacks. She remembered seeing a white policeman in her armored vehicle shoot at a young girl. She said the officer told her: "A snake is a snake, young or old."

"That meant I was a snake too because I was the only black in the vehicle." Naapo recalled.

Now she was going into the heart of Johannesburg's white suburbs, where virtually the only blacks are maids, gardeners and delivery men. Though she had visited white homes many times to negotiate servant disputes, she felt out of place, as if she were wearing the wrong clothes at a formal party.

Thompson was cool but polite. She was wary of Naapo, who had her own doubts about how willing this madam was to take Mary back.

Naapo suggested that the problem was a mere miscommunication.

"You're right," Thompson said. "Mary was *not* dismissed."

According to Thompson, Mary had walked out in a huff the day after the baby-sitting incident. But Mary had been given the entire afternoon off the previous day, Thompson said, and had been given adequate advance notice of the baby-sitting duties for the couple's 15-month-old son.

"She left me literally overnight—just disappeared. She said she never wanted to see this place again," Thompson said. Her fair face was reddening.

Mary shook her head. She said she had gone to visit a friend in the hospital that afternoon. She did not consider that time off—and then she was told to baby-sit until 10 p.m. without a break.

Mary conceded that when "the master"—Richard Thompson—phoned to say he would be getting home later than 10, she told him she was going to lock the baby in the house and go outside to her quarters to sleep. But of course she stayed with the child, she said.

"I was just tired and cross," she said.

Naapo cut in to ask both women how their relationship had been over 13 years.

"Very good," Thompson said.

"Very nice, OK," Mary said.

Thompson smiled. "She's been like a mother to me. I call her my black mother. She's the grandmother to my child."

Mary cut in and said: "Yes, you are like my own child." But then she turned to Naapo and said coldly: "But they gave me a good reminder that I'm black and I don't belong here."

"Did they say so verbally?" Naapo asked.

"No, it's just the way they acted. Madam wants me to die here and go out in a coffin. . . . I'm old and stupid, that's what they think. Old things get thrown away."

Thompson rolled her eyes. "Now, really Mary, you're insulting me. Please don't," she said.

Suddenly the young boy, Jonathan, appeared in the living room and rushed toward Mary. The old woman gave out a cry and swept the boy in her arms and kissed him. "Oh, I've missed you, my baby!" she said.

Thompson's face softened. Mary looked over and begged her to let her visit the boy regularly, no matter what happened between the two of them.

"Oh, Mary, of course you can. You know you're always welcome here," Thompson said.

Everyone fell silent. Finally, Naapo spoke: "There is a lot of love in this house. Can't we consider the future and forget these little troubles?"

Mary and her madam looked at each other. The boy gurgled in Mary's lap. Both women nodded.

It was agreed that Mary would get a full month's pay for the partial month worked, her pension, plus 400 rand for a sewing-maching attachment Thompson had promised her. She had earlier given Mary a sewing maching, along with the TV set.

Thompson handed two checks to Mary, who said, "Oh, thank you, thank you, Madam."

Naapo asked Thompson if she would rehire Mary right away.

Thompson said she would have to talk to her husband and give an answer the following week. She was already interviewing new maids.

Mary kissed Jonathan goodbye. Everyone shook hands, relieved to be done with the whole awkward thing.

Mary was not optimistic about a definitive answer from Thompson. "That child is so disorganized, she'll never make up her mind."

She asked Naapo to take her to the sewing-machine outlet right away. She was eager to get the new attachment. The two women got in the car and drove quickly from the white suburb.

A MOTHER MUST LIVE FOR HER SONS

THURSDAY, DECEMBER 15, 1988

SOWETO, SOUTH AFRICA—Twice, three times, Cecilia Ngcobo tried to wake herself. Each time she fell back into a slumber. She had come home from the night shift at dawn. Now it was 11 a.m. Time to get up.

Wake up, Mama Cecilia, said her granddaughter. The girl fetched some hot tea. Now the old woman was awake. It was already hot. There was so much to do, so many troubles descending like summer smog on her and her sons.

She had to go visit Chris in prison. The twins, Gerry and Bheki, were slipping in and out of the gray matchbox house, always wary of the security police. Her youngest son, Moses, 13, had been grabbed on the arm by a policeman the week before, and his mother had to yank him back into the house.

The security police want the sons of Cecilia Ngcobo. The midnight visit and ransacked house are etched into the routine of her daily life. She knows well the way to prison, just as she knows the many ways of maneuvering to keep her sons safe and alive after years of detentions.

By night, Ngcobo mops floors and cleans toilets inside a skyscraper in downtown Johannesburg. By day, she makes the rounds that every detainee mother must make—back and forth to prison, to the lawyers, to the police, and then back home to hold the house together as the police paw through the bedrooms and haul away books and papers.

It is a regimen that permits only snatches of sleep. "There is no sleeping time in Soweto," Ngcobo repeats often.

No one in "The Struggle"—the anti-apartheid movement—sleeps well these days. Since June 1986, at least 32,000 activists have been detained without charge or trial, according to human rights groups. An estimated 1,000 of them are still in detention. Among them is Chris Ngcobo, who turned 26 in prison. More detainees are rounded up every day.

Ngcobo, a stout woman of 53, has lost track of the number of times the police have visited her four-room house. Throughout South Africa's black townships, police raids are so common that people remark casually to their friends, "The System visited the house last night," as if to say, "The postman passed just now."

The System has visited Ngcobo many times, and much has been lost. In December 1984, her eldest son, Jabulani, was killed by the South African army in neighboring Swaziland, where the young man had fled to join the outlawed African National Congress. Cecilia Ngcobo found out about it when she saw his photo in the newspaper; he was identified by the authorities as a "terrorist" who had engaged in unspecified "terrorist activities."

She spent three months' wages to travel to Swaziland and spent two days persuading the authorities to let her see the body. Her son's body had more than one hundred bullet wounds, she says. She wondered why a man had to be shot so many times. "He even had bullet wounds in his hands," she recalls now.

Jabulani had made the entire family a target. Early on the morning of June 12, 1986, the first day of the ongoing state of emergency, security police dragged Bheki, now 28, from his bed at 4 a.m. while his mother was at work. He did not emerge from detention for 13 months. After searching for Chris the next three days, the police found him sleeping in a dormitory bed and hauled him away. He is still in Soweto's Diepkloof Prison.

Exactly one year after Bheki's detention, on the day in June 1987 when the emergency was renewed for another year, Bheki's twin, Gerry, was found hiding in a safe house in Soweto after an informer turned him in. He was detained for three months.

The family was not notified of the detentions. Like thousands of other detainee parents, Cecilia Ngcobo spent several days inquiring at local police stations before stumbling across official records of her sons' detentions.

The police did not need warrants to take the Ngcobo men away. Nor did they charge them with crimes. (After his release, Gerry was charged with possessing banned literature, but was acquitted in February.) Detainees have no right to see lawyers or family members, though many—including the Ngcobos—are ultimately granted such privileges.

Cecilia Ngcobo often wonders why, if her sons are considered dangerous enough to lock up for months and years, they are not charged with crimes and taken to court. Liberal white politians have asked the same kind of questions in Parliament. The authorities have replied that the judicial system is not equipped to deal quickly with "suspected revolutionaries" who must be taken off the streets at once.

"The ordinary laws of the land . . . are inadequate to enable the government to ensure the security of the public," President Pieter W. Botha told Parliament in ordering the state of emergency.

A government booklet that attempts to justify detentions says: "When national interests are of greater importance than individual interests, some rights of the individual must be curtailed."

Law and Order Minister Adriaan Vlok has told Parliament that police must be able to detain people without legal encumbrances when "it is absolutely necessary for the maintenance of public order [and] the safety of the public."

In a comment that has astounded detainee mothers like Ngcobo, Vlok also said that activists are detained for their own safety and to end the state of emergency.

Cecilia Ngcobo, laughing despite her troubles, wondered how tossing her sons in jail for no stated reason would protect them—and from what?

And how, she asked, does their detention end the emergency rule that allows them to be jailed in the first place?

Her sons are not criminals, she said. Gerry is an organizer for the legal black transport workers' union. Bheki is unemployed and looking for work. The police have repeatedly searched the house for banned ANC literature and automatic rifles, Ngcobo said, but they have found nothing.

South Africa's Human Rights Commission has said the real purpose of emergency rule is to intimidate blacks and to crush peaceful dissent by artificially declaring black political opposition a crime. (The government does not detain right-wing whites who openly oppose its policies.) Court hearings and civil rights are inconvenient and time-consuming, the commission has said, and so they are swept aside.

"We are all subject to the whims of soldiers and policemen," the Detainees Parents Support Committee said last year. The government no longer has to listen to DPSC criticism; it effectively banned the group's anti-apartheid activities in February.

The detainees' group was once able to assist Ngcobo. Now she is on her own. She would like to quit her job to devote more time to her sons, but she supports 20 family members who sleep on her floors every night—three sons, six daughters and all of her grandchildren.

And still the police come. Earlier this year, they kicked down the door and took away her books, including her Bible. More recently, she said, they demanded that she tell them where to find Bheki and Gerry. She refused. They asked for her sons' passports. She refused that demand, too.

Even Moses, just 13, is afraid to stay in the house some nights. He was dragged from bed recently, his mother said. A security officer shouted at him: "Careful, boy, you're growing up to join the ANC. We are watching you."

"Even when Moses is away [hiding], I'm so afraid for him I can't sleep," Ngcobo said, squeezing the boy's hand. "He's so tall, he looks older."

She says she screams at the police, orders them out of her house. They do not frighten her, she said. Nor does she fear the punishment dealt out to others who have spoken out against detentions—a black youth murdered in Johannesburg and a black woman shot in the eye in the Cape, both by mysterious gunmen never caught by the police.

"For my husband, for myself, I am not afraid. They only want my sons," Ngcobo said. "Before, I was always afraid, always worrying. But since they killed my first son, I know the world is evil. I accept it."

She accepts, too, the narrowing of her personal life. Friends no longer visit, for they fear the security police will detain them. Her husband, Maxwell, a trucker, avoids political matters and thus shuns the driving force in the lives of his wife and children.

"My husband wants nothing to do with these troubles—we need his salary," Ngcobo said. "But my sons are committed to the struggle. I am proud of them. They have suffered so much, now I want to suffer for all of them."

She hugged Moses and went on: "My sons are making a difference, working for something good. One day change will come and everything will be all right. I will live to see that day. My sons are bringing that day closer to me."

It was almost noon now. Ngcobo's eyes were red from lack of sleep.

Her ankles were swollen. After 20 years as a cleaning woman, she has high blood pressure and arthritis.

She gulped her tea, trying to make her body come alive. She had to go see Chris in prison that afternoon and then be at work downtown by 6 p.m. There would be no time to sleep.

It hurt her to see Chris in prison and not be able to touch him because of the Plexiglas barrier in the visitors' room. But she took heart at the way he ignored the orders of the prison guards, as if they were invisible and only he and his mother were in the room.

"Chris is cheeky, like me," she said.

Ngcobo sighed and remembered what Chris had told her during their last visit: "Don't worry about me. Watch out for yourself, Mama, you look tired."

She had to admit it: She was exhausted. But the police had come just the week before, looking for Gerry. And Moses was certain to be snatched if she did not get him out of Soweto. She could not let the System wear her down now.

Tonight, perhaps, if the buses were running on time, she would be home from work by 5 a.m. If all was quiet, she would steal some sleep before the next knock of the police at the door.

A BAR OWNER QUIETLY PROSPERS WITHIN THE SYSTEM

FRIDAY, DECEMBER 16, 1988

BY DAVID ZUCCHINO

SOWETO, SOUTH AFRICA—Peggy "Bel-Air" Senne was born in a shebeen. He figures he'll die in one, too.

In South Africa's black townships, a shebeen is a place of booze—a bar, a tavern, a nightclub or a hole in the wall that serves drinks. In Soweto, the nation's largest township, the king of the shebeens is Peggy Senne, a bow-legged little man with a gravelly voice and blood-shot eyes from too many cigarettes and too many late nights out.

Booze is Senne's life, and he is proud of it. He calls himself a bootlegger, and the backyard shebeen called Peggy's Place has made him richer than most white men.

"I was born in a shebeen," he says, sucking on a cigarette in the cool of his living room, where the clinking of glasses and the hum of conversation filter in from Peggy's Place out back. "I went to school on shebeen money, got married on shebeen money, bought my first Bel-Air automobile on shebeen money. My kids went to college on shebeen money."

If there is a success story in Soweto, it might as well be Peggy Senne. He has thrived within apartheid's boundaries, a black man grown great in a one-color world. Born into segregation, he has chosen to flourish within it, not fight to escape it.

There are many blacks like Peggy Senne in South Africa. They accept their lot, and profit nonetheless. They build their lives quietly, within bounds, leaving to others the terrifying struggles of liberation and revolution.

Senne is wealthy enough that he could afford a big apartment in the so-called gray areas of downtown Johannesburg, where people of color have breached apartheid's walls. He could even afford to pay a white man to buy him a house in the exclusive white suburbs, where a few well-to-do blacks have infiltrated.

He stays instead in Soweto, for it took him a long time to arrive. His family was evicted in the 1950s from a palce called Sophiatown, then evicted again in the early 1960s from an eyesore known as the Western Native Township. In 1962, he found himself dumped into a four-room matchbox house in Soweto.

So naturally he opened a shebeen. It began in his dining room with a few crates of beer. Now he sells 8,000 cases of beer a week, plus huge quantities of liquor and wine. The little house has since grown up around the shebeen. Senne now owns one of the biggest homes in Soweto, with a separate two-story living wing and a big garage.

The white authorities cracked down on his new shebeen, of course, but not in the bloody racial clashes that have ruptured South African society for so long. They would simply confiscate his cars or his beer in return for allowing him to remain open.

CHALLENGING THE SYSTEM

In his own cautious way, Senne fought back. In 1979, he formed the Soweto Tavern Association to represent the shebeeners against the authorities. By 1984, he had persuaded the white government to legalize shebeens and charge them licensing fees and taxes. He had challenged the system, quietly but persistently, and finally it gave in.

"We all struggle in our own way," he says.

Senne has since stayed out of politics. He doesn't want any trouble. He just wants to sell his booze and see his customers have a good time.

"Look, I'm a shebeener, not a politician," he says. "Don't ask me political questions. I just take what comes. You've got to survive, man."

Even so, racial politics engulf Soweto. Senne does what he must do. When the young radicals who call themselves "comrades" order him to shut down in support of a boycott or a strike, he obeys. He does not reopen until they tell him to. He does not, however, encourage young people to drink at Peggy's Place. He prefers mature customers, who don't talk politics.

He often wonders why the comrades are so bitter and so willing to suffer for their cause. He believes that a black man is far better off in South Africa now than when he was their age.

'SKY'S THE LIMIT'

"Our new generation sees no improvement," he says. "But if you ask me, things are much better—and they'll continue to get better. Before, you couldn't even buy the car you wanted. You couldn't form a company or apply for a loan. Now, the sky's the limit. I can go down to the white bank and take out a loan. They don't care what color I am, long as my credit's good."

Senne offers himself up as proof that a black man can prosper despite apartheid. As a boy, he worked in his parents' shebeen. His mother was a maid. His father couldn't buy a car.

"My father rode a bicycle. I have seven cars," he says. He claims to be the first black man in South Africa to drive an American car—a Chevy Bel-Air in the 1950s. Now his main car is a silver 1988 Mercedes-Benz.

Senne wears his success. On this particular evening he wears a yellow cardigan over a golf shirt, mustard slacks, tassled loafers, tinted shades and gold—gold necklaces, gold bracelets, gold rings and a gold wristwatch.

There are three main avenues to wealth in the townships. One is elected office in the township council, where graft and bribes enrich a black man willing to serve within apartheid's edifice. Another is construction—for the thousands of blacks who can afford expensive additions to their little township homes.

A third avenue is booze, either a liquor store or a shebeen. A township is a place of joy and despair, and thus liquor is always required. Senne prides himself on his ability to recognize the distinctive drinking habits of blacks, and to profit from them.

"A black doesn't drink like a white man," he says. "A white man can drink at home. A black man, he has to drink in a place where there's people and talking and noise. And a black man wants to be able to drink early in the day if he wants to, and all night if he wants to do that."

For those reasons, Peggy's Place opens early and closes late. "We're like a police station—we never close," he says. He and his wife take separate vacations so that Peggy's Place can always be open.

Resting on a sofa, Senne smokes his cigarette and totals up his blessings. He has a loving wife, Dorothy, better known as Cookie. He has four children—one a lawyer, he says proudly—and seven grandchildren. When he dies, he says, he will die a satisfied and comfortable man.

In the kitchen, Cookie is preparing dinner, humming softly. Inside Peggy's Place, some customers have already ordered drinks. The sound of their laughter is soothing.

Life is sweet, says Peggy Senne, looking out his living-room window at men unloading cases of beer from a truck guarded by a man with a shotgun. The beer bottles reach the floor of his garage with a satisfying clink, like the sound of money in the bank.

A TENTATIVE STEP TOWARD FREEDOM

SATURDAY, DECEMBER 17, 1988

BY DAVID ZUCCHINO

SPRUITVIEW, SOUTH AFRICA—David Mkhabela has taken his leave of Soweto. After years of fear and intimidation, of corruption and filth, he has made his escape from that sad black reservoir.

Home now is a fine, modern brick house he has built in a place called Spruitview, known to all as a "model township" for South Africa's black elite.

Here, in a stretch of expensive homes rising from the grass veld 19 miles south of Johannesburg, live the first blacks officially allowed out of the cramped townships—freed from the areas created decades ago as black labor reserves.

So David Mkhabela, his supervisor's salary invested in a new home and a new life, finds now that he has escaped only Soweto, not South Africa. He is the first urban black South African in 75 years to actually own the ground beneath his home, but he has taken only one tentative step on the long and uncharted journey to true liberation.

And in doing so, he has broken with the great black masses and also with his two brothers, both revolutionaries who have suffered greatly at the hands of the white security police.

Mkhabela has invested in apartheid reform, but without illusions. Like other successful blacks, he has cautiously accepted a less onerous form of racial segregation. The white authorities have endorsed Spruitview as the first of several clean, efficient "upmarket"—and still segregated—black living areas. Blacks who can afford it are moving in.

Some blacks believe that those in Spruitview have somehow abandoned the township resistance movement, but for many the alternatives had become unbearable.

"I had to get out of Soweto. I could no longer survive there," Mkhabela was saying in the cool living room of his new home, 27 miles and a political chasm away from his tiny matchbox house in Soweto outside Johannesburg. He spoke like a man released from prison, but on parole.

As a black man who works as a supervisor for white-owned Anglo

American Corp.—the mining and industrial colossus viewed by some blacks as an exploiter of black labor—Mkhabela had become a target. The young township revolutionaries who call themselves "comrades" had threatened him and his family. They demanded that everyone in Soweto honor the many "stayaways"—work boycotts—they call to protest apartheid.

But Mkhabela, who is 40, had an important position and a family to support. He had worked too hard for too long to lose his job over a political protest.

"Those youngsters were quite angry, quite threatening," Mkhabela said. He mentioned their "people's courts," kangaroo courts where township justice is meted out with floggings and sometimes with executions. "They would introduce a new law and you would be guilty of violating it."

He refused to sacrifice his job. But moving to another cramped, volatile township near Johannesburg was out of the question. Each one, like Soweto, has a housing shortage so acute that the waiting list for homes runs into the thousands.

In late 1986, South Africa offered another of its slowly evolving apartheid reforms. Blacks were given "freehold rights" to own residential land in urban South Africa for the first time since 1913.

Except for the handful of blacks who fell through bureaucratic cracks in rural areas, blacks were not allowed to own property in South Africa under the Natives Land Act of 1913 for fear that property rights would lead to political rights. A black could own a home in a black area, but the land it rested on had to be rented from the government—a policy some blacks called "the bricks but not the dirt."

With freehold rights now available, a handful of blacks with money have begun to flee the townships for clean, spacious Spruitview. Mkhabela was the first, moving into his 76,000 rand ($36,000) home in January. Of the 100 families who have followed, at least 90 have come from Soweto in search of safety and peace.

The new cars driven by Mkhabela and his neighbors carry a bumper sticker: "SPRUITVIEW—The New Garden Suburb for Peace and Security."

Although Spruitview is South Africa's only completed "model township," others are planned. Since Mkhabela got his title in January, more than 400 other blacks have acquired titles to their homes in existing townships, according to Alec Weiss, a government housing official in Pretoria.

Spruitview is a centerpiece of the government's "hearts and minds" strategy designed to improve black living conditions while maintaining strict racial segregation. The strategy is coupled with an iron fist policy of smashing both violent and peaceful dissent through the government's looming security apparatus and emergency rule.

The government's deputy minister of economic affairs, T. G. Alant, said recently that freehold rights and other reforms were creating "an affluent black middle class, which serves as an inspiration to other blacks of what can be achieved."

Those blacks, he said, are a hedge against "the [black] anarchists [who] are bound to totally destroy the existing structures and then capitalize on the chaos."

In Spruitview, men such as Mkhabela resent being portrayed as government supporters. They regard Spruitview as only one step toward dismantling—rather than modifying—apartheid. They say they differ from the revolutionaries only in tactics and timetables, not in goals. They believe that they will achieve full political rights in their lifetimes.

"Something must replace this system because there is no hope for black people under the present state of affairs," Mkhabela said. "For the government, reform means trying to buy time. For me, it means moving ahead to a better life. We are showing that a black man can do better. He doesn't have to live in a matchbox house."

Mkhabela has chosen a life far different from that of his defiant brothers. Their divergent paths are one small measure of the divisions within a vast black nation of 26 million.

One brother, Ismail, is an activist in the Azanian People's Organization, the black consciousness movement founded by the black martyr Steve Biko. Ismail has been detained many times; his wife gave birth to their child while she was in detention. He once told his brother that he did not intend to die of natural causes but as a soldier fighting for black revolution.

Mkhabela's other brother fled Soweto after the 1976 student riots and joined other exiles fighting South Africa from neighboring Botswana.

"My brothers belong to the movement," Mkhabela said. "I highly appreciate their actions. Without their struggle, things would seem normal. And of course nothing is normal for black people in South Africa."

Mkhabela has struggled in his own way. Twelve years ago, he decided he wanted to work at either Anglo American or IBM after working a series of menial jobs. So day after day, he pestered the two companies. Finally, Anglo offered him a job reserved by custom for blacks: security guard.

He took it. Soon he was demanding to be moved up to something more challenging. "I confronted them by asking if my color was a stumbling block," he said.

Anglo eventually moved him to an entry-level position in the transport department. After seven years with the company, he was promoted to supervisor in charge of licensing company vehicles. He now directs a staff of 19, five of them whites.

"On paper, I am above the whites," Mkhabela said. "But in reality, they don't report to me but to other whites. If you are a black, they move you away from direct supervision of whites. They have to nurse their feelings."

He now fears that he has reached his ceiling at the company, despite its declared policy of promoting blacks to traditionally white jobs. "It's frustrating to know you can do your boss' job, but to get constantly shoved sideways while the whites move up. So I make a lot of noise," he said.

In Spruitview, at least, Mkhabela believes that he has taken charge of his own life. His new home and lot are more than double the size of his Soweto matchbox, which cost 1,300 rand ($620). The water, electricity and telephone service are reliable. The roads are paved. The garbage is collected regularly. He no longer worries about crime and political strife.

In his living room, Mkhabela sat on a new sofa next to walls painted a light salmon. The house smelled of new paint and carpets. A color TV and a stereo system had been set up. In the kitchen, a black housekeeper fussed over Mkhabela's 3-year-old daughter, Joan. Out back, black construction workers bought sodas from a small snack shop he runs from his garage.

In Soweto, he said, he could not have run such a shop without paying enormous bribes to black councilmen who dole out franchise rights. In Spruitview, he paid a nominal sum for a trader's license.

But in other ways, not much has changed. His five children still go to poorly run "Bantu" schools reserved for blacks. There are white schools close by, but the Mkhabela children must attend school in cramped Katlehong township down the road. There are mixed-race private schools available, but they are in Johannesburg, too far away.

Mkhabela wants to start a private school in Spruitview, but he has encountered government resistance. The message is clear: Black children should go to black schools. He senses apartheid's walls closing in again.

"If this is a so-called elite area, why shouldn't we have elite schools?" he asked, though he knew the answer.

He sighed and rested his head against the back of the sofa. It was the end of another long day—the hour's drive to work and back, the struggle to complete a new house, the bills to pay. He had too many battles: to raise himself up, to fight the system in his own quiet way.

Anyway, he said softly, it was better than Soweto. He smiled and raised Joan to his lap. He had chosen the right path—he was certain of that. He was certain of something else, too. When his girl was grown, no one would tell her where to live.

FOR MANY, STRUGGLE IS FOR WORK

SUNDAY, DECEMBER 18, 1988

BY DAVID ZUCCHINO

UITENHAGE, SOUTH AFRICA—Every morning for nine months, Patrick Stalli was there at the gate. He would walk the four miles from home in the dark and join the thousands of other jobless black men pressing against the fortified gates of the towering Volkswagen plant.

Every day for nine months, he walked back home without a job. One morning, the white foreman said he needed 20 men. Thousands surged for the gate. Stalli pushed and clawed. Somehow his body popped through the tiny opening. He had a job.

"I was so desperate. I would do anything for a job. A little fighting and pushing was nothing to me," Stalli said recently, riding a bus at dawn to his 4.98-rand-an-hour ($2.08) job as a press operator who cuts out upholstery for car seats.

For millions of black South Africans, the concerns that eat away at their daily lives have little to do with the struggle for political rights or the faltering, bloody war of black revolution. Protest and confrontation are remote concepts. Life boils down to the basics—a decent house and a job, any job.

Officially, the unemployment rate for registered black workers is 14.7 percent. But private research groups put the actual unemployment rate at up to 30 percent of adults among South Africa's 26 million blacks, or nearly five times the white rate. In the hardscrabble eastern Cape, where Uitenhage forms a dingy island of auto plants and tire factories, black union leaders say the unemployment rate is nearly 50 percent.

Earlier this year, a research firm asked blacks in nearby Natal province to list their most pressing fears. Ninety-four percent of those polled led with the fear of losing their jobs. Only 49 percent said they worried about living under white rule. Just 8 percent said they had a "great desire" for more political rights.

Patrick Stalli, 28 and the possessor of an eighth-grade Bantu education prescribed to blacks by whites, does not dream the dreams of black freedom and black rule.

He wants to make enough money to repair his dilapidated car, to afford a bottle of beer when he gets off work.

He wishes his matchbox township house were nicer or at least bigger. He longs for the six friends and relatives camping out in his spare bedroom to find their own place to live.

Most of all, Patrick Stalli hopes he can hold on to his job. He has been laid off twice because of a soft car market, and each time he felt the sting of hunger and despair. He is back full-time now, but only until the next union strike or the next retrenchment.

"I am most fortunate to have a job," he said, dropping heavily onto an old sofa at home, exhausted after another 9-hour shift. "All of my friends, they are begging me to find them work at the plant. But even this job is not enough. I need overtime just to have enough food to eat."

Like most blacks, Stalli supports an extended family of 20 or more people. An enduring African tradition requires those with jobs to support those without. Stalli sends money to his parents and siblings and the parents and siblings of his wife. The relatives and friends staying with him eat away at his meager food supplies.

A longing for something better gnaws at him. He is driven by ambition—but for himself and his family, not for the millions of dispossessed blacks across the land. He cannot carry their burdens. He has no time or energy for protests and boycotts and political meetings. It is enough to worry about his own affairs.

"This job doesn't support me in the way I want to live," he said. "It just keeps me alive to come to work the next day."

It was payday, and Stalli opened his envelope inside his darkened home after work one evening. He could not understand where all his money went. With overtime, he had grossed 501 rand over two weeks. But deducted from his paycheck were income taxes, medical insurance, pension payments, union dues and unemployment insurance—plus deductions to the township for his rent and utilities. That left 296 rand to see him through the next two weeks.

In the house, a visiting union shop steward named Mlami Magioimesi tried to console Stalli. He mentioned that things had been much worse before the black union—the National Union of Metalworkers of South Africa—was formed in 1986. Until 1979, black unions were not permitted in South Africa.

"Power—political power, economic power—comes from the union," Magioimesi said. "The government knows that. It knows we have the power now to affect the national economy."

White corporations pushed the government to allow black unions in order to address their workers as a coherent body, to avoid wildcat strikes and uncontrolled strife. But now the government, stung by the unions' militancy and their ability to halt production, is trying to crush them. It has restricted Cosatu, the Congress of South African Trade Unions, from political activity. It detains union leaders without charge for months at a time. It is trying to ram through legislation restricting the right of unions to strike. And it uses the police to break up job actions.

Even Volkswagen, a progressive employer by South African standards, has not moved fast enough for the union men like Magioimesi. Of the plant's 7,600 employees, 5,600 are low-paid, hourly workers. All of them are black. The remaining 2,000 are higher-paid, salaried employees. With a small but growing number of exceptions, they are white.

"Job reservation may be scrapped," Magioimesi said, referring to the recently rescinded law that prohibited blacks from holding skilled jobs reserved for whites. "But it's still there, only in a more subtle form. If you're black, it's still very difficult to move up."

Even so, many South African academics predict that black revolution will one day come not from the barrel of a gun, but on the factory floor. The South African Institute of Race Relations speaks of a "silent revolution" triggered by black unions and the black workforce. Blacks drive the economy with their labor. As consumers, they determine white marketing strategies by the beer they drink, the clothes they buy, the types of food they eat.

"The worker's life and the political life are one and the same. Through unity comes liberation," another black shop steward, William Smith, told Stalli at the plant the next day.

Stalli nodded, but he did not care much for political theory. He supported the union. Without it, he knew, he could be fired for no reason. When the union told him to strike, as it did only last June, he obeyed. But really, he confided, he didn't think strikes accomplished much. He would rather be working.

□□□

Kwanobuhle township woke up. Dogs barked. Donkeys brayed. It was 4:30 a.m.—time for Patrick Stalli to go to work.

Stalli stepped over the sleeping forms of his friends and relatives. He washed his face and brushed his teeth from a pail of cold water filled from a tap outside. His pregnant wife, Valencia, cooked breakfast on a paraffin stove. Stalli listened to the morning news on a radio powered by a car battery. The house has no electricity or plumbing.

Pulling on his blue Volkswagen overalls, Stalli took a few bites of corn porridge and gulped down a cup of instant coffee. His wife handed him his lunch packed into a plastic grocery bag, and Stalli walked down a dirt road to the bus stop.

It was now 5:30 a.m. The bus was late. A long queue had formed—auto workers with their grocery bags of food, domestics with their faces streaked a ghastly gray from skin lightener creams. Already, unemployed men were lounging on Kwanobuhle's street corners. At last the bus arrived.

It was an important day. After work, Stalli would take his driver's test. If he passed, he would be able to apply for a higher-paying job as a forklift driver. The job was so important to Stalli that he had taken lessons from driving school on his own. He still owed the One Way Driving School 100 rand for four lessons.

On the assembly line inside, Stalli went through the monotonous motions of laying the mold, stretching the fabric, cutting the fabric. His movements were crisp and economical. He prides himself on not losing his concentration.

His white supervisor, Jeff Humphries, watched him. He said Stalli seemed ready for a promotion to the bonding machine that adheres the upholstery to car seats. That assembly line job pays the same as a forklift driver's.

"He's a good, dependable worker," Humphries said. "He knows what he wants. He wants to move up."

Humphries mentioned that he would recommend moving Stalli up the line to the bonding machine the next month. But he said nothing to Stalli.

After the shift, Stalli went out and passed his driving test. He needed only the driving school certificate to apply for the forklift job, but he couldn't get it until he paid for the lessons.

On the way out of the plant, Stalli seemed distracted. He did not suspect that he might soon be promoted up the line. Anyway, he was determined to get off the line and move up to the reasonably stimulating job of driving a forklift.

Outside the plant, some of the men from the union were talking politics. Stalli ignored them and walked on to the bus stop, his head bent in thought. He was wondering how a man working the line was going to save up 100 rand.

THIRTEEN

ANATOMY OF AN AIR CRASH

1989 WINNER IN THE EXPLANATORY JOURNALISM CATEGORY

"For a distinguished example of explanatory journalism that illuminates significant and complex issues . . . ."

The Dallas Morning News
David Hanners
William Snyder
Karen Blessen

Perhaps the most troubling of David Hanners's findings is that "seven men died in part because the 'adequate level of safety' the National Transportation Safety Board said didn't exist in 1977 still didn't exist in 1986. Nor does it exist today."

Every time a plane crashes in this country, as word of the tragedy is quickly relayed to news organizations and to relatives of the victims, a solemn scenario is played out at the crash site: Amid the wreckage of the airplane stands an investigator from the National Transportation Safety Board, bending now and then to examine a piece of debris. The charred and twisted fragments around him are the pieces of a complicated puzzle he must solve.

It is hard *not* to be fascinated by the mystique of the lone investigator as he "kicks tin." But besides the highly visible work that goes on in the field, the rest of the process by which the NTSB investigates such crashes is little understood. It is a process that involves teams of experts, high-tech sophistication, old-fashioned detective work and, frequently, politics.

I had long been fascinated by that process and its implications for air safety in this country. In early November 1985—just three months after the crash of Delta Airlines Flight 191 at the Dallas/Fort Worth International Airport—I sent a memo to my editors suggesting we take an in-depth, behind-the-scenes look at how the NTSB investigates air crashes.

I thought the simplest, clearest way to do this would be to follow one investigator as he examined one crash, from start to finish. We would walk on the crash site with him as he did the first time, follow him through the subsequent investigation and analysis and be there in Washington when the five members of the NTSB made their findings of probable cause of the crash.

The NTSB agreed to our proposal, but we had a problem in selecting the kind of crash that would show a "typical" investigation. After discussing our objectives with Warren Wandel, the NTSB air safety investigator assigned to us, we came up with four criteria the crash would have to meet before we would choose it for our project.

1. The crash should involve multiple fatalities.

2. The crash should involve a multiple-engine airplane.

3. There should be some communication between the pilot and the control tower so we would have transcripts of the final communication.

4. The crash should be outside the Dallas area and should be relatively unnewsworthy in Dallas. The reasoning behind this point was that we didn't want to have the board in the position of explaining to our local competitors why I and our photographer, William Snyder, were being granted access to the crash site and they were not.

With the criteria set, we waited. And waited. And waited. Then, at 10:30 on Friday night, April 4, 1986, Wandel called. A New Jersey–bound business jet operated by the Singer Corporation had crashed near the tiny community of Redwater, Texas, killing all seven people aboard. Wandel asked if we wanted to go to the crash site.

My wife and I had plans for the weekend. The weather was lousy (indeed, the plane had crashed during a driving thunderstorm). I was getting ready for bed and didn't relish the thought of having to leave for East Texas at 3 a.m. Saturday to traipse around in a muddy pasture for days.

But I decided to go, and for the next 22 months that call had a dominating influence on my life.

As Snyder and I met Wandel the following morning and walked to the crash site with him, we got our first close-up view of an airplane crash. It wasn't a pretty sight.

The airplane, a twin-jet Israel Aircraft Industries 1124A Westwind 2, had crashed nose-first into the ground at more than 640 miles per hour. There wasn't much left of the plane, crew or passengers; just shards of metal strewn around a crater 10 feet deep and 15 feet wide in an East Texas pasture. The plane exploded on impact.

As the other members of the investigation team arrived at the crash site, Snyder and I also got our first, abrupt introduction to the air crash investigation community. We quickly learned it was a small, closed community that was suspicious of outsiders, particularly reporters and photographers.

We heard every you-reporters-get-it-wrong horror story. Aviation safety was an extremely complex story, I told them, and it wasn't always easy to grasp the finer points quickly, as we are often forced to do on deadline. Looking back, getting the aviation community to trust us was perhaps our biggest hurdle on this project.

Wandel accepted us quickly enough; we were there because of "orders from Washington," he reasoned, and I believe he thought that educating the media about his job would make things easier for everybody.

We met other members of the crash inquiry team—representatives of the Federal Aviation Administration, the aircraft owner and manufacturer, insurance companies and others. These people were not accustomed to letting a reporter and photographer in on their private meetings and discussions. While most were cordial and reasonably tolerant, a few were openly hostile. The Singer Corporation refused to cooperate with our project in any way.

As a reporter with only a notebook and pen, I found it easy to eventually fade into the background. I felt that because this was a long-term project, I could give the people more "room"—I wouldn't have to pepper them with questions all at once. I would have months to ask them. By giving them this freedom, I think they came to trust me more. Eventually, I became just another person in the room.

For Snyder, who was laden with cameras and other photo equipment, the task of getting the team to relax around him wasn't as easy. To get them over their uneasiness with the camera as quickly as possible, Snyder shot a lot of frames early so the team members would get used to the sound of the shutter. In time, they got more comfortable with the camera around, and Snyder, too, faded into the background.

At the crash site it wasn't difficult to find things to photograph. The project's photographic challenge came later, however, when Snyder had to find drama in events that didn't have a lot of action—"nonvisual situations," as Snyder called them.

As the investigation progressed, we followed Wandel across the country. We went with him to Duncanville, Texas, where the crash debris was laid out on a hangar floor to "reconstruct" the wreckage. There wasn't much to put back together. We traveled to Phoenix,

Arizona, where the Westwind 2's two jet engines were dismantled and inspected for damage. We also went to the NTSB headquarters in Washington, where we interviewed people who worked on other aspects of the inquiry, such as examining weather conditions and air traffic control communications at the time of the crash.

The NTSB issued a 600-page factual report on the crash in June 1987. Although the finding of probable cause was still eight months away, I felt that I had enough material to start writing. The paper's editor's had not yet decided whether the project would be published as a series or as a special section. I began writing what I thought would be a four-part series.

The challenge in writing about the investigation was the difficulty in presenting highly technical and complex information in the simplest and clearest way so readers would stay with it. Moreover, the story had to be told in human terms without being maudlin. Toward this end, I decided that the only relative of the crash victims that I would feature would be the pilot's widow. She was cooperative, and her comments, interspersed throughout the piece, helped break the "technical tension" that tended to build up in the piece.

The subject matter lent itself to the style of a detective story: It started with a puzzling crash and then, slowly, pieces were put together to solve the puzzle.

As the stories were being edited, Karen Blessen, a graphic artist at the paper, began working on ways to tell the story through graphics. She started with a map showing air traffic control routes in East Texas and the path of the ill-fated jet. Once it was decided to publish the project in a 12-page special section, the opportunities for graphic illustrations were greatly increased.

The graphics involved an enormous amount of research, and Blessen soon encountered the same problem I had come across—how to make complicated information easy to understand.

Blessen studied maps and weather data with NTSB officials. The resulting graphic that was published on the section's cover was an uncluttered but informative piece of art.

After nearly two years of investigation, the board scheduled its hearing on Tuesday, February 2, 1988. By the following Sunday, *The Dallas Morning News* hit the streets with something no newspaper had ever had: a comprehensive, behind-the-scenes look at an NTSB crash investigation.

—David Hanners, William Snyder and Karen Blessen
The Dallas Morning News

THE FINAL FLIGHT OF 50 SIERRA KILO

SUNDAY FEBRUARY 7, 1988

BY DAVID HANNERS

The phone rang. It was trouble.

Warren Wandel was used to getting phone calls at home that meant trouble. As an air safety investigator in the Fort Worth office of the National Transportation Safety Board, Wandel's phone often brought news of some calamity, of death from above.

This call came at 8:14 on Friday evening, April 4, 1986. A Federal Aviation Administration official told Wandel that a business jet, shortly after takeoff from Dallas' Redbird Airport, had disappeared from Dallas/Fort Worth air control radar somewhere over East Texas.

With the call came the beginning of the post-mortem of 50 Sierra Kilo, a process that would take 22 months and one that would produce a chilling final entry: That seven men died was a tragedy; that the system allowed them to die was a travesty.

Even as Wandel was on the phone, the Bowie County Sheriff was reporting that a plane had crashed near Redwater, a tiny community tucked in a wooded corner of Northeast Texas not far from Texarkana.

The 38-year-old Wandel, a helicopter gunship pilot in Vietnam and a 6-year veteran of the safety board, jotted down the particulars on a white tablet that is never far from his phone: The aircraft was an Israel Aircraft Industries 1124A Westwind 2, registration N50SK ("50 Sierra Kilo") and operated by the Singer Corp.

The plane left Dallas, bound for New Jersey. Over East Texas, the plane encountered bad weather and the pilot asked permission to climb to a higher altitude to get above the turbulence.

An air traffic controller gave him the clearance, but the pilot never acknowledged. Moments later, the plane crashed in a field.

The pilot's flight plan listed six people aboard; later, it would be learned there was a seventh. None survived.

From his home in East Fort Worth, Wandel set in motion a government agency credited by some as the world's most elite corps of accident investigators and criticized by others as a cumbersome, powerless bureaucracy often hamstrung by politics.

For nearly two years, Wandel and his team of experts would spend countless hours trying to piece together the airplane's final moments, figure out what happened and make recommendations that might prevent the same thing from happening to somebody else. It is a job that is part detective work, part science, part common sense, part luck.

But as Wandel hung up the phone and sat for a moment on the edge of his chair, he knew there was a chance that, like a few of the 380-plus crashes he had investigated, there might be parts to this puzzle he could never find. There would be questions that only the crew of 50 Sierra Kilo could answer, and they were dead.

What Wandel did know intrigued him: A sleek business jet equipped with modern weather radar and flown by two experienced pilots took off from Dallas, flew straight into the middle of a terrible storm and crashed with all of hell's fury in a bucolic Texas pasture.

All Wandel had to do was figure out why

□ □ □

The odyssey of 50 Sierra Kilo started before dawn that Friday morning when Kenneth Lee Hetland rose from his bed, rubbed the sleep from his eyes and shuffled to the shower. He dressed quietly so as not to disturb his wife, Virginia, and their three young daughters.

He bent down to kiss his sleeping wife goodbye. Sunrise was still more than two hours away when Hetland climbed into his car for the hour-and-15-minute drive up the New Jersey Turnpike from his home in the quiet town of Willingboro, N.J., to Teterboro Airport, one of the busiest general aviation airports in the country.

Hetland was a pilot for the Kearfott Division of the Singer Co., and on this Friday, April 4, he was scheduled to fly five executives to Dallas for a business meeting. While Singer was synonymous with sewing machines, it was now diversified high-tech. Kearfott, based in Little Falls, N.J., manufactured a wide range of electronic equipment for aircraft, particularly for the defense industry.

Kearfott was bidding for a subcontract on a project headed by LTV Missiles & Electronics Group in Grand Prairie. LTV had a $180 million contract to develop a new battlefield missile for the Army, and Kearfott sought a $2.5 million subcontract to build the missile's tail fin controls.

As the 35-year-old Hetland neared Teterboro, he could see off to the right the lights of New York City glistening in the early-morning chill. In a few moments he would turn onto Moonachie Avenue and would be at Kearfott's large, white hangar on the airport's south perimeter.

Hetland had been flying for 10 years and had been with Kearfott since August 1979. He had logged more than 7,300 hours in the air in everything from small planes to DC-3s to business jets.

Like most pilots, flying was something Hetland couldn't get enough of. In fact, he had originally been scheduled to fly a different trip this day, but had switched with another pilot at the last minute because the flight to Dallas would allow him to get back home in time to fly a Friday night mission with his U.S. Air Force Reserve unit. He was a loadmaster on a C-141 cargo plane.

Inside the hangar, illuminated by the brilliant lights, was the jet he would fly to Dallas, a white and beige Westwind 2.

The Westwind 2 is $4.6 million worth of ritzy business jet (in terms of dollars, Westwinds represent Israel's biggest annual export to the United States), and it was designed to meet the needs of corporations that wanted something bigger than a LearJet but smaller than, say, a Lockheed JetStar.

The Westwind 2 met that need in style. It had a large cabin, by "bizjet" standards anyway, good headroom and legroom, a galley, bar, closet—even an airline-type flushing toilet. With a wingspan of 44 feet and a length of 52 feet, the Westwind 2 can fly intercontinental distances at speeds up to 449 mph.

Fifty Sierra Kilo, which rolled off the Tel Aviv assembly line in 1981, was a graceful, elegant aircraft, with its long, slender fuselage and thin, bullet-shaped fuel tanks at the tips of the wings located midplane. Aft and above the gently swept wings were a pair Garrett turbofan jet engines.

Hetland's co-pilot on this flight would be Steven Fulop. At 22, Fulop was several years Hetland's junior, but he had logged almost 240 hours more flight time in Westwind 2s than Hetland.

As the aircraft was towed out of the hangar under an overcast sky, the executives who would be making the 8:30 a.m. trip began arriving one by one from their homes in suburban New Jersey: Martin Chen,

44, a program director from Kinnelon; Frank Schmitt, 43, a senior pricing administrator who lived in Cranford; Robert Imfeld, 59, a contract manager who lived in Nutley; and William Pasechnick, 49, of Little Ferry, a program manager.

A fifth executive scheduled for the trip, contract negotiator Donald McBride, 47 of Totowa, missed the flight, but made commercial arrangements to join his colleagues in Dallas.

Fifty Sierra Kilo's three-hour flight to Dallas' Redbird Airport was uneventful. When the executives arrived shortly before 10:30 a.m., they were greeted by Kearfott's central region manager, Tom R. Mahoney, who drove them to Grand Prairie.

Hetland and Fulop did what corporate pilots often find themselves doing: waiting. They passed part of the time at an aircraft serving facility at Redbird, getting a bid to paint Kearfott's JetStar.

It had been raining off and on in Dallas, and at 11:28 a.m., one of the pilots phoned the FAA's Dallas Flight Service Station at Love Field to get a weather briefing and update his flight plan for the 2:30 p.m. return trip.

The news wasn't good. The briefer told him he could expect thunderstorms locally and throughout his route through Northeast Texas and Arkansas. The cells would continue building during the afternoon.

He thanked the briefer and hung up. Hetland and Fulop then asked some employees of Aviall, an aircraft servicing facility, about a good place to get a haircut, borrowed a car from Aviall (they put 13 miles on it) and drove off.

□ □ □

Hetland and Fulop, their hair freshly cut, returned to Redbird Airport by early afternoon. At 2 p.m., one of the executives called the airport and told the crew that a meeting was being delayed and that they wouldn't be done in time to make the scheduled 2:30 p.m. return. He told Hetland the executives would take a commercial flight back home, and Hetland and Fulop were to fly the Westwind 2 back on their own.

Hetland called Kearfott's flight operations office and told them of the developments. The operations office told them that if the executives could be done by late afternoon and they could be "wheels up" from Dallas by 7 p.m. (that would make it almost a 20-hour workday for Hetland and Fulop) that they should stay and wait for the meeting to end.

Even as ground crews topped off the Westwind 2 with 600 gallons of jet fuel, the weather was worsening. It had rained and hailed at Redbird; FAA tower manager Nick Melton's van had been dented by the hail.

At 5:14 p.m., a member of the Kearfott crew—it's unclear which pilot placed the weather calls—phoned the Dallas Flight Service Station to revise the flight plan and get an update on the weather. Regina Pickering, a flight service specialist, handled the call.

She alluded to a line of storms that was, at the time, to the south of the Dallas/Fort Worth area and ran to the northeast. But she told the pilot that once the crew got outside the immediate Dallas area, weather wouldn't be a problem.

She told them to call back just before they left to "see what this line is going to do."

Clarence H. "Ozzy" Osborne Jr., Aviall's supervisor at Redbird, told the pilots they could call his company's private weather service, WSI Corp. of Bedford, Mass. At 5:28 p.m., the Kearfott pilots logged onto WSI's system and got an automated briefing for the route between Dallas and Teterboro. The briefing included something the FAA briefing didn't: a weather notice called a Convective SIGMET (short for Significant Meteorological Information, a warning of hazardous flying conditions) covering the central and eastern United States.

At 5:30 p.m., the automated weather briefing complete, Hetland and Fulop logged off the computer and waited for their passengers to arrive. A few minutes before 7 p.m., the executives—including McBride, who had flown commercially to Dallas—arrived, and they were pumped; they had a memorandum of agreement on the missile subcontract and all it needed was the signature of Kearfott officials back East.

They loaded their luggage and climbed aboard. Cutting it close to the 7 p.m. fly-or-stay deadline ordered by Kearfott's flight operations office, Fulop was the last aboard, securing the hatch behind him.

The rain and the wind had stopped, but it was overcast as 50 Sierra Kilo waited on the ramp. As Hetland radioed Redbird tower, asking for an Instrument Flight Rule clearance to Teterboro, he began turning the wheels of the nation's air traffic control machine.

Although it may not be apparent to a commercial airline traveler, the sky above Dallas/Fort Worth is a symphony with pilots as the string section and air traffic controllers as the conductors.

But unlike a symphony's lone conductor, this production has a series of conductors, each responsible for a different passage, a different slice of airspace.

Imagine an 80-mile-wide stop sign with D/FW airport at the center. The north, south, east and west sides of the sign are the routes aircraft take out of the area, while the northeast, southeast, southwest and northwest sides are the "gates" into the area. Each of these sides is monitored by a separate air traffic controller, whose job is to keep an orderly flow of traffic and make sure airplanes don't run into each other—in short, to keep the symphony in harmony.

Permission to take off comes from Redbird Tower. Once the aircraft is airborne, Dallas/Fort Worth Departure Control, which monitors the airspace within a 40-mile radius, assumes control.

Fifty Sierra Kilo, like many other commercial, corporate and private aircraft, was equipped with a transponder, a device that sends a code identifying the aircraft on air traffic control radar screens. As a transponder-equipped aircraft takes off, it appears as a flashing blip on the controller's screen—with an accompanying "data block" identifying its type, registration number, speed and altitude.

As an eastbound aircraft banks and heads over Lake Ray Hubbard, near the eastern boundary of the airspace ruled by departure control, it is "handed off" to a controller at the Fort Worth Air Traffic Control Center. The Center, as it is called, controls aircraft flying in a 174,000-square-mile chunk of airspace extending as far north as Kingfisher, Okla., and as far south as Temple, in Central Texas.

The eastern route of that imaginary stop sign is called the "Lake Low" area, so named because the area begins just east of Lake Ray Hubbard and because aircraft in that zone fly at lower altitudes. As aircraft pass through that region and gain altitude, they are directed to one of the eastern route's three high altitude exit routes: Texarkana High, Shreveport High or Alexandria High.

Hetland had requested the Texarkana route on his flight plan. Now, as he sat on the apron at Redbird, he was waiting for permission to take off. Within moments, it came.

"We'll see ya," Hetland acknowledged as he released the brakes.

Fifty Sierra Kilo rolled onto Runway 13—5,452 feet of concrete and the longest of Redbird's two runways. A Westwind 2 can take off in just under 4,000 feet, but as controllers in the glass tower remarked later, 50 Sierra Kilo's roll seemed to take forever.

Finally, with only about 500 feet of strip left, the nose lifted and the airplane lumbered into the air. At 6:56 p.m., 50 Sierra Kilo was airborne, headed homeward on a trip it never would complete.

□ □ □

Precisely as the Westwind 2 was taking off from Redbird Airport, the National Weather Service's National Aviation Weather Advisory Unit issued Convective SIGMET 2C, warning of severe weather over East and North Central Texas, including portions of 50 Sierra Kilo's intended route.

The crew of the Westwind 2, however, never heard it. Transcripts of air traffic control radio frequencies later showed that the warning was not broadcast on any of the frequencies while 50 Sierra Kilo would have been listening to them.

At 7:00:35 p.m., as the Westwind 2 gained altitude and headed eastward, Hetland radioed D/FW Departure Control for directions to avoid the weather that was dumping rain east of Dallas. He gave the first hint of trouble, asking for radar directions because "our radar is not doing very well this evening."

The departure controller provided the directions and, at 7:02 p.m., "handed off" 50 Sierra Kilo to the Lake Low controller at the air route center.

The departure controller never mentioned 50 Sierra Kilo's possible radar problem to the Lake Low controller, and neither did the crew, at least not in so many words. But 10 seconds after getting handed over to the Lake Low controller, 50 Sierra Kilo radioed, ". . . If, uh, you help us pick our way through here, we'd appreciate it."

At 7:06 p.m., the Lake Low controller handed off 50 Sierra Kilo to the Texarkana High controller: nothing more was said about radar.

The weather over North Central Texas was getting rougher, and other aircraft in the area were going to great distances to escape the storms.

A flight of three U.S. Air Force C-141 cargo planes had to turn north, going 230 miles out of their way to avoid the weather. A Republic Airlines flight and three Braniff flights had to divert from their course to avoid the storms.

All the aircraft were equipped with weather radar, which was showing parts of the storm over East Texas in brilliant red, the color used to indicate the most severe storms.

There's an axiom among pilots, in fact, about the colors on the radar: "Green is mean, yellow can hurt a fellow, red is dead."

One of the Braniff pilots later would describe the thunderstorms, some 25 to 40 miles in diameter, as "almost completely red."

□ □ □

Don Ruggles and Donny LaRue, slammed and battered about in the cockpit of a twin-engine Beechcraft Baron, were in the grip of the same storm as they approached Texarkana.

The 50-year-old Ruggles, a retired Army lieutenant colonel who flies a charter air service out of Texarkana, had flown LaRue to Houston to pick up a 325-pound piece of equipment that needed to be delivered that night to a railroad crew in Arkansas.

LaRue, 35, wasn't overly fond of flying anyway. But the Texarkana railroad maintenance and construction company he owned required him to fly fairly frequently—mostly in small planes and into small airports.

The Beechcraft hit the storm about 10 miles northeast of Longview. Ruggles and LaRue saw cumulus clouds towering up to 30,000 feet; arthritic bolts of lightning arched from cloud to cloud.

"I knew that I was not going to penetrate what I saw ahead to the northeast—at any altitude," said Ruggles. "Since I was cleared to (descend to) 3,000 feet, I felt like at least I could get below the cloud level and could have visual contact with any severe weather at that point."

But as Ruggles approached from the southwest, passing over Wright Patman Lake about eight miles southwest of Texarkana, he hit heavy rain, hail and severe turbulence. Engulfed in dark, thick, boiling clouds, he lost sight of the ground below.

What happened next was a heart-stopping acrobatic act few pilots live to tell about.

Ruggles was at 2,000 feet and traveling 160 mph. In the wink of an eye, his airspeed shot up to 250 mph and the Baron fell into a 60-degree bank to the right and dropped more than 1,000 feet. The aircraft then went into a 180-degree turn and the airspeed plummeted to 70 mph, far too slow for the Baron to stay airborne. The honking of the aircraft's stall warning horn flooded the tiny cockpit.

Ruggles tried to radio for help but the Baron was bucking so badly he couldn't hold the microphone. Now he was only 600 feet off the ground and in the middle of a pilot's worst nightmare: he was out of control in a bad storm, with no idea where he was—or how to get out of it.

He had lost control of his aircraft to a dark conspiracy of meteorology and aerodynamics. He regained control of the Baron—he's still not sure just how he did it—and managed to land safely at Texarkana Airport.

Ruggles had logged more than 10,000 hours in airplanes and helicopters, spanning almost 30 years. He describes the incident matter-of-factly:

"I would describe the conditions as severe updrafts and downdrafts and probably some wind shears," he said. "We just simply could not maintain the aircraft in a straight and level attitude. We were in such severe turbulence that we could not monitor our instruments very well."

LaRue translates for the layman:

"We were bouncing around every which way—upside down, backwards and forwards and every way you could ever imagine. It's the worst storm I've ever been through, no doubt. I fly a lot and those kinds of things you don't forget real regular."

□ □ □

Fifty Sierra Kilo was climbing to cruising altitude, and about 12 minutes into the flight, Hetland asked permission to fly directly to Texarkana. A few minutes later, the Texarkana High controller radioed back: "Five Zero Sierra Kilo, roger, when able, cleared direct Texarkana on course, maintain flight level three three zero (33,000 feet)."

Meanwhile, other aircraft were requesting permission to deviate from their flight paths to get around the storm. At 7:17 p.m., 21 minutes into the flight, the controller asked 50 Sierra Kilo: "How's your ride through there?"

"Uh, some uh, light bumps every now and then," Hetland responded, "but we've topped it."

"You remember what the tops were right along there?" the controller asked, referring to the top altitude of the clouds.

"Well, off to our left they're still building, uh, there's toppin' out about 38, 39 (38,000 or 39,000 feet), but off to the right where we were just passing through there, she's uh, topping out about 36 to 37," Hetland said.

The ride was getting much rougher, though, and a minute later, Hetland was directing full attention to flying while Fulop took the radio, requesting permission to climb to 39,000 feet to get above the turbulence that was knocking the plane around. Fulop's voice was tinged with nervousness.

Before the Texarkana High controller could grant the request, he had to check with the controller in charge of the adjoining airspace, who was at the Memphis Air Route Traffic Control Center. The delay must've seemed an eternity for the two men in the cockpit of the Westwind 2. At 7:19:51 p.m., 23 minutes into the flight, an agitated Fulop radioed: *Center, Westwind 50 SK need to get up!*

Ten seconds later the Texarkana High controller cleared the plane to climb to the higher altitude.

There was no immediate response from 50 Sierra Kilo. Twelve seconds later came a brief, unintelligible transmission. Played back later, the garble sounded to some like "negative thrust."

A little more than a minute later, the controller told 50 Sierra Kilo that he had lost the plane's transponder signal from his radar screen, but there was no response. Over the next four minutes, the controller tried 12 times to raise the Westwind 2.

Each call met silence. The radio crackled with the transmission of other flights on this Friday night. But there was only silence from 50 Sierra Kilo, a silence that left the controller with a knot in the pit of his stomach.

□ □ □

DeWayne Cannon looked at the darkened heavens and heavy rain over his head and uttered a silent curse. The 8 p.m. cookout he had planned for his Webelos Scout pack in Redwater looked as though it would have to be called off.

But when he got to his pack's meeting place in Texarkana, he found that some parents already had dropped off their kids. Cannon called the home of the boy who was to host the cookout. He got a pleasant surprise: It wasn't raining in Redwater. The cookout was back on.

Soon after he started the 16-mile drive along Texas Highway 67 to Redwater, Cannon began to regret his decision. The storm seemed to follow them, and it began raining harder. Cannon slowed to 35 mph.

"It was extremely dark," said Cannon. "And it was raining so hard. Even the windshield wipers wouldn't keep the windows clear."

About a mile east of Redwater, a couple of Scouts in the back seat, 10-year-olds Chris Stanley and Kyle Lutgen, looked to the north and caught a brief glimpse of something screaming out of the low, mean clouds.

In an instant, the darkened sky was filled with a horrific, violent orange explosion that shook the car and those inside it. Cannon, imagining lightning or a tornado had struck a nearby natural gas storage tank, reacted instinctively: He pushed the accelerator to the floor and got the hell out of there.

"It was violent," Cannon said. "It scared everybody. You coulda heard a pin drop in that car with the Scouts."

But as Cannon and his Scouts later would learn, what they saw was neither tornado nor bolt of lightning, but perhaps nonetheless an act of God.

It had been an airplane. As they had groped through the storm, they had witnessed the last tragic moment of the flight of 50 Sierra Kilo.

'KICKING TIN': THE SEARCH FOR PIECES

SUNDAY, FEBRUARY 7, 1988

BY DAVID HANNERS

The rain the night before had flooded Interstate 30, delaying Warren Wandel more than an hour. But the rain had stopped by the time he pulled his government-issue red Ford Tempo off beside the pasture.

The morning of April 5, 1986, was turning into another overcast, muggy East Texas day as Wandel retrieved the black briefcase from the car's trunk and headed past the yellow police barrier that Bowie County sheriff's deputies had strung around the 83-acre field.

Just as Wandel had envisioned the night before, sheriff's deputies had arrived within moments after the crash of the Westwind 2 corporate jet. They had sped there, lights flashing through heavy rain, intent on rescuing survivors. But they had found no life to save.

The wreckage was so brutally twisted that some metal pieces were indistinguishable as to their original purpose and design. Lying in the midst of the debris of 50 Sierra Kilo were body fragments of the seven Kearfott employees who had been aboard.

Wandel, one of 89 air safety investigators for the National Transportation Safety Board, lit another Merit Menthol 100—not his first that morning—as he shook hands with Bowie County Sheriff Thomas Hodge.

Hodge and his deputies had conducted an all-night vigil at the scene, about two miles north of the tiny community of Redwater, shielding the site from the curious; Hodge and his deputies were looking haggard.

Wandel himself had only about five hours' sleep. He had been called a little after 8 p.m. the night before, but by the time he had arranged security at the site, put together his investigation team and ordered various pieces of evidence preserved, it was midnight before he turned in.

Wandel arrived at the Northeast Texas crash scene from Fort

Worth, one of 10 NTSB field offices around the country. The safety board was established in 1976, 10 years after the Department of Transportation was born. Essentially, the NTSB absorbed the personnel and duties of the Bureau of Safety of the Old Civil Aeronautics Board, the predecessor of the Federal Aviation Administration.

To ensure that the NTSB remained an "independent" agency, Congress gave it broad investigatory powers but no regulatory authority. The board could make safety recommendations to the FAA (or other agencies regulating transportation), but those agencies were not bound to accept the recommendations.

The board's recommendations involving "black boxes," the cockpit voice recorders and flight data recorders that often provide valuable details about airline accidents, provide ready examples. As far back as 1978, the NTSB had recommended the FAA require cockpit voice recorders in turbine-powered airplanes capable of carrying six or more people. In 1982, the safety board broadened its recommendation to include flight data recorders. Only recently has the FAA proposed rules requiring additional types of aircraft to carry black boxes.

Neither device would have answered *all* the questions in the crash of 50 Sierra Kilo, but they certainly wouldn't have hurt, Wandel thought as he made his way to the old school bus the sheriff's office used as a command center.

Wandel surveyed the gently rolling pasture. Except for a few small trees, a utility pole here and there and the crater of 50 Sierra Kilo in the center, the landscape was quiet and green, deceptively tranquil.

"Do we have witnesses?" Wandel asked Hodge, blowing smoke out of the corner of his mouth.

The Texarkana sheriff explains that he already has gotten the names of people who believe they saw the airplane or the actual crash. They will be interviewed later.

Key investigators accompany Wandel to the makeshift command center. One by one they duck their heads and climb aboard the converted bus: J. C. Pierce and Chuck Dawson of the FAA's district office in Dallas; Tom Mahoney, the Singer Co. executive who saw the victims off from Redbird Airport only minutes before the crash; Hodge; a couple of deputies; and a representative of the Bowie County medical examiner's office.

Wandel's first words are for Mahoney. "As the operator of the aircraft," he says, "I would like to have a representative of your flight operations division as a member of our team." Mahoney jots down notes and nods in agreement.

"Whoever comes down needs to bring all the aircraft maintenance records," Wandel says.

As everyone strains to listen over the din of the generator outside, the investigator gives an update on what is known about the flight so far.

"It appears we may be dealing with a straight-line descent, and if that's the case, we may have had an intact plane on impact," he says. "The thing I want to do today is establish all four corners—the two wing tips, the nose and the tail."

Wandel asks if any remains have been removed, and the man from the medical examiner's office replies that they haven't. "We had the doctor from Texarkana come in, and he said he couldn't find enough remains to send in for a toxicology report," the man says.

Wandel looks out the bus windows to the crater and turns to Hodge. "I know we're not going to get it finished today, and probably not tomorrow, so we're going to need continuous security," he says.

"I was afraid you'd say that," said Hodge, only *half*-jokingly.

Sadly for Hodge and his deputies, crash scene security was not a new experience. Some of the same deputies, in fact, had spent their New Year's Eve about eight miles away, protecting the wreckage of a DC-3 that had crashed, killing singer Ricky Nelson, his fiancée and five members of Nelson's band. Only the two pilots had survived.

Wandel put down his paper and pen and looked up. "Well," he said. "Let's go take a look at our crater."

In investigator parlance, this process is called "kicking tin." Wandel flips open his sample case and pulls out work gloves, a 35mm camera, a microcassette recorder and some Baggies.

The sky has begun to clear, but the ground is still muddy underfoot. Slinging the camera around his neck. Wandel snaps his fingers and pops his fist into an open palm as he and Pierce lead the group to the crater.

Wandel is tall, about 6 feet 2 inches, and his blue short-sleeved jumpsuit with the NTSB official seal makes him appear even taller.

Wandel, a native of San Antonio, became a pilot at 19 and flew Army helicopters in Vietnam. He logged 700 hours of combat time, flying Huey and Cobra gunships. He was shot down once and crashed once.

After leaving active military duty, Wandel was an aviation safety officer for Bell Helicopter in Iran from 1977 to 1979, getting out after Shah Mohammed Reza Pahlavi was deposed and the Ayatollah Ruhollah Khomeini came to power.

Since joining the safety board on St. Patrick's Day 1980, he has investigated more than 380 accidents. Herbert W. R. Banks, head of the board's field operations, once paid Wandel perhaps the ultimate compliment: "If I ever went down in an airplane, I'd want Warren Wandel to be the one investigating it."

Wandel walks to the edge of the oval-shaped crater. Fifty Sierra Kilo's final resting place is a jagged hole gouged in red East Texas clay about 15 feet across and 10 feet deep. Twisted debris, none of it very large, sticks out of the mud in the crater and encircles the outside. More debris is spread in an erratic pattern to the north.

Sticking out of opposite sides of the crater are the shallow, muddy troughs where the plane's wings hit. Each trough is filled with long strips of torn metal, and at the end of each groove is a crumpled mass, the remainders of the Westwind 2's wingtip fuel tanks.

Wandel kneels at the edge of the crater and surveys every inch of the hole. He stands up, walks a short distance and scans the shards of white airplane skin and other indistinguishable pieces that litter the pasture.

He crosses his arms, furrows his brow. "Hhhmmmm," he says audibly.

The air is filled with the sickening sweet smell of mud saturated with jet fuel. Sprouting amid the debris are several small orange flags that mark places where deputies have located, but not yet removed, human remains.

There's precious little left when meteorology, physics, aerodynamics and bad luck gang up on an airplane. Fifty Sierra Kilo hit the ground at high speed, its nose almost straight down.

At impact, the aircraft's nose dug into the soil, compressing the rest of the fuselage behind it, rippling it like an accordion.

It hit with roughly the explosive force of 3 pounds of dynamite, enough to pulverize a 14-ton granite boulder. But as Isaac Newton said, for every action, there is an opposite and equal reaction. The kinetic energy built up at impact had to be released. Like a tightly coiled spring suddenly released, the fuselage sprang back with explosive force, violently ripping apart everything inside the airplane.

It had all happened in a fraction of a second. Mercifully, the seven victims probably never felt death.

Judging from this, it's probably the leading edge of the tail," Wandel says as he looks over a piece of metal. He picks through the large shards one by one, turning them over, examining them, looking for anything that might provide a clue.

Investigators call pieces that provide clues "Easter eggs." Some Easter egg hunts turn up more eggs than others.

Wandel makes his first climb into the muddy crater, trying to find solid footing and gingerly trying to avoid getting cut on the sharp metal. "I got my last tetanus booster during *191*," he says, referring to the Aug. 2, 1985, Delta crash at D/FW Airport.

The largest piece of metal in the hole is one of the jet's two engines, and it is badly deformed. The other engine is a few feet away. While they were once large, complex machines, the crash has compressed them into piles of crushed metal little bigger than a beer keg.

Wandel kneels down to take a closer look at the engine resting outside the crater. He studies it, contemplates it from different angles and then fixes his gaze on it head-on, almost as if he could stare 50 Sierra Kilo's secrets out of it.

The first day of a major field investigation is spent documenting the layout of the wreckage—establishing the "four corners" as Wandel had said on the bus. The aim is to find if the plane was intact on impact, or whether it broke up in flight.

Pierce, a sandy-haired, boyish-faced aviation safety inspector with the FAA, will diagram the wreckage. Clipboard in hand and measuring tape in tow, he sketches out the crash site, measuring how far the large pieces of debris are from each other and the crater.

There is a curious piece to the puzzle. Located 360 feet to the south of the impact crater is the Westwind 2's left horizontal stabilizer and elevator, the parts of the tail that control the aircraft's movement up or down. As Wandel and Pierce crouch to study it, they notice an unusual dent in the stabilizer's leading edge.

It appears the piece fell off just before the crash, but why? Did something hit it and break it off? Was the attachment bolt defective, or was it overstressed? And where is the right stabilizer and elevator? Wandel will have the parts analyzed at a metallurgy lab.

Pierce and Wandel measure 50 Sierra Kilo's heading at impact (275 degrees) and the angle at which it hit (82 degrees, nose down).

There are at least eight segments of any NTSB investigation, and the FAA—as well as aircraft manufacturers, engine manufacturers and other—participates.

They document the history of the flight and crew members' duties; they study the wreckage and the accident scene; they investigate the engines, as well as the aircraft's instruments and hydraulic, electrical, pneumatic and other systems.

Other team members investigate air traffic control involvement, while others look at weather and human performance. Others study survival factors, which won't take long in this crash.

Although the NTSB has the authority in the field, the participants are ever-mindful of who *really* has the regulatory power: the FAA.

"We call *them* the 'guys in the pink berets,' " jokes the FAA's Pierce, his voice taking on a mock effeminate lisp, his wrist hanging limp. The NTSB's Wandel laughs, but not real loudly.

□ □ □

At lunchtime, as investigators eat fast-food fried chicken, a breeze blows slowly, bringing an eerie calm to the crash site.

The fates seem capricious in what is torn apart and what isn't when a large airplane crashes. Large pieces of metal dot the pasture, but between them lie tiny bits and pieces, indistinguishable now in their deformity.

It is a fertile garden of disaster. Strands of wiring lie here, a few rain-soaked playing cards lie there. A shredded Diet Pepsi can lies on the ground, while a few feet away, the door of the Westwind 2's cabin refrigerator lies flattened—the row of small cans of tomato and orange juice that line the shelf flattened neatly along with it.

Nearby, stuck partly in the mud, a $50 bill flaps limply in the breeze.

A page from a Jeppesen pilot handbook has been charred and torn from its binding, but only a few feet away, a thick stack of computer printouts lies undamaged, still held together by a rubber band.

There's a seat cover, a patch of golden carpet, a Lipton tea bag, individual sticks of Wrigley's Juicy Fruit and spearmint gum, a page from a magazine, a nickel.

□ □ □

After lunch, deputies are issued large green plastic bgs and rubber gloves. The remains of the seven victims and personal effects are the only things that will be removed from the site on this first day of the investigation.

The remains will be sent to the Southwestern Institute of Forensic Sciences at Dallas and then on to the FAA's aeromedical lab in Oklahoma City. Wandel will learn there isn't enough of the remains for toxicological analysis.

By early afternoon, a gaggle of reporters and photographers has gathered on the road, outside the yellow "Sheriffs Line Do Not Cross" ribbon stretched atop the fence. It is time for Wandel to become official press spokesman.

He doesn't mind the role, but it's not one of his favorite parts of the job either. Accidents often are hard to explain even after months of investigation, let alone after a few hours in the field, and invariably, he complains as he walks to the fence, the first question reporters always ask is "What caused the crash?"

He gets to the fence, notebooks are poised, cameras click and microphones are thrust into his face. The first question: "What caused the crash?"

With practiced patience, Wandel says he doesn't know and explains what is known so far. His talking head will be on the evening news and his picture in the morning paper, giving the stock line that is part of almost any NTSB news conference in the field: "We're just getting the investigation started, and it will be several months before we can determine the cause."

After the news conference ends, the *whomp-whomp-whomp* of a helicopter can be heard in the distance. Within moments, Don Ruggles—the private pilot who flew a Beechcraft Baron through the storm the night before and lived to tell about it—lands his helicopter near the crash site and offers his help.

Wandel is anxious to get into the air to spot the missing right horizontal stabilizer. He realizes his chances of spotting it from the air are slim, but he climbs into Ruggles' chopper and the two take off.

He hovers over the crater, snapping photos and getting a bird's-eye view of the scene. Still, no sight of the missing piece; he and Ruggles return to the crash site.

The afternoon sun now seems more unbearable than ever. This is the hot, dirty, smelly, sweaty, unpleasant part of an air safety investigator's job. Wandel knows that many of the pieces to the puzzle of this crash probably will be found by people sitting in air-conditioned offices studying mounds of weather data and air traffic control transcripts.

"We know we have very severe weather in the area at the time of the crash," he says, lighting another cigarette and looking out over the wreckage. "We know weather's going to be a factor."

Again, he walks from piece to piece, stopping a moment to examine a fragment, to dictate a note into his recorder. He kneels down and focuses his camera on what is left of a seat belt, examining it for points of stress and failure.

"The seat belts are tested to withstand 9 Gs (9 times the force of gravity) . . . but here, we're talking about 300 or 400," he said, flipping the belt over. "But it's all kind of immaterial after 40 Gs. Forty is the human limit."

□ □ □

A shower and a change of clothes had washed away the red East Texas clay and the ugly smell of fuel-soaked mud. Wandel looked and felt like a new man.

It was 6:13 p.m. and the sun was still high outside, but inside Wandel's room at the Holiday Inn in Texarkana, the squat air conditioner was making little headway against the heat.

Wandel sat barefoot on his hotel bed, legs crossed yoga-style, with a phone cradled between his ear and shoulder. The telephone is his constant lifeline to other members of the investigation team. He is tying up loose ends, touching bases after Day One of the field investigation.

One of his tasks is to order the preservation of air traffic control and weather radar tapes. Those tapes will be needed later when the board's meteorologists and air traffic control specialists begin their analyses.

Both sources of radar information are important, mainly because neither gives the complete picture. Air traffic control radar doesn't see—or "paint," in radar vernacular—weather well, and weather radar doesn't see aircraft.

Correlate data from both sources, however, and an investigator can get a good picture of what happened.

Within a few minutes, the rest of the crowd enters the room for the day-end briefing. Pierce of the FAA sits down in a big red chair near the bed. He is joined by two new representatives who will monitor the inquiry, Lee Martin and Shields B. Craft.

Craft, a tall, white-haired man with a grandfatherly manner, represents Associated Aviation Underwriters, the Dallas company that insured the airplane.

Martin, a portly former military transport pilot who spent 16 years with the Civil Aeronautics Board and then the NTSB, is now an El Paso–based consultant and has been retained by the Singer Corp.

Pierce has spent part of his day interviewing witnesses, and he has also put together a thumbnail sketch of the ill-fated flight's history. The FAA investigator notes, among other things, that a sample of the Jet A fuel from the same truck that serviced the Westwind 2 at Redbird will be analyzed.

Even the flight crew's last meal comes under scrutiny, on the off-chance they may have eaten tainted food. "Both pilots ate sandwiches from the same tray," Pierce reports.

Pierce turns his attention to comments the pilots made to people at Redbird, comments that wouldn't have been given a second thought had 50 Sierra Kilo not crashed.

"The crew was telling everybody that if they didn't get off by 7 (p.m.), they were staying the night. They rotated at 6:56.

"The tower at Redbird also says they had an unusually long takeoff roll—they rotated 500 feet from the end of the runway," continues Pierce. "There's nothing unusual about the flight except the takeoff roll and the crew's hurriedness to take off."

Wandel begins filling them in on what he has found out about the weather. "National Weather Service radar in Longview said he was seeing hail on the radar, which is unusual," said Wandel.

"And the storm here was pretty bad, obviously," he said. "It was raining and hailing so hard that shortly after the accident . . . all the deputies had to retreat to their cars. They also had a confirmed tornado close to the crash site."

The subject turns to a question that will remain through much of the investigation in the months that follow: Why did 50 Sierra Kilo fly into bad weather?

"We've got some other aircraft in the area, but they're all diverting around it or asking permission to divert," he said. He has no quick answer.

Wandel recounts how much fuel was aboard the aircraft, its heading, the pilot's request to climb to a higher altitude, the fact he was given clearance to the altitude but didn't respond, and the time the plane last appeared on radar—7:19:49 p.m.

Give or take a few seconds, the flight of 50 Sierra Kilo had lasted just 26 minutes.

"The only thing we're missing right now that we haven't readily identified is the right horizontal stabilizer and elevator, but I think we're going to find it in the crater," Wandel said, pausing a moment to look up from his pad. "It's probably there in a form we don't recognize."

The meeting in Wandel's hotel room breaks up about an hour and a half after it began. In a moment, Wandel is on the phone again, updating his bosses on the investigation.

"I don't see a lot there that impresses me," he tells them.

□ □ □

It was only 9:28 a.m., and already the sun had burned away the early morning overcast. Two new arrivals join the investigation team this Sunday morning, Day Two of the field investigation. Peter B. Baker, 30, a senior product safety engineer with Garrett Turbine Engine Co., will help extricate 50 Sierra Kilo's two engines from the field. They will be shipped back to his office in Phoenix for the engine tear-down, which can provide crucial clues in the probe.

The other arrival is Darwin Hess, the white-haired head of technical services for Israel Aircraft Industries in the United States. The 54-year-old Hess has flown in from Wilmington, Del.

This afternoon, trucks and workers from Air Salvage of Dallas are to begin picking up the wreckage. It will be placed in large wooden crates and hauled away to the firm's huge facility in Lancaster, where, in a few days, the investigation team will reconvene to sort through the wreckage.

But for now, Wandel and the others stand around the bed of a pickup parked under a shade tree a couple of hundred yards from the crater. The investigator pulls on rubber gloves and begins going through the victim's personal effects.

Deputies had placed the items, many of them still wet from the rain, in plastic evidence bags the day before. Some bags contain key chains, others a watch or personal papers, credit cards, driver's licenses, business cards and wallets.

Wandel sits on the truck's lowered tailgate and, working with the long, thin blade of a knife, meticulously separates the wet pages of papers. When he's done, the personal effects are released to Singer's representative, and papers belonging to the flight crew go into a cardboard box.

Shortly after 11 a.m., Hess finds the missing right horizontal stabilizer. As Wandel had guessed the night before, the piece, virtually unrecognizable, was in the crater with the rest of the mangled debris.

The "four corner" puzzle is now complete. "We're in fat city," Wandel smiled as he finished his work on the truck's tailgate.

Today's break is burgers, fries and soft drinks. Baker, meanwhile, has been walking around the crater, picking up fan blades from the engines. The inside of a jet engine is filled with rotating spools lined with scores of small fan blades, each slightly larger than the cover of a paperback book. The way the titanium blades are broken off, dented, pitted or bent can tell an engineer much about what happened to the engine.

These blades appear to have been ripped from the spools, thrown by centrifugal force at impact.

That means the spools were spinning when 50 Sierra Kilo crashed, but it doesn't necessarily mean that the engines were producing thrust. There's a chance the spools were simply "windmilling," or being spun by the airflow like a child's pinwheel.

In the field, Baker knows only one thing for sure: Only a detailed analysis in Phoenix will unlock the engines' secrets.

Shortly after lunch, a backhoe is inched carefully to the edge of the impact crater, and in slow, jerking motions, the operator lowers the machine's bucket into the hole to begin digging out debris. Wandel and the others stand on the opposite edge of the crater, watching, shouting directions.

As the first load is laid unceremoniously beside the crater, Wandel walks over to look at the debris, turning the metal fragments over with his hand to inspect both sides.

In this phase of the investigation, no object is too small or too innocuous to be studied. In fact, the tiniest light bulbs—actually the filaments inside them—can provide clues about a crash.

Wandel kneels down and picks up a small piece of blue and black plastic. It is the power switch to the Westwind 2's coffee maker, located in the front part of the passenger cabin. Wandel pries off the back to reveal a small, intact light bulb no bigger than half the size of an aspirin capsule.

He uses a folding magnifying glass to examine the wisp of a filament inside the tiny bulb. It is stretched wickedly out of shape, but it is still attached to the two support wires at the base.

That small light bulb already has told Wandel that at least some of the electrical systems aboard the airplane had power when it crashed. The reason: If a bulb is off when it impacts at high speed, the thin filament wire shatters. But if the light is lit when it impacts, the filament is hot and malleable; it stretches instead of breaking.

Later, he will have the bulb photographed with a close-up lens, and it will yield even more. The NTSB's Canadian counterpart, the Canadian Air Safety Board, has done extensive research into filament stretching. The Canadians have even published a reference book demonstrating how many G forces it takes to obtain various degrees of stretching.

"The worst filament bending in the Canadian study is 4,000 Gs, and it looks *better* than ours," he says later. In a loose way, the tiny light bulb has quantified what Wandel has suspected: The impact forces were not just unsurvivable but also unimaginable.

More sifting and more examining, and the team calls it a day. Monday would be a lot like Sunday, which was a lot like Saturday. There would be more debris unearthed, cleaned and crated.

But in the early morning hours Monday, 50 Sierra Kilo indirectly claimed an eighth victim. At 4:30 a.m., Hess, Israel Aircraft Industries' representative in the investigation, suffered a heart attack and died in his hotel room.

Although only 54, Hess had suffered a heart attack six months earlier, and in November 1985, he had undergone bypass surgery. He had mentioned none of that to Wandel, and it troubled the investigator. "If I'd known about his heart problems, I would've never let him out in that field," Wandel said.

By midafternoon Tuesday, the last crate of debris had been loaded onto a flatbed truck for the drive to Air Salvage's hangar in Lancaster. Wandel, Pierce and the others were packing for the drive home. The yellow police tape that cordoned off the pasture was torn down, and the deputies that had guarded the site since Friday night headed home.

Except for the crater that marred the middle of the field, all the outward signs of 50 Sierra Kilo were now gone. Once again, the breeze was silent, save for the chirping of birds and the occasional whine of a tractor-trailer far in the distance.

□ □ □

Early Wednesday morning, Wandel was back in his cubbyhole of an office on the seventh floor of the Federal Building in downtown Fort Worth. Stacks of flight manuals, books, boxes of debris and tattered brown folders pregnant with papers made the office appear even smaller.

"We have a joke around here that when the weight of a folder equals the weight of the wreckage, you can write the report," Wandel laughs. It's not unusual for the four investigators in the Fort Worth office to handle more than 30 active cases at any one time.

Wandel's office is filled with commendations, contradictions and humor. Despite the room's apparent disarray, Wandel is a man who is well-organized, perhaps a product of his accounting background (he has a bachelor's degree in accounting from the University of Texas at San Antonio) and years of disciplined military flying.

Some papers on his desk are held together with a plastic clip that says "Stop Smoking," an impotent reminder to Wandel, who lights up another Merit. A blackboard hangs from the far wall, and its faint white chalk etchings are quick sketches of a jet engine's innards. A sign on the blackboard declares:

This is not Burger King. When you enter this office, you will not have it your way. You will get it my way or you'll never get the son-of-a-bitch at all.

That first morning back after the accident, Wandel briefed his boss, Armand Edwards, who then headed the 11-person NTSB office in Fort Worth. He then briefed officials at NTSB's Washington headquarters.

On Thursday, April 10, Wandel sat down at his desk to fill out NTSB Form 6120.19A, an eight-page report due five days after an accident. The preliminary report doesn't have findings of fact or recommendations. Rather it is a who-what-when-and-where report of the accident.

It is computer-coded, so the crash of 50 Sierra Kilo—now officially NTSB Accident/Incident No. FTW86MA058—could be easily entered, indexed and retrieved in the safety board's computer.

He wrote a four-paragraph, 366-word narrative summary, ending with the sentence: "The investigation is continuing."

He came to the page where he had to fill in numbered computer codes to describe what happened. In the first blank, he filled in the number 240, the code for "in-flight encounter with weather." In the second blank, he wrote 250, for "loss of control—in-flight."

He came to the third blank. The code, were it not for the tragedy of the seven lives lost and the grief that had been visited on people's lives, appeared almost comical in its stilted, bureaucratese attempt to describe a plane crash.

"230," Wandel wrote. "In-flight collision with terrain."

HIGH-TECH SLEUTHS FIND 'SMOKING GUN'

SUNDAY, FEBRUARY 7, 1988

BY DAVID HANNERS

It didn't take a Ph.D. in meteorology to figure that weather was going to play a major role in the investigation of the crash of the Israeli 1124A Westwind 2.

Warren Wandel knew that much. The weather had been terrible that night and, as the National Transportation Safety Board's lead investigator in the accident, one of the first things Wandel did was call in the board's top meteorologist.

His four days of "kicking tin" at the crash site had told Wandel much. But there were still three perplexing questions to answer before the riddle of 50 Sierra Kilo would be solved: What exactly was the weather over East Texas, why did the crew fly into it, and what happened to the plane inside the storm?

□ □ □

Five days after the crash, Gregory Salottolo was on his way to Texas to try to answer the first of those questions. The 40-year-old Salottolo, a professorial type with red hair, round wire-rimmed glasses and a thick mustache, enjoyed the four or five times a year he was able to leave his tiny, windowless Washington office and get out in the field.

As the NTSB's senior meteorologist, Salottolo knew that nearly 45 percent of all general aviation accidents were weather-related. But from what Wandel had told him on the phone, Salottolo also knew the crash of 50 Sierra Kilo was clearly different from the 400-plus previous investigations in which he'd participated.

"For a high-performance jet to get involved in a thunderstorm and then crash, that is a little unusual," said Salottolo. "A jet at 37,000 feet going straight into the ground—no, we haven't had many of those."

He began by getting surface maps, radar maps and logs, satellite pictures, written statements, upper air data, forecasts, copies of weather advisories and SIGMETS (for SIGnificant METeorological information, a warning of hazardous flying weather) and other material from the National Weather Service. He interviewed forecasters. The Federal Aviation Administration provided data.

After several weeks of analyzing the data, the weather picture began emerging. The weather the night of April 4 was, in a word, rotten.

A line of intense thunderstorms stretched through East Texas; from 7 p.m. to 7:20 p.m., the National Severe Storms Forecast Center in Kansas City, Mo., issued no fewer than *seven* severe weather reports covering East Texas and reporting wind and hail damage.

Meteorologists measure storm intensities in VIP (for Video Integrator Processor) levels, with VIP level 1 being the weakest and VIP level 6 being the strongest. A VIP level 6 storm can drop in excess of 7 inches of rain an hour.

Salottolo found that the Westwind 2 encountered VIP 2 and 3 storms near Mount Pleasant. When the plane disappeared from radar at 7:22 p.m. southwest of Texarkana, it was surrounded by raging storms.

A VIP level 5 storm was about 13 miles southeast of the jet. A VIP level 4 cell was centered 15 miles to the west. Eight miles to the northeast was the core of a VIP level 6. (By comparison, it was a VIP level 4 storm in which a Delta L-1011 crashed in August 1985 at Dallas/Fort Worth Airport, killing 137.)

Salottolo estimated that the storms were rising at a rate of nearly 1,000 feet *per minute.* At the altitude 50 Sierra Kilo was flying, 37,000 feet, the plane was, at best, capable of climbing only about 700 feet per minute.

Salottolo plotted 50 Sierra Kilo's path on weather maps. The resulting computer-drawn series of diagrams chills Wandel; it is a graphic representation of a tiny airplane flying into big trouble.

"That's a level 3 storm and he went right through it like he nailed it," Wandel says, looking on Salottolo's diagram at the storm cell near Mount Pleasant. "That tells you his radar ain't working worth a. . . . No one would go through that."

□ □ □

Thus the second key question: Why did Kenneth Hetland and Steven Fulop, two experienced pilots with more than 10,000 hours' flying experience between them, fly into bad weather?

Bad weather on the day of the crash had prompted the National Weather Service and the FAA to issue a flurry of severe weather warnings; whether the crew had gotten that information was another matter. Mike McMullen, NTSB's chief air traffic control specialist until he recently left the board, and the FAA's Ken Peppard hoped to find out.

A pilot planning a flight under instrument flight rules is required to telephone the nearest FAA Flight Service Station and file a flight plan. An FAA specialist then briefs the pilot on the weather, including adverse conditions, current forecasts along the route of the flight, winds aloft, any special notices and reports from other pilots in the area.

Before takeoff, Hetland and Fulop made two calls to the FAA's Dallas Flight Service Station at Love Field, the first at 11:28 p.m. and the last one at 5:14 p.m.—1 hour and 42 minutes before takeoff.

During the last call, the crew was briefed by Regina Pickering. In a statement she gave McMullen and Peppard on April 12, Ms. Pickering said she gave the pilot a summary of the weather activity contained in Convective SIGMET No. 46C, which had been issued at 4:55 p.m.

A transcript of her briefing told a different story, however, McMullen and Peppard found. The recording of the briefing showed she never mentioned the SIGMET to the crew.

"So basically, the only thing you're showing on your radar is in the general area of Dallas?" the pilot asks on the tape.

"Well, the general area here, and it does run like I said, up across Blue Ridge then the northwest corner of Arkansas and movement only about 15 (knots) and it hasn't really been moving very much," Ms. Pickering responded.

"It's been sorta redeveloping," she continued, "so I don't really think it's gonna have time to move across your route of flight any other than right here in the Dallas area. . . ."

(The FAA declined *Morning News* requests for an interview with Ms. Pickering. She was transferred to the Fort Worth Automated Flight Service Station a few months after the crash.)

The transcript also showed Ms. Pickering didn't tell the pilots about Alert Weather Watch No. 66, which was in effect for the area at the time. The reason: Although the watch had been plotted on one of the three large maps in the Flight Service Station, whoever posted it apparently failed to update the expiration time. Ms. Pickering told McMullen and Peppard that she believed the notice had expired, so she never mentioned it.

The two investigators could find no indication that the crew ever learned of Convective SIGMET 2C, which was issued just as 50 Sierra Kilo was taking off. A review of the air traffic control tapes showed the notice was not read on any frequencies while the Westwind 2 would have been listening to them, although the FAA requires SIGMETs to be broadcast on all local frequencies at least once if the area covered by the SIGMET is within 150 miles.

And although the SIGMET and Alert Weather Watch should have been transmitted over the voice band of the Texarkana VHF radio beacon at 15-minute intervals, no indication could be found that it was.

The investigation has turned up its first "smoking guns." The FAA is holding them.

Another important piece of the puzzle came in the tape of conversations between 50 Sierra Kilo and air traffic controllers. About 4 minutes into the flight, Hetland told a departure controller, Gregory D. Hood, that he "would like vectors around these buildups, we would appreciate it, our radar is not doing very well this evening."

Singer-Kearfott's flight procedures prohibit crews from flying with a faulty radar. The Westwind 2 was equipped with a Collins WXT-250A color weather radar, which, if working properly, would have shown the storms in shades of green, yellow or red, with red being the most severe.

Wandel would have no opportunity to check the radar unit itself. By virtue of being in the nose of the plane, it was the first thing destroyed in the crash. But an audit of the airplane's repair and maintenance history—part of any NTSB investigation—showed 50 Sierra Kilo's radar had been repaired four times since November 1981, the last time on April 11, 1985, about a year before the crash.

Investigators listened to air traffic control tapes for 50 Sierra Kilo's flight to Dallas to see if Hetland or Fulop had said anything about their radar on that phase of the flight. They hadn't.

The FAA air traffic controller's handbook says that keeping aircraft separated is the controller's primary duty, and passing along weather information is secondary, a task to be done as time permits.

When Hetland told Hood about the radar problem, Hood obliged and diverted the plane around some storms near Dallas. But when Hood "handed off" 50 Sierra Kilo to en-route controller Emery J. Beaulieu, the controller made no mention to his colleague of the plane's possible radar problem.

Nor was Hood required to pass along the information. As Wandel pointed out in his report, Beaulieu, the en-route controller, had no indication that 50 Sierra Kilo's crew members "were not providing their own weather avoidance."

About six minutes into the flight, Hetland told Beaulieu: ". . . if, uh, you help us pick our way through here we'd appreciate it."

Beaulieu said he would, but air traffic control radar doesn't show weather well. He told the crew: "If you see anything you need to deviate off that heading, just go right ahead and do it."

At shift change, as Beaulieu briefed his replacement, Steven C. Wooten, he pointed out VIP level 5 and 6 storms in the Texarkana area and said pilots had been asking to deviate around the weather.

While briefing Wooten, Beaulieu singled out a lone aircraft—probably 50 Sierra Kilo—making a beeline for the storm that other aircraft were giving a wide berth.

"Well," Beaulieu remarked to Wooten, "he's going, looks like he's going straight through it. . . ."

□ □ □

Eleven days after the crash, Wandel had called the members of his investigation team to Air Salvage of Dallas for the layout of the wreckage. The 8-acre salvage yard, near Lancaster airport and actually guarded at night by a lion named Bozo, is littered with bent and battered wings; 50 Sierra Kilo was the newest arrival.

Laying out the wreckage from the 7-ton Westwind 2 is like fitting together a big jigsaw puzzle with pieces that are deformed or even missing. But it can yield evidence of mechanical failure or other clues of how or why a plane has crashed.

"The priorities, as far as the layout goes . . . need to be to lay out the flight control system—flight surfaces, actuators, push-pull rods, everything," explained Wandel. "We need to see what shape they (the crew and aircraft) were in."

The plane's control surfaces—flaps, ailerons, tail, elevator—are moved by small actuator jackscrews, or threaded rods. By measuring the extension of the rods, Wandel could determine the aircraft's configuration at the moment of the crash—flaps up or down, spoilers open or closed, landing gear lowered or retracted.

Those present include Peter Baker from Garrett, the engine manufacturer, and L. E. Martin, the retired NTSB investigator now working as a private consultant for the plane's owner. Both had been with Wandel at Redwater.

Joining them are three new parties to the investigation: Louie Casias of Israel Aircraft Industries; Stewart Nicolson, Kearfott's chief pilot; and Joseph Cucinotta, head of aircraft maintenance for Kearfott.

The men gather in a conference room inside Air Salvage's office and get Wandel's update of the investigation. His recap of the weather clearly troubles Nicolson. Hetland and Fulop were more than fellow pilots; they had been friends.

"If he was in the core of this thing," Nicolson says, looking at Wandel's rough map of the storms on a blackboard, "Christ, he was going for a ride."

Wandel sets his cassette recorder in the middle of the conference table to play the tape of 50 Sierra Kilo's communications with air traffic controllers in the minutes before the crash.

The men seated around the conference table grow silent and heads lower as if bowed in prayer, straining to hear the voices on the tape. They listen as the crew's voices go from cool to tense as the aircraft encounters the storm. They hear Fulop's desperate plea for permission to climb to a higher altitude: "Center, Westwind 50 SK—need to get up!"

There is one last, unintelligible transmission from the aircraft. Wandel believes it sounds like "negative thrust."

"Are we talking about engine thrust?" asks Wandel, referring to the possibility that both engines failed. "Is it two statements? Is it 'negative' to the center and 'thrust' to the co-pilot?"

Nicolson isn't so sure. "It sounds like 'trouble' to me, not 'thrust,' " he says. "But whatever it is, they're in deep. . . . They're in trouble."

Wandel assures him the tape will be analyzed by the NTSB's lab in Washington.

Out in the warehouse, men wearing work gloves pick through the boxes, pulling out twisted parts, knocking the mud off and then laying them on the floor.

While J. C. Pearce of the FAA has begun calculating the aircraft's weight and balance measurements, Wandel and Baker sort out the rain-soaked pages of the pilot's log, placing a paper towel between each page to dry them out.

The information in the log will be important later when Wandel compiles his report, which will include a history of the flight crew, their experience in the aircraft they were flying, and how much they had flown in the last months, days and hours before the crash.

By the end of the day, the vaguest hint of an outline of an airplane has begun to take shape on the cement warehouse floor. The first day of work here is done; there will be at least a couple more.

"I still can't help but think the cause of this accident isn't in these boxes," Wandel said, looking out over the floor, out the large door and to the twilight sky above. "It's out there in that thunderstorm."

□ □ □

Paul Turner works in audiophile heaven. The walls of his Washington office—a place called the "tempest room" with walls of 2-inch steel to keep out stray electronic signals—are lined with audio equipment that would make a heavy metal rocker plead for mercy.

Two weeks after the crash, Wandel took the tape of 50 Sierra Kilo's transmissions to NTSB headquarters in hopes that Turner, head of the board's audio lab, could decipher the last, garbled message he thought was "negative thrust."

Turner (who retired in 1987) and colleague James Cash spend most of their time analyzing tapes from cockpit voice recorders, one of the "black boxes"—actually they are bright orange—carried aboard most modern airliners. (The Westwind 2 wasn't equipped with a recorder, nor did regulations require one.)

Analyzing the short transmission on the tape could provide an important clue. While field investigators may get most of the headlines, people like Turner and Cash can come up with many of the "Easter eggs," those pieces of an air crash puzzle that complete the picture.

Like the Air Florida crash in January 1982 in Washington. Shortly after takeoff, the Boeing 737 jetliner crashed into the 14th Street Bridge and plunged into the icy Potomac, killing 78 people.

In listening to the cockpit voice recorder, fished from the Potomac a week after the crash, the 57-year-old Turner sensed that something just didn't sound right.

His hunch was right. His analysis showed that the engine noises in the background indicated the plane's two jets were producing only about 85 percent of the power needed for takeoff. An iced-over sensor was telling the crew they had enough power.

Turner and Cash loaded Wandel's cassette into one of their tape players and listened to it again and again, playing it for a couple of hours.

They sped it up. They slowed it down. They turned the noise into electronic spikes and valleys that they printed out on paper. They called in a "fresh" set of ears, an engineer trainee from across the hall, to listen.

They agreed the words sounded like "negative thrust." However, "our confidence level is low," Turner wrote in his subsequent two-page report.

One thing Turner and Cash did find, though: a 12- to 13-hertz-per-second modulation in the crew member's voice. Something was shaking the plane and that vibration could be heard in the speaker's voice.

Turner had no idea what was causing it. That was Wandel's job.

□ □ □

The Egyptian scientist Hero is credited with building the world's first jet engine, a crude steam-driven motor built around 100 B.C. Nearly 2,000 years later, Garrett Turbine Engine Co.'s successful TFE731-series of engines—two of which powered 50 Sierra Kilo—is considered among the most reliable and efficient power plants in business aviation.

One day shy of the two-month anniversary of the crash, Wandel was at Garrett's sprawling plant in Phoenix for the teardown of the plane's engines. Wandel and his colleagues had been able to piece together much about the weather and why the crew of 50 Sierra Kilo might have flown into it. But answers to the third key question remained murky: What had happened to the Westwind 2 inside the storm?

Obviously, the plane had gone out of control, but why? Did the engines stop running—"flame out" in flying parlance—and leave the crew without power? And if so, why did they flame out?

Inside Garrett's giant repair and overhaul facility, Wandel, Casias, Baker and other Garrett engineers gathered around two sealed wooden crates that held the remains of 50 Sierra Kilo's two turbofan engines, serial numbers P-77401 (left) and P-77402 (right).

"These are going to be aardvark teardowns," warned Garrett's Baker, rolling his eyes. "We're going to border the new frontiers of tear-down techniques—hammers and hacksaws."

A modern turbofan like the TFE731 is a complex, finely tuned feat of engineering consisting of thousands of expertly machined parts meticulously assembled with precise tolerances. You wouldn't have known that, though, looking at the squat mass of mud-encrusted metal as it was lifted out of its wooden crate.

The purpose of this exercise in grime is to determine if the engine was producing thrust at impact—"turnin' and burnin' " as jet engineers put it.

A turbofan is basically a tube filled with spools of compressor fans, fuel injectors and igniters, which act like spark plugs. A large fan at the front (hence the name) sucks air into the "tube," or core; the air is compressed and accelerated by the fans; and fuel is added and then ignited.

Wandel already knows the spools were turning because at impact, centrifugal force ripped many of the compressor blades from the spools. Whether the engine was producing thrust—burning—is another matter. The spools may have been freewheeling or "windmilling," simply moving in the airflow like a child's pinwheel.

Working in a cordoned-off area with an armed security guard standing by, the men began taking apart the engine. Each step, each part, is photographed for the record.

It is dirty, noisy work and the air is filled with the staccato *zzip-zzip-zzip* of air wrenches. It is hard work, too; the impact squashed the engine—normally about five feet long and a yard in diameter—into a mass roughly the size of a beer keg.

In the adjacent work bay, two technicians in white lab coats use precision tools to make minute adjustments to a TFE731 the firm uses for testing. It is an incongruous scene, for as the two men tinker with the $400,000 machine, 50 Sierra Kilo's right engine is being hammered, chiseled, pried, sawed, blowtorched and wrestled apart.

The workers are looking for evidence of "metalization." An engine producing thrust is hot and at impact, the turbine blades will grind against the containment rings. Heat melts the tips of the blades and the molten metal splatters—metalization—on the inside of the rings.

A "metalized" ring has a blotchy, semishiny look, as if painted with a can of silver spray paint with a defective nozzle. The molten metal fuses with the ring and cannot be scratched off.

Different parts of the engine leave the experts with different opinions. "It's clean," said Casias as he looks at one part. "It wasn't grinding or anything like that."

"This thing was burnin'," Baker said as he looked at another part on the same engine.

"It's turning," allows Wandel. "But nobody said he's got a fire back there. I don't think the fat lady's sung yet."

After several hours of sawing, prying and sweating, the exhaust section of the right engine's turbine is freed and examined. The fat lady sings: no splotches, no metalization. Fifty Sierra Kilo's starboard engine wasn't running when it crashed.

The next day will be spent on the port engine, and it, too, will lack any metalization. The engines were undamaged but not producing thrust at impact, Garrett officials will write in their 109-page formal report. Left unanswered is the question of *why* they flamed out.

With the day's sweat and grime washed off and the Phoenix sun outside set on slow broil, Wandel and the others seek refuge at a nearby hotel's watering hole.

It's no surprise the discussion revolves around the crash, which spawns an academic debate over whether 50 Sierra Kilo's crew could have recovered if both engines were out.

Wandel doubts it. He figures the plane was going too fast, perhaps 400 knots (approximately 460 mph), it was in the thick of a severe thunderstorm, the crew probably couldn't tell up from down and restarting engines can be difficult even in the best of circumstances.

"And," Wandel adds, lifting his drink, "there's a difference between going 400 knots in level flight and going 400 knots straight down."

"Sure is," Baker said. "When you go straight down, the sky ends."

□ □ □

As the government investigation moved along, Virginia Hetland settled back into her Willingboro, N.J., home and began rebuilding her life.

She was 18 and Kenneth Hetland was a handsome 22-year-old airman at nearby McGuire Air Force Base when they met at her sister's wedding in 1972. They wed 10 months later.

They had three daughters, ages 5, 7 and 10, and Hetland's sudden death left all of them with emptiness and—particularly for Mrs. Hetland—anger.

"Anger is one of the emotions you go through, but it's not aimed at him. I know that whatever happened was not his fault," said Mrs. Hetland. "At the beginning, you're angry at God. But you realize it was an accident, and accidents happen."

She took her husband's remains to his Minnesota home for burial. A hard rain was falling as she boarded her flight in Newark, N.J. "The last thing I wanted to do was get on that plane," she said later.

Years before, Hetland had told his bride-to-be that he wanted the song *My Way* sung at his funeral. "Ever since he told me that, I've hated that song," Mrs. Hetland said.

It was sung at his funeral.

She returned to Willingboro and began the tasks left for survivors, such as changing names on accounts and tending to legal affairs. While Mrs. Hetland was sifting through the couple's safety deposit box, she found a will that her husband had written in longhand a couple of months before the crash. In simple, straightforward language, he left everything to his wife and kids.

Her lawyer later would tell her the unwitnessed will was invalid. There was a cruel irony, too, that didn't go unnoticed by Mrs. Hetland. When she flipped the paper over, she noticed it: Her husband had written his will on the back of a photo of a Westwind 2.

□ □ □

In mid-March 1987, Wandel sat down in front of the word processor in his Fort Worth office to write his factual report.

The crash had occurred almost a year before, but work had gone slowly because, for one, it had been a perplexing investigation. Also, Wandel had had several other accidents and incidents to investigate since April 1986—more than 30, in fact. Two out of three could be handled with a few phone calls, but the remainder sent him from Montana to Mexico, from Connecticut to Marfa, Texas.

An NTSB factual report in a major crash like the Westwind 2 can run hundreds of pages long. It covers history of the flight, injuries, damage to aircraft, other damage, witnesses, and then information about crew, aircraft and weather.

The report also covers aids to navigation, communications, airport and ground facilities, flight recorders, wreckage, crew medical information, medical and pathological data, fire, survival aspects, tests and research, and additional data.

Once the factual report is completed, the investigator in charge writes an analysis and proposes recommendations for fixes. The report is then sent to NTSB headquarters in Washington, where department heads scrutinize it and make their additions or deletions.

The five presidentially appointed members of the NTSB board, chaired by James E. Burnett, may then convene a hearing on the accident, although there is no hearing in the majority of the 3,000-odd crashes the board investigates each year. The board determines the probable cause of the crash and lists any factors that may have contributed to the accident.

Wandel spread the stacks of folders out before him. Among the material he had gotten was a series of calculations and test data from the aircraft manufacturer in Tel Aviv.

Using Wandel's actuator measurements, engineers for Israel Aircraft Industries said 50 Sierra Kilo was configured for level flight. However, the landing gear was down and wing spoilers raised, an indication the crew may have tried desperately to slow their descent.

The question of what caused the engines to flame out still nagged him, and Wandel had asked the manufacturer if it was possible for the Westwind 2's wings, located ahead and just below the engines, to disrupt airflow into the engines if the airplane's nose rose too high.

It could, the manufacturer responded, but the airplane would have to be outside the "flight envelope," the boundaries of speed, attitude, altitude and other limits in which an airplane can fly. Outside that "envelope," almost anything could happen. There was little doubt 50 Sierra Kilo was outside the envelope.

Israel Aircraft Industries said the 12- to 13-hertz buffet Turner discovered could be caused by "aerodynamic excitation" when the wings began losing their lift. It was possible that the airplane was at such an acute angle the wings no longer provided lift, and it was violently shaking the plane.

The engineers also estimated that during the dive, the stick forces—the amount of pressure the crew would have had to exert on the control stick to pull the plane level—would have been as high as 200 pounds.

"The two guys are going to have to damn near have their feet on the instrument panel," said Wandel.

"And the problem is, you've got to know which way to pull or push on the stick," he said. "The attitude instruments have tumbled during the upset. . . . You've got to remember that they're sitting inside this environment with no way of knowing which way is up. You don't know which way you're going. At this point, they're just along for the friggin' ride."

The manufacturer even calculated the top speed the plane may have reached in its dive: 559 knots, or 642.8 mph (at sea level, the speed of sound is 750 mph). The fastest dive that a Westwind 2 had recovered from during flight testing was 448 mph, the engineers noted.

The investigation had uncovered some procedural smoking guns, but some of the evidence remained circumstantial. There was no one piece, no one statement Wandel could point to, as with the broken engine attachment bolt that led to the crash of the American Airlines DC-10 in Chicago in 1979 or the iced-over sensor cited in the 1982 Air Florida crash in the Potomac River.

"It's awfully frustrating knowing that something happened that you can't put your finger on," Wandel said. "Every investigator would like to have the piece in his hot little hands and say, 'This is the piece that did it.' Unfortunately, that doesn't happen as much as we'd like."

And an NTSB report is no place for speculation. As Wandel is quick to note, three of every four crashes the board investigates winds up in court somehow, somewhere. (So far, a number of lawyers, representing 50 Sierra Kilo's five passengers, have expressed interest in seeing the board's final report.)

"To figure out one of these things," Wandel said in a moment of reflection, "give me someone who is one-quarter engineer, one-quarter pilot, one-quarter psychologist. . . ."

He paused to think.

"And one-quarter soothsayer would help," he said. "There are a few investigators who say that when they die and go to hell, they're going to look up the pilot and ask him what *really* happened."

On the afternoon of April 21, 1987, 382 days after the last flight of 50 Sierra Kilo, Wandel boarded a commercial flight at D/FW Airport to carry his completed report to Washington. As with most commercial flights he takes, he rode jump seat in the cockpit.

The forecast called for thunderstorms as the jetliner taxied to the runway. When the pilot switched on his on-board weather radar just before takeoff, it malfunctioned. The pilot taxied back to the ramp for repairs.

As they sat in the cockpit while technicians fiddled with the radar, the pilot turned to Wandel and apologized. "Pardon the inconvenience," he said, "but we've got to get this fixed."

"Hey, don't worry about it," Wandel said with half a laugh. "I'm carrying a report here on the *last* guy who tried to fly through a thunderstorm with a malfunctioning radar."

SYSTEM ALLOWS 50 SK TO FLY BLINDLY TO DEATH

SUNDAY, FEBRUARY 7, 1988

BY DAVID HANNERS

By bureaucratic standards, the sentence was straightforward:

"In this era of sophisticated weather detection and tracking systems . . . the Safety Board believes that current systems for passing information rapidly to the aviation user apparently remain unable to assure an adequate level of safety."

So said the National Transportation Safety Board in its report on the April 4, 1977, crash of Southern Airways Flight 242 near New Hope, Ga. The DC-9, with 85 people on board, flew into a violent thunderstorm, lost power in both engines and crashed as the crew tried an emergency dead-stick landing on a highway.

Seventy people died. In its report 11 months later, the NTSB said a key factor contributing to the crash was "limitations in the Federal Aviation Adminstration's air traffic control system which precluded the timely dissemination of real-time hazardous weather information to the flight crew."

In essence, the NTSB was saying that while everyone on the ground knew the weather was bad, the air traffic control system failed to get that information to pilots whose very survival depended on it. The board made six recommendations to the FAA that, the NTSB believed, could significantly improve the situation.

On April 4, 1986—nine years to the day after the crash of Southern Airways Flight 242—50 Sierra Kilo flew blindly into a violent thunderstorm, lost power in both engines and crashed near the small East Texas community of Redwater.

All seven on board died. The dead left behind six grieving widows and 19 sons and daughters.

The irony of 50 Sierra Kilo was that seven men died in part because the "adequate level of safety" the NTSB said didn't exist in 1977 still didn't exist in 1986. Nor does it exist today.

When 50 Sierra Kilo fell prey to the same faulty system, its seven fatalities pushed the toll to 252 people whose deaths NTSB investigators attributed to a large degree to poor communication of weather information to airborne flight crews.

The FAA, in fact, still has not taken final action on the key recommendation the NTSB made to the agency after the Southern Airways accident.

That the crash of 50 Sierra Kilo happened at all was a tragedy; that nine years wasn't enough time to correct a lethal gap in the system was a travesty.

□ □ □

Any air safety investigator worth his salt will tell you that very few crashes are the result of a single, catastrophic event. Rather, most airplane accidents are the inevitable conclusion of a chain of events.

So it was with the last flight of 50 Sierra Kilo. In his investigation into the crash, Warren Wandel, the NTSB's investigator-in-charge in the accident, found that 50 Sierra Kilo's fatal chain was a long one that included a problem-plagued air traffic control system, equipment malfunctions and mechanical limitations.

And plain bad luck.

The chain of events began almost two hours before takeoff on that fateful Friday:

- At 5:14 p.m. when the crew called the FAA's Dallas Flight Service Station to get a briefing on the weather, the briefer failed to mention two different kinds of severe weather notices posted for areas on the jet's route, a breach of FAA procedure.
- At 6:56 p.m., as the Westwind 2 took off from Dallas' Redbird Airport, a severe weather advisory called a Convection SIGMET (for SIGnificant METeorological Information) was broadcast, but the crew was tuned to the departure control frequency and didn't hear the warning.
- Moments after takeoff, the crew asked an air traffic controller to direct them around turbulence in the immediate Dallas area because their aircraft's radar was "not doing very well this evening."
- At 7:02 p.m., as 50 Sierra Kilo winged eastward, the first air traffic controller "handed off" the plane to another controller without mentioning the plane's reported radar malfunction—nor did regulations require him to.

- At 7:02:10 p.m., the plane's crew told the second controller they would like help "pick(ing) our way through here," referring to storms.
- At 7:06 p.m., the second controller handed 50 Sierra Kilo over to a third controller. Again, no mention was made of the plane's radar problem or the two requests by the crew for help in avoiding bad weather.
- As 50 Sierra Kilo continued eastward, the FAA's Texarkana VOR navigation beacon station should have been broadcasting at 15-minute intervals two different severe weather notices for aircraft in the area. The notices were never transmitted, the NTSB found.
- Although at least two air traffic controllers noticed the airplane was headed for an area of precipitation displayed on their radar screens—and they knew other aircraft had been asking to divert around the area—the controllers made no attempt to warn 50 Sierra Kilo. Again, FAA regulations didn't require them to.
- At approximately 7:17 p.m., 50 Sierra Kilo encountered extreme turbulence. It was dark out, but had the crew been able to see—or if the plane's radar had been working properly—they would have found themselves almost completely surrounded by towering storms that were growing at an alarming rate.
- At 7:18 p.m., the crew asked to climb from 37,000 to 39,000 feet to get above the turbulence. By the time clearance was granted, it was too late. At 7:19:51 p.m., the plane's agitated co-pilot radioed: *Center, Westwind 50 SK need to get up!*
- Once inside the storm, the Westwind 2 was battered out of control, and the plane lost power in both engines, making recovery from its dive perhaps humanly impossible.

Individually, the links of seemingly unrelated, even innocuous occurrences appeared harmless enough. Collectively, though, the links formed a lethal chain; 50 Sierra Kilo's luck had run out. At 7:22 p.m., the Westwind 2 slammed into a rain-soaked East Texas pasture.

In analyzing an accident's chain of events, investigators try to find the link where the chain can be broken and the accident avoided.

"In this crash, there's a lot of points where a decision could've been made that would've prevented the accident," Wandel said. "Any one of them, or any combination of two, and the accident doesn't occur."

Timely weather information was a key factor. The safety board believed the crew couldn't be faulted for not trying to get a good weather briefing. During the day, they had gotten four different briefings from three different sources.

But had they gotten adequate information in their last, critical briefing, they would have known about the severe weather along their intended route. With such information, they might have taken a different route home or even stayed in Dallas.

If they had heard the Convective SIGMET advisory that was broadcast as they took off, they would have learned about the bad weather that lay ahead.

Had their radar worked properly, they could have seen the weather electronically. But the NTSB believed that even with a faulty radar, the air traffic control system should have been able to divert the aircraft around the storms. The crew did make two requests to two different controllers for help.

But the crew didn't know about the bad weather. They couldn't see it out their cockpit windows or on their radar, and the air traffic controllers said nothing of the weather systems over East Texas.

Change perhaps any one of those events, Wandel figured, and the accident doesn't happen. But in a world of "ifs," one thing appears certain to Wandel: Once the Westwind 2 encounters the storm at about 33,000 feet, its fate is sealed.

"The point where it gets irrevocable is where he breaks out at 33," Wandel said. "He's in that canyon. He can't out-climb it, he can't turn around. He's going to try and ride it, which may be his only option."

□ □ □

On Feb. 2, 1988, 669 days after the crash of 50 Sierra Kilo, the five members of the National Transportation Safety Board gathered around a table in Washington to discuss the crash, hammer out the probable causes and make recommendations to the FAA for changes.

After quizzing Wandel for about an hour and a half, the board ruled there were nine "findings" of probable cause. The first was the partial failure of the Westwind 2's on-board weather radar. The next four involved weather; the board said 50 Sierra Kilo had run into thunderstorms, turbulence, gusts and downdrafts.

The question, then, became one of *why*—why did an experienced pilot and co-pilot fly their plane and passengers into violent weather?

In the four remaining findings of probable cause, the board blamed the FAA—in particular, the agency's Dallas and Shreveport Flight Service Stations—for mistakes that, in the NTSB's analysis, led to the crash.

Because the weather briefer gave an improper briefing and failed to tell the crew about the hazardous weather advisories in effect for that evening, the crew "was probably misled" into thinking that the weather along their intended route wasn't as bad as it actually was—or as bad as had been forecast.

In addition, the board attributed the failure of Dallas Flight Service Station personnel to update the expiration time of the Alert Weather Watch and the failure of the Shreveport Flight Service Station to broadcast advisories over the Texarkana VOR as probable causes.

In a 16-page summary of their findings, board members agreed that Hetland and Fulop "would have been taxed to the limit" in trying to save their doomed plane. "The crew was faced with multiple emergency situations: a dual engine flameout, possible interruption of electrical power, erratic or erroneous altitude displays, darkness, flashing lightning, extreme turbulence, and severe airframe icing," the board said.

The NTSB will make four recommendations to the FAA. The NTSB has no regulatory authority, and the FAA will have 90 days to respond to the recommendations. The FAA can take them or leave them; as one safety board spokesman put it, "We regulate by raised eyebrow."

The post–50 Sierra Kilo recommendations call for one change in the FAA's Airman Information Manual (AIM), the bible of basic flight rules; two changes to the Air Traffic Control handbook; and a plea that the FAA speed up plans to improve timely dissemination of hazardous weather information to pilots.

Currently, if any number of certain onboard equipment conks out while a plane is in flight, the AIM requires pilots to inform an air traffic controller of the problem. Strangely, on-board weather radar—a piece of equipment now often commonplace in modern aircraft—is not presently one of the items whose malfunction must be reported.

The board recommended that the AIM be amended to include weather radar on the list of reportable malfunctions.

As an air traffic controller at a facility like Fort Worth Air Route Traffic Control Center monitors an airplane, he watches it on radar. Next to the radar scope is a stack of skinny plastic cards, each holding a paper data strip representing an individual aircraft the controller is currently handling.

The stack is ever-changing, with new strips of information being added and others being subtracted as planes fly into or out of the controller's particular slice of airspace.

Each strip contains a bit of pertinent information about each plane, including whether the pilot has reported any malfunctions of on-board equipment. Again, on-board weather radar is not on the list of deficiencies required to be noted on the strip, and the board recommended that the FAA change the Air Traffic Control handbook to include it.

The crew of the Westwind 2 had told the first air traffic controller they dealt with that evening that their radar was having problems, but the information stayed with him. Had the radar problem been a required entry on the data strip on April 4, 1986, it is doubtful that 50 Sierra Kilo could have been handled by two subsequent air traffic controllers who had no knowledge that something was wrong on board the airplane.

□ □ □

"No accident has to happen," said Wandel one afternoon in his office as he reviewed the crash. "This did not have to happen. Why did it happen? We have several bits of weather information, and none of it gets to the flight crew."

That issue—timely dissemination of hazardous flight information to pilots—was the subject of the remaining two and perhaps most important of the recommendations issued by the NTSB after the crash of 50 Sierra Kilo.

"The National Weather Service forecast was excellent, and dissemination to the agencies was good," said Wandel. "The breakdown occurs at the FAA level when it comes to disseminating that information to the end user."

The NTSB recommended that the FAA speed implementation of a program called Hazardous In-Flight Weather Advisory Service, or HIWAS.

HIWAS is a high-tech computer system that continuously broadcasts severe weather information over navigational frequencies that pilots can tune in at their convenience. It can transmit a range of weather reports, including urgent warnings.

Currently, only air traffic facilities in Houston, Miami and Jacksonville, Fla., have the $7 million computerized system, and the FAA had hoped to have 53 more stations in operation, covering the entire 48 contiguous states, by the end of this year.

The NTSB said year's end wasn't quick enough and urged the FAA to expedite implementation of HIWAS. The FAA, meanwhile, says that technical and fiscal problems have set the program back, perhaps several years. In fact, FAA spokesperson Joann Sloan said the complete HIWAS network may not be in place until 1995.

Until that time, it appears air traffic controllers still will play a role in disseminating hazardous weather information to pilots. It is the size of that role that is one of the sources of controversy.

Controllers currently can get hazardous weather information from five different sources.

At most major airports, the first of these sources is a group of surface wind shear detection devices located on the airport grounds.

Controllers also have access to SIGMETS (and more severe Convective SIGMETS), which are issued by the National Weather Service and teletyped to the traffic control center.

Another source is a Center Weather Advisory, issued by meteorologists at 20 air route traffic control centers in the continental United States.

The controllers also can get weather reports from pilots in the air—called PIREPS—and pass those along to other pilots.

Lastly, located in front of the controller is his radar scope. The radars are designed to identify aircraft, but they also can detect precipitation. The ability to "see" weather on these scopes is limited, however. A controller can't differentiate, for example, between storm intensities. In other words, the radar doesn't know the difference between a VIP level 1 storm or a VIP level 6 storm—just that precipitation exists.

And on top of that, the controller can't see weather and aircraft simultaneously. To "see" weather, the controller must adjust the display, which removes the aircraft information.

Up-to-the-minute weather information is particularly critical to pilots because most storm systems that pose hazards for pilots are born, live and die in a matter of minutes. And if the problem of timely dissemination of weather information that arose in the crash of 50 Sierra Kilo sounded familiar to the safety board and the FAA, it was for good reason: Since 1974, the NTSB had made 93 recommendations to the FAA involving weather-related problems.

At least 14 of those recommendations, rooted in six crashes and one incident of severe turbulence, involve the dissemination issue.

The six accidents claimed 245 lives; 50 Sierra Kilo made it 252.

In seven of the 14 recommendations, the NTSB deemed the FAA response "acceptable" and considered the matter closed. Five more—including some dating back to 1974—remain open with no final FAA action taken.

In two other recommendations, the NTSB considered the FAA's response "unacceptable."

At least part of the problem has been technological. After a 1973 accident involving an Ozark Airlines airplane in St. Louis, which killed 38, the safety board recommended in 1974 that the FAA develop and install an air traffic control radar capable of locating severe weather and displaying turbulence. That recommendation remains "open."

The board made similar or related recommendations after the Southern Airways crash in Georgia in 1977 and after the June 1980 crash of an Air Wisconsin flight over eastern Nebraska, which killed 13.

While the FAA has agreed to work toward developing a radar system that can show aircraft and various weather intensities in a single display, there have been problems. In a July 1983 response to one of the Air Wisconsin crash recommendations, the FAA said that while tests of a dual-purpose radar screen were "successful," there was concern that the display had "too much clutter" and "could not satisfy the needs for graphic data . . . in a legible manner."

The FAA said development efforts would continue. But the speed at which those efforts have been made—and the mounting toll of lives lost in the interim—has been criticized by some in the aviation community, Congress and elsewhere.

Tight federal funds may be part of the explanation. Some of the critics, however, contend that at the heart of the problem is a fundamental battle between the NTSB and FAA over just how much responsibility an air traffic controller should shoulder.

Section 91.3(a) of the Federal Aviation Regulations (FAR) says that the pilot-in-command ultimately is responsible for his aircraft. And Section 7110.65D of the FAA's air traffic control handbook firmly establishes that a controller's primary duty is to maintain proper "separation" and keep aircraft from colliding with each other.

Other duties, such as broadcasting weather information to aircraft, are to be handled "to the extent possible" and as time allows. Historically, the FAA has not only fought to keep separation as the controller's first priority, but also has battled tenaciously to keep controller responsibility—and the agency's legal liability—to a minimum.

For example, in the 1973 Ozark crash at St. Louis, one of the NTSB's recommendations was that air traffic controllers be allowed to deny approach and landing clearances and takeoff clearances "when they (controllers) deem an operations hazard is present."

FAA officials rejected the proposal, saying they didn't believe controllers should assume such responsibility and that controllers weren't trained or qualified to make such judgments about weather.

The FAA also has fought efforts to experiment. In the wake of the 1980 Air Wisconsin crash, for example, the safety board asked the FAA to undertake an experimental program to see if it was technically and operationally possible to have air traffic controllers provide both separation and severe weather condition information to aircraft.

The FAA minced no words in its response: "All the information we have derived from experience, user input, and meteorological state-of-the-art, indicates conclusively that the final decision-making authority (concerning weather avoidance) should rest with the pilot-in-command.

"The FAA will continue its effort to upgrade the quality and timeliness of weather information that we provide the pilots," the response continued. "However, our dedicated involvement in weather-related activities has provided no evidence indicating that transfer of the decision-making authority, from pilot to controller, is warranted or would, in any way, increase safety."

By and large, controllers aren't eager to see their duties or responsibilities increase. "We can't get in the cockpit and fly the thing. There's a point of responsibility that rests with the pilot," said Anthony Skirlick, a controller in Los Angeles whose testimony before Congress has made him one of the more outspoken controllers.

"It's very limited what we can do," said Skirlick. "We have very poor radar weather depiction. It's dependent upon the pilots to fill in the gaps. On one hand, the pilots want us to get in the cockpit and fly the thing for them, and on the other hand, they don't.

"We're damned if we do and damned if we don't."

□ □ □

Congress has expressed concern over the issue of timely dissemination of severe weather information to flight crews. In August 1985, U.S. Rep. George E. Brown Jr., then-chairman of the Subcommittee on Transportation, Aviation and Materials, asked Congress' investigative arm, the General Accounting Office, to look into the matter.

Although the 31-page report was prepared *before* the crash of 50 Sierra Kilo, the picture that GAO auditors drew was a partial blueprint of the series of events that led to the fatal crash.

"Limitations in the existing aviation weather system hinder timely detection and dissemination of potentially hazardous weather conditions and can result in insufficient weather information being available to pilots . . . ," the GAO said.

"We also found that hazardous weather warnings are frequently not provided to pilots as soon as they are available because controllers are too busy separating aircraft during peak traffic periods," the agency said.

For an air traffic control system billed as the most advanced in the world, the communication problem seemed like something out of the Stone Age.

"Under existing procedures," the GAO reported, "the teletyped strips of paper containing weather information are given to one controller by the supervisor to read to pilots on his radio frequency. When finished, the controller passes the strips to the next controller position in the arrival and departure sequence.

"If they (controllers) are busy separating aircraft," the report noted, "the warnings are delayed, and in some cases not given."

The report said the average time taken to disseminate SIGMET and

Center Weather Advisories at D/FW was 23 minutes. The last flight of 50 Sierra Kilo lasted just 26 minutes.

GAO auditors said an aircraft could miss SIGMET and Center Weather Advisory broadcasts altogether if it is "leaving airspace where the warning has not yet been transmitted but is entering airspace where the warning has already been read." Precisely the same scenario provided one of the links in the crash of 50 Sierra Kilo.

The final NTSB recommendation stemming from the crash of 50 Sierra Kilo would require air traffic controllers to "frequently" broadcast significant hazardous weather reports if they pose a threat in their area. Currently, a controller need only broadcast it once, as time permits.

Some of the problems cited by the GAO involved the 1978 deregulation of airlines and controller workload and training, three items that have become sensitive issues with the FAA after President Reagan fired nearly 11,500 of the nation's air traffic controllers for an illegal strike in 1981.

After the strike, the nation's airports, departure control facilities and en-route centers have been left with fewer controllers, and training at the FAA Academy in Oklahoma City was put into high gear.

The result, critics contended, was that a growing corps of less-experienced controllers was responsible for routing an ever-increasing flow of air traffic.

For its April 1986 report, the GAO polled 3,282 controllers nationwide about how they felt about the weather training they had received at the academy. More than half—55 percent—said they believed their training for controlling aircraft in bad weather was less than adequate.

Fifty-three percent of the controllers polled said they occasionally do not provide weather notices to flight crews; one in five said they often *decline* to give weather notices, the report said.

Moreover nearly two-thirds of the controllers interviewed by the GAO at the nation's five busiest airports, including D/FW, said they delay or don't relay weather information to pilots because they are too busy separating traffic.

The information in the GAO report came as a shock to some congressmen. "We're very concerned about this issue, but more than concerned, we have to do something about it," said U.S. Rep. Robert A. Roe, chairman of the Science, Space and Technology Committee, which oversees aviation issues in the House.

Roe, D-N.J., has more than a passing interest in the crash of 50 Sierra Kilo. Singer's headquarters is in his district. Two of the plane's victims were his constituents.

"Do we become indignant and become upset with it?" Roe asked. "I would say Congress is upset with the whole damn air transportation system, to say the least. The whole attitude that surrounds the air controller issue . . . has been festering for three or four years. This is a major national issue."

□ □ □

Virginia Hetland had waited anxiously 22 months for the NTSB's final report. Since the accident that killed her husband, she had packed up the couple's three young daughters, sold the house in Willingboro, N.J., and moved to Newark, Del., about an hour's drive northeast of Baltimore.

It was a time in her life that called for all the inner strength she could muster, and much of that strength was anchored by her unfailing belief that whatever had happened to 50 Sierra Kilo had not been her husband's fault.

"There is no doubt in my mind that he did everything he could," she said some months after the accident. "It was totally out of his hands."

A few, quiet others believed differently. To them, FAR 91.3(a) was the final word; regardless of the circumstances, Hetland alone shouldered the ultimate responsibility for his aircraft.

The pilot is dependent on a variety of inputs upon which he must base his decisions—inputs like the instruments in front of him. But what if one of those instruments malfunctions, through no fault of the pilot and without his knowledge? Is the faulty, perhaps fatal decision the pilot might make as a result of that malfunction necessarily his fault?

Through advancing technology, the nation's air transportation support system, including weather briefers and air traffic controllers, has become a critical aspect of the pilot's inputs; in some cases, that support system can be just as important as any dial or light on the instrument panel. And if that input fails, is the pilot's resulting decision necessarily his fault?

Hetland had done all the system had asked of him. He had gotten a weather briefing from the FAA that he had every reason to believe was complete. When his radar failed, he told an air traffic controller. When turbulence made the ride rough, he asked for help getting around it.

But when Hetland—the living, breathing "end user" the bureaucrats refer to in this whole debate—was forced by circumstances to ask something of the system, it failed him, his co-pilot and his five passengers.

All Virginia Hetland knew was that her husband had awoken early one chilly spring morning, kissed her goodbye, and she never saw him again. For nearly two years, she had lived quietly with the grief, the emptiness, the anger and the sore, nagging angst that only a widow of the sky can know.

When the NTSB report came out last week, absolving Hetland of any blame and saying he and the others were but victims of circumstances far beyond their control, it affirmed to the world what the young widow had known all along.

Within minutes of the board's findings, Mrs. Hetland learned by phone what had been most important to her—that her husband wasn't at fault. As she turned out the light that night to go to sleep, for the first time since that horrible stormy Texas night of April 4, 1986, a part of her could finally rest.

Kenneth Hetland's death still hurt, no government report could ever change that. But Wednesday, his widow vowed, would be the first day of the rest of her life.

FOURTEEN

DEATH IN THE DARK

1989 WINNER IN THE SPECIALIZED REPORTING CATEGORY

"For a distinguished example of reporting on such specialized subjects as sports, business, science, education, or religion . . ."

The Orange County Register
Edward Humes

U.S. military officials see important strategic advantages to flying helicopters under cover of darkness. But we've killed 134 of our own soldiers, Edward Humes reports, by forcing pilots to use goggles that weren't designed for flying.

On the night of February 12, 1987, a Marine Corps helicopter flew into a hill. Straight and level, never wavering from its course, the helicopter drove into the ground as if propelled by a hammer. The three Marines on board died.

No mechanical failure caused the crash. Nor was anything suspect about the crew: The Marines at the controls were experienced combat pilots, the best of the best. They had flown through the same desolate canyon in southern Orange County countless times. They knew that hill as surely as they knew the drive home from work.

So why were they dead?

The Pentagon couldn't—or wouldn't—explain that mystery.

More than a year and a half would pass from the time I was rousted from bed to cover that crash to the day I sat back in my chair in the newsroom, appalled at the answer I finally found buried in forgotten reports on disasters long past: Those Marines died because they couldn't see. And they were not alone.

In an age of Star Wars lasers and Stealth bombers, it is hard to imagine a topic that sounds more eye-glazingly prosaic than "night-vision goggles." But as a few routine questions about these binocular-like, light-amplifying goggles ballooned into a lengthy hunt fueled by many Freedom of Information Act requests, the strategic importance of these devices—and their deadly flaws—slowly drew into focus.

The deaths of three Marines in Orange Country led to evidence that the goggles' inadequacies were linked to dozens of crashes and hundreds of deaths and injuries elsewhere. As the reports on other, similar crashes slowly filtered in, I learned that the military's night-vision goggles were intended for truck drivers and ground troops and were unsuited for flying. Yet fly with them the military did—and the flying continues.

"If it's war, it's 'Come as you are,' " one general told me. "We go with what we've got. And we train the way we'll fight." The general, along with virtually every other senior military official I interviewed, believed this was an acceptable way of operating, even if it meant more accidents and deaths during peacetime training. We need the goggles to counter the numerically superior but goggleless Soviets, the Pentagon planners say—and we can't wait for better, safer equipment.

This uniformity of opinion was one of the major obstacles to reporting "Death in the Dark," along with secrecy and pressure on whistle-blowers to keep silent—hurdles commonly erected whenever the Pentagon perceives a reporter or a story as "negative." All these obstacles stem from the Pentagon's extremely efficient system for withholding information from the public, a system that can make obtaining the most basic facts on an event about as pleasant as root-canal, but more time-consuming.

The foremost obstacle is the secrecy that shrouds military safety investigations. Whenever there is a crash or death in the military, officials clamp the lid on the flow of information, purportedly to encourage witnesses to make candid admissions about safety problems. (Some in the military consider this disingenuous: The only common form of retribution occurs when servicemen get too candid. When some of the stories broke, Marine Corps authorities launched investigations, not of the reported problems, but to find out who leaked the stories.)

Whether or not the military's position on secrecy of safety investigations is valid, the effect is to bar the media and the public from learning the circumstances and causes of fatal accidents in the military. Months or even years pass before reports on an accident are released by the military—long after interest and headlines have faded.

Getting more immediate information is next to impossible. The investigators are barred from talking to the press, as are witnesses. Some talk anyway, at their own peril. Occasionally, forthright field commanders feel it is their duty to inform the public, but they are bucking an immense tide of silence. It took me six months to confirm that the February 1987 accident involved the use of night-vision goggles. Marine spokesmen would say only that the crash occurred during "routine night training."

The military's attempts to stop the flow of information sometimes border on the absurd. When reporting on U.S. military maneuvers in Panama during the height of tensions between General Noriega and the Reagan Administration, I was forbidden by a U.S. Marine colonel from asking the troops "any political questions." The colonel instinctively struck at the essence of my story, which was to show the contradiction of staging war games when real warfare was a trigger-pull away. Of course, this was all the kids in the jungle wanted to talk about. I never really had to ask.

This is not to say all military reporting is unpleasant and confrontational—I have enjoyed specializing in this field. Many of my stories, some included here, were possible only because of the cooperation of military officials who believe in the value of openness, even when it hurts. In Orange County especially, Major General D.E.P. Miller, head of the Third Marine Aircraft Wing, is a strong advocate of the public's right to know.

Because the military possesses men like Miller who believe openness and even criticism can help the military, I had hoped that "Death in the Dark" could lead to reform by revealing a deadly problem long kept secret. Perhaps it will—in March, the House Armed Services Investigation Subcommittee began a probe of night-vision goggles, with the stated purpose of reducing the number of accidents that occur each year with the devices.

But so far, nothing has changed. A daunting wall of expert opinion has been assembled by the Pentagon, constructed of officials who find no fault with night-vision goggles, who blame all the many crashes on human error and who ignore the fine print of their own accident reports. Those in the military who believe otherwise have been criticized, ridiculed and, in a few cases, driven from the military they once loved. Sad to say, only one thing has changed in the five months since "Death in the Dark" was published December 7, 1988: the death toll.

By the end of December, 134 servicemen had died on night-vision flights. As of mid-May 1989, that number was 155.

—Edward Humes
The Orange County Register

MILITARY KNEW NIGHT GOGGLES WEREN'T MEANT FOR HELICOPTERS

SUNDAY, DECEMBER 4, 1988

BY EDWARD HUMES

At least 134 servicemen have died and 62 military helicopers have crashed in the past 10 years while pilots wore light-amplifying night-vision goggles the Pentagon knew were unsafe, a six-month investigation by the Register has found.

In crash after crash, highly qualified Army, Marine Corps and Air Force pilots wearing the goggles at night flew their helicopters blindly into mountains, wires, trees, oceans and one another, military records show.

Most of the crashes occurred during difficult, ground-skimming flights, while pilots peered through outdated, jury-rigged goggles never intended or fully tested for flight.

The goggles were designed and tested for ground troops and truck driving. Their designers and manufacturers never considered them flightworthy.

The Pentagon has blamed all but two of the night-vision goggle crashes on pilot error—a finding that has allowed flying with them to continue uninterrupted. A Pentagon spokesman said there are no common links to the crashes that would justify grounding the goggles.

But several recent crashes and the goggles' inadequacies have led Rep. Frank McCloskey, D-Ind., a member of the House Armed Services Committee, to request a congressional investigation of goggle safety next year. That request is pending.

The Register examined more than 50 military crash reports spanning a decade, declassified at the newspaper's request and obtained through the federal Freedom of Information Act. The newspaper also reviewed military manuals, training guides and internal safety publications and interviewed dozens of pilots and night-vision experts.

This research showed that Pentagon officials were well aware of the dangers, yet chose to risk flying with infantry goggles because of the tactical advantages night flying offers.

"I kept saying, use these for the mission they were designed for—driving," said former Army engineer Edward Firth, who presided over development of the infantry night-vision goggles before retiring in 1978. "They just don't give you enough to fly at high speeds. . . . It was an Army decision to put them in helicopters. They are aware of the risks."

Firth said the maximum safe speed limit for a person using the goggles is 35 mph, far less than typical helicopter speeds of 100 mph or more.

Manufacturers have never considered the infantry models suitable for flight because pilots cannot see in the dark well enough to fly at typical helicopter speeds of 100 mph and above, according to company spokesmen at ITT Electro-Optical Products in Roanoke, Va., Varian Image Tube Division in Palo Alto, and other goggle makers.

"ITT's position is that we don't endorse Generation II (infantry goggles) for flight applications," said Jim Eder, an ITT night-vision program manager. "If you have an alternative, I wouldn't want anyone to use Generation II."

In fact, at least two multimillion-dollar lawsuits filed by crash victims or their next-of-kin have been dismissed because manufacturers warned the military that the goggles were not flightworthy, court records show. The devices were not defective, the courts ruled, they were simply being misused.

In dismissing a case this year against ITT Electro-Optics Division—filed by the families of victims in the 1984 Marine crash in Korea—a New York federal judge wrote that the only legitimate defendant in a goggle-related crash would be the US government, for knowingly ordering men to fly with the devices.

However, such a case against the government can never be filed, US District Court Judge Peter K. Leisure wrote, because the military is immune from lawsuits by servicemen.

Military officials tacitly acknowledge safety problems by saying accidents should decrease during the next three years, when the old infantry goggles gradually are replaced by improved, state-of-the-art systems designed specifically for pilots.

Both types of goggles electronically amplify starlight and moonlight, displaying green-colored images of night landscapes on two tiny video screens embedded in a binocular-like goggle. The new pilot goggles are two to four times more powerful than the old devices. They offer clearer vision, and, unlike the infantry goggles, are lightweight and fit flight helmets.

But they are twice as costly and will remain in short supply for at least three years, according to Pentagon procurement schedules, which are four years behind because of technical and budget problems.

In the meantime, Army and Marine spokesmen said the ability to fly at night—even with flawed goggles—is crucial to national security, and cannot wait for better technology.

"We believe we have to keep doing this so we can be ready when the time comes," said Lt. Gen. Charles H. Pitman, deputy chief of staff for Marine Corps aviation, who was involved with goggle flying from its inception.

Pitman said the military does all it can to make flying with the infantry goggles as safe as possible. Pilots are trained to compensate for the inadequacies of the goggles—such as poor depth perception and no peripheral vision. Crashes have happened when aircrews failed to fly within the goggles' limitations, Pitman said.

"If they had followed procedures in each of these accidents we've had . . . and used common sense, the accidents wouldn't have occurred."

But night-vision experts and other pilots question the findings of pilot error, and say lives are endangered every day the military flies with goggles originally designed for the infantry.

"Goggle flying was one hairy experience after another," said Clyde Emery, a retired pilot who taught instructors at the Army's flight school at Fort Rucker, Ala., and who was one of the Army's most experienced goggle pilots before he quit in 1981. "It's one of the reasons I retired. We were killing people . . . and I wanted to live another 20 or 30 years."

Emery said pilots routinely "cheated" while flying on goggle missions by taking them off and flying without them—without telling superiors.

"We did it to survive," he said.

Pilots need light-amplifing goggles for night flying because almost all of the nation's military aircraft—jets and helicopters alike—were designed for combat in daylight. The goggles were seen as an inexpensive, easy way to convert even the oldest helicopters in the fleet to night-time troop carriers, tank-killers and cargo haulers, said Lt. Col. Robert Verona, product manager at the Army's Night Vision and Electro-Optics Laboratory at Fort Belvoir, Va.

But the goggles now being used by pilots were developed in the mid-1970s for infantry soldiers, truck drivers and tank crews. They never fully were tested for flightworthiness or air safety, and "were not developed to be compatible with aviation usage," according to an Oct. 17, 1983, crash investigation report by the Army Safety Center at Fort Rucker, Ala.

In the past 10 years, the Army has had 41 major crashes during goggle flights, the Marine Corps has had eight and the Air Force has had three. Six of the most recent occurred during the use of goggles designed specifically for pilots; the rest involved infantry goggles. Some of the crashes involved more than one helicopter.

Of all the services, only the Navy refuses to fly helicopters with the infantry goggles. The Navy never has approved their use in aircraft, Pitman said.

Hazards posed by night-vision goggles are many and well-known to the Pentagon, according to some of the military's own manuals and crash-investigation reports.

"For a number of years the PVS-5s (infantry goggles) have met with mixed reviews and marginal success in the field," wrote Army night-vision expert Tim Neal in a May 1983 article in the US Army Aviation Digest. ". . . The facts are that they are heavy, ill-fitting, poor performing and give some of us claustrophobia. PVS-5 limitations have been documented precisely."

Other drawbacks include:

- Loss of peripheral vision.
- Impaired depth perception.
- Blurred eyesight.
- Disorientation.
- Visual illusions.
- An inablility to read vital instruments and gauges.

- A tendency for the goggles to be blinded in cloudy weather.

The goggles have other problems as well: Helicopters had to be flown so slowly on some goggle missions that they began to stall or rock up and down—a constant danger when the ground is less than 25 feet below.

Bright lights—such as flares or explosions typical in battle—cause the goggles to shut down, much like the pupil of the human eye closes. While that problem lasts only a second or two after the light dims, it still can be deadly. A helicopter moving at 120 mph travels more than 200 feet in a second and a half.

Until the cause was pinpointed in 1983, the simple act of switching on radio equipment inside a helicopter caused goggles to shut down for several seconds. That problem has since been fixed, officials said.

Because they cover the sides of the face, the goggles eliminate peripheral vision.

"Scotch-tape the tube from an empty toilet-paper roll on each eye, and you'll know what flying with goggles is like," said George Small, an instructor pilot for the Army at Fort Campbell, Ky., who retired last month after 20 years of flying in the military.

The grainy images created by the goggles often fail to show clouds, dust or blowing sand until a helicopter is completely engulfed in weather that blocks out moonlight and starlight, rendering the goggles useless.

That failure was reported in at least 20 of the fatal accidents in which goggles were used, records show.

Because the infantry goggles were not designed to be compatible with flight helmets, they are clumsy, heavy and tiring for fliers to use. They must be attached to the pilot with cumbersome, makeshift straps and rubber tubes—what the commander at El Toro Marine Corps Air Station, Maj. D.E.P. Miller, calls "a bandaid fix that isn't worth a damn."

Verona and safety officials in both the Army and Marine Corps said they are working hard to decrease the dangers of goggle flying. The Marines recently opened a new safety laboratory in Yuma, Ariz., for simulating hazards while training pilots to fly with night-vision goggles, and the Army is expected to follow suit.

"We know these goggles are not the best, but if you give me a choice between flying in the dark with them or without them, I'll scream, 'Give me those goggles,' " said Capt. Russell James, an Army spokesman and helicopter pilot. "To survive in combat, we've got to fly low at night. That's why we use them."

"It's a dangerous mission, but we have to do it," Verona said. "There will be accidents."

Marine helicopter pilots at Tustin Marine Corps Air Station and elsewhere say the infantry goggles are far better than none at all.

"When I go out flying at night, I want to wear goggles," said Maj. Pete Todsen, a CH-53D Sea Stallion pilot at Tustin. "They are a good friend."

A push to increase goggle flying in the last five years coincides with skyrocketing numbers of crashes and deaths. While military-aviation safety has improved overall, the incidence of crashes in which pilots wore night-vision goggles has shot up, from 7 percent of all fatal Army helicopter crashes in 1981 to more than 25 percent in 1987, records show.

Through May of this year, five of 12 fatal Army helicopter crashes occurred while night-vision goggles were in use—more than 41 percent of all Army helicopter crashes.

However, Army officials have produced alternative statistics examining crashes by fiscal year that suggest night-vision crashes have decreased: from 12 in fiscal year 1987 to six in fiscal year 1988.

The goggle crashes are strikingly similar to one another, an analysis of 10 years' worth of Army, Air Force and Marine crash-investigation reports shows.

Mechanically-sound helicopters careened into obstructions as pilots attempted to navigate with the miniature, light-amplifying video screens embedded in their goggles.

Thirty-three of the crashes occurred when moonlight and starlight levels dipped below the point where the goggles could function adequately—something that happens quickly and without warning, literally leaving pilots in the dark, crash reports show.

"It's like putting on a pair of dark glasses at twilight, then trying to see," Small said. "When the light levels are low, which they frequently are, it's a joke. They are not safe."

"They (pilots) should be driving tanks with these things, not flying helicopters . . . that's why they're crashing," said former Marine Capt. Art Conroy, who retired as a pilot at Tustin in 1986, in part, he said, because of fears over flying with goggles. He is now a government contractor in Washington, D.C.

Goggle-related crashes include three fatal accidents in 1987 involving Orange County–based Marine Corps helicopters. Two of the crashes occurred when the helicopters on "routine training missions" slammed into cloud-shrouded hillsides that pilots could not see, according to Judge Advocate General investigation reports by the Marine Corps. The third helicopter hit the side of an aircraft carrier. Eight Marines were killed in those accidents and another 24 servicemen were injured.

In a typical goggle disaster, First Lt. Chris Toburen, 27, of Laguna Hills flew his Tustin-based helicopter into a mountain at Camp Pendleton in September 1987. He and the other three Marines on board were killed.

Investigators found that an unexpected cloud layer had caused Toburen's goggles to shut down—one moment he could see the terrain below him clearly; 10 seconds later, he could not. Investigators also concluded that Toburen and his crew were not properly familiarized with their goggles before the mission, and that "there is an inability to see clouds while wearing NVGs (night-vision goggles)."

Nevertheless, pilot error—the fact that Toburen flew into clouds he could not see—was deemed the primary cause of the crash.

The first item on a list of safety recommendations arising from the crash: "No further restrictions to training or operations are warranted regarding night-vision goggle . . . missions."

The worst crash involving goggles occurred in Korea in 1984, when a Tustin-based Marine helicopter on maneuvers flew into a mountain its pilot never saw, the Marine report on that crash says. Twenty-nine servicemen died.

Night-vision goggles also were in use when the abortive 1980 Iran hostage-rescue mission ended in a fiery collision at the "Desert One" rendezvous point, where eight servicemen died when a Navy helicopter struck a transport plane.

And most recently, goggles intended for the infantry were being worn during an October midair collision between a Camp Pendleton–

based helicopter and another Marine helicopter on maneuvers in Arizona. Despite a nearly full moon and apparently ideal conditions for flying with goggles, the crews aboard the helicopters never saw one another, Pitman said, and all 10 servicemen on board were killed. That crash still is under investigation by the military.

It was the 10th fatal collision between aircraft during night-vision flights, crash-investigation reports show.

Mechanical failures were not to blame in these or the other crashes. The pilots simply did not or could not see what killed them, records show.

". . . Night-vision goggles were not developed to be compatible with aviation usage, restricting vision to a narrow field of view," one military-safety panel reported after a non-fatal 1983 Army helicopter crash in which a pilot flew into power lines he could not see.

In one of only two occasions in 10 years in which the military has blamed goggles for an accident, the panel from the Army Safety Center concluded the crash on July 18, 1983, "impossible" to avoid because of the goggles' limitations.

In virtually all other crashes since then—even those with identical equipment under similar circumstances—military crash investigators and boards of review have blamed pilot error, not goggle problems, records show. The error, according to the reports, was that pilots and crew failed to fly within the limitations of the goggles.

But an Army flight-manual excerpt attached to a July 1983 Army Safety Center crash report says the infantry goggles "were adopted as an interim pilot's night vision system without formal development testing/operational testing for aviation use and with full knowledge that it did not fully meet aviation-user requirements."

Pitman confirmed that such flight testing was skipped, and that the military has learned the good and bad points of night-vision goggles through using them in the field.

It took five years, 10 crashes and 21 deaths for the Army to learn in 1983 to modify the infantry goggles so pilots could read their instrument panels; the Marines waited until after the crash that killed 29 to modify theirs, according to Bob McLean, the Army human-factors expert who developed the modified goggles.

This modification consists of cutting away portions of the goggles' face mask with shears, rewiring them, and strapping them to flight helmets with rubber tubes, straps and velcro.

Had flight testing been done, Pitman said, such modifications would have been made sooner.

Normally, the Marine Corps needs Navy approval to use an aviation system, because the Navy owns all the Marines' aircraft and designates Marine pilots as naval aviators. The Marines were able to get around that requirement in the case of goggles, Pitman said, "because they are not part of the aircraft—the pilot wears them."

Without Navy authorization for the goggles, they had to be bought with "green dollars"—money allocated to the green-uniformed ground forces of the Marines—rather than "blue dollar" Navy money, Pitman said. Then the aviation branch of the Marines borrowed the goggles from the infantry, he said.

In the process, flight-testing normally required by the Navy was skipped, as it had been skipped earlier by the Army, records show.

Use of the infantry goggles by pilots was supposed to be a short-term measure until goggles designed specifically for fliers could be developed and fielded—originally set for 1983. But after 10 years, the 15,000 infantry goggles now in flight use still are the mainstay for night flying in the military, officials said.

Even the improved pilot goggles are a compromise system, Verona said, acknowledging that anything that restricts a pilot's vision and depth perception is potentially dangerous. Pitman said the military hoped someday to have foward-looking infrared sensors installed on all helicopters so the goggles could be dispensed with.

"We don't have the systems that are necessary," Small said. "They're trying to do this on the cheap."

NIGHT-FLYING CAPABILITY ESSENTIAL TO US SECURITY, MILITARY SAYS

SUNDAY, DECEMBER 4, 1988

BY EDWARD HUMES

Pentagon officials and military-helicopter pilots say an ability to fly combat missions at night is essential to US security and that night-vision goggles often are the only way to get the job done.

"While they have limitations, they give us more capabilities than we had without them," said Lt. Gen. Charles H. Pitman, deputy chief of staff for Marine Corps aviation. ". . . We belive we have to keep doing this so we can be ready when the time comes."

No other nation has mastered the art of night flying, giving the US a potentially enormous edge in combat, agreed Maj. Tim McKeever, spokesman for the Army Training and Doctrine Command at Fort Monroe, Va.

"The Russians do not have a very strong night-fighting capability, either on the ground or in aviation," he said. "They are deeply concerned about our night-fighting capability.

"Given the fact that we are outnumbered (by Warsaw Pact troops and aircraft) . . . flying at night with night-vision goggles sort of evens the odds," McKeever said.

While acknowledging some of the failings in night-vision goggles, Pitman said investigators are justified in blaming 52 night-vision crashes and the resulting 134 deaths in the past 10 years on pilot error.

"If they (pilots) had followed procedures with each of these accidents we've had . . . and used common sense, the accidents wouldn't have occurred," Pitman said.

He said the military forbids goggle flying unless the weather is clear enough to allow sufficient moonlight and starlight for the goggles to function.

And, he said, pilots are taught how to escape safely from blinding clouds.

He said the Marine Corps was replacing the pilots' oudated goggles, designed for ground troops, as quickly as it could with better pilot goggles. The military also is altering cockpit lighting on its helicopters; current lighting systems interfere with goggles, Pitman said.

"I think we've done a very good job considering the circumstances," he said.

Army officials said the military began flying with infantry goggles because it could not wait for newer, better technology.

He said goggles were the only way to overcome shortcomings inherent in military helicopters. Most were designed 10 to 30 years ago and lack the sophisticated radar or infrared sensors built into the more modern jet aircraft. But they still must fly the same low-altitude, radar-dodging missions.

Capt. Russell James, an Army spokesman and UH-60 Blackhawk helicopter pilot at Fort Campbell, Ky., said the goggles enable pilots to land in darkness without tipping off the enemy. Landing lights would be needed without goggles, he said.

"The idea of turning on a spotlight—that's a shoot-me sign if I've ever seen one," he said.

One of the pilots' major concerns, however, is how the goggles will perform in combat. Army attempts to fly helicopters in large combat formations led to several crashes last year, and pilots say the bright explosions and flares of the battlefield will blind pilots wearing goggles.

The enemy also can shine spotlights as a deliberate countermeasure to goggles.

"That's one of the things we worry about," James says. "Spotlights could blind us . . . It's like someone put their hands over our eyes."

NIGHT-VISION GOGGLES CAN BLIND PILOTS TO DANGERS IN THE SKIES

SUNDAY, DECEMBER 4, 1988

BY EDWARD HUMES

Blindness took them without warning.

One moment, moonlit hilltops rolled by 200 feet below. The next, clouds enveloped their military helicopter in a dark fist, blotting out moon, stars, horizon, sight. Cockpit windows became black mirrors, revealing nothing.

Pilot and crew knew they had moments to react, to turn or climb from their blind path. Straining to see, they peered through the artificial eyes of night-vision goggles, devices that amplify evening's meager light hundreds of times.

Under ideal conditions, such goggles make moonlight gleam with dazzling brightness, painting a glowing green picture of the night-dark landscape below. But conditions were far from ideal this night—the clouds were thick, the moon obscured. And the men learned that the mechanical eyes they relied on were not so reliable after all.

The mountain was visible only a few seconds before the crash, a shadowy mass, black as a coffin lid, rising in front of them. Their helicopter was swatted to earth with crushing force as the pilot tried, too late, to veer away.

And then, finally, there was light—the fiery brightness of burning wreckage that drew other helicopters to the scene like moths to a candle.

The date was March 24, 1984. A Marine Corps helicopter from Tustin on maneuvers in South Korea struck a cloud-shrouded mountain and burst into flames. Twenty-nine men died; none survived.

It happened again Sept. 3, 1987: another mountain, another group of Marines dead, this time four at Camp Pendleton.

And again Feb. 12, 1987: three Marines killed in Trabuco Canyon in another fiery meeting of mountain and helicopter.

A similar sequence of events led to crashes in May 1988, November

1986, December 1984, April 1978, and 28 other times in the past decade. All of them involved Army, Air Force or Marine helicopters that simply ran into the ground.

On 10 other occasions, helicopters ran into other aircraft. Eight times, the unseen obstacles were power cables. And there were dozens of other minor accidents in which death and destruction barely were averted.

All of these accidents had a common theme: They occurred while pilots wore night-vision goggles.

In all but six out of 52 cases, the goggles in use were outdated, jury-rigged devices designed for ground troops and truck drivers, not pilots.

The Pentagon has been aware the goggles are inadequate for flying for at least 10 years, when crashes began occurring during routine flights, according to 50 military crash-investigation reports and other documents obtained by the Register through the federal Freedom of Information Act.

An analysis of a July 1983 crash by the Army Safety Center in Fort Rucker, Ala., baldly states that the ground-troop goggles "are not compatible with aviation," and the retired Army scientist who presided over their development, Edward Firth, said they were designed for driving vehicles no faster than 35 mph.

Even before the crashes, the goggles' manufacturers and the Army's own night-vision experts warned that the infantry goggles were inadequate for flight.

The long string of night-vision accidents has led to safety improvements in procedures, training and helicopter lighting. But the miltary does not believe flying with goggles should be curtailed or stopped, said Lt. Col. John Reitz, the Army's Pentagon spokesmen for night-vision goggles.

"In the last two years, no accidents (that occurred during goggle flights) were directly attributable to night-vision goggles," he said. "There were no common links."

Military officials blame most of the crashes on pilot error, contending that pilots fail to fly within the goggles' limitations.

This finding allows flying with the infantry goggles to continue while the military gradually converts to a newer, safer type of goggle design specifically for pilots. These pilot goggles remain in short supply.

More than 15,000 pairs of the infantry goggles are now being used at military bases nationwide. Helicopter pilots at the Tustin Marine Corps Air Station fly with them nightly. Pilots wear them occasionally at the Los Alamitos Armed Forces Reserve Center, officials said.

The military uses the goggles because most of its helicopters were designed 10, 20, even 30 years ago, built primarily for daytime combat, without sophisticated radar or guidance systems. Tremendous casualities in Vietnam and deadly new anti-aircraft weapons developed since then have forced pilots to fly these helicopters at night on ground-hugging, radar-evading missions for which they never were built.

The goggles represent a kind of ad-libbed pilot's aide, a quick way to increase helicopters' nighttime capabilities simply by strapping something on a pilot, said George Small, an Army night-vision goggle instructor who retired last month at Fort Campbell, Ky.

But there are problems, he said.

"When you're over a desert, where there's little contrast, or when the light levels are low, you can forget it," he said. "They are not safe."

"When you're wearing those goggles, you lose your peripheral vision, you lose your balance, you lose your depth perception," said former Marine Capt. Art Conroy, who flew Sea Stallion helicopters at Tustin until his retirement in 1986. "When there's an overcast, forget it. You can't see. And then when something happens, they call it pilot error.

"I think there should be some questions about that."

The first fatal night-vision goggle crashes on record—discounting one attributable to helicopter breakdown—were in April and July 1978.

Two Huey training helicopters were destroyed and six Army fliers killed while training with the goggles at Fort Rucker, Ala., where all Army pilots earn their wings.

In both cases, sudden fog obscured moonlight, reducing the goggle image to the equivalent of a television without an antenna—all static and sparks.

This was to become the hallmark of night-vision crashes—unwitting entry into bad weather. It's a deadly trap the goggles repeatedly bait for pilots because the devices are incapable of seeing clouds or fog, according to several Army and Marine reports on crashes.

At the same time, the tight face masks of the infantry goggles barred pilots from seeing their instruments, leaving them unable to tell whether they were descending, turning or flying on a level course.

Deprived of sight, the helicopter pilots in both 1978 crashes became disoriented and ran into the ground. Pilot error was blamed in both cases, although one crash-investigation report also conceded that "environmental factors" played a role.

After 10 crashes and 21 deaths, Army night-vision experts in 1983 learned they could improve safety by cutting away the face-mask portion of the goggles, allowing pilots to peer underneath at instruments during crucial moments. The Army and the Air Force then banned use of the full face-mask goggles that same year.

But the Marine Corps, which had been pursuing a separate night-vision program, failed to adopt this change—until after the March 1984 crash and 29 deaths in Korea, according to Conroy and Bob McLean, an Army human factors expert at the Abderdeen Proving Grounds in Maryland.

The use of the full face-mask goggles was not addressed in the official Marine investigation report on the crash. This report, a Navy Judge Advocate General's investigation, written by Marine Maj. Michael Powers, then of the Tustin Marine Corps Air Station, only noted that clouds obscured moonlight so much that the goggles could not function properly.

The squadron commander on the Korea maneuvers, Lt. Col. James Schaefer, also formerly of the Tustin base and an early advocate of goggle flying, was chastised in the report for failing to abort the mission because of cloudy weather.

Four years earlier, Schaefer, then a major, was the pilot whose helicopter collided with a plane during the ill-fated Iran-hostage rescue mission—a mission conducted with the infantry goggles.

Former Marine pilot Conroy was slated to be co-pilot on the helicopter that crashed in Korea but was pulled off flight duty at the last minute in favor of a senior officer who needed the additional flight time, Conroy said.

"It could easily have been me dead and burned on that hill. . . . We were not prepared to be flying with goggles on a mission like that," he said. "It was absolutely criminal."

Cutting away the face masks of the goggles did not eliminate the other problems with the ground-troop goggles. Their poor performance in low light continued to lead to crashes.

In at least 20 crashes, including two of last year's crashes in Orange County, goggles were blinded by cloudy weather, according to 10 years of reports on night-vision goggle crashes.

As helicopters fly into the fringes of clouds, the goggles try to compensate by increasing the brightness of their video images. Pilots cannot tell they're in trouble until the clouds completely engulf them, cutting off all light, according to Lt. Col. Robert Verona, night-vision goggle product manager at the Army's Center for Night Vision and Electro-Optics at Fort Belvoir, Va.

"It can be insidious," he said. "It can suck you right in."

Theoretically, pilots are expected to notice they are flying into clouds by seeing halos around objects, indicating haze, or by watching for shadows on the ground that could be cast by clouds, military documents and safety experts say.

The Orange County Marine crashes were blamed on pilot error because investigators determined that pilots failed to watch for these danger signs. But Conroy and former Army instructor pilot Clyde Emery, who taught night-vision flying from 1978 to 1981, said that was laughable.

"There's no way you're going to know until it's too late," Conroy said. "They weren't designed for that."

"The best thing you can do when you're in clouds is slap them (the goggles) off," Emery said. "And if you're good at unusual-attitude recovery, you'll survive. Maybe."

An Army report on a Dec. 19, 1985, crash in Germany describes trying to land a helicopter with night-vision goggles on a cloudy night as flying "into a black hole."

Ten days earlier, on Dec. 9, 1985, a US Army UH-60 Blackhawk helicopter, searching for another chopper downed in South Korea, struck high-voltage power lines 225 feet off the ground. It had been flying at a cautious 23 mph. The rotors were ripped off the helicopter, which plunged straight down, impaling itself on a dead tree, killing a Korean door gunner and critically injuring the three US fliers on board.

The moon was only a sliver that night—6 to 7 percent of a full moon, too little for the goggles to function properly. At least a fifth-full moon is required, although the Army lets its pilots fly with special infrared search lights when the moon is smaller, Verona said.

The pilot, Warrant Officer Thomas Getsy, said the wires were invisible until the crash: "I saw this big white strand come across the cockpit. . . . Then the rotors came off all at one time."

The verdict of investigators: The crash was caused by Getsy's error. He should have avoided the wires.

But in a virtually identical accident July 18, 1983, in Germany, investigators drew a seemingly contradictory conclusion—one of two times an accident has been blamed on the goggles' inadequacies.

An Army OH-58 Kiowa on a night-vision goggle training flight also struck power lines, this time under even better conditions—a brightly moonlit night and traveling at about 30 mph. The helicopter suffered major damage but stayed aloft until severe vibrations forced the instructor pilot, Chief Warrant Officer Richard Pratt, to make an emergency landing.

Before touching down, he lost power and hit the ground so hard the chopper's tail was torn off. The two men on board suffered minor injuries.

"I was looking out and could not see the wires," Pratt reported.

In blaming the crash on environmental and equipment factors, meaning the goggles, investigators made this finding: "Night-vision goggles were not developed to be compatible with aviation usage, restricting vision to a narrow field of view and making it impossible for Pratt to detect wires."

Excerpts from a 1983 Army training manual attached to the crash investigation say, "Normally, wires are impossible to see at night with or without the night-vision goggles."

The difference is: When flying at night without goggles, pilots are required to stay high enough to avoid wires. With goggles, they are required to fly low, "nap-of-the-earth" missions designed to avoid radar.

To improve safety, they fly the routes in daylight, jotting down wire locations, mountains and other hazards on maps. Then they use their notes as references while flying at low altitudes on night-vision goggle flights.

Pilots normally will not have the opportunity to fly routes in advance in combat.

Pilot error also was blamed for a midair collision in Kentucky that killed 17 Army fliers in March. With peripheral vision blocked by the goggles, there was little chance to see the collision in the making until the last moment, investigators said, just as Pratt failed to see the wires that downed his chopper. Yet this time, the dead flight crews were blamed.

Night-vision goggles give pilots such poor vision that they would be medically disqualified from flying if their natural eyesight was that bad, according to the sworn statement of an Army instructor pilot consulted during the investigation of the Kentucky crash.

The pilot, David Heaton, begged his superiors to accelerate delivery of goggles designed specifically for flying as a means of reducing accidents, according to his statement attached to the crash-investigation report.

Pilot error was cited in another accident, when the goggles made starlight reflected in water appear to be stars in the sky, according to an Army Safety Center report on the crash.

Two fliers were severely injured in 1985 during a flight in Salt Lake City when this common goggle illusion sent them careening into Great Salt Lake. The pilot thought he was flying on a level course.

When six Army fliers hit an island and died while flying over Lake Michigan near Detroit in 1983, a surviving helicopter crew reported that the goggles made a small island on the lake look like fog. The other helicopter had barely pulled up in time when the lead chopper crashed. The verdict: pilot error.

"I don't believe in the term pilot error in these cases," said Matthew Ellis, a former Army officer, now a private helicopter safety consultant in Tennessee. "These pilots and field commanders are doing a tremendous job overcoming the limitations of the goggles. Sometimes you go out and everything is fine. But the problem is the next time you fly, those limitations will come up and bite you on the ass.

"And you may not have done anything different."

He said the finding of pilot error in so many goggle crashes glosses over the severe hazards the goggles pose for servicemen.

Even so, many pilots said they would rather have the infantry goggles than none at all. Old hands remember night flying in pre-goggle days in Vietnam, where there were two choices, each equally terrifying: You flew high and became an easy target for enemy radar, or you lit up the sky with flares and spotlights and became an easy target for ground troops. Compared to that, the infantry goggles are a godsend, they say.

"I don't think there's a guy who flew in Vietnam who wouldn't have flown with night-vision goggles if he could have," said Lt. Col. Michael D. Ryan, commander of the Marine Aviation Weapons and Tactics Squadron One at Yuma, which teaches other marine units how to best use night-vision goggles. "You could have sold them for all the money those guys had."

"We use them because we can see," said Capt. Mike Saunders, a AH-1 Cobra pilot at Camp Pendleton. "Before . . . we had dark."

But Emery said many military pilots love the goggles only because they represent such a marked improvement over flying in the dark—overlooking the fact that night flying without goggles is often safer because the missions are slower and more cautious. With goggles, pilots are often required to fly the same high-speed, low-altitude missions flown in daylight, he said.

Efforts are under way to improve safety, officials said. The Army has changed flight procedures and helicopter lighting systems in response to recent accidents. The Marine Corps forbids passengers on flights using the infantry goggles, and allows passengers with the new pilot goggles only on nights when lighting is good.

In January, the Marine Corps opened a special training lab at Yuma, Ariz., to teach night-vision safety by simulating hazards. Lt. Rick Mason, the Navy physiologist assigned to the lab, said it was first proposed after the Korea crash but has just received funding.

Army and Marine officials say they will replace most of the infantry goggles with new ones designed for pilots by 1991 or 1992. They have been available since 1982 and originally scheduled for delivery in 1984. A few thousand have been distributed, but infantry goggles still are used in the vast majority of night flights and are the primary kind used at Tustin and El Toro.

The new pilot goggles have received rave reviews from pilots, and safety experts say they will reduce accidents. Although they operate better in dim light and do not blur vision as badly as the infantry goggles, they still share all the other shortcomings, and they are even more vulnerable to cloudy weather.

More exotic goggles are being designed that will be mounted inside flight helmet visors, adding infrared sensors and other navigational aides, but they are years off and primarily intended for jet pilots.

In the meantime, while budget priorities lie with more sophisticated weapons systems, the helicopter pilot will have to struggle with goggles built for truck drivers.

"Give him a set of goggles that is not the state of the art . . . and you do not have to be mental giant to realize that something is going to happen," Heaton wrote in his statement attached to reports on the March midair collision.

"Until we do this (replacement), accidents like this will continue to happen."

A PEOPLE IN PERIL

ANCHORAGE DAILY NEWS

Anchorage Daily News staff.

CAMPAIGN FOR BUS SAFETY

THE LOUISVILLE COURIER-JOURNAL

The Louisville Courier-Journal staff.

THE COLOR OF MONEY

THE ATLANTA JOURNAL-CONSTITUTION

Bill Dedman, 28, began newspaper work at the age of 16 as a copy boy for *The Chattanooga Times.* He worked as a reporter and editor at several small and mid-sized papers in Tennessee and Missouri before joining *The Atlanta Journal-Constitution* as a staff writer in April 1987.

A CARTOONIST'S TICKLE AND JAB

CHICAGO SUN-TIMES

Jack Higgins, 34, has been drawing cartoons for the *Chicago Sun-Times* since February 1980, first on a freelance basis, and since July 1984 as a staff cartoonist. He covered the 1980, 1984 and 1988 Democratic and Republican national conventions, and he was a 1986 Pulitzer Prize–finalist.

THE GREAT TAX GIVEAWAY

THE PHILADELPHIA INQUIRER

Donald L. Barlett, 52, and James B. Steele, 46, have worked together as an investigative reporting team at *The Philadelphia Inquirer* since 1971. They earned a Pulitzer Prize in 1975 for national reporting on the Internal Revenue Service. Other investigations have included subjects such as American foreign aid and the energy crisis.

THE PALESTINIAN UPRISING

THE WASHINGTON POST

Glenn Frankel, 39, has completed his two-and-a-half-year assignment as bureau chief in Jerusalem. He joined *The Washington Post* in 1979 as chief of the Richmond, Virginia, bureau and has served as assistant foreign editor and southern Africa correspondent before being posted in Jerusalem.

GORBACHEV'S GRAND PLAN

THE NEW YORK TIMES

Bill Keller, 40, became Moscow bureau chief for *The New York Times* in January 1989 after serving there as a correspondent since December 1986. Before joining the *Times*'s Washington bureau in April 1984, Mr. Keller worked at *The Dallas Times-Herald,* the *Congressional Quarterly Weekly Report* and *The* (Portland) *Oregonian.*

RESCUE ATTEMPT

ST. LOUIS POST-DISPATCH

Ron Olshwanger, 52, is a part-time photographer and full-time owner of MMI, a wholesale furniture showroom in St. Louis. After volunteering as assistant chief of the Red Cross Disaster Service, he began taking photographs of fires and other disasters, mainly for fire department training programs.

A CLASS ACT

DETROIT FREE PRESS

Manny Crisostomo, 32, joined the *Detroit Free Press* in 1982, working first as an intern and later as a staff photographer. A native of Guam, he previously worked as a photographer for the *Pacific Daily News* (Guam) and at the *Jackson* (Michigan) *Citizen Patriot.* He has made an ongoing photographic documentary of troubled youth.

CITY GOVERNMENT'S FOLLY AND FRAUD

CHICAGO TRIBUNE

Lois Wille, 57, joined the *Chicago Tribune* as associate editorial page editor in January 1984 and was promoted to editorial page editor in 1987. She worked for 22 years at the *Chicago Daily News* as a reporter, national correspondent and associate editor until it ceased publication, and from 1978 until 1983, she was associate editor at the *Chicago Sun-Times*.

LITERARY HEROES AND 'CREATIVE WRITING'

THE NEWS AND OBSERVER

Michael Skube, 45, started his journalism career writing freelance book reviews and other articles while employed by the U.S. Customs Service in Miami. Later he covered government and politics for the *Winston-Salem Journal* and contributed a Sunday column to *The Atlanta Journal-Constitution* before joining *The News and Observer* in 1982.

THE PEOPLE'S REPUBLIC OF CHICAGO

CHICAGO TRIBUNE

Clarence Page, 41, has been a columnist and a member of the editorial board at the *Chicago Tribune* since July 1984. He first joined the paper in 1969 as a reporter. In 1972, he contributed to a series on vote fraud that won a Pulitzer Prize. After eleven years at the *Tribune,* Mr. Page interrupted his newspaper career to work for four years at WBBM-TV in Chicago.

BEING BLACK IN SOUTH AFRICA

THE PHILADELPHIA INQUIRER

David Zucchino, 37, was named Africa correspondent for *The Philadelphia Inquirer* in 1986. From October 1982 to July 1984, he was a correspondent in the Middle East. Before joining *The Inquirer* in 1980, Mr. Zucchino worked for the *Detroit Free Press* and *The News and Observer* of Raleigh, N.C.

ANATOMY OF AN AIR CRASH

THE DALLAS MORNING NEWS

David Hanners, 33, began his journalism career as police reporter at the *Amarillo* (Texas) *Globe-News* in 1977. He rose to be chief of the paper's Randall County bureau before leaving in 1980 to become federal courts reporter for the *Brownsville* (Texas) *Herald.* He joined *The Dallas Morning News* in 1982 as a general assignment reporter.

William Snyder, 29, had his first photograph published when he was 13. In 1982 he covered the Miami riots and the Super Bowl for *The Miami News.* A year later he moved to *The Dallas Morning News* as a staff photographer.

Karen Blessen, 37, joined *The Dallas Morning News* in 1986 after working as a freelance illustrator and designer. As a designer at *The Morning News,* she works on large, specialty design projects.

DEATH IN THE DARK

THE ORANGE COUNTY REGISTER

Edward Humes, 31, joined *The Orange County Register* in 1985 as a general assignment reporter and now is assigned to the metropolitan staff where he concentrates on coverage of the military. He previously worked for *The Texas Observer* in Austin, the *Pine Bluff* (Arkansas) *Commercial* and the *Tucson Citizen* in Arizona.

ABOUT THE EDITOR

Kendall J. Wills is completing the Asian field study portion of a Gannett Foundation fellowship, based at the University of Hawaii. A native of Milwaukee, he previously worked as assistant editor of the Op-Ed page at *The New York Times.*

"Israel Haunted by Comparison with South Africa," by Glenn Frankel, January 25, 1988. Reprinted with permission of *The Washington Post*.
"Palestinian Children of the Stones," by Glenn Frankel, February 7, 1988. Reprinted with permission of *The Washington Post*.
"Arab Uprising: Drawing the Populations into War," by Glenn Frankel, March 20, 1988. Reprinted with permission of *The Washington Post*.
"Nightmare on the West Bank," by Glenn Frankel, April 14, 1988. Reprinted with permission of *The Washington Post*.
"High Backing Seen for Assassination," by Glenn Frankel, April 21, 1988. Reprinted with permission of *The Washington Post*.
"Israel Turns to Detentions as Weapon Against Uprising," by Glenn Frankel, May 13, 1988. Reprinted with permission of *The Washington Post*.

Pulitzer Prize nominating letter for Bill Keller of *The New York Times*. Courtesy of *The New York Times*.
"In the Gauntlet of Democracy: A Soviet Editor Takes Knocks," by Bill Keller, June 18, 1988. Reprinted with permission of *The New York Times*.
"Soviet Change vs. The Worker's Security," by Bill Keller, May 10, 1988. Reprinted with permission of *The New York Times*.
"In Stalin's City of Steel: Change Confronts Inertia," by Bill Keller, August 16, 1988. Reprinted with permission of *The New York Times*.
"Armenian Capital Is Roused by Call for New Freedom," by Bill Keller, September 5, 1988. Reprinted with permission of *The New York Times*.
"Gorbachev's Grand Plan: Is It Real or a Pipe Dream?" by Bill Keller, December 5, 1988. Reprinted with permission of *The New York Times*.
"From Soviet Quake: Echoes Widen," by Bill Keller, December 18, 1988. Reprinted with permission of *The New York Times*.

Introductory essay on spot news photography by Ron Olshwanger. Reprinted with permission of Ron Olshwanger. One photograph by Ron Olshwanger of a firefighter trying to revive a child, published in *The St. Louis Post-Dispatch*. Reprinted with permission of *The St. Louis Post-Dispatch*.

Introductory essay on feature photography by Manny Crisostomo. Reprinted with permission of *The Detroit Free Press*.
Twenty photographs by Manny Crisostomo in *The Detroit Free Press*, June 26, 1988. Reprinted with permission of *The Detroit Free Press*.

Pulitzer Prize nominating letter for Lois Wille by the editors of the *Chicago Tribune*. Reprinted with permission of the *Chicago Tribune*.
"Don't Muzzle Aldermanic Stupidity," by Lois Wille, November 18, 1988. Reprinted with permission of the *Chicago Tribune*.
"Another Good Idea to CUSS Out," by Lois Wille, February 19, 1988. Reprinted with permission of the *Chicago Tribune*.
"How to Get Low-Cost Homes in the City," by Lois Wille, March 22, 1988. Reprinted with permission of the *Chicago Tribune*.
"Election Board Caves in to a Swindle," by Lois Wille, April 7, 1988. Reprinted with permission of the *Chicago Tribune*.
"One Hit, Then Betrayal in Springfield," by Lois Wille, July 3, 1988. Reprinted with permission of the *Chicago Tribune*.

"How City Hall Copes with Reform," by Lois Wille, November 22, 1988. Reprinted with permission of the *Chicago Tribune.*
"Must City Aldermen Obey the Law?" by Lois Wille, November 25, 1988. Reprinted with permission of the *Chicago Tribune.*

Introductory essay on criticism by Michael Skobe, *The News and Observer* of Raleigh, NC. Reprinted with permission of *The News and Observer.*
"Shouldering the Burden of the Southern Writer," by Michael Skube, February 21, 1988. Reprinted with permission of *The News and Observer.*
"Western Lit from Milton to Zane Grey (and Others)," by Michael Skube, June 12, 1988. Reprinted with permission of *The News and Observer.*
"North to Alaska with James Michener," by Michael Skube, July 3, 1988. Reprinted with permission of *The News and Observer.*
"A Most Excellent Man, on the Face of It," by Michael Skube, July 17, 1988. Reprinted with permission of *The News and Observer.*
"T. S. Eliot's Solitary Search for Salvation," by Michael Skube, November 6, 1988. Reprinted with permission of *The News and Observer.*
"Larry McMurtry Still the Best in the West," by Michael Skube, November 13, 1988. Reprinted with permission of *The News and Observer.*
" 'Creative Writing' and the English Department," by Michael Skube, December 11, 1988. Reprinted with permission of *The News and Observer.*

Introductory essay on commentary by Clarence Page, the *Chicago Tribune.* Reprinted with permission of Clarence Page.
"The People's Republic of Chicago," by Clarence Page, June 26, 1988. Reprinted with permission of the *Chicago Tribune.*
"Thanks for Being Honest, Jimmy 'The Greek'—Too Honest," by Clarence Page, January 20, 1988. Reprinted with permission of the *Chicago Tribune.*
"Tawana Brawley, Twice a Victim," by Clarence Page, June 19, 1988. Reprinted with permission of the *Chicago Tribune.*
"Dr. King's Legacy: The Way Is Clear, the Will Is Uncertain," by Clarence Page, April 6, 1988. Reprinted with permission of the *Chicago Tribune.*
"A Breach in TV's Cycle of Ignorance About Black Life," by Clarence Page, February 24, 1988. Reprinted with permission of the *Chicago Tribune.*
"The Mayor Stands By His Man—and Looks Like a Heel," by Clarence Page, May 4, 1988. Reprinted with permission of the *Chicago Tribune.*
"A Deplorable Effort to Help Dentists Shun AIDS Victims," by Clarence Page, June 15, 1988. Reprinted with permission of the *Chicago Tribune.*

Introductory essay on feature writing by David Zucchino, *The Philadelphia Inquirer.* Reprinted with permission of David Zucchino.
"Out of Challenge Came Death," by David Zucchino, December 11, 1988. Reprinted with permission of *The Philadelphia Inquirer.*
"A Bond of Necessity for Black and White," by David Zucchino, December 12, 1988. Reprinted with permission of *The Philadelphia Inquirer.*
"A Mother Must Live for Her Sons," by David Zucchino, December 15, 1988. Reprinted with permission of *The Philadelphia Inquirer.*
"A Bar Owner Quietly Prospers Within the System," by David Zucchino, December 16, 1988. Reprinted with permission of *The Philadelphia Inquirer.*
"A Tentative Step Toward Freedom," by David Zucchino, December 17, 1988. Reprinted with permission of *The Philadelphia Inquirer.*

"For Many, Struggle Is for Work," by David Zucchino, December 18, 1988. Reprinted with permission of *The Philadelphia Inquirer.*

Introductory essay on explanatory journalism by David Hanners, William Snyder, and Karen Blessen, *The Dallas Morning News.* Reprinted with permission of David Hanners, William Snyder, and Karen Blessen.
"The Final Flight of 50 Sierra Kilo," by David Hanners, February 7, 1988. Reprinted with permission of *The Dallas Morning News.*
" 'Kicking Tin': The Search for Pieces," by David Hanners, February 7, 1988. Reprinted with permission of *The Dallas Morning News.*
"High-Tech Sleuths Find 'Smoking Gun,' " by David Hanners, February 7, 1988. Reprinted with permission of *The Dallas Morning News.*
"System Allows 50 SK to Fly Blindly to Death," by David Hanners, February 7, 1988. Reprinted with permission of *The Dallas Morning News.*

Introductory essay on specialized journalism by Edward Humes, *The Orange County Register.* Reprinted with permission of Edward Humes.
"Military Knew Night Goggles Weren't Meant for Helicopters," by Edward Humes, December 4, 1988. Reprinted with permission of *The Orange County Register.*
"Night-Flying Capability Essential to US Security, Military Says," by Edward Humes, December 4, 1988. Reprinted with permission of *The Orange County Register.*
"Night-Vision Goggles Can Blind Pilots to Dangers in the Skies," by Edward Humes, December 4, 1988. Reprinted with permission of *The Orange County Register.*